CASKET EMPTY:
God's Plan of Redemption
through History

New Testament Study Guide

David L. Palmer

Copyright © 2016 David L. Palmer
All rights reserved.

ISBN: 0692758127
ISBN 13: 9780692758120

To my family

Table of Contents

Preface

My participation in the CASKET EMPTY project is living testimony to the grace of God and the body of Christ. Any writing project requires significant institutional and personal support. I am grateful for the gift of Gordon-Conwell Theological Seminary where I first learned that the Bible is God's redemptive story with Jesus at its center. I also gained there a lifelong set of friendships and partners in the gospel that have lasted for decades. Above all, my gifted and godly wife, Dr. Christine Palmer, who serves as adjunct faculty in Old Testament at Gordon-Conwell, with whom I share the wonder of God's Word. She has generously shared her own profound insights into Scripture and has been a constant source of encouragement in helping me to see the connections between the Old and New Testament. My first class in seminary was Hebrew with Dr. Gary Pratico. I wept within the first five minutes as he introduced us to the living God through the name "Micah," which means: "Who is like the LORD?" I sat next to Carol Kaminski in that course. I am thankful for our friendship, and the delight in Scripture and the church that we share together with her husband Matt. Her invitation to develop the New Testament portion of CASKET EMPTY has been a remarkable privilege. Her leadership, vision, and enthusiasm for this project have been invaluable. Our mutual friend, Dr. Jay Sklar, Dean of Faculty at Covenant Seminary, was instrumental in suggesting our collaboration.

Several other institutions and ministries have provided the opportunity for this material to be developed, taught, and refined. The content of this study guide was first presented at a Pastor's Conference hosted by the Harold John Ockenga Institute and the Shoemaker Center for Church Renewal at Gordon-Conwell in 2011. Dr. David Horn and his dedicated staff, especially Saemi Kim, created a meaningful time for everyone. I cherished the opportunity to teach CASKET EMPTY to the Navigator's student leadership at the University of Cincinnati. Their hunger for God's word stirred my own. Inter-Varsity Christian Fellowship invited me to spend an intensive week with their campus staff serving throughout New England. Together we shared profound moments in contextualizing the New Testament mission for today. Logos Bible software offered me the opportunity to share a draft of the material on expectations at their Pastorum conference in Chicago, IL. Training Leaders International allowed me to share this material with ethnic church pastors from Africa, Europe, the Middle East, and Asia over several summers in Athens, Greece. I want to thank Darren Carlson for his visionary leadership in prioritizing theological education to end the famine of the Word of God. I also want to thank Dr. Panagiotis Kantartzis, who invited me to present CASKET EMPTY at a Pastor's conference and preach at the First Evangelical Church in Athens, Greece. His ministry vision has opened my eyes to see God's mission in the world today. Dr. Ryan Reeves, Assistant Dean of Gordon-Conwell in Jacksonville, FL, has graciously invited me to teach this material as a graduate level New Testament Survey course for several years. I am also grateful to my colleagues in the Division of Biblical Studies who have given me the gift of teaching this material at the main campus in Hamilton, MA. These have been precious times where God has met with us in the classroom.

Kenwood Baptist Church of Cincinnati, OH has been my ministry home throughout this project. I am privileged to serve Jesus Christ there as Senior Pastor, along with a very gifted and dedicated ministry team. This material was first presented to our Young Adult class, who pushed me further with their love for the historical context. A weekly men's Bible study over the past five years has provided a generous and engaging setting to work through the study guide in detail. These brothers have shaped the presentation in countless ways. God's renewed humanity in Christ is on display at Kenwood with fourteen native languages, four generations, and a wide range of social and educational backgrounds. We are striving together to announce the good news of the gospel and to join God's mission in the world.

Several people have made vital contributions toward the completion of this study guide. Dr. Carol Kaminski, Professor of Old Testament at Gordon-Conwell, read the entire manuscript several times and provided countless recommendations to improve the clarity of expression and to highlight the theological connection with the *Old Testament Study Guide*. She also invested a very generous portion of her time in editing and preparing the manuscript for publication. Sarah Sulek used her God-given ability in graphic design to make the New Testament timeline come alive, and graphic designer Nicole Rim provided the artwork for the New Testament Study Guide cover. Lois and Katie Bascom read early drafts of chapters and greatly improved my style. Lyle Fiore reviewed the final manuscript with care. Stephenie O'Connell edited the companion power point presentation and provided outstanding support from CASKET EMPTY Media. Whitney Cahan read the entire manuscript with keen editorial skill and checked every Bible reference for accuracy in citation. The competent staff of the Hebrew Union College and the Mason Public Library supplied much needed resources. Our beloved children, Salome and Jonathan, attended the first Pastor's Conference, and took copious notes as full participants, even at a young age. They share with their parents a great appetite for God's Word and are now growing conversation partners in the greatness of Jesus Christ who died and rose again. Finally, two extremely generous Christian families opened their homes by the sea as a quiet refuge for writing. Looking out over beautiful sunlit waves, I could often imagine the coming day when "the earth shall be full of the knowledge of the LORD as the waters cover the sea" (Isa. 11:9).

David Palmer
July, 2016

Introduction

The Bible is one redemptive story that begins in Genesis and concludes in Revelation. God inspired sixty-six different books, written in three distinct languages, over thousands of years, to reveal his single story for the whole world. He inspired human authors from different continents, ages, and social classes, to address us all. The overarching unity of the Bible is found in the revelation of the identity and character of God and his saving plan for humanity in Christ. The CASKET EMPTY Bible series seeks to help people understand God's plan of redemption through history—with Jesus at its center.

The Bible is *one redemptive story*. When we read the Bible, we come to know the incomparable person of the living God. His ways are higher than ours. He is both just and the justifier of the ungodly. We also come to know ourselves. We are made in the image of God. Yet we are fallen through the deception of sin. In the Bible we learn of God's redemptive plan for all peoples that comes to climactic fulfillment in the death and resurrection of God's Son, Jesus Christ. We find the provision for our forgiveness in the death of Christ on the cross. We discover a sure hope of eternal life through his resurrection. We find newness of life as we are transformed by the Holy Spirit. All study of the Bible should lead us to praise and worship the Lamb who was slain for us (Rev. 5:9-10).

The Bible is one redemptive story *through history*. The Bible begins with the creation of the world and ends with the consummation of all things. There is no time, place, or human experience outside the Bible's frame of reference. There is no person, people group, or society for whom the Bible is irrelevant. As we have seen from our study of the Old Testament using the acronym CASKET, God's saving purpose is revealed through six periods in the Old Testament that begin at CREATION and continue with the call of ABRAHAM and the covenant God makes with his descendants at SINAI. God's redemptive plan advances in the period of KINGS when the monarchy is established and King David is promised everlasting kingship. Despite the judgment of EXILE, God's plan remains certain as the final period of TEM-PLE concludes with partial restoration and a vivid picture of future hope. As we journey into the New Testament to see how God's plan of redemption is fulfilled in Christ, we will see that history still matters. The Bible is not a timeless catalogue of abstract principles to be applied. It is the historical narrative of God's saving actions. If the events of the Bible did not actually occur in history, our faith is futile and we are still in our sins. Above all, if Christ has not been raised, then "we are of all people most to be pitied" (1 Cor. 15:19).

The Bible is one redemptive story through history *with Jesus as its center.* Jesus' life, death, and resurrection are given more literary space than any other topic in the entire Bible. Jesus told the religious leaders of his day that Moses "wrote of me" (John 5:46). Jesus' disciples claim: "We have found him of whom Moses in the Law and also the prophets wrote, Jesus of Nazareth" (John 1:45). Jesus repeatedly showed his disciples from Scripture "that he must go to Jerusalem and suffer many things from the elders and chief priests and scribes, and be killed, and on the third day be raised" (Matt. 16:21; cf. Matt. 17:22-23). On the road to Emmaus, Jesus taught his disciples that the Scripture was about his death and resurrection (Luke 24:26-27). This reminds us that Jesus is at the very center of God's plan of redemption in the Bible.

An important passage for our study is 1 Cor. 15:1-4. Paul summarizes the gospel or "good news" of God. The gospel contains God's royal announcement that Jesus is the Messiah and Son of God. The gospel represents the truth upon which believers stand. The gospel provides the means "by which you are being saved" (1 Cor. 15:2). Paul solemnly testifies to the central truth of God's gospel. The death and resurrection of Christ are the focal point: "For I delivered to you as of first importance what I also received: that Christ died for our sins in accordance with the Scriptures, that he was buried, that he was raised on the third day in accordance with Scriptures" (1 Cor. 15:3-4). This passage provides the theological content for our acronym and the controlling cover images for the CASKET EMPTY Bible study series. The death of Jesus (represented by the cross on the cover of the Old Testament Study Guide), and his resurrection (represented by the empty tomb on the cover of the New Testament Study Guide) provide us with the orienting center of the biblical story. As we will see, Jesus fulfills the Old Testament hope and accomplishes God's redemptive plan. His resurrection marks the beginning of the new creation. He is the seed of Abraham. He fulfills the law given at Sinai. He is the promised Davidic king. He brings about the return from exile. He builds a living temple for God's own presence that will never be destroyed. In Jesus the Messiah, all of God's promises are "Yes" and "Amen" (2 Cor. 1:20).

The order of the New Testament books

As we begin our study of the New Testament, the first thing that I would like you to do is open your Bible to the Table of Contents. You will notice that there are twenty-seven books of the New Testament, beginning with Matthew and ending with Revelation. There are four different types of material in the New Testament: Gospels (4), History (1), Letters (21), and Prophecy (1). The first four books of the New Testament are called gospels, since they focus on the good news that Jesus, the promised Messiah, has come. The four gospels are Matthew, Mark, Luke, and John. The gospel writers faithfully record the birth, life, public ministry, death, resurrection, and exaltation of Jesus the Messiah.

The second type of material is history. This does not mean that other New Testament books are not historical records, but rather, the book of Acts is identified as history since Luke records the narrative of historical events that take place after the ascension of the Messiah. Luke faithfully presents the ongoing activity of the exalted Jesus in the world through his followers as they proclaim the gospel to all nations by the empowering presence of the Holy Spirit.

The third type of material consists of letters. There are twenty-one letters. The letters are written to early church communities who share faith in Christ. These letters provide instruction on Christian doctrine, identity, and how the people of God are to live as followers of Jesus. As you read through the New Testament letters, it is important to realize that they are not arranged in chronological order. Instead, the twenty-one letters are grouped together by author, such as Paul (13 letters), the writer of Hebrews (1), James (1), Peter (2), John (3), and Jude (1). For each author, the letters are arranged by descending length. For example, Romans is the first of Paul's letters in the New Testament, not because it is the earliest or the most important but because it is the longest. Philemon is Paul's final letter, not because it is the last or the least important but because it is the shortest.

The fourth type of material is prophecy. There is one book of prophecy, Revelation. This book contains an extended vision of Christ's present rule and future glory. Revelation looks toward the culmination of history at the return of Christ. Evil will be defeated and the serpent condemned. The Bible, which began with the Garden of Eden, will end with the City of God as the New Jerusalem descends and God dwells with his people forever.

The acronym EMPTY

The acronym CASKET has helped us to read the Old Testament as one redemptive story and to locate the various books within their historical context. The acronym EMPTY will help us to do the same for the New Testament. God's plan of redemption in the New Testament has been divided into five distinct periods with each period having its own heading and date: EXPECTATIONS (430-6 BC), MESSIAH (6 BC-AD 33), PENTECOST (AD 33-65), TEACHING (AD 33-95), and YET-TO-COME (AD 95-Return of Christ). Each heading describes what takes place in the particular period, and the first letter of each heading makes up the acronym EMPTY.

Key turning points in the redemptive plan of God

Each period is "marked off" by a key event. Just as civilizations organize their history according to important leaders and decisive events, God instructs us to remember key moments within his redemptive plan (Deut. 5:15; Isa. 46:8-9; Luke 24:6-7; 2 Tim. 2:8). Within each period, we will identify the key dates and events that advance God's saving purpose in Christ. We also want to learn the books of the New Testament that pertain to each period. If you are able to memorize the acronym EMPTY, along with the dates, key events, and people for each period, this will provide a framework for you to learn about the fulfillment of God's redemptive story in the New Testament. The complete acronym CASKET EMPTY will provide you with a concise way for remembering the entire sweep of the Bible with Jesus at the center.

Why the acronym CASKET EMPTY?

CASKET EMPTY reminds us that the death and resurrection of Jesus are the focus of God's saving purpose as revealed in the Bible. "For as in Adam all die, so also in Christ shall all be made alive" (1 Cor. 15:22). Jesus is the beloved Son sent forth from the Father's love to die for us (John 3:16). Eternal life is to know Jesus Christ whom the Father has sent into the world (John 17:3). Jesus is "the Lamb of God, who takes away the sin of the world" (John 1:29). Peter says that Jesus "bore our sins in his body on the tree, that we might die to sin and live to righteousness. By his wounds you have been healed" (1 Pet. 2:24; cf. Isa. 53:5). Paul writes that "God shows his love for us in that while we were still sinners, Christ died for us" (Rom. 5:8). CASKET EMPTY draws our attention to the cross of Christ (1 Cor. 2:2; Gal. 6:14).

CASKET EMPTY also points us to the empty tomb of Christ as the dawn of God's new creation. His resurrection demonstrates that his offering for sin has been accepted (Luke 24:5-7). The power of death has been defeated (Heb. 2:14; Rev. 1:17-18). The accuser has been thrown down and "there is therefore now no condemnation for those who are in Christ Jesus" (Rom. 8:1; cf. Rev. 12:10). Christ's resurrection is the "firstfruits of those who have fallen asleep" and the guarantee of our own resurrection (1 Cor. 15:20). You may recall from our study of the Old Testament that Abraham had "resurrection faith." He believed that God would bring life out of that which was dead (Gen. 15:6; cf. Rom. 4:16-22). This "resurrection faith" characterized the early church, as it does believers today; we are those who believe that God raised Jesus from the dead (Rom. 4:23-25). The resurrection of the Messiah, which is represented in the title for this Bible study series, is central to the Christian faith.

Furthermore, CASKET EMPTY causes us to embrace the death and resurrection of Christ as the model for Christian discipleship and the pattern of New Testament ethics. Jesus says: "If anyone would come after me, let him deny himself and take up his cross and follow me" (Matt. 16:24). We are called to imitate Christ's death in our daily behavior and attitudes, and walk according to the new life offered to us in Christ (Phil. 2:5-11). Paul prays that "I may know him and the power of his resurrection, and may share his sufferings, becoming like him in his death, that by any means possible I may attain the resurrection from the dead" (Phil. 3:10-11).

Finally, CASKET EMPTY helps us to communicate God's great redemptive story for all peoples. Only when we stand in awe of God's global purpose are we willing to offer our lives in grateful response (Rom. 12:1-2). Only when we behold the saving work of Christ can his love compel our dedicated missionary service (2 Cor. 5:14). Only when our hearts exult in Christ alone are we prepared for an eternal celebration of the redeemed who will declare: "Worthy is the Lamb who was slain, to receive power and wealth and wisdom and might and honor and glory and blessing!" (Rev. 5:12). We join with "every creature in heaven and on earth and under the earth and in the sea, and all that is in them, saying, 'To him who sits on the throne and to the Lamb be blessing and honor and glory and might forever and ever!'" (Rev. 5:13).

The New Testament timeline

This study guide is designed to be used with the New Testament timeline. Make sure that you have a copy of the timeline open as you read this book. It is available at www.casketempty.com. It will also prove very rewarding to have the Old Testament timeline nearby as well. Whenever I teach CASKET EMPTY, whether in a local church, seminary classroom, small group study, mission context, or pastor's conference, I like to set up the two CASKET EMPTY banners in the room. Having both timelines open will help you to discover the biblical and theological connections that unite God's redemptive purpose in Christ. As you read this study guide, I would encourage you to look up Bible references that are cited. All quotations are taken from the English Standard Version (ESV), unless otherwise indicated.

Five pictures represent the five time periods

Before starting with the first chapter on EXPECTATIONS, it is important for you to locate the five pictures on the timeline that represent each period in the acronym EMPTY. Memorizing the pictures along with the dates for each period will help you grasp the storyline of the New Testament. A summary of each period is provided below.

The picture for EXPECTATIONS is the visionary cloud

The visionary cloud for the period of EXPECTATIONS represents the expectation of God's messianic King and his kingdom. The blue crown inside the visionary cloud has been taken directly from the period of KINGS in the Old Testament; it represents the Davidic king from the line of Judah. The period of EXPECTATIONS spans the time from the last of the Old Testament prophets, Malachi (430 BC), until the birth of Christ (6 BC). This period is often referred to as the intertestamental period. There is a sovereign movement of history through a series of four earthly kingdoms leading toward the kingdom of God (Dan. 2:1-45; 7:1-28). Throughout this intertestamental period, God builds expectations for the coming of the Messiah. He preserves his people from compromise and draws the nations to himself. God leads his people to search the Scriptures to await the hope of Israel at just the right time.

The picture for MESSIAH is the blue crown

The blue crown for the period of MESSIAH represents the righteous reign of God in his Son Jesus, the Messiah. This icon has been taken directly from the Old Testament timeline, showing that Davidic kingship is fulfilled in Jesus. The period of MESSIAH begins with the birth of Jesus (6 BC) and continues until his death and resurrection (AD 33). Jesus is the promised Messiah, the son of David, the son of Abraham (Matt. 1:1; cf. Gen. 12:1-3; 2 Sam. 7:12-16). God's plan of redemption through history is now fulfilled in Christ. Jesus announces that the time is fulfilled and the kingdom of God has arrived (Mark 1:14-15). Jesus demonstrates the kingdom in word, deeds, and in a life of obedience. Jesus' death atones for the sin of the world and his resurrection dawns the new creation (Matt. 20:28; Isa. 53:11).

The picture for PENTECOST is the fiery cloud

The fiery cloud for the period of PENTECOST represents the pouring out of God's Spirit upon the church at Pentecost. This icon carries forward an important element from the Old Testament timeline. You will remember that the cloud of the divine presence, which had once filled the tabernacle and temple, had departed due to Israel's sin (Ezek. 9-11). Now the exalted Jesus Christ pours out the Holy Spirit upon all peoples, men and women, young and old, rich and poor (Acts 2; cf. Joel 2:28-32). The Holy Spirit is God's personal, empowering presence. The Spirit fills all who believe, resulting in lives of righteousness, mission, and service. The witness of the early church begins in Jerusalem, extends to Judea and Samaria, and reaches to the end of the earth (Acts 1:8).

The picture for TEACHING is a scroll

The scroll for the period of TEACHING represents the teaching of the early Church. This icon is designed to look like a smaller version of the Torah scroll. The teaching ministry of the church must include the Old Testament. God promised in the Old Testament that one day all nations of the world would seek to learn the Word of God as it goes forth from Jerusalem (Isa. 2; Mic. 4). Jesus commissions his disciples to be teachers of the nations (Matt. 28:20; 1 Tim. 2:7). Most of the New Testament books are letters sent to early Christian communities in an ever-expanding sphere of witness to the truth that Jesus is Lord and Savior (Eph. 4:21). These letters provide instruction on living as God's people in the world.

The picture for YET-TO-COME is the New Jerusalem

The New Jerusalem coming down from heaven for YET-TO-COME represents the City of God. The tree of life is visible and accessible in the middle of the city. The New Jerusalem reveals to us that God's redemptive story for all peoples, which began in the Garden of Eden, ends with a city. The City of God comes down like a bride adorned for her husband (Rev. 21). Inside the gate, the water of life flows from God's throne (Rev. 22). God and the Lamb have restored access to the tree of life. Testimony to Christ will extend as an innumerable multitude from every nation is gathered unto Christ (Rev. 7). There will be no more evil, sin, or curse. The blessing of God's presence, which had been lost in Eden, has now been restored forever (Gen. 2-3; Rev. 22).

As we begin our study of the New Testament, my prayer is that the CASKET EMPTY material would cause your love for God to grow, that your heart and mind would be captivated by the person and work of Christ, and that the Holy Spirit would use your life in his service wherever he might call you. I pray that you might experience, together with all of God's people, "the immeasurable greatness of his power toward us who believe, according to the working of his great might that he worked in Christ when he raised him from the dead" (Eph. 1:19-20). Amen.

Chapter 1
EXPECTATIONS

The period of EXPECTATIONS simply explained

THE PERIOD OF EXPECTATIONS covers the time between the end of the Old Testament and the beginning of the New Testament. This period is often referred to as the intertestamental period. There are over four hundred years between Malachi and Matthew. Many people wrongly imagine this as a period of divine silence or inactivity. To be sure, there is no inspired prophetic voice during this time adding to the canon of Scripture. However, just as God uses the four hundred years of slavery in Egypt to prepare Israel for redemption through the Exodus, our God will use these four hundred years to prepare the world for redemption through his Son. Throughout this period, God builds expectations for a coming king both in Israel and among the nations. The nations of the world are brought into greater contact with God's people and are given access to his Word. God's people are humbled through suffering, yet rescued and refined to await the fulfillment of his promises.

There is a sovereign movement of history in EXPECTATIONS according to God's word given to the prophet Daniel in the sixth century BC. You may remember that the Babylonian King Nebuchadnezzar had dreamt of a statue with a head of gold, chest of silver, thighs of bronze and feet mixed with iron and clay. Then, a stone cut without human hands strikes the statue, smashing it to pieces that are blown away by the wind. The stone, however, rises like a great mountain and fills the earth. God had given Daniel the interpretation of this vision as a sequence of four earthly kingdoms: Babylon,

Persia, Greece, and Rome. The stone represents a fifth kingdom, the kingdom of God, which will supplant all others and endure forever.

Daniel himself later dreams of a storm-tossed sea. Four terrifying beasts arise from turbulent waters: a lion, a bear, a leopard, and a final beast with iron teeth and horns. These creatures exercise dominion with violence and terrorize those under their rule. Suddenly the heavens open, God is seated on a glorious throne, attended by the host of heaven. The dominion of the beasts is removed as a fifth figure, a Son of Man, approaches God's throne. He is human, yet divine; he is a royal, image-bearing Son. He receives an everlasting kingdom that will never be destroyed. All peoples, nations, and languages will glorify him. As with the vision of the statue, the four beasts are interpreted as the rulers of Babylon, Persia, Greece, and Rome. The fifth ruler is the Messiah, the Son of Man, who reigns over the kingdom of God. Daniel 7:13-14 is perhaps the single most important Old Testament text for the period of EXPECTATIONS. The sequence of these kingdoms pointing toward the everlasting reign of the Son of Man is displayed on the Old Testament timeline at the bottom of the EXILE column and builds expectations for the coming of the Messiah and the establishment of his everlasting kingdom.

For many readers of the Bible, the period of EXPECTATIONS is vague and unfamiliar. The five bold headings in this section on the timeline will help you to follow the movement of God's redemptive plan. You should briefly identify these on the New Testament timeline. The first key movement in the story is that Israel becomes part of the Greek world. This takes place in 330 BC through the Greek ruler known as Alexander the Great. Through Alexander's conquests, God sovereignly brings the nations of the world into contact with his people. Foreign nations who inhabit rival narratives of the world are introduced to the one, true and living God who has revealed himself in Israel.

The second key movement is that Israel suffers greatly as wars are fought between Alexander's successors. Despite these hardships, we see that God remains at work in the world. He moves the heart of a Greek king to guard the sanctity of the Jerusalem Temple. He even inspires a Greek king to sponsor the translation of the Bible into Greek so that the nations might have access to God's Word.

The third key movement in EXPECTATIONS is that God delivers Israel through the Maccabees. While living under a dominant Greek culture, God's people struggle with compromise. Conflict over Greek culture erupts with violence. Suffering reaches new depths when a Greek ruler named Antiochus IV Epiphanes desecrates the Jerusalem Temple and makes biblical faith illegal. Thousands are put to death, yet God delivers his people through a priestly family named the Maccabees in 167-164 BC. The temple is rededicated and foreign rule is removed.

The fourth movement in the storyline is when Israel is humbled by the return of Roman rule. The descendants of the Maccabean family prove to be kings just like the nations. Their internal fighting over succession leads to direct Roman intervention. The Roman general Pompey besieges Jerusalem and enters the Holy of Holies, bringing Israel back under foreign rule in 63 BC. Israel is humbled by Roman rule established by Caesar Augustus through his client king, Herod the Great. Herod's violent rule and vast building program deepens suffering and stirs hope for God to act again.

The fifth bold heading under EXPECTATIONS on the timeline is the most important as Israel expects the Messiah, awaiting the Old Testament promises of God. The prophetic sequence of kingdoms is nearly complete. Babylon, Persia, Greece, and Rome have had their day. God's people know from Scripture that the next movement of history will be the kingdom of God and the everlasting reign of the Son of Man. During this time of eager expectation, God's people search the Scriptures. God's promises are studied, taught, and prayed. The hope of Israel fills the hearts of God's people. The kingdom of God will come. A royal Son of Man will rule. The Son of David will sit upon the throne. Atonement for sin will be made. A new covenant will be inscribed upon the human heart. The Holy Spirit will be poured out upon all peoples. The blessing of Abraham will extend to all nations. There will be a resurrection from the dead. There will be a final judgment and evil will be condemned. God will create a new heavens and a new earth in which righteousness dwells. As the period of EXPECTATIONS comes to a close, the next movement of redemptive history can only be the birth of the Messiah, when the fullness of time has come.

The key dates for this period are 430 BC and 6 BC. 430 BC is the approximate date for the last Old Testament prophet Malachi. 6 BC is the approximate date for the birth of Jesus the Messiah. Several other dates are important during this period. In 330 BC, one hundred years after the end of the Old Testament, Alexander the Great defeats the Persian Empire. This marks the transition to Daniel's third kingdom, namely, Greece. In 167-164 BC, God delivers his people through the priestly family known as the Maccabees, and the temple is rededicated. In 63 BC, the Roman general Pompey besieges Jerusalem and enters the Holy of Holies. This marks the transition to Daniel's fourth kingdom, namely, Rome.

The biblical books that provide the background for this period are the entire Old Testament, especially the prophetical books. This is because the Old Testament books are read, studied, and prayed during this period as God's people await the fulfillment of what he has promised. Other important non-canonical documents that help us to understand this period are the works known later as the Apocrypha, especially the books of 1-4 Maccabees. These documents are Jewish works written in Greek during the intertestamental period. They were not regarded as divinely inspired in antiquity, but they are valuable primary sources for this time period. The Apocrypha is included in several study versions of the Bible (such as the NRSV), so it is readily accessible as a useful resource. The books 1-4 Maccabees will be cited by the abbreviation, *Macc.,* along with the specific reference. Other important sources we will use for this period are written by the Jewish historian Josephus, who lived from AD 37-100. His major works, *Jewish Antiquities* and *The Jewish War,* provide us with an important ancient account of this period. I will cite these works by the abbreviation *Ant.* or *War* followed by the book and paragraph number. The works of Josephus are readily available in translation and online.

New Testament timeline

The icon for the period of EXPECTATIONS is the prophetic visionary cloud. This reminds us of the visions God gave Israel's prophets. The blue crown in the center represents God's coming Messiah, who brings the Old Testament expectations into focus (Isa. 52:7; Zech. 14:9; 1 Pet. 1:10-12). There are ten facets to Israel's EXPECTATIONS listed near the lower section of this column on the New Testament timeline. These are like carefully crafted edges of a diamond of hope. They are like stars that form a single great constellation called redemption. They are the substance of what Paul will call "the hope of Israel" (Acts 28:20).

God builds expectations for a coming King...

This large bold heading on the timeline identifies God's major redemptive activity during the period of EXPECTATIONS. God is at work to prepare the stage of history and the hearts of all humanity for the revelation of his beloved Son. Notice the rising blue arrow on the timeline. The line connects us to the end of the Old Testament timeline and the blue crown of the Messiah. This reminds us that the New Testament is a continuation of the Old Testament narrative. Throughout EXPECTATIONS, the line rises toward the Messiah's birth, as hope grows stronger. At certain points, the line becomes very light, almost disappearing from sight. Yet God remains active, even during times of great suffering. When the line becomes visible again, the intensity of the color deepens. The blue line eventually sharpens into an arrow pointing to the birth of the Messiah. His royal blue will eventually spread out across the New Testament timeline "for the earth will be filled with the knowledge of the glory of the LORD as the waters cover the sea" (Hab. 2:14). Notice that the rulers of the earth also appear in their own likeness on coins across the timeline. Though often making great claims, they appear in a subdued and colorless grey. They cannot help but look ahead. They grow smaller and less significant as God's redemptive plan moves forward toward the reign of him who rules forever and whose glory never fades. To him alone, it will one day be announced: "the kingdom of the world has become the kingdom of our Lord and of his Christ, and he shall reign forever and ever" (Rev. 11:15).

Roadmap to the chapter

As you read through this chapter, I would encourage you to keep the New Testament timeline in front of you, as it will help you locate important people and events. This will be particularly important for this chapter on EXPECTATIONS, since you will encounter a good deal of unfamiliar material. You must be patient in reading this first chapter. Remember that God's people waited for four hundred years to see how his plan of redemption would unfold. I will guide you through the key events that help us to see how God is working in this period. Each heading given in this chapter has been taken directly from the timeline. Additional Bible references are given throughout the chapter. Passages from the Apocrypha will be cited in the NRSV. Quotations from Josephus will be provided so that key events and persons might be more vivid and memorable.

Israel becomes part of the Greek world

Our first bold heading under EXPECTATIONS advances God's redemptive plan, as Israel becomes part of the Greek world. Greece is the third kingdom in Daniel's prophetic vision, after Babylon and Persia. At the end of the Old Testament, Israel exists as a small province within the vast Persian Empire, which stretches from India to Egypt. During the time of Ezra and Nehemiah, the Persians knew Israel only as part of the province "Beyond the River" (Ezra 4:10). Real power flowed from Persepolis. Tribute from the nations filled Persian treasuries, as dignitaries were welcomed through the monumental Gate of All Nations. Within God's sovereign plan, Persia will soon be overthrown and Israel will become part of the Greek world through the conquests of Alexander the Great (Dan. 2, 7). As a result, the nations are given increased exposure to the people of God and the treasure of his Word. The momentous events of this period shape the cultural expectations of the broader Greco-Roman world. These cultural expectations create an alternative narrative out of which many would be called to believe in the God of Israel. We must remember that the biblical narrative of redemption always encounters rival, counterfeit narratives. When people are brought inside the biblical story through faith, these competing narratives are overturned, redirected, and in some aspects even redeemed.

Persian wars with Greece

The Persian wars with Greece alter the geopolitical landscape of the intertestamental world. We rehearse briefly here some of the earlier history of the Persian Empire during the last period of the Old Testament since it sets the context for the period of EXPECTATIONS. The Persian king Darius I (522-486 BC) was a conquering warrior who extended the boundaries of the Persian Empire. You may recall that God had moved Darius early in his reign to pay for the rebuilding of the Jerusalem Temple (Ezra 6:1-12). An image of Darius I on a coin can be seen on the timeline. Darius tries to conquer the Greek Empire, but he is defeated at the famous battle of Marathon. The Persians lose 6,400 men and the Athenians only 192. After the victory, a Greek soldier named Pheidippides runs twenty-six miles back to Athens and collapses after uttering the phrase: "We have won!" His route serves as the inspiration for the modern marathon today.

Ten years after Marathon, the Persians return under Darius' son and successor, Xerxes (486-465 BC). His Persian name *Xshayarsha* means "ruler of men." In Hebrew, this name is transliterated as *'Akhashewerosh*, which is rendered as Ahasuerus in many English versions of the Bible (Esth. 1:1). In Greek, his name is transliterated as *Xerxes*, which is rendered as Xerxes in some English versions of the Bible. Although Xerxes and Ahasuerus sound very different, they are actually just the Greek and Hebrew attempts to transliterate the same Persian name. Xerxes vows to avenge his father's defeat. He conscripts the largest army ever assembled, with contingents from forty-six different subject nations, and more than four thousand ships. Xerxes' massive force approaches the Hellespont, the narrow waterway dividing Asia and Europe. He orders two floating bridges to be built so that his army could cross the sea. When a sudden storm breaks up the bridges and powerful currents wash them away, an enraged Xerxes orders his commanders to lash the sea three hundred times with a whip for not obeying him. He drops iron shackles into the water for not yielding to his glory. He promptly beheads the builders and demands new bridges be made.

As Xerxes crosses over into Greece, Persian ambassadors spread out in advance to ask for "earth and water" as signs of surrender. When the Spartan king Leonidas is asked to lay down his weapons, he famously replies: "Come and take them." The Spartan force of three hundred men holds a narrow pass for several days. A local herder named Ephialtes betrays them and leads the Persians around a mountain path to surround the Spartans. All three hundred Spartans die, except one who commits suicide after reporting the results of the battle. Xerxes orders the corpse of Leonidas to be decapitated, although his body was later recovered and buried with honor.

The Persian army arrives in Athens in the fall of 480 BC. After plundering artwork and sculpture, they burn the city. The Persian navy moves to finish the war against the remaining Greek fleet. The Greek statesman Themistocles cleverly lures the Persian fleet into the narrow straits opposite the island of Salamis by dispatching a false message of surrender to Xerxes. The Persian king launches his force while he sits upon a golden throne on the shore to observe the battle. The battle of Salamis begins just after dawn. The size of the Persian fleet proves a hindrance in the narrow straits and is decimated against the more maneuverable Greek warships. Xerxes groans at the disaster and tears his royal robes. He leaves in disarray and rushes back toward the Hellespont in a forced march of forty-five days. Upon his return to Susa in 479 BC, Xerxes selects Esther as his new queen in place of her banished predecessor (Esth. 2:16-17). The character of Xerxes makes it clear why Esther feared to come before the king (Esth. 4:11). The story of Esther reveals how God sovereignly protects his people in a violent and hostile world. Although Esther takes place near the end of the Old Testament, this will prove one of the great lessons of the intertestamental period as well.

The golden age of classical Greek culture

The Greek victory in the Persian wars leads to the golden age of classical Greek culture. This is important in our study of the intertestamental period because Greek culture creates a set of rival expectations to the biblical hope, as we will see. Upon the ruins of the burned Acropolis, the Athenian statesman Pericles embarks on a lavish building program. The centerpiece is a temple, known as the Parthenon, dedicated to the virgin goddess Athena Parthenos. The architectural statement of the Parthenon is extremely well conceived. There are no straight lines in the entire structure due to subtle optical refinements. From a distance, the Parthenon looks perfect to the human eye. At each end, a triangular pediment holds life-sized sculptures. The eastern pediment depicts the birth of Athena from the head of Zeus; the western pediment shows the contest between Athena and Poseidon for the honor of becoming the patron deity of the city. The four sides of the Parthenon contain brightly painted sculptures carved in high relief. Each side is devoted to historical or mythical battles. Along the exterior walls of the inner temple, a continuous frieze in low relief extends some 524 feet. The Parthenon frieze contains 192 figures to immortalize the number of Athenians who fell at the battle of Marathon. The Parthenon frieze also shows an intermingling of human with divine figures in sacred procession to the entrance of the temple. Once inside, the Parthenon houses a towering gold and ivory statue of Athena over forty feet high. The statue is adorned with removable gold plates weighing forty-four talents, nearly 2,500 pounds. The goddess Athena thus embodies a considerable part of the treasury of Athens. The Parthenon is regarded as the high point of classical art and an enduring symbol of Greek culture.

Greece also experiences a golden age in philosophy, art, literature, and science. This is the era of the philosophers Socrates, Plato, and Aristotle. The sculptor Phidias reaches a new level of technical achievement. His forty-three foot gold and ivory statue of the Greek god Zeus would later be included in the Seven Wonders of the World. The historians Herodotus and Thucydides flourish at this time. The poets Aeschylus, Sophocles, Euripides, and Aristophanes compose plays that are still performed today. The philosopher Isocrates boldly claims that Greece has been given the role of teaching the whole world. This confident posture of Greek culture toward the rest of the world could exist only in isolation from the people of God. This would soon change under God's sovereign hand.

New Testament timeline

You may want to locate the picture of the Parthenon on the timeline under this section, as it will remind you of this competing cultural and religious vision. It is against the backdrop of this very temple that Paul will one day proclaim that the "the God who made the world and everything in it, being Lord of heaven and earth does not live in temples made by man" (Acts 17:24; cf. Gen. 1:1). This is why the Parthenon is also depicted on the timeline's map at Athens, recalling Paul's message to the Athenians with this backdrop in view. You will find a brief description of the Parthenon given on the back of the timeline under the theological key section.

Alexander defeats Persia, establishing Greek rule in the East

The next movement of the story in this period is when Greek rule is established in the East. Alexander the Great is the son of Philip II, king of Macedon. He is privately tutored by Aristotle in the classical tradition and receives extensive military training. When his father is assassinated in 336

BC, Alexander inherits at age twenty a well-trained Macedonian army, superior weaponry, and a corps of able commanders. After spending two years consolidating his power in Greece, Alexander sets off to conquer the Persian Empire now led by King Darius III. Alexander deliberately retraces the route of Xerxes across central and northern Greece. In 334 BC, he crosses the Hellespont with thirty thousand soldiers and five thousand cavalry. He hurls his spear on land and dances around the tomb of Achilles, the great hero of the Trojan War. Alexander viewed himself as the new Achilles; he even slept with a copy of Homer's *Iliad* throughout his entire campaign.

Beginning near the site of ancient Troy, Alexander sweeps across the province of Asia in a series of military victories. He finally encounters a large Persian army under the command of Darius III at Issus in 333 BC. The Persian forces number over 100,000, with Darius positioned at their center; the Macedonian forces number only 40,000. When Alexander perceives a weakness in the Persian formation, he rushes his cavalry straight toward Darius' chariot. The Persian king flees the battle, leaving his mother, wife, and two daughters behind. Darius sues for peace, offering ten thousand talents for the safe return of the royal family and a political alliance. Alexander refuses and reminds the king that since he has prevailed in battle, Darius should address him as King of Asia and not as an equal.

Alexander moves down the eastern Mediterranean coast to cut off the Persian naval forces and consolidate the western half of the Persian Empire. He besieges Tyre and captures the island city after an extended seven-month siege in 332 BC, constructing an artificial landmass that would forever connect the island to the mainland. Darius again sends envoys, offering ten thousand talents, all the territory from the Euphrates to the Aegean, and his daughter in marriage. Alexander replies that he has no need of money or land and that he would marry Darius' daughter only if he wished. Darius gives up hope for peace and prepares for war. Alexander forays into the interior of Syria, capturing a number of places, occupying some by force, and bringing others to terms. He moves south, capturing Gaza on the coast after two months. It is important to remember that Jerusalem is nearby and can be reached after a ride of one or two days.

Israel becomes part of the Greek world precisely at this point. Alexander prepares to meet a delegation from Jerusalem. Israel's high priest at the time, Jaddua, asks God's people to pray for protection. God gives the high priest a vision and instructs him to open the gates of the city and to meet Alexander dressed in his high priestly garments. When Alexander sees the high priest of Israel, he bows down before him in reverence. His commanders are astonished and question why he honors this man. Alexander replies that he had seen this very person in a dream wearing these distinctive garments, while he was still in Macedonia. Having seen no other dressed like him, Alexander honors the God who gives such a priesthood and becomes convinced that he conducts his army for a divine purpose. Jerusalem's religious leaders produce a scroll of the prophet Daniel to show Alexander that God had promised that one of the Greeks would destroy the Persian Empire (Dan. 8). Alexander offers a sacrifice to God in the Jerusalem Temple and allows God's people to follow their ancestral laws (Josephus, *Ant.* 11.325-339).

Alexander's generous terms are consistent with those he bestowed upon the other cities who receive him. His offering in the temple of Jerusalem and treatment of the priests are similar to his honoring of the gods of Greece, Tyre, Egypt, and Babylon. The truly distinctive element of this encounter is the Word of God. The LORD had revealed to Daniel the prophetic sequence of kingdoms for this period (Dan. 2, 7). Daniel had seen another vision of a ram with two horns (Dan. 8:3-4). The ram had charged west, north, and south, claiming all lands under its feet. No one could oppose it. The ram represents the Medo-Persian Empire that extends precisely in these directions. Daniel had then seen a male goat come rapidly from the west without even touching the ground (Dan. 8:5). The goat ran straight at the ram, striking it with great rage and trampling it to the ground. No one could rescue the ram from its power. God had given Daniel the interpretation of the vision: "As for the ram that you saw with the two horns, these are the kings of Media and Persia. And the goat is the king of Greece. And the great horn between his eyes is the first king" (Dan. 8:20-21). The details of Daniel's vision correspond exactly with the character of Alexander's campaign. God's redemptive purpose through history includes the progression of kingdoms that will prepare Israel and the rest of the world for his Messiah.

After granting Israel the right to live according to their laws, Alexander founds the city of Alexandria in Egypt. This city would become the largest and most important of the twenty cities, which he would found named

Alexandria. The city would become a center of culture and learning. It would become second only to Rome in size and wealth. Alexander then presses further into the eastern Persian Empire, crossing the Euphrates and Tigris Rivers unopposed. Darius III raises another massive force and prepares to meet Alexander on the plain of Gaugamela (in northern Iraq) in 331 BC. Although heavily outnumbered, Alexander outmaneuvers the Persian army. The Great King is enveloped with intense hand-to-hand fighting and is the first to flee the battle. The terror on the face of Darius is captured in the mosaic of Alexander found at Pompeii. The Persian center collapses and the confused force is crushed. Alexander moves swiftly to capture Babylon, Susa, and Persepolis and their enormous treasuries without opposition. He claims 180,000 talents of gold, a staggering figure some two centuries in the making. Alexander pursues Darius, using forced marches over hundreds of miles of rough terrain. He eventually finds Darius close to the point of death, having been fatally stabbed by his own allies. Alexander sends his body back to Persepolis and gives him a royal burial in the tomb of his ancestors. The Persian Empire ends in the summer of 330 BC as Alexander establishes Greek rule in the East.

Alexander's campaigns would inspire all future makers of empires in the Greco-Roman world of the New Testament. Alexander had embarked upon an unrelenting twelve-year campaign, eventually reaching all the way to India. Covering a total distance of more than 22,000 miles, he never lost a battle though often heavily outnumbered. His tactics are studied today in military academies and he is considered one of the greatest tactical battlefield commanders of all time.

For our study of EXPECTATIONS, Alexander's conquests bring East and West into greater contact with each other. Alexander makes several attempts to synthesize the cultures he conquers and bring them together under his sole rule. He officiates at the marriage ceremony of ten thousand Macedonian soldiers to Persian noblewomen to create a new ruling class for his empire. He experiments with wearing Persian royal dress. He requires his soldiers to pay him homage in the Persian gesture of bowing down in reverence, which they heartily refuse. As a result of his campaigns, the Greek world is exposed to the God of Israel. This encounter produces wonder and admiration for many Greeks as they learn of a people who worship one God and whose sacred writings contain the history and purpose of God for all of humanity. The first recorded exchange is between the Greek philosopher Aristotle and an Israelite sage. Aristotle is impressed that the Jewish sage speaks Greek and has the soul of a Greek. In the end, Aristotle concludes that the Jewish sage had instructed *him* rather than the other way around. This fascinating incident encourages us that the world often feels wonder when they first encounter the God of the Bible. We need to be reminded that the responsibility for instructing the nations and bringing them together under a single ruler has been entrusted to the people of God and not to the world (Isa. 2:1-4; Matt. 28:19-20; Eph. 1:22).

New Testament timeline

I would encourage you to take a few moments to locate several icons on the timeline for this section. First of all, you will see a picture of an attacking soldier, which has been taken from the Old Testament timeline. This icon represents attack from a foreign power, which in this case recalls the Persian wars with Greece. Second, you should locate the coins bearing Alexander's image on the timeline under EXPECTATIONS, and it is on the back of the timeline accompanied by a brief description. This coin represents the rule of Alexander (332-323 BC). Third, the picture of a leopard is taken from Daniel's vision in the Old Testament. It indicates that Alexander's defeat of the Persian Empire ushers in the third kingdom in Daniel's vision. Lastly, you should have already located the picture of the Parthenon; this icon represents the influence of Greek culture and its competing religious worldview.

Israel suffers in wars of Alexander's Successors (Dan. 11)

Our second bold heading under EXPECTATIONS is Israel suffers in wars of Alexander's Successors. God's people must learn to trust in him, even when a series of violent wars between Alexander's successors are fought across their land. Despite these hardships, God remains at work in the world. He controls the rise and fall of nations. He will even inspire a Greek king to translate the Scriptures into Greek. As Prov. 21:1 declares: "The king's heart is a stream of water in the hand of the LORD, he turns it wherever he will."

Alexander dies suddenly in Babylon in 323 BC at age thirty-three, never having returned to Greece. His vast plans for the future are found among his documents. He intended to assemble a huge navy and campaign against Carthage, build a network of roads and harbors across North Africa, erect vast temples at key religious centers, dedicate a tomb for his father which would rival the pyramids of Egypt, and intermarry peoples in order to bring the world into harmony and the bonds of kinship. Although the LORD uses Alexander to advance his sovereign purpose, the role of uniting all peoples under a single ruler belongs to the Messiah (Ps. 2:8; Dan. 7:13-14). When four of his generals ask at his deathbed to whom he would leave his kingdom, Alexander replies: "To the strongest." This recalls the prophetic word of Daniel: "The goat became exceedingly great, but when he was strong, the great horn was broken, and instead of it there came up four conspicuous horns toward the four winds of heaven" (Dan. 8:8). Daniel had prophesied that the Greek kingdom would be divided among those who are not his heirs: "As soon as he has arisen, his kingdom shall be broken and divided toward the four winds of heaven, but not to his posterity, nor according to the authority with which he ruled, for his kingdom shall be plucked up and go to others besides these" (Dan. 11:4). We now turn our attention to consider what takes place next in fulfillment of Daniel's prophecy.

His four generals abandon Alexander's plans and devote their energy to fighting one another to become sole ruler. These generals are known as Alexander's *Successors*. Their struggle for power rages over the next two centuries. Since they are Alexander's successors, the coin depicted on the timeline for their rule is Alexander, which represents the continuation of his Greek rule through them. The four generals will soon be reduced to two. Ptolemy will rule from Alexandria in Egypt (note that the P in Ptolemy is silent, pronounced *Tolemy*). Seleucus will rule from Antioch in Syria. Since these two important generals may be unfamiliar to you, they can be easily distinguished by remembering that **P** is for **P**tolemy, who rules where **Pha**raohs had been on the throne in Egypt. S is for Seleucus who rules from Syria. Their descendants, who are known as the Ptolemies and the Seleucids, confront each other in a series of six Syrian Wars. Imagine a map with a large, well-equipped army in Egypt and another large, well-equipped army in Syria. Where will the fighting actually take place? The land of Israel lies in between these competing powers. Israel suffers greatly during this period under the tracks of marching armies. Her sons are conscripted for battle. Her resources are plundered. God's people suffer the incalculable collateral damages involved in hosting war. The Ptolemies and Seleucids are the kings of the north and the kings of the south in Dan. 11.

Ptolemaic rule over Israel (301-200 BC)

Ptolemy I combines the Greek cultural and intellectual tradition with Egyptian religion and mythology. His dynasty would endure for nearly three hundred years until its last monarch, Cleopatra VII, commits suicide after Mark Anthony's defeat by Octavian in 31 BC. Israel becomes incorporated into Ptolemy's kingdom in 301 BC. Although God's people suffer greatly during this period, God continues to build expectations by providing the nations of the world greater access to his Word.

Ptolemy II sponsors translation of the Bible into Greek (LXX)

Ptolemy II is remembered as a man of learning and culture. Under his patronage, the library of Alexandria acquires and disseminates encyclopedic learning to the broader Greek world. Alexandrian customs officials would search merchant ships for books. All books would be taken into custody so that copies could be produced for the library. The library of Alexandria grows into the largest in the world; it contains a vast collection of works ranging from philosophical treatises to cookbooks. At this time, Ptolemy II learns of the worth of the Bible and the need to translate it into Greek. He sends a letter to the high priest in Jerusalem, requesting that their law be translated into Greek from the Hebrew original.

The high priest selects six learned men from each of the twelve tribes. These seventy-two translators are brought from Israel to Egypt where they are hosted by the Greek king and lavishly supplied. During an extended seven-day banquet, King Ptolemy poses a series of ethical questions to the translators in a stylized symposium. Each of their answers makes explicit reference to God. Ptolemy proclaims that these men excel in virtue and understanding, for they give glory to God in all things and proclaim his sovereign hand over all nations. The work of these translators takes place on the island of Pharos, located off the coast of Alexandria. Their version becomes known as the translation of the seventy, the Septuagint, commonly identified by the Roman numerals LXX (with seventy-two being simplified to seventy). This is the first large-scale translation project in the ancient world.

New Testament timeline

You will notice a picture of the lighthouse of Alexandria on the timeline's map under the period of TEACHING. Ptolemy II built the lighthouse on the island of Pharos, the very place where God's word was being translated. The lighthouse was 450 feet high, the second tallest man-made structure in the world, just shorter than the Great Pyramid of Giza. The signal fire of the lighthouse would radiate a beam of light more than one hundred miles. The *unending light of God's Word* now becomes available to the nations under God's sovereign hand on this same island.

The significance of the Septuagint is that the Word of God becomes available to a much broader Greek-speaking audience. The translation also meets the needs of Greek-speaking Jewish communities outside the land of Israel. The Septuagint seeks to be faithful to the original Hebrew text and to strike a middle position between excessive literalism and dynamic equivalence. The Septuagint defines many key biblical terms in Greek. This is the version often read and quoted by the New Testament writers when they cite the Old Testament. You will notice that I refer to this translation on several occasions in our study of the New Testament. Philo of Alexandria, a Jewish commentator born a generation before Christ, records that the translators prayed that all of humanity might benefit from these beautiful commandments and that their lives might be corrected by living according to the Scriptures. The Word of God remains the most widely translated document in the history of the world. There is an urgent remaining need for those who have never heard the words of the living God in their native language. May the LORD raise up translators in our generation who are called to complete this sacred task.

Seleucid rule over Israel (198-142 BC)

Israel falls under Seleucid rule after Antiochus III defeats the Ptolemaic general Scopas in 198 BC at Baneas. Antiochus III is the great-grandson of Alexander's general Seleucus. Like Alexander who built twenty cities named

Alexandria, Seleucus founds sixteen cities named Antioch after his son Antiochus. One of these cities will be the place where believers in Christ are first called Christians (Acts 11:26). The church of Antioch will be a major supporter of Paul's missionary journeys. For now, Antiochus III extends his rule across Asia Minor into Greece, drawing the attention of the emerging Roman power. Rome demands that Antiochus recognize the right of the Romans to protect the Greeks in Asia. After the Romans declare war, Antiochus is defeated and forced to renounce his territory on the western side of the Taurus Mountains. He is also required to pay a staggering war indemnity of fifteen thousand talents. His son Antiochus IV grows up as a hostage in Rome as a pledge of future payments.

Antiochus III grants Israel to live by their ancestral laws

When Antiochus III first expands his rule into Israel, the inhabitants of Jerusalem receive him and supply his army. In return, Antiochus III issues a series of royal decrees to benefit Jerusalem. He remits taxes and provides funds for the offerings made in the Jerusalem Temple. Three of these decrees have been preserved by indirect transmission (Josephus, *Ant.* 12:138-153). They provide another fascinating window into how the nations of the world are amazed at their first encounter with the people of God. Antiochus III grants Israel a number of significant provisions, including the right to order their society according to their ancestral laws, namely, the sacred Scriptures. He provides wine, oil, frankincense, and cedar from Lebanon. He even publishes a decree to guard the sanctity of the Jerusalem Temple from defilement by foreigners or desecration through prohibited sacrifices (*Ant.* 12.145-146). The picture of the Ten Commandments on the timeline will remind you of this favorable ruling by Antiochus III that enables Israel to live according to God's Word.

However, the benevolent posture of Seleucid rule toward Israel does not last. Antiochus III is killed attempting to plunder the temple of Elymais in Persia in order to replenish his exhausted treasury. His son Seleucus IV rules in his place. When Seleucus IV is murdered a few years later, his brother Antiochus IV rules in his place (175-164 BC). His reign produces a time of terror and great distress in Israel. Despite the intensity of suffering, God remains faithful to his promises. He does not allow his people to be completely destroyed by a hostile culture, and he will deliver Israel once again.

God delivers Israel through the Maccabees

Our third bold heading for the period of EXPECTATIONS teaches us that God delivers Israel through a priestly family, known as the Maccabees. God does not allow the lamp to go out in Israel because of the covenant he had made with David (2 Chron. 21:7). His people must remain in the world because God's redemptive purpose through Israel has not yet been fully realized. During this time, God's people struggle with compromising their faith under pressure from the surrounding culture. The conflict of worldviews erupts in violence. Israel's suffering reaches new depths when Antiochus IV desecrates the temple and makes biblical faith illegal. Thousands are put to death, yet God delivers his people through the Maccabees and the temple is rededicated.

New Testament timeline

You may want to take a moment to locate the picture of a hammer on the timeline that represents this period. The Hebrew noun *makkebet,* meaning "hammer," is the nickname given to Judas Maccabeus whom God raises up to rescue his people. This picture, along with its description on the back of the timeline, will help you to remember the Maccabean victory over Antiochus IV.

Conflict in Israel over attitude to Greek culture

We have already seen several positive reactions from the nations of the world when they encounter the God of Israel. They discover for the first time the identity, character, and purpose of God. He is incomparable in the beauty of his holiness, power, and mercy. Sadly, this encounter with the nations can have a negative influence on God's people, as they become enthralled when they are exposed to pagan culture. In the wake of Alexander's conquests, Greek cultural institutions and aspirations spread widely. The Greeks bring an idolatrous, self-glorifying perspective on this world. Man is the measure of all things. The highest forms of Greek cultural achievement are heroic deeds, athletic competition, and exhilarating entertainment in the theater and hippodrome. Greeks offer a rival mythology of many gods whose sexual immorality and vice are reflected in their devotees. Temples for the gods and heroes are built to house their images. Idolatrous worship secures protection and honor for each particular location. Greeks also present an alternative educational philosophy and curriculum based on their own literature and understanding of success. The Greek vision of cultivating leadership emphasizes bodily training in athletics, and rhetoric as the art of public speaking. These are the skills required to secure participation, status, and employment in a rapidly changing world. Paul will later renounce reliance on Greek rhetoric to ensure that the proclamation of the gospel does not rely on human technique, but on the power of God and his Word (1 Cor. 1:18-31; cf. Jer. 9:23-24). Paul will use the image of an athlete to illustrate the real importance of training in godliness (1 Cor. 9:24-27). For now, we need to see that this dominant, aggressive Greek culture produces a tremendous conflict in Israel.

The conflict over Greek culture erupts when Jason, the brother of the high priest Onias III, offers 360 talents of silver to be appointed the new high priest. Antiochus IV readily assents and grants Jason the high priesthood, along with the authority to shift Israel toward the Greek way of life. Jason's reforms introduce new customs contrary to God's laws. God's people "Hellenize" through their adoption of foreign ways. Jason establishes a gymnasium in the heart of Jerusalem to educate a new ruling class. The gymnasium emphasizes athletic training and exercise. These are done in the nude wearing a distinctive Greek hat. The Greek word *gymnos* means "naked." The place where these exercises are held is called a *gymnasium*. The powerful attraction of sports and entertainment proves irresistible even for those dedicated to serving God. The priests ministering in the sanctuary begin to be distracted. They eventually neglect their ministry to God that they might not miss the wrestling events and the discus throw (*2 Macc.* 4:10-15). The allure of dominant, human-centered culture can be intoxicating, even to those who are well-versed in the Word of God. As I write these words, I am soberly reminded that my own society has embraced and valued sports and entertainment among our highest forms of prestige. It grieves me to consider that thirty seconds of advertising during the Super Bowl could fund our entire church ministry for four years or send dozens of missionaries to the field.

Antiochus IV plunders the Temple forcing Israel to abandon the laws of God

Antiochus IV grows elated at the initial successes of his reign. He assumes the grandiose title Antiochus *Epiphanes,* meaning "God manifest," although later Greek writers would call him *Epimanes* meaning "Madman." He launches an aggressive policy of political and cultural expansion. He claims all of Syria, Palestine, and Phoenicia, sparking a new war with Ptolemaic Egypt. After Antiochus has himself crowned King of Egypt, the Roman Senate sends Gaius Popilius Laenas to protect Roman interests. Antiochus greets the Roman envoys and offers his hand in friendship. Popilius refuses, asking him first to read the decree of the Senate that he places in his hand. The decree demands Antiochus' immediate withdrawal. Standing at the head of a large army, Antiochus asks for the opportunity to call his friends and consider what he should do. Popilius slowly draws a circle around him in the sand with his staff. He tells Antiochus that he should make his final decision before he steps out. This confrontation is the origin of the idiom "to draw a line in the sand." A stunned Antiochus yields and withdraws in rage.

Antiochus leaves Egypt and vents his anger by attacking Jerusalem. The account of his brutality is preserved in 1-2 Maccabees. Antiochus' soldiers slaughter young and old, men and women, infants and children. Within three days, eighty thousand are killed. The atrocities escalate even further when Antiochus enters the Jerusalem Temple and seizes vessels, offerings, and 1,800 talents of silver (*2 Macc.* 5:11-16, 21). He then issues a decree throughout Jerusalem and Judah, making the practice of biblical faith illegal. He prohibits burnt offerings and sacrifices; he requires Israel to profane the Sabbath; and he defiles the sanctuary. God's people are forced to sacrifice unclean animals and to leave their sons uncircumcised. Antiochus decrees death for anyone who refuses to obey the king's command (*1 Macc.* 1:44-50).

Antiochus sends an Athenian senator to enforce his decree. The people, land, and sanctuary are desecrated to an almost unimaginable degree. The Jerusalem Temple is filled with revelry. The altar is covered with abominable, desolating offerings. People are forbidden to keep the Sabbath, observe the festivals, or even confess themselves to be Jews (*2 Macc.* 6:1-6). It is hard for us to imagine the level of persecution God's people experience under the hand of Antiochus IV.

The prophet Daniel had predicted the anguish of these days. He had seen a "horn" that would become swollen with pride. The regular burnt offering would be abolished and the sanctuary overthrown. The horn would throw truth to the ground (Dan. 8:9-12). By Antiochus' decree, God's people are forced to participate in processions to Dionysius, the god of wine and drunkenness. They are required to adopt a different calendar, marking each month with Antiochus' birthday. They are pressured to offer pagan sacrifices and eat forbidden foods. Those who refuse to adopt the Greek way of life are killed. Two women are paraded around the city for having circumcised their children and are thrown down from the wall with their sons. Others secretly try to observe the Sabbath, only to be found out and burned to death (2 Macc. 6:7-11). An elderly man named Eleazar, together with seven brothers and their mother, are tortured for refusing to eat forbidden foods. Antiochus strips the aged man and flogs him. His body is tortured with various instruments. When he falls, a guard kicks him in the side and shouts at him to obey the king's command. As guards pour a burning liquid into his nostrils, Eleazar lifts his eyes toward heaven and utters a final prayer that God might purify the land (4 Macc. 6:2-11, 24-29).

New Testament timeline
This period is represented on the timeline by the coin depicting Antiochus IV, also known as Antiochus *Epiphanes*. Take a few moments to locate this coin, along with the brief description of his rule on the back of the timeline. Antiochus is remembered for his violent and outlandish behavior, especially his forcing Israel to abandon God's laws and adopt the Greek way of life. He is identified as the arrogant horn throwing truth to the ground in Daniel's prophecies (Dan. 8:9-14; cf. 2 Macc. 5-7; 4 Macc. 6-17).

December 164 BC the temple rededicated (*Hanukkah*)
Although many compromise their faith, thousands in Israel refuse to obey the king. When invited to sacrifice and eat forbidden foods, a priest named Mattathias declares that even if all the nations under the king obey him, he and his family will live according to God's law (1 Macc. 2:19-22). When one of his kinsmen steps forward to obey the king, Mattathias burns with zeal for God like Phineas long before (Num. 25:7-13). He kills his fellow Israelite

who is about to sacrifice to foreign gods. Mattathias then cries out in his town, calling everyone who is zealous for God to join him and his sons (*1 Macc.* 2:24-27).

Mattathias' third son Judas, nicknamed *Maccabeus* ("the hammer"), defeats Antiochus' forces over the next three years. Before the decisive battle at Beth-Zur, Judas prays to God, the Savior of Israel, to deliver his people, remembering what God had done through David to defeat the boastful Goliath (*1 Macc.* 4:30-33). After Antiochus is defeated, Judas and his soldiers reach the Temple Mount. They weep to see the altar profaned and the gates burned. Thickets grow in the courts and the priestly chambers are in ruins. Judas selects godly priests to cleanse the sanctuary and remove anything that has defiled it. They take unhewn stones and rebuild the altar. They consecrate the courts and make new holy vessels, such as the lampstand and table. They offer incense on the altar and light the lamps. They place the bread of the Presence in the temple and hang the curtains. Early in the morning on December fourteenth, 164 BC, they offer the burnt offering on the altar and restore the worship of the LORD in Jerusalem (*1 Macc.* 4:47-53). The temple is rededicated three years from the day it had been desecrated. This celebration is known as the Feast of *Hanukkah* (meaning "dedication" in Hebrew). This key event is represented on the timeline by the picture of the lampstand with branches, known as the *menorah.*

During this period, God's people learn the important lesson that cultural compromise threatens their very existence in the world. The persecution under Antiochus IV refines them in the furnace of affliction. Israel is preserved, despite her disobedience, because of God's promises to Abraham and David. In Scripture, suffering proves redemptive under God's sovereign hand (Job 5:17-18; Prov. 3:11-12; Jer. 30:11; 31:18-19). God's mercy continues, even in the midst of discipline, and he does not forsake his people (2 *Macc.* 6:12-16). God delivers Israel at this time through the Maccabees. He grants them victory over numerically superior armies. He defeats the tyrant through the blood of his saints. Shortly after learning of the defeat of his army, Antiochus IV dies while plundering temples in Persia (2 *Macc.* 9). Although making great boasts, Antiochus' coin remains grey on the timeline. He cannot help but look ahead. God cannot be mocked forever. The sacrificial death of the martyrs is the decisive means God uses to overthrow tyranny; their death is described like a sacrifice, a ransom for the sin of the nation (*4 Macc.* 17:20-22). We need to remember that the LORD is at work during the period of EXPECTATIONS—he is preparing the hearts of Israel and the nations for his beloved Son who will offer his life once for all. He will one day tell his disciples: "the Son of Man came not to be served but to serve, and to give his life as a ransom for many" (Matt. 20:28; cf. Isa. 53:10-12).

Hasmoneans rule "until a true prophet arises"

After the Maccabean victory in 164 BC, the family of Mattathias, later known as the Hasmoneans, rules over Israel. (You can remember the identity of the Hasmoneans by connecting them with Hanukkah, since both terms start with the letter H.) The Hasmoneans initially view themselves as a temporary leadership provision "until a true prophet arises" (*1 Macc.* 4:46; 14:41; cf. Deut. 18:15, 18). After Judas Maccabees dies in 160 BC, four years after the rededication of the temple, his youngest brother Jonathan leads the nation. In 152 BC, Jonathan is named both governor and high priest by the new Seleucid Greek ruler, Alexander, the son of Antiochus IV. Jonathan's attempt to hold both offices of governor and high priest sparks a negative reaction among many devout Israelites, since this would only be permitted for the Messiah. Some scholars suggest that this event causes a number of priests to withdraw under the leadership of the "Teacher of Righteousness," which will result in the formation of the Essene community at Qumran. We know about this religious group through the discovery of the Dead Sea Scrolls. In the Scrolls, Jonathan is referred to as "the Wicked Priest" and frequently contrasted with the "Teacher of Righteousness." Other lay leaders withdraw to form a surrogate priesthood devoted to the study of the Scriptures; they even apply the ritual requirements of the priesthood to their everyday life. This marks the beginning of the group that will become known as the Pharisees. Aristocratic supporters of Jonathan's high priesthood will become the Sadducees. We will learn more about these groups in the following chapter. For now, it is important to realize that God's people not only suffer under foreign Greek rule, but there is continued unrest within Israel over ungodly leadership that threatens the existence of the people of God.

Simon, the last of the five Maccabean brothers, eventually succeeds Jonathan. Under his leadership in 142 BC, the last remnant of the Greek

Seleucid garrison is defeated and "the yoke of the Gentiles is removed from Israel" (*1 Macc.* 13:41). Israel becomes an independent state again. This is the first time God's people have experienced any degree of independence since the exile. Their initial euphoria, however, is short-lived. The Hasmonean rulers expand territory, yet they offend many in Israel. Like many who are entrusted with leadership, they find worldly attractions irresistible. The Hasmoneans adopt Hellenistic models of kingship and opulent patterns of court life. They use double names, one Hebrew, another Greek; they mint coins with Greek images of power. They build the cultural institutions of the pagan world like theatres, gymnasiums, and stadiums across the land.

Popular resentment against the Hasmoneans increases over the next century. John Hyrcanus (135-104 BC) refuses when a prominent Pharisee asks him to lay aside the priesthood and be content with leading the civil government. Hyrcanus' son, Alexander Jannaeus (103-76 BC), proves even more brutal. Tempers flare during the Feast of Tabernacles when pilgrimage crowds pelt him with citrus, because he improperly officiates the temple liturgy. He responds by sending his soldiers into the crowd, resulting in the deaths of six thousand people. Alexander later crucifies eight hundred Pharisees in Jerusalem. He kills their wives and children before their eyes, and then watches their death while drinking and lying down with his concubines (Josephus, *War* 1:97). The Dead Sea Scroll community laments Alexander as a brutal man, who carried out revenge and hanged living men from trees, referring to these mass crucifixions.

The bitter disappointment with the Hasmoneans deepens Israel's longing for the righteous rule of the coming Messiah. This hope finds expression in a collection of eighteen prayers written during the first century BC that are associated with the Pharisees. These prayers are filled with allusions from the Old Testament prophets, especially passages from Isaiah and Jeremiah. The Old Testament passages in these prayers serve as a poignant reminder that God's people are learning to search the Scriptures with rising expectations for God to act again.

Israel is humbled by the return of Roman rule

Our fourth bold heading describes how Israel is humbled by the return of foreign rule. The Hasmonean ruler Alexander Jannaeus dies in 76 BC. His widow, Salome Alexandra, rules for nine years (76-67 BC); she is remembered as a competent and pious queen. Her two sons, Hyrcanus II and Aristobulus II, fight bitterly for succession. The violence of their rivalry brings Israel to the brink of a civil war and turns Jerusalem into a fortress. Both brothers appeal to the Roman general Pompey, who is campaigning in the East. This crisis brings Israel under direct Roman control in 63 BC. The few decades of independence under the Jewish Hasmonean leaders collapse under a crushing new foreign power. The Roman Republic itself is transformed during this era through civil war into an empire. Roman rule is exercised over Israel through the client kingship of Herod. During this period, God's people suffer greatly and in humility search the Scriptures to find hope. Since the arrival of Roman rule marks the fourth kingdom of Daniel's prophecy, this further heightens expectations that the next movement of God's redemptive plan will be the arrival of the kingdom of God and his Messiah.

New Testament timeline

This period of Roman rule is represented on the timeline by the ten-horned beast, which is taken directly from the Old Testament and recalls the fourth kingdom in Daniel's prophecy (Dan. 2:40-44; 7:17-22). Daniel had seen the fourth kingdom, which was terrifying and strong, with iron teeth devouring and breaking in pieces. This picture will help you remember the violent Roman rule of this period, yet since it is the fourth kingdom, it builds expectations that God will soon establish his everlasting kingdom.

Pompey besieges Jerusalem and enters the Holy of Holies 63 BC

Gnaeus Pompeius Magnus (106 BC-48 BC), commonly known as Pompey, becomes a successful general and political leader during the late Roman Republic. Pompey rises through his military conquests and his disregard for traditional political limitations based on age or class. After victories in Africa, Pompey demands a triumph. Trying to upstage his superiors, Pompey rides in a chariot towed by an elephant, representing his exotic African conquests. However, the elephant would not fit through the city gate! Pompey achieves further victories in Spain and Gaul. He helps to suppress the slave revolt led by the gladiator Spartacus. In a violent display of Roman power, six thousand slaves from Spartacus' army are crucified at regular intervals for nearly two hundred miles along the Appian Way leading into Rome. Pompey is elected to the highest public office of consul at only thirty-five years of age. Two years later, he is given command of a naval task force to suppress piracy in the eastern Mediterranean. The conservative faction of the Senate remains suspicious of him, but Pompey's supporters, including Julius Caesar, insist that he should be given control over the sea and the coasts for fifty miles inland. By the end of the summer of 66 BC, his forces sweep through the Mediterranean. In 64 BC, Pompey marches into Syria; he deposes the Seleucid Greek ruler, Antiochus XIII, and reconstitutes this area as a Roman province. He then moves south and establishes Roman supremacy in Phoenicia.

Pompey's next decisive victory takes place in 63 BC. As the civil war in Israel escalates between the Hasmonean sons Hyrcanus and Aristobulus, both appeal to Pompey with large gifts. Pompey sides with Hyrcanus, largely through the intervention of the Idumean Antipater, who is the father of Herod the Great. This marks the beginning of a lasting relationship between Rome and the house of Herod, as we will see later in our study. Pompey besieges Jerusalem by erecting a siege ramp on the north side of the temple. After three months, Roman battering rams breach the city wall. As Roman forces enter the city, many priests are slain even as they continue their service at the altar. Thousands are killed by the unrestrained brutality of Roman plunder (Josephus, *War* 1:150-152). Pompey exercises his right of conquest and enters the Jerusalem Temple. He sees the lampstand, table, vessels made of gold, a great quantity of spices, and thousands of talents dedicated to the LORD. However, he is astonished that there is no idol or image of the God of Israel and leaves wondering who is worshiped in Jerusalem. His entrance desecrates the Jerusalem Temple and profanes the holy place. The date of 63 BC on the timeline thus represents an important year in the period of EXPECTATIONS, as it marks the moment when Israel is humbled by the return of foreign rule under Rome. The fourth kingdom of Daniel's prophetic vision now rules the land.

Remember that Daniel had depicted the fourth kingdom as a mixture of iron and clay (Dan. 2:40-44). It was strong and warlike, yet brittle and difficult to hold together. We see this dynamic throughout Roman history, from the very beginning when Romulus kills his brother Remus, to the rise of Caesar Augustus who rules a society that is worn out with civil war. Daniel also describes the fourth beast as "terrifying and dreadful and exceedingly strong. It had great iron teeth; it devoured and broke in pieces and stamped what was left with its feet" (Dan. 7:7). As we will see, Rome will rule Israel with both violent brutality and a rapidly changing cast of characters.

For those who know the Scripture well, however, the arrival of Roman rule causes Israel's hope and expectations to rise. God's people know that the fourth kingdom will be followed by the kingdom of God and his Messiah. His kingdom will never be destroyed. The stone cut without human hands will crush all rival kingdoms and become a great mountain filling the earth. There is great hope, therefore, even in the midst of great adversity, for God is at work accomplishing his plan of redemption through history. God's king is surely coming, the glory of Israel and a light of revelation to the nations.

Julius Caesar transforms the Roman Republic into an Empire

The Roman world is violently transformed during this period from a republic into an empire. Roman society changes from a *res publica* ("public thing") to an empire ruled by an *imperator* ("emperor" or "conquering general"). It is helpful to review briefly the background that led to this change. The city of Rome had been established in 753 BC. The Latin poet Vergil wrote Rome's national epic poem called the Aeneid. The poem recounts how the Trojan prince Aeneas fled the burning city of Troy after the Greek victory in the Trojan War. Following a long journey, reminiscent of the travels of the Greek hero Odysseus, the Trojan prince lands in Italy and founds a new settlement in Latium, which grows to become the city of Rome. According to Roman myth, the twin brothers Romulus and Remus were the offspring of Rhea Silvia and Mars, the god of war. They were abandoned at birth, but suckled by a she-wolf and raised by a shepherd. The founding of Rome begins with bloodshed as Romulus kills his brother Remus after arguing over whether to found the city on the Palatine or Aventine Hill. Rome is first ruled by a series of kings, with the last king being overthrown in 509 BC. The city became a republic ruled by two consuls, along with elected magistrates in the Senate. For centuries, aristocratic families shared power and resisted the consolidation of power under a single ruler. During the first century BC, this would dramatically change in the person of Julius Caesar, thus setting the historical context for our study of the New Testament.

Julius Caesar was born into an upper-class family with an elite pedigree. He later formed a political alliance with Pompey and a wealthy leader named Crassus. This alliance steadily gained political power, but was opposed by the Senate. Caesar's great military victories in Gaul bring him military power and public honor. His popular appeal eventually leads him into conflict with Pompey, who realigns himself with the Senate after the death of Crassus in 53 BC. When the Senate orders Caesar to step down from his military command, he famously refuses by crossing the Rubicon River into Italy under arms in 49 BC with the defiant phrase "the die is cast." The following year, he defeats Pompey in Greece, and is later named *dictator* ("one who leads") for life in 44 BC. He initiates a series of vast public building projects, social reforms, and the Julian calendar that still serves as the basis of the solar calendar used by most of the world to this day.

Despite his accomplishments, Caesar's enemies in the Senate remain. An organized conspiracy of more than sixty men assassinates Julius Caesar a month later in 44 BC, on the "Ides of March" (March 15). He is stabbed twenty-three times before finally collapsing at the base of a large, marble statue of Pompey. Republican leaders, including Brutus and Cassius, rush into the streets and exclaim: "People of Rome, we are once again free!" The assassination of Julius Caesar does not revive the Roman Republic, but actually launches a protracted civil war that resolves in empire. Julius Caesar is deified after his death and given the title *Divus Iulius* ("the divine Julius"). The appearance of a comet for seven days during games held in his honor is interpreted as Caesar taking his place among the gods. Julius Caesar is the first Roman ruler to be honored in this way and this marks the beginning of the imperial cult. This will be a significant counterfeit religious belief that we will encounter throughout the New Testament as Jesus is proclaimed the true divine Son of God and Savior of the world.

Caesar Augustus rules as first Roman emperor (27 BC-AD 14)

Julius Caesar names his adopted son and grandnephew Gaius Julius Caesar Octavian (later called Caesar Augustus) as his sole heir. He is eighteen years old when Julius Caesar is assassinated. The young Octavian quickly forms a political alliance with the Roman general Mark Anthony to fight against Republican forces, led by Brutus and Cassius. The decisive engagement takes place over two battles in October 42 BC at Philippi in northern Greece. Thirty-six legions of experienced Roman soldiers fought against one another, with over 100,000 men on each side. Cassius, Brutus and countless ranks of Roman nobility die on the battlefield. Philippi is resettled with military veterans and renamed a Roman colony. We will encounter the vibrant Christian church in this city later in our study (Acts 16:12; Phil. 1:1).

After Octavian's victory at Philippi, civil war continues between Octavian and Mark Anthony. A final confrontation takes place in 31 BC at Actium in western Greece. During the battle, Mark Anthony and his Egyptian ally, Cleopatra, flee to Egypt where they both commit suicide. Octavian returns to Rome where he is hailed as *imperator* ("conquering general") at the age of thirty. He is celebrated as savior, benefactor, and the one who brings peace to the world. He begins a vast public building program in Rome. His architectural style projects stability, power, and authority. Monumental projects like his Mausoleum and the Temple of Apollo communicate a sense of grandeur and opulence, casting a vision of optimism for the future. Large public spaces, such as the Forum, display Roman glory and the image of Octavian as a savior in time of need. Toward the end of his life, he would claim to have received Rome as a city of bricks and left it a city of marble.

In 27 BC, the Senate honors Octavian by naming him *Augustus* ("Exalted" or "Venerable One"). His official title was *Imperator Caesar Divi Filius Augustus* ("Emperor Caesar, Son of the Divine One, Exalted"). A laurel crown identifies him as Rome's savior and an inscribed shield announces his virtues and pious works for the gods and country. He is proclaimed as the one who brings *Pax Romana* ("Roman peace") to the entire world. An altar of peace is decorated with the imperial family to signify that the nations of the world have been united under the rule of a single man.

Augustus is regarded as the first Roman emperor. Although preferring the title of "first citizen," he holds tremendous power through his various offices: he is the head of the senate and presides at senatorial meetings; he is the chief priest of Roman state religion; he holds consular power with authority equal to the chief executive; he is supreme commander of all Roman legions; and he has tribunal authority to veto any act or proposal by any magistrate within his dominion. This is the Caesar Augustus we will encounter in the

New Testament who will issue a decree that all the world should be registered (Luke 2:1).

Augustus presents the spread of Roman imperial rule as a benefit to the whole world. Although openly acknowledging and imitating the superiority of Greek culture in religion and the arts, Augustus utilizes the Roman gifts of government and war to subjugate the nations. Roman armies impose peace by conquering the proud. The echoes of Dan. 2 and 7 resound as a divine witness against such a claim. Despite his vast accomplishments, Augustus represents yet another rival version of human power. The LORD God of Israel has already determined that the Son of Man will rule over all peoples (Dan. 7:13-14). The desire of all nations will be found through faith in him alone. He will conquer his enemies by offering his life for theirs upon a Roman cross. His death will secure their forgiveness. His resurrection will bring them everlasting peace.

Herod rules as "King of the Jews and Friend of the Romans"

Caesar Augustus extends Roman rule through a relationship of patronage called "client kingship." This system of patronage relies upon local leadership to maintain order and collect tribute. As Roman power increases in the east, Antipater, an Idumean leader and father of Herod, proves exceptionally skilled at exploiting the benefits of patronage. The Idumeans live in the area of ancient Edom, southwest of Jerusalem. They are descendants of Esau, later called Edomites, and traditional enemies of Israel. Around 120 BC, the Hasmonean rulers forcibly convert the Idumeans to Judaism. In 47 BC, Herod's father, Antipater, provides military support when Julius Caesar is under siege in Alexandria. Julius Caesar rewards Antipater with Roman citizenship and makes him governor of Judea. Antipater appoints his son Herod as governor of Galilee at age twenty-five, and his elder brother Phasael as governor of Jerusalem.

The assassination of Julius Caesar and the poisoning of Antipater bring political instability to Rome and Judea. Herod first allies himself with the Republican leaders, Brutus and Cassius, who support his claim to rule Judea. However, Cassius strips the land of Israel for funds and abandons Herod just prior to the battle at Philippi. Antigonus, the last of the Hasmoneans, claims the throne of Judea. With the help of the Parthians (the term used at this time for the ancient Persians), he is named king and high priest in 40 BC. Herod boldly makes his way to Rome where the Senate declares him "King of the Jews." He returns to Jerusalem and captures the city in 37 BC. He crucifies his rival, Antigonus, and then beheads him, and kills forty-five members of the Sanhedrin who had supported him.

During the long civil war between Mark Antony and Octavian, Herod first allies himself with Antony. After Antony's defeat at Actium, Herod pledges his support to Octavian. He risks everything by appearing before Caesar on the island of Rhodes. He approaches Octavian in the dress of a commoner and lays down his crown. He asks Octavian to consider "not whose friend, but how loyal a friend, I have been" (Josephus, *War* 1.390). Deeply moved, Octavian places the crown upon Herod's head with his own hands and publicly confirms his kingdom. A lasting friendship is forged between the two leaders. Herod becomes second only to Marcus Agrippa in Caesar's affections. He is publicly recognized as "King of the Jews and Friend of the Romans." Herod never forgets that his kingship is based on Caesar's patronage. He demonstrates his loyalty in conscious imitation of Caesar's dress, architectural style, and manner of living. Even Herod's own monumental tomb outside Jerusalem, the Herodion, is built to resemble Caesar's Mausoleum in Rome.

For our study, it is important to realize that Herod and his descendants come to power exclusively through Roman patronage. Herod owes his kingship to the decree of the Roman Senate. He is the son of an Idumean father and Nabatean mother. This is the Herod we will encounter in the gospel narratives who rules as King of the Jews and Friend of the Romans (Matt. 2:1-19; Luke 1:5).

New Testament timeline

You may want to take a few moments to review the main points on the timeline that we have rehearsed thus far. We have noted that this period is represented by the ten-horned beast from Daniel's prophecy. You should also identify the red crown next to the following line on the timeline: Herod rules as "King of the Jews and Friend of the Romans." The red crown, which has been taken directly from the Old Testament, represents illegitimate kings.

Herod is named King of the Jews and he will rule as king of Judea when Jesus is born, but he is not the promised king from the line of Judah.

Caesarea is founded and the Jerusalem Temple is lavishly renovated

Herod's vast building projects reveal his complex identity as client king of the Jews. For his Roman patrons, he builds public buildings in Jerusalem and names them Caesareum and Agrippeum. He rebuilds the capital of Samaria with six thousand Roman colonists and names the city Sebaste (the Greek equivalent of Augustus). At the city center, he dedicates a large temple to Caesar. His greatest attempt to honor his patron is the founding of an entirely new city on the coast named Caesarea. The city is conceived as a new capital for Roman trade in the East. With the help of Roman engineers and new construction technologies, like concrete that hardens when exposed to water, he creates an expansive artificial harbor into the Mediterranean Sea. Huge towers at intervals along the harbor are adorned with statues of Caesar's family. A temple to Caesar rises upon the ground that dominates the city center. The temple houses a statue of the emperor and another of the goddess Roma. Herod adorns the city with a theater, forum, and royal palace connected to a hippodrome. He institutes festival games every fifth year, and calls them Caesar's Games. Contestants in athletics, music, and theater receive lavish prizes for first, second, and third place (Josephus, *War* 1:415). The Apostle Paul will later be imprisoned for two years in Herod's palace at Caesarea while awaiting trial (Acts 23-25).

For his Jewish subjects, Herod's greatest projects take place in Jerusalem. Like Caesar's attempt to beautify Rome, Herod rebuilds Jerusalem on an opulent scale. He expands the walls of the city, adding three defense towers named after his friend Hippicus, his brother Phasael, and his wife Mariamne. He decorates his royal palace in Jerusalem with marble, sculpture, and detailed ornamentation. His most ambitious project is the renovation of the Jerusalem Temple. Herod begins the project in 23 BC by enlarging the area surrounding the temple with massive retaining walls. The largest stones quarried weigh more than five hundred tons. The Temple Mount platform becomes the largest public square in the ancient world and could accommodate 200,000 people. The outer courtyard is surrounded with colonnaded porticoes providing shade and space for public teaching. Herod constructs the Royal Portico on the southern side of the Temple Mount as a magnificent, two-story structure with 162 solid columns. Those who go up to Jerusalem for the major pilgrimage festivals would reach the Royal Portico through an arched, marble staircase.

The Herodian Temple Mount and sanctuary reflect the architectural plan of the tabernacle, and Solomon's temple (Exod. 25-31; 1 Kgs. 8). The entire design communicates graded holiness when moving closer toward the sanctuary. The majority of worshipers would reach the Temple Mount through a monumental staircase with two sets of beautiful, carved gates. This area is later described as the Beautiful Gate (Acts 3:2). Worshipers ascended through a decorated passageway and emerged within the outer court of the Temple Mount. The vast outer courtyard of the Temple Mount was paved with variegated marble paving stones. This large area was known as the Court of the Gentiles. A carved, stone wall, four and a half feet high, surrounded the sanctuary proper, allowing access to ethnic Israelites alone. Thirteen stone slabs at equal intervals, written in Greek and Latin, announced the law of ritual purity and warned that no foreigner was permitted to enter the Holy Place. Two of these stones have been found in recent excavations. Worshipers ascended further by steps to the court of the sanctuary, passing through one of nine gates overlaid with silver and gold. This area, known as the Court of Women, was open to all Israelites, men and women. Israelites would enter here to complete a vow, offer special prayers, and join in festival singing. Moving further toward the sanctuary, fifteen semicircular steps ascended to a platform where Levitical singers would lead public worship. Just behind them, an ornate gate rose seventy-five feet high and was overlaid with Corinthian bronze. A wealthy Alexandrian Jew named Nicanor is remembered for making such a remarkable gift to adorn the sanctuary.

Israelite men and priests could pass through the Nicanor gate. This area was known as the Court of the Israelites. Beyond this area, priests offered daily offerings upon the altar, according to a regular rotation in the Court of the Priests. The sanctuary itself was located in the center of the Temple Mount, accessed by twelve additional steps. Solomon's temple had been built on this very place, over the rock upon which Abraham had been instructed to offer his beloved son Isaac (2 Chron. 3:1; cf. Gen. 22:2). The front façade of the sanctuary proper rose nearly 150 feet high, covered with polished marble and gold. An enormous open gate revealed that the interior of the sanctuary was completely covered with gold. Inside the Holy Place, accessible only to the priests, stood the golden menorah, the table of the showbread, and the altar of incense wrought with artistic skill. An elaborate woven veil separated the Holy of Holies, accessed only once per year by the high priest on the Day of Atonement. Jewish tradition remembers Herod's Temple in Jerusalem as the most beautiful structure ever built. This is the temple that Jesus will visit as a child. He will teach publicly in these courts. He will one day reveal that "something greater than the temple is here" (Matt. 12:6), referring to his own presence.

Despite Herod's economic, military, and architectural accomplishments, Israel never fully embraced Herodian kingship. He is scorned for his non-Israelite (Idumean) ancestry. His ruthlessness, heavy taxation, and collaboration with Rome foster deep resentment. His domestic life is filled with betrayal and murder. Augustus once remarked that he would rather be Herod's pig than his son. Herod's increasing paranoia leads to the execution of his sons whom he suspected of plotting against him. He even murders his wife Mariamne, the Hasmonean queen who brought the legitimacy he so craved. In 4 BC, he executes his son Antipater just five days before his own death. The suffering under Herod comes to vivid expression in the testimony of a Jewish delegation sent to Rome pleading for change. When Caesar grants the representatives permission to speak, they do not conceal the horror of Herodian rule:

> He was not a king whom they had to bear with but the most savage tyrant who ever lived. Many had been executed by him, and the survivors had suffered so much that they envied the dead. Not only had he tortured individual subjects, but whole cities; he had crippled his own towns and embellished those of other people; he had shed the life-blood of Judea to gratify foreigners. Depriving them of their prosperity and their ancestral laws, he had reduced the people to poverty and utter lawlessness. The fact was that in the course of a few years, the Jews had endured more calamities at Herod's hands than their ancestors had endured in all the time since they left Babylon (Josephus, *War* 2.84-86).

Roman rule through Herod brings God's people to their lowest point. Notice how the delegation equates the oppression under Herod to the entire time period since the exile from Babylon. God's people are moved to remember and rehearse the sovereign intentions of their Creator and Redeemer. God had promised through Moses and the prophets that the period of EXILE did not mean ultimate rejection but divine discipline that would be followed by restoration. God would protect and refine his people through a series of four successive kingdoms: Babylon, Persia, Greece, and Rome. The fifth kingdom, the kingdom of God, must come next. Israel is stirred at this time with an unparalleled intensity to hope in the Old Testament promises of God.

Israel expects the Messiah: awaiting God's Old Testament promises

We have traversed the unfamiliar ground of the intertestamental period to arrive here. Our fifth and final bold heading is by far the most important for the period of EXPECTATIONS. God sovereignly builds expectations that he will act again to redeem and save his people. He has sustained his people through adversity. He has humbled them through afflictions. He has reminded them to put their trust in him alone. God's people now search the Scriptures to find hope. The hope of Israel looks toward the decisive, saving action of Israel's God. The prophets portray God's coming as a second Exodus. God will reach out his hand a second time after four hundred years (Isa. 11:11; cf. Gen. 15:13). The Exodus from Egypt forms the template for the redemption that is to come. The Lord had stirred the hearts of his people with the promise that he would act again: "Fear not, for I am with you; be not dismayed, for I am your God; I will strengthen you, I will help you, I will uphold you with my righteous right hand" (Isa. 41:10). Recalling the crossing of the sea, the Lord had declared: "When you pass through the waters, I will be with you; and through the rivers, they shall not overwhelm you" (Isa. 43:2; cf. Exod. 3:12).

The hope of Israel is unique in the ancient world. It is inspired by prophetic vision, not by human invention. Israel's prophets refer to time as either the "former days" or the "latter days" (Deut. 4:30; Isa. 2:2; Jer. 23:20; Dan. 2:28; Hos. 3:5). The "latter days" (or "end times") is Old Testament language used to describe the time when God would act again after the period of EXILE. God's saving action is also signaled by the expression "the day of the LORD" or simply "on that day" (Isa. 13:6; Jer. 46:10; Ezek. 30:3; Joel 2:1; Zeph. 1:14; Mal. 4:5). Although there are various aspects and scriptural images, the hope of Israel forms a single, coherent vision that anticipates the coming day of God's salvation.

New Testament timeline

There are ten key expectations that form the hope of Israel. These are listed on the lower-left corner of the New Testament timeline, along with key Scripture passages. You will also notice a cluster of icons representing these expectations. The blue crown represents the kingdom of God, the royal Son of Man, and the Son of David. The altar represents atonement for sin. The picture of a heart with the law inside it represents the new covenant. The fiery cloud represents God's presence poured out at Pentecost. The gift represents God's gracious blessing promised to Abraham that is extended to the nations. The empty tomb represents the hope of resurrection. The two trees recall God's judgment, and the hope of new creation. Each picture has been taken directly from the Old Testament, underscoring that God's people are waiting for the fulfillment of what God has promised.

You should become deeply familiar with this list, as it will help you to understand the hope of Israel, which is our goal for the period of EXPECTATIONS. Each of these ten expectations should be considered a vital feature of the whole. Israel hopes for such things because God has promised them in his Word. There is a historical and theological progression within this great prophetic expectation. The hope of Israel is absolutely essential for understanding the identity of Jesus as Messiah. The hope of Israel will compel the expansion of early Christian mission. The hope of Israel will also provide the shape and content of Christian theology, as we will see. We will present each aspect of the hope of Israel to conclude the period of EXPECTATIONS. If you have read through the Old Testament Study Guide, you should be familiar with many of these expectations that are so central to God's plan of redemption through history.

The Kingdom of God as the coming reign of God

The first aspect of the hope of Israel is the kingdom of God as the coming reign of God. Israel has known the LORD God as Creator, Redeemer, and King (Isa. 43:15; 44:6). God alone is Creator in Genesis (Gen. 1-2). He alone is Redeemer in Exodus (Exod. 1-15). God's reign as King is celebrated after the crossing of the Sea with the acclamation that "the LORD will reign forever and ever" (Exod. 15:18). Israel's great confession calls the people to worship the LORD alone: "Hear, O Israel: The LORD our God, the LORD is one" (Deut. 6:4). The hope of Israel expects that one day all peoples will know and worship the LORD alone. This hope for the reign of God comes to clear expression in the proclamation by the prophet Zechariah: "The LORD will be king over all the earth. On that day the LORD will be one and his name one" (Zech. 14:9). Zechariah prophesies in the sixth century BC as the Old Testament draws to a close. His final chapter concerns the coming day of the LORD (Zech. 14). All nations will be gathered to Jerusalem. The LORD himself will appear and stand upon the Mount of Olives. The earth will tremble and darkness will cover the land on an utterly unique day. Living waters will flow out from Jerusalem to the east and to the west. As a result, the LORD God will be king over all the earth. He will be the only one. The idols of the nations will be overthrown as the nations stream to worship the God of Israel and all peoples will be "holy to the LORD."

Zechariah 14:9 holds an important place within Israel's liturgical life. This verse is recited at the ending of a prayer that closes each of the three daily synagogue services and reflects language used in the Jerusalem Temple liturgy at this time. This prayer is called the *Aleinu* prayer (lit. "it is upon us"); God's people were entrusted with a sacred obligation to worship him alone. The prayer begins with the confession that the Lord is King and there is none besides him. The prayer then moves to declare that "the LORD is God in the heavens above and on the earth beneath, there is no other" (Deut. 4:39). The prayer continues in petition that the glory of God would one day be revealed and false gods be removed. The prayer asks that all of humanity will call upon God's name and all the wicked will turn in repentance. The prayer lifts up hope that all the inhabitants of the world would glorify God's name and that every knee must bow and every tongue confess that the LORD is God. This prayer, spoken more than one thousand times per year, ends in expectation that all nations might accept the yoke of God's kingdom and that he would reign forever and ever. This expectation is based on the Scripture: "The LORD will be king over all the earth. On that day the LORD will be one, and his name one" (Zech. 14:9).

The royal Son of Man vision

The second aspect of the hope of Israel comes from Daniel's vision of the royal Son of Man (Dan. 7:13-14). We are now familiar with the prophetic sequence of four kingdoms that ends with the arrival of the kingdom of God (Dan. 2:44-45). This vision explains the rise and fall of kingdoms from the time of the exile through the intertestamental period. In Dan. 7, the prophet Daniel sees four terrifying beasts coming up out of the sea. Each one is a hybrid, mixed creature bent on violence. The first is like a lion with eagles' wings, standing like a man. The second is like a bear, raised up on one side with three freshly consumed ribs in its teeth. The third is like a leopard with four wings of a bird, having four heads and wielding dominion. The fourth beast has great iron teeth and ten horns, devouring, breaking in pieces, and stamping what remains with its feet. These beasts are interpreted as the kings who would reign over four coming kingdoms. The deathly reign of the beasts ends with the life-giving vision of the LORD upon his throne. Daniel sees the LORD enthroned as the Ancient of Days in purity and holiness. Myriads of the heavenly host stand ready before the King of glory. The LORD brings judgment upon the beasts and removes their dominion from the earth. The next sentences are some of the most breathtaking in the entire Bible:

> I saw in the night visions, and behold, with the clouds of heaven there came one like a Son of Man, and he came to the Ancient of Days and was presented before him. And to him was given dominion and glory and a kingdom, that all peoples, nations, and languages should serve him; his dominion is an everlasting dominion, which shall not pass away, and his kingdom one that shall not be destroyed. (Dan. 7:13-14)

The Son of Man is distinguished from the beasts by his humanity. Just as the ancient serpent is described as "more crafty than any other beast" (Gen. 3:1), rulers whom he inspires share his likeness. Pride, arrogance, and unbridled human power always degrade and desecrate the image of

God. In contrast, the Son of Man comes as a new Adam -- a royal, image-bearing Son. The Son of Man is also distinguished by his divinity. He comes to God's throne with the clouds of heaven that signify the divine presence (Exod. 24:16; 40:34; 1 Kgs. 8:10-11; Ps. 104:3; Ezek. 1:28). The most remarkable decree is announced—the LORD gives the Son of Man dominion, glory, and an everlasting kingdom. All peoples and languages worship him (Gen. 12:3; 49:10). His dominion will never pass away or be destroyed (2 Sam. 7:14; Ps. 2:8). Here we see a vivid picture of our Messiah. The kingdom of God will be established through him.

The Son of David restored to the throne

The third aspect of the hope of Israel is that the Son of David would be restored to the throne. The LORD's promises to David in 2 Sam. 7 stand behind this specific expectation. After the LORD had given him rest from all his enemies, David seeks to build a house for the LORD. The LORD reminds David of all that he had graciously done for him. Instead of David building a house for the LORD, the LORD promises that he would build a house for David. He promises to raise up David's offspring after him who would reign forever. The LORD promises a unique Father and Son relationship with the Son of David. He promises never to withdraw his steadfast love. Unlike Saul, whose sin prompted the LORD to remove his Spirit and take away the kingship, the Son of David will receive divine discipline for Israel's sin with stripes and blows from men. His kingship, however, will never be removed. It will be made sure and will be established forever (2 Sam. 7:12-16).

The LORD is faithful to place Davidic kings on the throne throughout the period of KINGS. The Psalms often celebrate God's covenant promise to David (Pss. 2:6-8; 89:3, 35; 132:11). Yet as we have seen, the sin of the Davidic kings leads to the divine discipline of exile, with the last Davidic king being taken to Babylon in 586 BC. Nevertheless, David's line continues through the exile with King Jehoiachin and his sons (Jer. 52:31-34), along with his grandson Zerubbabel (1 Chron. 3:17-19). The LORD's prophets look to the time when the LORD would raise up a righteous Son of David from this line who would reign as God's anointed king forever. After the punishment of exile, the prophet Jeremiah sees the glorious time of his appearance:

> Behold, the days are coming, declares the LORD, when I will raise
> up for David a righteous Branch, and he shall reign as king and deal
> wisely, and shall execute justice and righteousness in the land. In his
> days Judah will be saved, and Israel will dwell securely. And this is
> the name by which he will be called: 'The LORD is our righteousness.'
> (Jer. 23:5-6)

The prophet Amos similarly proclaims that after the exile, the LORD will rebuild the fallen house of David: "In that day I will raise up the booth of David that is fallen and repair its breaches, and raise up its ruins and rebuild it as in the days of old, that they may possess the remnant of Edom and all the nations who are called by my name" (Amos 9:11-12). The expectation that a Son of David would rule over God's people is a strongly attested feature of the hope of Israel (Isa. 4:2; 9:7; 11:1, 10; 16:5; 55:3; Jer. 30:9; 33:15-17; Ezek. 34:23-24; 37:24; Hos. 3:5; Zech. 12:8-10; 13:1). God's people will one day be ruled by a Davidic king in fulfillment of the covenant with David, which could not be broken (Jer. 33:15-17).

Atonement for sin

The fourth aspect of the hope of Israel awaits atonement for sin. Just as Adam's sin exiled our ancestors from the Garden of Eden, Israel's sin brought them into exile from the land. Israel's prophets long for the day, however, when full atonement for sin would be made, and God's relationship with his people restored. This expectation comes to sublime expression in Isa. 53 in the atoning work of the Servant of the LORD. The Servant would carry the sin of the nation. He would bear Israel's griefs and carry their sorrows; he would be smitten by God and be wounded for their transgressions. He would be crushed for their iniquities, and by his stripes they would be healed. The prophet Isaiah proclaims: "All we like sheep have gone astray; we have turned—every one—to his own way; and the LORD has laid on him the iniquity of us all" (Isa. 53:6). The Servant would be a sacrificial lamb led to the slaughter; he would utter no word, like a sheep is silent before its shearers. The Servant would have his grave among the wicked, even though no deceit was found in him. Isaiah sees that the divine solution to Israel's unrighteousness is found in the Suffering Servant, whose atoning sacrifice will justify the many:

> Yet it was the will of the LORD to crush him; he has put him to grief; when his soul makes an offering for guilt, he shall see his offspring; he shall prolong his days; the will of the LORD shall prosper in his hand. Out of the anguish of his soul he shall see and be satisfied; by his knowledge shall the righteous one, my servant, make many to be accounted righteous, and he shall bear their iniquities. (Isa. 53:10-11)

This deeply moving passage depicts how the will of the LORD will ultimately prevail over the sin of his people. The servant of the LORD, a royal Son, grows up like a shoot out of dry ground. This is the imagery of a future Davidic king (Isa. 11:1). He does not attract our attention with his physical form or beauty. He is despised and rejected by his own and is a man of sorrows. Yet Isaiah explains that the sorrows the Servant carries are ours. He is stricken by God and afflicted. He is pierced for our transgressions and crushed for our iniquities. While each of us has gone our own way, the LORD has laid on him the iniquity of us all. The Servant is cut off from the land of the living. He dies with the wicked and is buried with the rich, although he has done no violence. His life is offered as a guilt offering. After his substitutionary death, the Servant will be raised from the dead. He will see his offspring and prolong his days. After his resurrection, the Servant will make many to be accounted righteous. In the end, the Servant is highly exalted because he bore the sin of many. Isaiah 53 remains one of the most important passages in the entire Bible and is one of the most frequently quoted in the New Testament.

The prophet Daniel also announces that God would provide atonement for sin. While exiled in Babylon for many years, Daniel reads the Scripture in Jeremiah concerning the seventy years of exile (Dan. 9:1-2; cf. Jer. 25:11-12). He turns his face toward the LORD in humility and offers repentance and confession for the sin of the nation. He proclaims the LORD's faithfulness and confesses Israel's unfaithfulness. He recognizes that calamity has come upon Israel due to their sin, disobedience, and rebellion against God. He pleads with the LORD that his anger may turn away and that the face of God might shine upon his people again (Dan. 9:3-19; Num. 6:25). The angel Gabriel responds to Daniel's prayer with further revelation. Rather than seventy years of exile, God has decreed seventy "sevens" for the ultimate realization of his redemptive plan. Six climactic purposes are announced in Dan. 9:24: "Seventy weeks (lit. "sevens") are decreed about your people and your holy city, to finish the transgression, to put an end to sin, and to atone for iniquity, to bring in everlasting righteousness, to seal both vision and prophet, and to anoint a most holy place." Although the exact interpretation of Daniel's seventy weeks has produced differences among biblical commentators, the most important ideas of this passage are clear. The LORD comforts Daniel with the revelation of his sovereign intention to provide atonement for sin and usher in everlasting righteousness through the Messiah. Atonement for sin is a key aspect of the hope of Israel during the period of expectations. Without atonement for sin, there is no forgiveness, no return from exile, and no restoration of the covenant relationship with God.

The new covenant

The fifth aspect of the hope of Israel is the expectation of a new covenant (Jer. 31:31-34). God entered into a covenant with Abraham's descendants at Mount Sinai and required them to keep his holy laws (Exod. 20, 24). Yet God had warned Moses just before his death that the people would "forsake me and break my covenant that I have made with them" (Deut. 31:16). Through a long and turbulent history, the prophets define Israel's sin as breaking God's covenant (Jer. 11). Their covenant breaking eventually draws down the covenant curses as God's righteous judgment against sin (Lev. 26:14-39; Deut. 27:1-26; 28:15-68). This finally takes place in 586 BC when the temple in Jerusalem is destroyed and God's people are taken away into exile (2 Chron. 36). Yet God allows Israel's prophets to see beyond the judgment of exile to the time of restoration (Lev. 26:40-46; Deut. 30:1-14; Jer. 30-33; Ezek. 34, 36-37). Israel's sins will be forgiven through blood atonement, and the LORD will gather his dispersed people and make a new covenant with them.

The hope of the new covenant comes to stirring expression in the prophetic ministry of Jeremiah. He is an eyewitness of the last days of Judah. He urges the people to submit to the divine discipline of judgment being carried out through the Babylonians. The LORD repeatedly shows him that there is hope for the future. He even tells Jeremiah to buy a field as a sign of Israel's future in the land. In Jer. 29:11, the LORD proclaims: "I know the plans I have for you, declares the LORD, plans for welfare and not for evil, to give you a future and a hope." Jeremiah 31 opens with the covenant formula that the LORD would be their God, and "they shall be my people" (Jer. 31:1). The LORD announces to his people: "I have loved you with an everlasting love" (Jer. 31:3). Mourning will be turned into joy. Those who have been scattered will be gathered. The curse will be overturned into blessing. The LORD will ransom and redeem his people (Jer. 31:11).

Israel's future restoration completes Jeremiah's own prophetic calling. The LORD had told Jeremiah: "I have set you this day over nations and over kingdoms, to pluck up and to break down, to destroy and to overthrow, to build and to plant" (Jer. 1:10). In Jer. 31:28, the LORD declares: "as I have watched over them to pluck up and break down, to overthrow, destroy, and bring harm, so I will watch over them to build and to plant." The climax of this glorious future is expressed as a new covenant between God and his people:

> Behold, the days are coming, declares the LORD, when I will make a new covenant with the house of Israel and the house of Judah, not like the covenant that I made with their fathers on the day when I took them by the hand to bring them out of the land of Egypt, my covenant that they broke, though I was their husband, declares the LORD. But this is the covenant that I will make with the house of Israel after those days, declares the LORD: I will put my law within them, and I will write it on their hearts. And I will be their God, and they shall be my people. (Jer. 31:31-33).

Notice that several features of the new covenant are not new. The new covenant is between the same covenant partners, God and Israel. The new covenant is made by the same saving initiative of the LORD. The new covenant inscribes the same revelation of God's will. However, the new covenant does address the great problem of the old covenant, Israel's sinful heart. The problem with the covenant that God had made with Israel at Sinai was that they had broken it through their disobedience (Jer. 11). Despite the LORD's faithfulness, Israel had been unfaithful. The most striking feature of the new covenant is that God will write his law *on the hearts of his people,* which anticipates what God will do through his Spirit (2 Cor. 3:1-6). God will transform the heart of his people from disobedience to obedience. They will all know the LORD and reflect this knowledge in their life together. The new covenant will be based in the divine provision of forgiveness for sin. The hope of the new covenant rises in the gracious, sovereign declaration that God will "forgive their iniquity" and "will remember their sin no more" (Jer. 31:34).

While the expression "new covenant" occurs only in Jer. 31, we have also listed an important passage from Hosea on the New Testament timeline (Hos. 2:16-23). Hosea's own prophetic calling to marry an unfaithful wife embodies Yahweh's covenant relationship with unfaithful Israel. Hosea is called to show how Israel "went after her lovers and forgot me, declares the LORD" (Hos. 2:13). Hosea announces the coming judgment of exile when Israel will be banished like an unfaithful bride. The LORD promises to bring Israel back into the wilderness, the setting of the covenant making. He will reunite his banished bride within the lasting embrace of covenant and betroth her to himself forever:

> Therefore, behold, I will allure her, and bring her into the wilderness, and speak tenderly to her . . . And in that day, declares the LORD, you will call me "My Husband," and no longer will you call me "My Baal." For I will remove the names of the Baals from her mouth, and they shall be remembered by name no more. And I will make for them a covenant on that day with the beasts of the field, the birds of the heavens, and the creeping things of the ground. And I will abolish the bow, the sword, and war from the land, and I will make you lie down in safety. And I will betroth you to me forever. I will betroth you to me in righteousness and in justice, in steadfast love and in mercy. I will betroth you to me in faithfulness. And you shall know the LORD. (Hos. 2:14-20)

Another important passage for the hope of a new covenant is found in Ezekiel. The prophet Ezekiel addresses Israel from the land of exile. He had seen the divine presence depart from temple in Jerusalem due to the sinfulness and idolatry of the people (Ezek. 9-11). Ezekiel 16 depicts the relationship between God and his people as a faithless bride. His prophetic indictment reveals the graphic and pathetic nature of our sin before our faithful LORD. Israel's sin results in God's righteous judgment. After the judgment, the LORD will make atonement and an everlasting covenant: "I will remember my covenant with you in the days of your youth, and I will establish for you an everlasting covenant ... I will establish my covenant with you, and you shall know that I am the LORD ... when I atone for you for all that you have done" (Ezek. 16:60, 62-63). The promise of the new covenant is central to the hope of Israel. We will hear this language again in the upper room when Jesus tells his disciples: "This cup that is poured out for you is the new covenant in my blood" (Luke 22:20). Through his atoning blood, forgiveness is secured and the new covenant is established forever. God's people will be declared righteous in his sight. Then they will be filled with the Spirit to walk in newness of life. This is indeed the hope of Israel.

Pouring out of the Holy Spirit

The sixth aspect of the hope of Israel will be the pouring out of the Holy Spirit. Just as the Spirit of God breathed life into humanity in the Garden of Eden (Gen. 2:7), the Holy Spirit will renew humanity in the latter days. Isaiah sees the renewal of God's people by the presence and power of the Holy Spirit when he proclaims:

> For I will pour water on the thirsty land, and streams on the dry ground; I will pour my Spirit upon your offspring, and my blessing on your descendants. They shall spring up among the grass like willows by flowing streams. This one will say, "I am the LORD's," another will call on the name of Jacob, and another will write on his hand, "The LORD's." (Isa. 44:3-5)

The prophet Joel also describes a coming day when the Spirit would be poured out upon all nations, both men and women, rich and poor. In Joel 2:28-29, the LORD promises: "And it shall come to pass afterward, that I will pour out my Spirit on all flesh; your sons and your daughters shall prophesy, your old men shall dream dreams, and your young men shall see visions. Even on the male and female servants in those days I will pour out my Spirit."

The prophet Ezekiel sees the full effect of this renewal by the Holy Spirit. The Lord will purify his people and remove their idols. He will remove their heart of stone and give them a heart of flesh. He will pour out the Holy Spirit who will empower them to walk in God's ways:

> I will sprinkle clean water on you, and you shall be clean from all your uncleannesses, and from all your idols I will cleanse you. And I will give you a new heart, and a new spirit I will put within you. And I will remove the heart of stone from your flesh and give you a heart of flesh. And I will put my Spirit within you, and cause you to walk in my statutes and be careful to obey my rules. (Ezek. 36:25-27)

This remarkable renewal by the Holy Spirit will one day come to pass. All nations will receive the Holy Spirit. They will abandon their idols and learn to walk in God's ways. We will hear Joel's prophecy again in our chapter on PENTECOST when Peter proclaims that the pouring out of God's Spirit has been fulfilled (Acts 2:14-36). Ezekiel's image of the Holy Spirit empowering new lives of obedience is one of the most important passages for understanding Paul's missionary labor among the nations.

Blessing of Abraham to the nations

The seventh aspect of the hope of Israel is the blessing of Abraham to the nations. You will remember from our study of the Old Testament that the LORD had promised to bless all families of the earth through Abraham and his seed (Gen. 12:3; 18:18; 26:4; 28:14). Israel's prophets knew that they were serving the only true and living God of all the earth. God's election of Abraham when he was an idolater in Ur was an act of grace. God's grace and power were further displayed to Abraham and Sarah through the promise of descendants to an elderly, barren couple. God would use Abraham and his "seed" (Gen. 22:18; Gal. 3:14, 16) to bring the knowledge and blessing of God to the world.

In the light of Israel's restoration, the prophets anticipate the day when all nations will know and worship the LORD (Isa. 2:2; 19:21-25; 42:6; 60:1-3; 66:20; Zech. 8:20-23). The mountain of the house of the Lord will be established as the highest of mountains. The rock cut without human hands will fill the earth. As a result, the nations will come, bearing gifts in praise of the LORD (Isa 60:1-3, 6). They will stream toward Zion to worship the LORD and learn to walk in his ways, saying: "Come, let us go up to the mountain of the LORD, to the house of the God of Jacob, that he may teach us his ways and that we may walk in his paths" (Mic. 4:2). Zechariah also declares that Jerusalem would one day be a blessing to all nations (Zech. 8:13). As we continue in God's plan of redemption in the period of MESSIAH, we will encounter magi from the east bearing gifts to worship the child born in Bethlehem. The nations will seek an audience with Jesus (John 12:20-21). His atoning death will bring blessing to the nations (Gal. 3:14). In PENTECOST and TEACHING, we will see the blessing of Abraham extend to all nations through faithful Christian mission to the ends of the earth (Acts 1:8).

Resurrection from the dead

The eighth aspect of the hope of Israel is the resurrection from the dead. Israel alone in the ancient world expects a bodily resurrection. Israel's God is the God of the living and not of the dead. God creates humanity for eternal life, but sin brings death (Gen. 2:16-17; 5:1-32). Only Israel's God could create new life from the dead. Abraham demonstrates "resurrection faith" when he believes that God would give children to his barren wife whose womb was "dead" (Gen. 15:6; cf. Rom. 4). God alone has this power to give life. God had spoken to Moses: "See now that I, even I, am he, and there is no god beside me; I kill and I make alive; I wound and I heal; and there is none that can deliver out of my hand" (Deut. 32:39). Several passages in the prophets anticipate a glorious resurrection to new life. Isaiah sees the day when God will prepare a rich feast for all peoples. He will destroy the veil that hides his glory from the nations. He will act to bring new life and destroy death forever:

He will swallow up death forever; and the Lord GOD will wipe away tears from all faces, and the reproach of his people he will take away from all the earth, for the LORD has spoken. It will be said on that day, "Behold, this is our God; we have waited for him, that he might save us. This is the LORD; we have waited for him; let us be glad and rejoice in his salvation." (Isa. 25:8-9)

The Lord takes the prophet Ezekiel in a vision to a valley filled with death (Ezek. 37), remembering that the most defiling thing for a priest is a human corpse. The LORD sets Ezekiel in the middle of the valley and asks: "Can these bones live?" (Ezek. 37:3). He responds in faith that the LORD alone knows. The LORD then commands him to prophesy over the bones: "Thus says the Lord GOD to these bones: 'Behold, I will cause breath to enter you, and you shall live. And I will lay sinews upon you, and will cause flesh to come upon you, and cover you with skin, and put breath in you, and you shall live, and you shall know that I am the LORD'" (Ezek. 37:5-6). The LORD explains the vision to Ezekiel as a future resurrection from the dead. God will open up the graves and raise his people from the dead. By this they will know that he is the LORD (Ezek. 37:12-14). God will put his life-giving Spirit within them, recalling the Spirit of God hovering over the waters (Gen. 1:2) and God breathing life into Adam (Gen. 2:6-7).

The prophet Daniel also sees the coming day when God would bring forth a general resurrection for those who have been buried in the earth. For some, this will lead to everlasting life. For others, this will lead to everlasting judgment: "Many of those who sleep in the dust of the earth shall awake, some to everlasting life, and some to shame and everlasting contempt. And those who are wise shall shine like the brightness of the sky above; and those who turn many to righteousness, like the stars forever and ever" (Dan. 12:2-3). As we will see, this hope of resurrection will first find fulfillment in Israel's Messiah. He will bear humanity's sin and death as the Suffering Servant, and then he will be raised from the dead as Israel's everlasting King. All who trust in him will receive eternal life and share in the resurrection from the dead.

Final judgment of the world and evil

The ninth aspect of the hope of Israel is the final judgment of the world and evil. When God creates the world and humanity in his image, he sees everything that he had made and "behold, it was very good" (Gen. 1:31). Through the serpent's deception, sin enters the world, distorting the image of God like a cracked mirror. Sin and evil are everywhere, especially in the human heart (Gen. 6:5). The earth is corrupted with violence (Gen. 6:11; Pss. 14:1; 58:2; Hab. 2:8). God pronounces a righteous judgment against evil (Gen. 6:5; 18:25). Israel's prophets look toward the day when God will judge the world with righteousness. Evil will be destroyed forever. The uniqueness of the God of Israel shines forth in this aspect of hope. God is holy and all his ways are just. He will purify the world by righteous judgment. This hope comes to expression throughout the Psalms and prophets. In Ps. 58:11 David prays: "Surely there is a reward for the righteous; surely there is a God who judges on earth." Psalm 96 summons all the earth to sing to the LORD! God is praised for his glory and power. The climax of the Psalm celebrates his righteous judgment:

> Worship the LORD in the splendor of holiness; tremble before him, all the earth! Say among the nations, "The LORD reigns! Yes, the world is established; it shall never be moved; he will judge the peoples with equity." Let the heavens be glad, and let the earth rejoice; let the sea roar, and all that fills it; let the field exult, and everything in it! Then shall all the trees of the forest sing for joy before the LORD, for he comes, for he comes to judge the earth. He will judge the world in righteousness, and the peoples in his faithfulness. (Ps. 96:9-13)

Isaiah also sees the LORD as a mighty warrior bringing righteous judgment on the earth. The vision of Isa. 63:1-6 is an awesome scene in which the LORD wears crimson-stained garments after treading the winepress of his own wrath. We are often tempted to minimize this aspect of hope, but it is crucial to the biblical story. The LORD God will solve the problem of evil. He will condemn sin and evil. We have already seen how he makes provision for forgiveness through substitutionary atonement. Without atonement, humanity faces God's righteous indignation. God's final judgment will be accurate. It will be a day of vengeance and vindication. It will in the end be an occasion of joy. The coming judgment of God will bring recompense on his enemies and salvation for his redeemed (Isa. 35:4; 40:10; 59:15-18; 61:1-3; 62:11; Jer. 51:6; Mic. 5:15; Nah. 1:5).

New creation of heavens and earth

The tenth and final aspect of the hope of Israel is the new creation of the heavens and earth. In Genesis, God creates the heavens and the earth and declares that his creation is "very good." Humanity is created in his image and likeness and commissioned to fill the earth with the knowledge of God (Gen. 1:28). Yet sin brings corruption to God's good creation (Gen. 3:14-19) and defaces humanity to fill the earth with violence (Gen. 6:5-7; Isa. 5:1-7; cf. Rom. 8:20-23). After God's righteous judgment against sin, God's people hope for a new creation where death and violence are no more. This comes to vivid expression in Isa. 65:17-19:

> Behold, I create new heavens and a new earth, and the former things shall not be remembered or come into mind. But be glad and rejoice forever in that which I create; for behold, I create Jerusalem to be a joy, and her people to be a gladness. I will rejoice in Jerusalem and be glad in my people; no more shall be heard in it the sound of weeping and the cry of distress.

Isaiah sees the full realization of God's purposes in a way that gathers together several important biblical themes of our study, especially from Genesis. The expression "I create new heavens and a new earth" closely echoes Gen. 1:1. Isaiah reminds us of God's joy over his creation. His redemptive plan begins with a garden and ends in an Edenic city, the New Jerusalem. There will be no anguish in the city or the tragedy of death. Humanity made in his image will enjoy the work of their hands. The curse of Gen. 3 will be overturned. God's people will enjoy intimate fellowship with him and hear his voice. The harmony even among animals is a poetic depiction that all of life will be renewed. The new heavens and earth will endure as a sanctuary of worship for the redeemed of all nations (Isa. 66:22-23). The hope of Israel does not expect a disembodied, individual, spiritual state. It is a corporate image where all nations are gathered to live meaningful lives forever in conscious praise of the LORD God Almighty, who is our Creator, Redeemer, and Savior. This is where the hope of Israel will lead us, and it will be accomplished in Jesus Christ.

As we conclude the period of EXPECTATIONS, we pause with wonder and awe at the way the LORD has prepared the stage of history and the hearts of humanity for the revelation of his Messiah. Throughout the intertestamental period, God builds expectations for a coming King. He has preserved and protected his people through a series of earthly kingdoms. He has gathered the attention of the nations and given them access to his Word. He has led his people to search the Scriptures in great anticipation of the coming day of salvation. The kingdom of God will come. The Son of Man will be revealed. The Son of David will be established upon his throne. Atonement for sin will be provided. A new covenant will be made. The Holy Spirit will be poured out upon all humanity. The blessing of Abraham will extend to all nations. The dead will be raised. Evil will be judged. God will create a new heavens and a new earth in which righteousness dwells. The hope of Israel focuses our attention on the coming Messiah, the Son of David, the seed of Abraham. His advent will change everything. As the period of EXPECTATIONS comes to a close, the next movement of redemptive history can only be the period of MESSIAH—when the fullness of time has come.

Chapter 2
MESSIAH Part 1

The period of MESSIAH simply explained

THE SECOND PERIOD of the New Testament is called MESSIAH because this period covers the life and ministry of Jesus, the Messiah, including his birth, public ministry, death, resurrection, and exaltation. His arrival marks the divine fulfillment of all that God has promised in the Old Testament. This period begins with an angelic birth announcement to an elderly couple named Zachariah and Elizabeth. Their son, who is to be named John, is identified as the messianic herald, born in fulfillment of God's word spoken through the prophet Malachi. He is the "Elijah-figure" who was to come; he is to prepare the way for the return of the LORD himself. The angel Gabriel also announces the birth of a son to a virgin named Mary, who is betrothed to Joseph from the line of Judah. Their son is to be named Jesus, for he will save his people from their sins. He is called Immanuel, "God with us," for his birth marks the return of God's presence. The significance of Jesus is highlighted by the unequaled space given to him in the Bible, with four gospels being devoted to recording the events associated with his birth, life, and death. Born in Bethlehem of Judea, Jesus is the promised Messiah, the son of David, who will reign on the throne of his father and establish God's everlasting kingdom. At his birth a star signals to magi from the nations that the Messiah has been born, and they bring gifts fitting for a King and bow down and worship him.

During the intervening years leading up to the public ministry of Jesus, Israel suffers the birth pangs of the Messiah after the death of Herod in 4 BC. There is great violence in the land and two thousand people are crucified. Caesar Augustus administers the will of Herod, establishing Roman rule through Herod's sons Archelaus, Antipas, and Phillip. After Judea is reduced to a Roman province ruled by procurators, four distinct religious groups in Israel (the Sadducees, Pharisees, Essenes, and Zealots) express hope for God's coming kingdom. The temple in Jerusalem remains central in this period, with Caiaphas serving as high priest. Rabbinic sages discuss and interpret the Torah, represented in the schools of Hillel and Shammai. A devout young Jew named Saul of Tarsus, later known as the apostle Paul, is educated in Jerusalem under Gamaliel. During the rule of the fifth Roman governor, Pontius Pilate, the time of waiting is over and the living God begins to speak again.

In AD 29 the word of the LORD comes to John in the wilderness. He proclaims a baptism of repentance, preparing the way of the LORD in fulfillment of the prophets Isaiah and Malachi. When Jesus is baptized by John, a voice from heaven declares that he is God's beloved Son. After triumphing over the temptations of the devil in the wilderness, Jesus announces that the time is fulfilled and the kingdom of God is at hand. He summons people to repent and believe in the gospel. As Jesus begins his public ministry in Galilee, he calls disciples to follow him. He gathers the following twelve disciples and designates them as apostles: Simon (Peter) and his brother Andrew; James, the son of Zebedee, and his brother John; Philip and Bartholomew; Thomas and Matthew; James, son of Alphaeus, and Thaddeus; Simon the zealot and Judas Iscariot.

Jesus preaches about the kingdom in his Sermon on the Mount. He demonstrates the kingdom through healings, casting out demons, and prophetic signs. Jesus acts with divine authority and fulfills the promises of Scripture in himself. He teaches about the kingdom in parables, inviting both the religious and sinners to believe and receive forgiveness in him. Jesus dines with sinners and outcasts, embodying that the kingdom is open to all who repent and believe. Through his parables Jesus reveals the arrival of the kingdom and the new life being offered, but he warns of judgment to come for those who reject his invitation.

As Jesus teaches his disciples about what it means to follow him, he calls forth a response of faith and confession that he is the Messiah, the Son of God. On his journey toward Jerusalem, Jesus makes known to his disciples that he must suffer, die and be raised on the third day. More than half of the literary space in the gospel narratives is devoted to Jesus' final week. Jesus offers himself on Friday as the atoning sacrifice for the sin of the world. Jesus' resurrection from the dead on Sunday morning signals that the power of sin has been broken and the new creation has dawned. His exaltation to the right hand of the Father means that he is vindicated as the righteous Davidic King, who reigns enthroned forever. After his resurrection from the dead and his appearing to many witnesses, Jesus promises the Holy Spirit to his disciples to empower them as his witnesses in the world. His disciples are to remain in Jerusalem therefore until they are clothed with power from on high. The period of MESSIAH ends with Jesus commanding his followers to make disciples of all nations—the global mission of the church is plainly set before them. Jesus' ascension and the outpouring of the Holy Spirit will be taken up in the book of Acts in the period of PENTECOST.

The three key dates for the period of MESSIAH are 6 BC, AD 29, and AD 33. The first date of 6 BC is the approximate date for the birth of Christ. A sixth century Christian named Dionysius Exiguus first developed the system of reckoning years with BC ("Before Christ") and AD (*Anno Domini* means "in the year of our Lord"). However, we know through coins, inscriptions, and other primary sources that Herod the Great died in 4 BC. Since Jesus was born approximately two years before Herod's death, scholars place his birth at 6 BC. AD 29 is the date for the word of the LORD coming to John. AD 33 is the approximate date for the death and resurrection of Christ. Some Christians propose a date of AD 30. The gospels record that Jesus was crucified at the time of the Passover on *Friday*. The fourteenth of Nisan (the date for the Passover in the Jewish calendar) occurs on *Friday* only in AD 30 and AD 33 around this time. We prefer the date of AD 33 in light of the whole sweep of New Testament chronology. The key people for this period are Jesus, John the Baptist, and the twelve disciples. Important Jewish leaders are Annas and Caiaphas, Herod the Great, and his sons Herod Archelaus, Herod Antipas, and Herod Philip. Key Roman rulers are the Roman emperors Caesar Augustus and Tiberius, and the Roman governor Pontius Pilate.

The New Testament timeline

As we begin to learn about the period of MESSIAH, it is important for you to notice the blue crown on the timeline. The blue crown represents the promised king from the line of Judah; it signals the rule of God over all peoples in Jesus, the Messiah. The blue crown recalls the period of KINGS in the Old Testament, especially God's promise of everlasting kingship to David's descendant (2 Sam. 7:12-13; 1 Chron. 17:11-12; cf. Gen. 17:6). The blue crown also marks the focal point of the prophetic visions during the period of EXPECTATIONS, which now comes to fulfillment in the Messiah. The opening verse of the New Testament tells us that Jesus is the Messiah, the son of David, the son of Abraham (Matt. 1:1; cf. Gen. 17:6; 2 Sam. 7:14). The central theme of Jesus' preaching is the arrival of the kingdom of God (Mark 1:15; cf. Dan. 2:44; Zech. 14:9).

Roadmap to the chapter

As we begin this chapter, we will be reading through the first four books of the New Testament, Matthew, Mark, Luke, and John, which are called gospels. The Greek word *evangelion* literally means "good news" and was used to announce a royal proclamation. The New Testament gospels announce God's good news for the world about his Son. The four gospels are the biblical books for the period of MESSIAH. They present the person, words, and work of Jesus, and are best seen as complementary accounts. While each gospel writer has a distinctive voice, we will attempt to hear the life of Christ as a single chorus of redemption. As we journey through the life and ministry of Jesus, Part 1 will survey Jesus' birth, and the intervening years prior to his public ministry, leading up the moment when the word of the LORD comes to John the Baptist. The chapter will conclude with Jesus' baptism and his victory over the serpent in the wilderness, which will prepare us for Jesus' announcement of the kingdom. Part 2 will follow Jesus' public ministry leading up to the climactic final week of his death and resurrection. The chapter will conclude with the disciples waiting in Jerusalem for the promised Holy Spirit, which will usher in the period of PENTECOST.

As you learn about this period, I encourage you to keep the New Testament timeline in front of you. Each point listed under MESSIAH will be discussed under headings that correspond to the main points on the timeline.

Additional Bible references are also given throughout the chapter. These provide key Old Testament background passages, along with other New Testament texts that deal with the same topic. You will benefit greatly from reading these verses along with this study guide.

God sends His Son into the world as messianic King

The bold heading at the top of the MESSIAH column on the New Testament timeline identifies God's major redemptive activity during this period. Notice how the rising blue arrow on the EMPTY timeline reaches its appointed goal with the birth of Christ. It is helpful to place the Old Testament and New Testament timelines together in order to follow this arrow through the whole of Scripture. You will see that arrow begins with the line of promise in Genesis at the beginning of the Old Testament timeline. The line turns blue with the promise of kingship to Jacob's son, Judah (Gen. 49:10) and extends through the line of Judah, culminating in the promises given to King David (2 Sam. 7:14). The line seems to fade during the period of EXILE, yet God's people are not without hope, for the line continues through King Jehoaichin's grandson, Zerubbabel. The line becomes visible again at the end of the Old Testament period pointing toward the coming MESSIAH. During the period of EXPECTATIONS, the line rises in the midst of great suffering; at moments it seems barely visible at all. At last, according to God's great redemptive plan "when the fullness of time had come," God sends forth his Son (Gal. 4:4).

Jesus the Messiah, the son of David, the son of Abraham

The New Testament begins with a stirring statement of subject and theme. Matthew 1:1 states that this is "the book of the genealogy of Jesus Christ, the son of David, the son of Abraham" (Matt. 1:1). Each phrase signals something important. First, Matthew reveals his conviction that Jesus is the Messiah. The Hebrew word *Messiah*, meaning "Anointed One," is translated into Greek with the noun *Christos*. The expression "Jesus Christ" or "Christ Jesus" occurs over two hundred times in the New Testament and represents the concise confession that God's promised Messiah has come. Second, Matthew announces that Jesus is the son of David (2 Sam. 7:14; Ps. 2:6-7). God's promise that the Son of David would have an everlasting kingship and universal dominion is at hand. Third, Matthew declares that Jesus is the son of Abraham (Gen.12:3; 18:18; 26:4). God's promise that all the families of the earth would be blessed through Abraham's descendants is now being realized in Christ.

These declarations about Jesus are introduced by the expression "the book of the genealogy." This is the equivalent of the Hebrew formula "these are the generations," a phrase that is used ten times in the book of Genesis to trace the movement of God's redemptive plan. By using this formula, Matthew is alerting us to the fact that God's decisive next step has begun in Jesus Christ. Matthew carefully arranges his genealogy to make a powerful point. His genealogy starts with Abraham (Matt. 1:2) and moves forward fourteen generations until David (Matt. 1:6). From David, he advances fourteen generations further until the exile (Matt. 1:11). From the exile, Matthew moves forward another fourteen generations to the birth of the Messiah (Matt. 1:17). The time of waiting is over. The time of fulfillment is here. The time for gathering Israel and bringing light to the nations has arrived (Isa. 49:6).

We sense the rising expectation of God's promised Messiah about to be fulfilled in the angelic birth announcements of John and Jesus. In Luke 1:5-7, we are introduced to an elderly priest named Zechariah and his barren wife Elizabeth. You will remember that God chose the elderly Abraham and his barren wife Sarah to bring forth a child of promise (Gen. 18:10-11). God is surely at work in the world again. The angel Gabriel appears to Zechariah during his ministry in the temple. He promises a son who is to be named John, meaning "Yahweh is gracious." This son will be the messianic herald who "will go before him in the spirit and power of Elijah, to turn the hearts of the fathers to the children, and the disobedient to the wisdom of the just, to make ready for the Lord a people prepared" (Luke 1:17). Gabriel's promise recalls the word of the LORD given through Malachi at the close of the Old Testament. The child who is to be born will be the Elijah-figure who was to come. He will be the prophetic messenger calling God's people to repentance before the great appearance of the Lord himself (Mal. 4:5-6). As we will see, John will prepare the people with a baptism of repentance as a voice crying out in the wilderness: "Prepare the way of the Lord" (Isa. 40:3; Mal. 3:1).

Six months later, God sends Gabriel to a young virgin named Mary, who is pledged to be married, with the joyous news: "the Lord is with you"

(Luke 1:28). When Mary is uncertain at the meaning of this greeting, Gabriel makes God's redemptive purpose plain:

> Do not be afraid, Mary, for you have found favor with God. And behold, you will conceive in your womb and bear a son, and you shall call his name Jesus. He will be great and will be called the Son of the Most High. And the Lord God will give to him the throne of his father David, and he will reign over the house of Jacob forever, and of his kingdom there will be no end. (Luke 1:30-33)

The name Jesus is the Greek form of the Hebrew name *Joshua*, meaning "Yahweh is salvation." The Lord comes into the world in the person of his beloved Son in order to save his people from their sins (Matt. 1:22; cf. Isa. 7:14). Jesus is the Son of God, uniquely born through the overshadowing presence of the Holy Spirit (Luke 1:35; cf. Gen. 1:1). He will sit enthroned on David's throne (2 Sam. 7:14). He will reign over God's people forever (Gen. 49:10). His kingdom will be everlasting (Dan. 7:14). In response to such a glorious announcement, Mary openly proclaims: "My soul magnifies the Lord, and my spirit rejoices in God my Savior" for "He has helped his servant Israel, in remembrance of his mercy, as he spoke to our fathers, to Abraham and to his offspring forever" (Luke 1:46-47, 54-55).

The next four subheadings on the New Testament timeline allow us to introduce each of the four gospels and to hear how each writer announces the coming of Christ in concert with Old Testament expectations. As we present the birth of Jesus, remember that these are things into which angels long to look. Open your eyes to see God's saving purpose on display before you. Give your best attention to the best news ever announced on earth. Receive God's greatest gift to you in Jesus Christ. Ask the Lord to fill your heart with faith and respond to him in love.

A virgin will give birth – Immanuel has come! (Matt. 1)

The gospel of Matthew presents Jesus as the fulfillment of the hope of Israel. Matthew possesses a deep familiarity with Scripture. Although he had worked as a tax collector when Jesus first called him (Matt. 9:9), he becomes an example of the "scribe who has been trained for the kingdom of heaven" and "who brings out of his treasure what is new and what is old" (Matt. 13:52). Matthew has almost as many explicit Old Testament quotations as all three of the other gospels combined. He is profoundly shaped by the Old Testament narrative, which he understands is coming to a climax with the birth of the Messiah. Beginning in verse 18, Matthew draws our attention to the extraordinary virgin birth of Jesus. Joseph and Mary are from the line of David. While they are engaged, Mary realizes that she is pregnant. As Joseph considers what to do, an angel of the Lord appears to him in a dream: "Do not fear to take Mary as your wife, for that which is conceived in her is from the Holy Spirit" (Matt. 1:20). Matthew explains the uniqueness of Jesus' birth as the fulfillment of what the Lord had spoken through the prophet Isaiah, "Behold, the virgin shall conceive and bear a son, and they shall call his name Immanuel (which means, God with us)" (Matt. 1:22-23; cf. Isa. 7:14). Matthew quotes Isa. 7:14 according to the Greek translation of the Old Testament (LXX). The Hebrew text uses the word *almah* that can mean "a young woman of marriageable age." In the biblical world, families would assume that such a woman would be a virgin. The Jewish translators of the Septuagint make this understanding explicit by translating *almah* with the Greek word *parthenos,* meaning virgin. The unique, virgin birth of Jesus heralds him as the new Adam, who has come into the world without sin.

In this passage, Matthew makes another breathtaking affirmation when he identifies Jesus as Immanuel, which means, "God with us" (*Immanu-el*). The name Immanuel indicates that the divine presence has returned with the birth of Jesus. You may recall from our study of the Old Testament that God had promised to be with his people, yet his presence had tragically departed from the temple due to Israel's sin (Ezek. 9-11). Matthew is the first Jewish writer since the exile to announce the return of God's presence. With the birth of Jesus, God's covenant presence with his people has been restored. Matthew openly proclaims the divinity of Jesus here and at the conclusion of his gospel. Jesus is Immanuel, "God with us" (Matt. 1:23), and he will later promise all who believe, "I will be with you" (Matt. 28:20).

Matthew records that magi (or wise men) see a star in the east. They travel a great distance asking: "Where is he who has been born king of the Jews? For we saw his star when it rose and have come to worship him" (Matt. 2:2). This star, which is represented on the timeline, marks the advent of

God's chosen king who will bring light to the nations and receive their adoration. Two thousand years before the birth of the Messiah, the patriarch Jacob prophesied that the tribute and worship of all nations would be brought to one of Judah's royal descendants (Gen. 49:10). Several hundred years later the prophet Balaam looked into the distant future and said: "I see him, but not now; I behold him, but not near: a star shall come out of Jacob, and a scepter shall rise out of Israel" (Num. 24:17). The prophet Isaiah saw that one day the nations of the world would come to the light of God's glory:

> Arise, shine, for your light has come, and the glory of the LORD has risen upon you. For behold, darkness shall cover the earth, and thick darkness the peoples; but the LORD will arise upon you, and his glory will be seen upon you. And nations shall come to your light, and kings to the brightness of your rising... They shall bring gold and frankincense, and shall bring good news, the praises of the LORD. (Isa 60:1-3, 6)

The magi follow the star to Bethlehem, a small town in the land of Judea where David had been anointed king by the prophet Samuel (1 Sam. 16). Several hundred years later, the prophet Micah had prophesied that the son of David, the coming messianic king, would be born in Bethlehem: "You, O Bethlehem Ephrathah, who are too little to be among the clans of Judah, from you shall come forth for me one who is to be ruler in Israel, whose coming forth is from of old, from ancient days" (Mic. 5:2). The magi follow the star to the infant Jesus in Bethlehem. Matthew tells us: "And going into the house they saw the child with Mary his mother, and they fell down and worshiped him. Then, opening their treasures, they offered him gifts, gold and frankincense and myrrh" (Matt. 2:11). These gifts signal that God's Messiah has been born. The adoration of the nations is his greatest tribute. The long night of exile is past. Immanuel has come. His advent brings good news to Israel and to all nations.

The gospel of Jesus, the Son of God, begins (Mark 1)
According to early church testimony, the gospel of Mark reflects a summary of Peter's preaching in Rome. Mark, whose Hebrew name was John, includes

a veiled reference to himself as the young man following Jesus from a distance, who ran away when he was arrested (Mark 14:51-52). John Mark was originally from Jerusalem. He joined Paul and Barnabas on their first missionary journey (Acts 12:25; 13:5) and later served Peter in Rome (1 Peter 5:13). The gospel of Mark is action-oriented, and gives special attention to Jesus' confrontation with demonic power. The narrative moves swiftly from scene to scene, with the transition word "immediately" occurring more than forty times. Mark's gospel starts with the bold announcement of the "beginning of the gospel of Jesus Christ, the Son of God" (Mark 1:1). He proceeds to show that this is in fulfillment of the prophet Isaiah, who had announced: "Behold, I send my messenger before your face, who will prepare your way, the voice of one crying in the wilderness: 'Prepare the way of the Lord, make his paths straight'" (Mark 1:2-3; cf. Isa. 40:3; Mal. 3:1). Mark draws our attention immediately to the royal announcement that Jesus is the Messiah, the Son of God. In him the hope of Israel is fulfilled. He is the royal, divine Son of God to whom kingship, authority, and power belong (2 Sam. 7:14; Pss. 2:7; 89:26-27). Mark identifies the beginning of the gospel in the ministry of John the Baptist, the messianic herald who is the prophetic voice in the wilderness. Through Malachi the Lord had promised: "Behold, I send my messenger, and he will prepare the way before me. And the Lord whom you seek will suddenly come to his temple; and the messenger of the covenant in whom you delight, behold, he is coming" (Mal. 3:1). In Isa. 40, the Lord had announced a day of comfort to Zion. After her sin had been punished and her iniquity pardoned, God himself would come again in glory. There would be a highway of redemption once again in the wilderness. The imagery depicts a dramatic second Exodus:

> A voice cries: "In the wilderness prepare the way of the LORD; make straight in the desert a highway for our God. Every valley shall be lifted up, and every mountain and hill be made low; the uneven ground shall become level, and the rough places a plain. And the glory of the LORD shall be revealed, and all flesh shall see it together, for the mouth of the LORD has spoken." (Isa. 40:3-5)

Mark identifies John the Baptist as the messianic herald and his gospel presents Jesus as the coming of the LORD himself (Isa. 40:9-11). In Jesus Christ, the Son of God, the second Exodus has arrived. All humanity will see it. The theological climax of Mark's gospel is heard in the confession of the Roman centurion at the foot of the cross: "truly this man was the Son of God!" (Mark 15:39).

Peace on earth through a "Savior who is Christ the Lord" (Luke 2:11)

The gospel of Luke is written by the only Gentile author in the New Testament. According to early church testimony, Luke was originally from Antioch. He became a believer in Christ and first joined Paul during his second missionary journey (Acts 16:10). His gospel, as well as his second volume, Acts, is dedicated to a patron named Theophilus. Luke provides a clear statement of purpose in an elegant prologue:

> Inasmuch as many have undertaken to compile a narrative of the things that have been accomplished among us, just as those who from the beginning were eyewitnesses and ministers of the word have delivered them to us, it seemed good to me also, having followed all things closely for some time past, to write an orderly account for you, most excellent Theophilus, that you may have certainty concerning the things you have been taught. (Luke 1:1-4)

Luke's gospel narrative advances through the eyes of individuals who are encountered by Christ. There are several people whom we know only through Luke. He shows a tremendous ability to notice people, record details about them, and unfold the impact Jesus has on their lives. At the same time, Luke addresses the global audience of the Greco-Roman world. Luke presents the birth of Jesus in connection with the decree of Caesar Augustus: "in those days a decree went out from Caesar Augustus that all the world should be registered" (Luke 2:1). Luke uses technical vocabulary for an imperial census to register people and property for taxation. In his *Res Gestae* ("Deeds Accomplished"), Augustus lists several censuses to confirm the increasing size and prosperity of his kingdom. You will remember from the previous chapter that Augustus styled himself as the one who brought peace to the world. He was hailed in inscriptions as "Savior and Lord." Coins from this time show Augustus crowned with the laurel of victory. He is depicted as ruler of the inhabitable world. The comet that appeared at the death of Julius Caesar was prominently displayed in architecture and coins. The comet was interpreted as Caesar having taken his place among the gods. As a result, Augustus was openly proclaimed *divi filius*, "Son of the divine one," or "Son of God." His birthday was celebrated as "the birthday of the divine one which has marked the beginning of the good news for the world."

In contrast to the *Pax Romana* ("Roman peace"), Luke offers a startling counter claim. In God's redemptive plan, Caesar's decree to register the inhabited world moves a young Jewish couple to Bethlehem. There in the city of David she gives birth to their firstborn son. Instead of a marble palace, this son is laid in a manger. Instead of wealthy courtiers, this son is greeted by common shepherds. Instead of benefitting one single ethnic group, this son is a cause of great joy for all people. Angels announce God's good news to a world longing to know the truth: "Fear not, for behold, I bring you good news of great joy that will be for all the people. For unto you is born this day in the city of David a Savior, who is Christ the Lord" (Luke 2:10). The armies of heaven appear with resounding praise: "Glory to God in the highest, and on earth peace among those with whom he is pleased!" (Luke 2:14). Jesus Christ is the true Son of God. He is the real King of the world. His gospel is for all people. He will bring peace to the world through his death and resurrection.

Joseph and Mary circumcise their son on the eighth day and name him Jesus (Luke 2:21). Forty days later, they dedicate him to the Lord at the temple and offer the gifts of the poor (Luke 2:24; cf. Lev. 12:6-8). Consider the humility and poverty of our Lord Jesus Christ, "that though he was rich, yet for your sake he became poor" (2 Cor. 8:9). There is no God like ours. When Joseph and Mary arrive in the temple courts, an elderly man named Simeon "who was waiting for the consolation of Israel" blesses God for his salvation (Luke 2:25). He declares that Jesus is "a light for revelation to the Gentiles, and glory to your people Israel" (Luke 2:32). Simeon's words echo the prophet Isaiah, that the Servant of the LORD would restore Israel from exile and be a light to the nations so that God's salvation would reach the end of the earth (Isa 42:6; 49:6). When an elderly prophetess named Anna sees Jesus, she thanks God and speaks to all who were waiting for the promise of redemption (Luke 2:38). Luke, himself a Gentile, understands the significance of this for his own story, and for all the nations. He will not only record the gospel of Luke, but also the work of the exalted Jesus in the book of Acts, as the gospel goes forth from Jerusalem to the ends of the earth (Luke 24:47; Acts 1:8).

"The Word became flesh and dwelt among us" (John 1:14)

The gospel of John is usually considered the last of the four canonical gospels. According to early Christian testimony, John published his gospel while living at Ephesus in Asia Minor. The apostle John takes great pains never to mention himself, often omitting his name from passages where he is explicitly named in the other gospels. Like the other gospel writers, he desires all of our attention to be on Christ. He prefers to describe himself as "the disciple whom Jesus loved" (John 13:23; 19:26; 20:2), meaning a person for whom Christ died. Jesus tells his disciples that "greater love has no one than this, that someone lay down his life for his friends" (John 15:13; cf. John 3:16).

John begins his gospel with a poetic prologue that evokes the rhythm and imagery of creation in Genesis: "In the beginning was the Word, and the Word was with God, and the Word was God. He was in the beginning with God. All things were made through him, and without him was not anything made that was made. In him was life, and the life was the light of men. The light shines in the darkness, and the darkness has not overcome it" (John 1:1-5). In this beautiful opening, John draws us to see Jesus as the Word, the divine Son of God, who is equal with the Father and the author of creation. He is uncreated, eternal, and full of light. He dispels darkness. The prologue reaches a climactic final stanza in John 1:14-18:

> And the Word became flesh and dwelt among us, and we have seen his glory, glory as of the only Son from the Father, full of grace and truth. (John bore witness about him, and cried out, "This was he of whom I said, 'He who comes after me ranks before me, because he was before me.'") And from his fullness we have all received, grace upon grace. For the law was given through Moses; grace and truth came through Jesus Christ. No one has ever seen God; the only God, who is at the Father's side, he has made him known.

John announces to the world that the Word of God has come in full humanity. The word translated here as "dwelt" is actually the Greek word meaning "tabernacled." John wants us to see the incarnate Jesus as the physical manifestation of the glory of God. He makes visible the invisible God. In Jesus Christ, God steps into history from the heavenly sanctuary of which the tabernacle was an earthly copy (Exod. 25:40; Heb. 8:5). Jesus is the only begotten Son from the Father. He is "full of grace and truth," two words reminiscent of the character of Yahweh in the Old Testament (Exod. 34:6; Ps. 86:15). He is the covenant mediator like Moses. He is the one who has made the Father known (lit. "exegeted" or "interpreted him"). Jesus will declare to his disciples: "Whoever has seen me has seen the Father" (John 14:9). John's prologue recalls the prophetic hope of Ezek. 43. Ezekiel had seen the glory of God depart from the temple due to the sin of the nation (Ezek. 9-11). Ezekiel ends with an extended vision of a restored sanctuary, the place of God's presence where he would tabernacle again in the midst of a forgiven and purified people (Ezek. 43-48). The vision ends with the promise that "the LORD is there" (Ezek. 48:35). According to John, this hope is now fulfilled in Jesus the Messiah.

John's gospel develops around a series of testimonies, prophetic signs, and extended discourses. There is a great deal of material that is unique to John. Each major unit is a complete presentation of Christ and therefore the gospel of John is aptly called the preacher's gospel. John is well aware of the other gospels, but he has structured his gospel with a very clear statement of purpose: "Now Jesus did many other signs in the presence of the disciples, which are not written in this book; but these are written so that you may believe that Jesus is the Christ, the Son of God, and that by believing you may have life in his name" (John 20:30-31). John proclaims that Jesus is the promised Messiah, the divine Son of God. Eternal life is found through faith in him alone. These are the profound truths that John seeks to make known to his readers. If these truths were described in detail, he considers "the world itself could not contain the books that would be written" (John 21:25).

In summary, we see that all four of the gospel writers share the conviction that Jesus is the promised Messiah, the Son of God. He fulfills the hope of Israel and brings salvation to the world. His birth marks the arrival of the kingdom of God, the return of God's presence, and the decisive next step in God's redemptive plan. This gospel announcement shines brightly in the light of the Old Testament teaching that there is only one Savior—the LORD (Isa. 43:3, 11; 45:15, 21-22; Ezek. 36:28). This is what the name *Yeshua* openly proclaims, that Yahweh (the LORD) is the one who saves. Jesus is the divine Son of God who comes to save his people from their sins (Matt. 1:22).

As we journey together through the gospels, keep your eyes closely on Jesus. Consider who he is, what he says, and what he does. Ask yourself what it would mean for you to follow him. Jesus is no ordinary person, no moral teacher. He is the Messiah, Son of God. He is Immanuel, God with us. Jesus invites each of us to receive him as our Savior. If you do not yet know Jesus as your Savior, I have written a personal invitation to you at the conclusion of this book, explaining how you can come into relationship with Jesus Christ today.

It is important to recognize that there is an interval of approximately thirty years between the birth of Christ and the beginning of his public ministry (Luke 3:23). The New Testament passes over the childhood of Jesus except for a single passage. In Luke 2:41-52, we learn that Jesus grew up within a devout Israelite family. Joseph and Mary brought their family to attend the Passover every year, in remembrance of the Exodus from Egypt. Jesus ate the Passover meal as a child, knowing that one day he would earnestly desire to eat this Passover with his disciples before he suffered (Luke 22:15). He shared in the Passover lamb, knowing that he was "the Lamb of God, who takes away the sin of the world" (John 1:29). At age twelve, we see Jesus among the sages at the Jerusalem Temple. He is listening and asking questions about the Scripture that he knew bore witness to him (Luke 2:46; John 5:39). All who heard him were amazed at his understanding (Luke 2:47). Luke, the physician, faithfully records that "Jesus increased in wisdom and in stature and in favor with God and man" (Luke 2:52). Luke's account leaves us at this point, with Jesus at age twelve (around 6 AD).

We now turn to consider what takes place in Israel during the intervening period up to the public ministry of Jesus. Many Christians have little direct exposure to the world in which Jesus lived. Yet this is the setting that God chose to reveal his salvation to the world. We have included the next two bold headings on the New Testament timeline to fill out the picture. This material may be summarized and adapted when teaching CASKET

EMPTY. You should feel free to present these two headings according to the needs and interest of the group you are leading. In my own experience, a working knowledge of Jesus' world helps us to know the audience that he addresses. It helps us to hear Jesus' compelling and distinctive voice. It also helps us to apply Jesus' words to our own contemporary context.

Israel suffers "birth pangs" of the Messiah

The years that follow have been summarized on the timeline as Israel suffers "birth pangs" of the Messiah. This heading refers to the violent era that is ushered in after the death of Herod in 4 BC. Israel's prophets used the image of a woman groaning in labor as a metaphor for the intense suffering that will immediately precede the day of the LORD and the revelation of his Messiah. The prophet Isaiah had announced a future time when "pangs and agony will seize them; they will be in anguish like a woman in labor" (Isa. 13:8; cf. Isa. 26:17; 37:3; 66:7; Jer. 30:5-7). These "birth pangs" will resolve in deliverance when the barren woman will rejoice (Isa. 54:1-8).

In our previous chapter we surveyed Herod's public successes and vast building program. Yet we also noted that as his reign progressed, his rule became increasingly destructive. Constant struggle over succession led to an atmosphere of suspicion and frequent changes to Herod's will. In 7 BC, he ordered the execution of his sons Alexander and Aristobulus. In 6 BC, Herod hears of the birth of the "King of the Jews" in Bethlehem from the magi who had traveled from the east (Matt. 2:1-3). He is troubled by news of a rival king, and enquires of the chief priests and scribes where the Messiah was to be born. Upon hearing that it was Bethlehem—the very place where the star had appeared—he instructs the magi to find the child and bring a report back to him. God warns the magi in a dream, and they return to their own country. In the meantime, God sends an angel to warn Joseph and Mary, who flee to Egypt (Matt. 2:13-14). When Herod discovers that he has been tricked by the magi, he orders the slaughter of infants in Jerusalem; every boy two years of age or younger is killed (Matt. 2:16-18). There is much lamenting in Bethlehem as parents mourn the slaughter of their children (Matt. 2:17-18; cf. Jer. 31:15).

Herod's violent rule continues, and in 4 BC, just five days before his own death, he executes his son Antipater. When rumor spreads that Herod was dying, two rabbinic teachers, Judah ben Zarifai and Mattityahu ben Margalith, urge their disciples to cut down the golden eagle that Herod placed over the entrance to the Temple Mount from the upper city of Jerusalem. An enraged Herod has to be carried to their public trial and orders that the teachers and their disciples be burned alive. Knowing that he was close to death, Herod tries to secure grief in Israel by locking up the most eminent citizens of Judea in the hippodrome of Jericho. He gives instructions to his sister Salome that "as soon as I die, kill them all; then unwillingly, every household in Judea will weep for me!" (Josephus, *War* 1.660). Immediately after Herod dies and before the army learns of his death, Salome quietly leaves the palace and releases the prisoners by reporting that the king had changed his mind.

Violence around Herod's death – two thousand crucified by Varus

After the death of Herod in 4 BC, the "birth pangs" intensify in the land of Israel. Herod's son, Archelaus, assumes kingship and executes three thousand people during the celebration of Passover. Roman regional governors descend into Judea to plunder Herod's estates. Populist figures in Israel, such as Simon the slave, claim kingship for themselves and devastate the land with marauding bands. Varus, the Roman legate of Syria, responds with a cruel and heavy hand. He has two thousand Israelites crucified for crimes against the state. While all this is taking place, Herod's sons travel to Rome and wait for Caesar Augustus to complete his assigned role as the one to carry out Herod's will. You may recall from our previous chapter that Caesar Augustus rules as Roman emperor during this period (27 BC-14 AD). He had established Roman authority in Israel by setting up Herod as client king. Augustus will be the one to determine Herod's successors.

Caesar administers the will of Herod through his three sons: Archelaus, Antipas, and Philip

Herod changed his will seven times over the course of his reign, depending on which wife and sons were in or out of favor. His final will balances rival claimants by dividing his kingdom among his sons: Archelaus is named king; his full brother Antipas and his half-brother Philip are named *tetrarchs* (meaning "ruler of one fourth") over different regions. Caesar Augustus listens to each claimant to the throne as well as a delegation that requests an end to Herodian kingship and the establishment of direct Roman rule. Augustus follows Herod's will with one significant change. Instead of naming Archelaus king, he is named *ethnarch* ("ruler of the nation") and is promised the title of king only if he proves worthy of the office. As we look briefly at Archelaus, Antipas, and Phillip, it is important to remember that each one begins to rule in 4 BC. Although they govern different geographical regions, the Roman emperor Caesar Augustus appoints them all. These three sons of Herod shape the political context for the gospels and heighten the expectation for godly leadership in the coming kingdom of God.

Archelaus ethnarch of Judea, Samaria, and Idumea (4 BC-AD 6)

Herod's son Archelaus becomes ruler of Judea, Samaria, and Idumea (ancient Edom), roughly half of Herod's kingdom. He is nineteen years old when he begins to rule. His reign begins with violence at the Passover and continues much the same. You will remember that Joseph and Mary had fled to Egypt from the rage of Herod (Matt. 2:13-14). When they had heard of Herod's death, they returned to Israel with their infant son. Their journey retraces Israel's Exodus from Egypt, in fulfillment of the second Exodus to come (Matt. 2:15; cf. Exod. 4:22-23; Hos. 11:1). God protects his beloved Son again by warning Joseph about Archelaus. Matthew tells us that when Joseph heard that Archelaus was reigning over Judea in place of his father Herod, "he was afraid to go there, and being warned in a dream he withdrew to the district of Galilee. And he went and lived in a city called Nazareth, that what was spoken by the prophets might be fulfilled: 'He shall be called a Nazarene'" (Matt. 2:22-23). The name "Nazarene" means "branch" in Hebrew and alludes to the promised Davidic branch who will come from the stump of Jesse (Isa. 11:1; cf. Jer. 23:5). God preserves Joseph and Mary during the tumultuous rule of Archelaus, and they settle in Nazareth (Matt 4:12-17; John 1:45-46). Archelaus is banished in AD 6 for incompetence after ruling nine years, never having received the title of king.

Antipas tetrarch of Galilee and Perea (4 BC-AD 39)

Herod's son Antipas is named tetrarch of Galilee and Perea. He is seventeen years old when he begins to rule. He rules for more than forty years. He is the son of Herod and Malthace, a Samaritan. He rules as tetrarch of Galilee and Perea during Jesus' public ministry and hears of his teaching (Matt. 14:1; Mark 6:14; Luke 3:1). John the Baptist will condemn Antipas' marriage to Herodias, the wife of his brother Philip, as being against God's law (Luke 3:19; cf. Lev. 18:16). Antipas will arrest John and bear responsibility for his gruesome death (Matt. 14:10; see Josephus, *Ant.* 18.116-117). Jesus will call Antipas "that fox" (Luke 13:32). Antipas will treat Jesus with contempt during his trial in Jerusalem (Luke 23:7-12; Acts 4:27). In AD 39, Antipas is accused of planning a revolt and is banished to Gaul, where he dies in misery.

Phillip tetrarch of northern territories (4 BC-AD 34)

Herod's son Philip is named tetrarch of the northern territories of Gaulonitis, Trachonitis, and the area around Paneas at the headwaters of the Jordan River. He is sixteen years old when he begins to rule. Philip is the son of Herod and Cleopatra of Jerusalem. He builds a new city and temple to Augustus near Paneas, naming the city *Caesarea Philippi* ("Caesarea of Philip"). Jesus will later withdraw to the district of Caesarea Philippi to ask his disciples: "Who do you say that I am?" (Matt. 16:15). Here Peter will confess: "You are the Christ, the Son of the living God" (Matt. 16:16). Philip will later die in AD 34, and his territory will be given to his nephew Herod Agrippa I.

The family tree of Herod, like any royal family, can be quite complex. There are several people named Herod in the New Testament. Male descendants are called Herod and female descendants are called Herodias. To summarize briefly, we note first of all that there is Herod the Great, King of the Jews, who is king of Judea at the birth of John and Jesus (Matt. 2:1-19; Luke 1:5). He dies shortly thereafter in 4 BC (Matt. 2:19). Next, there are three of Herod's sons: Herod Archelaus, who rules as ethnarch of Judea during Jesus' childhood and is banished in AD 6; Herod Antipas, who rules as tetrarch of Galilee and Perea during Jesus' public ministry and is banished in AD 39; and Herod Philip, who rules over the northern territories and dies in AD 34. Herodias is Herod the Great's granddaughter, whose ambition for power caused the death of John the Baptist (Matt. 14:3).

To complicate the matter even further, we will encounter two more Herods along the way in our study of the New Testament. Herod Agrippa I is the grandson of Herod the Great who rules as king from AD 41-44. He executes Jesus' disciple, James, the son of Zebedee, and then dies suddenly after failing to give God glory (Acts 12:23). Herod Agrippa II is the great-grandson of Herod the Great who listens to Paul's preaching about Christ (Acts 26:27-28). The Herodian royal family is completely dependent on Roman patronage for their power. As a group, they are mentioned in opposition to Jesus and attempt to trap him with respect to paying taxes to Rome (Matt. 22:16-17). They are depicted on the New Testament timeline under the period of EXPECTATIONS with a red crown as illegitimate kings.

Judea reduced to a Roman province ruled by procurators

The next bold heading on the New Testament timeline marks the moment when Judea loses independence and is reduced to a Roman province. After Archelaus is banished in AD 6, his territory becomes incorporated into the Roman Empire as the new province of Judea. Judea is ruled by a series of Roman procurators (or governors), appointed directly by the Roman emperor. Their primary responsibilities are to collect taxes, oversee building projects, administer justice, and maintain peace with the use of Roman legions or auxiliary forces under their command. Procurators hold the "the right of the sword" and possess sole jurisdiction over capital crimes. Coponius is appointed as the first procurator (AD 6-10), followed by Marcus Ambivulus (AD 10-13), Annius Rufus (AD 13-15), and Valerius Gratus (AD 15-26). The fifth Roman procurator, Pontius Pilate (AD 26-36), governs Judea during the ministry of Jesus and presides over his crucifixion (Mark 15:15). Roman governors often showed great disrespect for Israel's traditions and increased their own wealth through bribery and corruption. The reality of life under Roman rule increases hope for the coming one who would "proclaim good news to the poor" and "set at liberty those who are oppressed" (Luke 4:18; cf. Isa. 61:1).

Census of Quirinius – revolt by Judas of Galilee

Caesar Augustus sends Quirinius, a well-known Roman senator, to Judea in order to take a census of the new province. An earlier census under Quirinius' jurisdiction is connected with the birth of Christ, probably as Herod's reign was deteriorating and the Roman government sensed an imminent change of assets (Luke 2:2). Such censuses were carried out with the help of local tax collectors, who were despised as traitors of their own people. The census of Quirinius provokes a violent reaction in Israel. Judas of Galilee leads an armed revolt claiming that taxation is an introduction to slavery and exhorts the nation to assert their freedom. Although Judas attracts many, he is killed and his band dispersed (Acts 5:37). Josephus considers this revolt the beginning of a popular resistance movement that would ultimately bring the nation into a disastrous war with Rome in AD 66.

Sadducees, Pharisees, Essenes, Zealots seek God's righteousness

Now that we have been introduced to the political context, it is important to consider the religious context of Jesus' public ministry. There are four distinct religious responses to the world within Judaism at the time of Jesus. These groups are identified as the Sadducees, Pharisees, Essenes, and Zealots. It is helpful to briefly introduce these groups. They understand the problems of the world differently, and as such, they provide different solutions to repair what they perceived to be wrong with the world. At the same time, each of these groups share the hope of Israel and anticipate the coming kingdom of God.

The Sadducees

The Sadducees are represented on the New Testament timeline by the high priestly turban. They are a conservative, religious and political group drawn from upper class priestly and aristocratic families in Jewish society. The name Sadducee comes from Zadok, the high priest in the days of David and Solomon (1 Kgs. 1:34). The Sadducees control temple worship, and many are members of the supreme legal council called the Sanhedrin, which we will encounter during the trial of Jesus (Matt. 26:59). The Sadducees accept as binding only laws derived from the written text of the Torah, the first five books of the Bible. Their major opponents are the Pharisees; they disagree with them by denying the bodily resurrection, the doctrine of reward and punishment, and the validity of the Oral Law (Matt. 22:23-33). For the Sadducees, there is no problem in the world. This is a common view of those who hold power, wealth, and social status. Their solution is to maintain the status quo. The influence of the Sadducees continues during the early days of the church (Acts 4:1-2; 23:6-8), but it virtually disappears with the destruction of the temple in AD 70, leaving post-biblical Judaism to develop along Pharisaic lines.

The Pharisees

The Pharisees are represented on the New Testament timeline by a Torah scroll. They are an influential religious and political group during the time of Jesus. According to Josephus, there were six thousand Pharisees in Israel during the first century. They are a popular lay movement within Israel. The name Pharisee comes from the Hebrew verb *parash,* meaning "to separate." The name was understood as "those who separated themselves" from all sources of ritual uncleanness (Mark 7:1-23; Gal. 2:12). The Pharisees ate their common meals in the state of ritual purity normally required of the priesthood. Although often misperceived as extremely conservative, they perceive themselves as more liberal or lenient than the Sadducees in matters of ritual practice.

The Pharisees believe that God is the Creator who expresses his will to humanity in the text of Scripture. They interpret the Scriptures with the desire to maintain holiness and purity based on careful observance of the Torah (Matt 23:2-3). Their Scriptural interpretation and way of life is transmitted by generations of teachers and will eventually be known variously as the Oral Law, the tradition of the elders (Mark 7:3-5; Gal. 1:14), the works of the Law (Rom. 3:20-28; Gal. 2:16-3:10), or simply the *halakhah* ("way of walking").

The Pharisees understand faithfulness to the Torah as the prerequisite for Israel's visitation by God. Although some Pharisees come to believe (John 3:1; 19:39; Acts 15:5; Phil. 3:4-11), they frequently oppose Jesus in the gospels. The Pharisees take offense at the authority Jesus claims when he teaches in his own name (Matt. 7:29; John 3:1-3; 8:13). They reject his interpretation and application of the Scripture over issues such as: reverence for God (Matt. 22:34-40; Luke 5:17-26), Sabbath observance (Matt. 12:1-14), and ritual purity (Matt. 9:10-13; Mark 7:1-23). For the Pharisees, the problem is Israel's disobedience to the Torah. Their solution is the study, teaching, and practical application of the Torah. The Messiah will come and set everything right again. The Pharisaical point of view is preserved and transmitted in the vast collections of rabbinic literature including the Mishnah, Tosefta, Talmuds, and biblical commentaries called Midrash.

The Essenes

The Essenes are represented on the New Testament timeline with a storage jar used for scrolls. They are known for their extreme devotion and piety. They respond to a corrupt world by setting up an alternative community in the wilderness. They reject personal property, share common meals, and practice strict observance of the Torah. The name Essene comes from the Hebrew participle *oseh* meaning "doer" of the Law. The ritual practice of the Essenes is similar to the Sadducees and more conservative than the Pharisees. The Essenes practice a daily rhythm of life as liturgy. They begin every morning with ritual immersion in water, partaking of common meals after prayer, and then devoting the rest of the day to the study and interpretation of the Scripture. They practice strict community discipline and maintain ritual purity.

The beliefs and practices of the Essenes have been revealed in modern times with the discovery of the Dead Sea Scrolls in 1947. Nearly one thousand different texts have been discovered in caves near the Dead Sea. These texts were placed in storage jars and hidden during the early stages of the Jewish War with Rome (AD 66-70). Forty percent of the manuscripts are copies of the Hebrew Bible. These are the earliest copies of the Old Testament Scriptures that we have today. Although many texts are fragmentary, others are virtually intact, such as the great scroll of Isaiah. The discovery of the scrolls has greatly increased our confidence in the reliable transmission of the Bible over thousands of years. Thirty percent of the scrolls are non-canonical Jewish writings from the intertestamental period. This shows the widespread popularity of these works. Thirty percent of the scrolls are writings from the Essenes themselves. These documents describe their communal life, method of Scriptural interpretation, and ritual practice. The Essenes understood their community to be at the dawn of the age of redemption. They looked toward a consummating conflict between those identified as the sons of light and the sons of darkness. They interpreted the Old Testament prophets as predicting their own time and believed that the moment of divine fulfillment was imminent. For the Essenes, the problem was Israel's corruption and compromise with the world. Their solution was to withdraw into the wilderness and wait. They read, studied, and copied the Scriptures and prayed for God's Messiah to come.

The Zealots

The Zealots are represented on the New Testament timeline with a knife. The zealots believe that armed resistance is the proper response to Roman power. Their rallying cry is "No King but God!" The zealot movement begins with Judas of Galilee in response to the census under Quirinius. They represent a radical religious reaction to the world. One branch of zealots (nicknamed the *sicarii* or "dagger holders") would later terrorize Jerusalem by assassinating those who did not support the war against Rome. Jesus will openly reject this response in his teaching on non-violence (Matt. 5:39). Knowing that all who follow him find freedom (John 8:36), Jesus includes Simon, who had been a zealot, as one of his twelve disciples (Luke 6:15; Acts 1:13). For the zealots, the problem is Roman rule. Their solution is armed resistance. Their zeal for God will destroy Israel's enemies and pave the way for the Messiah to rule.

Annas high priest succeeded by his son-in-law Caiaphas

Alongside these religious responses within Judaism, it is important to keep in mind that Israel is ruled internally at this time through the high priest. According to Scripture, Israel's priesthood descended from the tribe of Levi and only descendants of Aaron could officiate at the altar. The high priest was responsible to lead all aspects of worship in the Jerusalem Temple, maintain accurate copies of the Scripture, and set the religious calendar. In the New Testament period, the high priest also functioned as a member of the Sanhedrin and oversaw the trial of religious crimes. In this period, Israel's high priesthood experiences a tumultuous era. Herod murders Aristobulus, the last of the Hasmonean high priests. He then transfers the high priesthood to the Babylonian family of Boethus. From the beginning of Herod's reign in 37 BC to the destruction of the temple in AD 70, twenty-eight different men are appointed as high priest. Instead of lifetime, hereditary appointment, the high priests of the first century are selected and deposed by the ruling powers. In AD 6, Quirinius appoints Annas as high priest of the newly formed Roman province of Judea (AD 6-15). Annas complies with Roman interests in the census, but he is deposed in AD 15 by the new procurator Gratus. Annas remains an influential religious and political leader through his sons, especially his son-in-law Joseph Caiaphas, who serves as high priest from AD

18-36. Annas and Caiaphas will plot the arrest and trial of Jesus whom they perceive as a threat to their own position and power (John 11:48-49; 19:12).

Hillel and Shammai are the leading rabbinic sages

The leading rabbinic sages at this time are Hillel and Shammai. They were probably among the sages with whom Jesus spoke at the Passover when he was twelve (Luke 2:41-46). Hillel came from Babylon and studied later in life despite great poverty. He is remembered for asserting the value of every human life, since God created the entire human family from one man, Adam. He reasoned that whoever saved a life saved an entire world. Shammai is remembered for his emphasis on studying the Torah as one's chief occupation. He taught his students to speak little and do much. Rabbinic texts preserve over three hundred practical topics that were debated between these two men and their disciples. The "house of Hillel" and the "house of Shammai" are the shaping influences in the development of the Oral Law. In matters of practice, Hillel usually takes the more lenient position and Shammai contends for a stricter position.

People of the Land and Diaspora rehearse the liturgy of hope

It is important to remember that the vast majority of Israelites at the time of Jesus were ordinary people. They too live in eager expectation of the promises of God. They are called the "people of land" in ancient texts. They are farmers, bakers, and tentmakers. They are mothers caring for their children. They are young men and women dreaming about their future in God's kingdom. The primary way that ordinary people learned the hope of Israel was through the liturgy of the synagogue, daily Scripture readings, and fixed prayers. Synagogue services were conducted three times per day. Weekly Torah readings were joined with a reading from the prophets called the *Haftorah*. The most important prayer was later known as the *Amidah* or standing prayer and contained a fixed pattern of praise, petition, and thanksgiving. This prayer is also known as the prayer of eighteen benedictions. It was recited more than one thousand times per year. It begins with praise to the God of Abraham, Isaac, and Jacob, and then expresses the hopeful longing that God will send a Redeemer to their descendants in fulfillment of his promises of old. We should never underestimate the importance of daily and weekly patterns of worship for shaping our hearts with the things of God. Jesus will reveal his true identity in Nazareth during the synagogue service reading the weekly prophetic portion from Isa. 61 (Luke 4:16-20).

During this period, most Jewish communities lived outside of the land of Israel. These people are collectively referred to as the *diaspora* ("dispersion"). Paul was a diaspora Jew from Tarsus (Acts 21:39). The geographer Strabo reports that the Jewish people had made their way into every city of the known world. The center of the diaspora community was the synagogue, often called a "place of prayer" (Acts 16:13). Many Gentiles regularly attended diaspora synagogues without becoming full converts; these people are known as God-fearers. Like the people of the land, diaspora communities learn and express their faith through the synagogue liturgy, Scripture readings, and prayers. Their prayers await the hope of Israel. They look toward the day when all nations would turn from idolatry, abandon their own national customs, and join themselves to the people of God (Isa. 2:1-4; Mic. 4:1-2).

New Testament timeline

You may want to take a few moments to locate the four icons on the timeline that represent the four main religious groups: the high priestly turban for the Sadducees, the scroll for the Pharisees, the Qumran storage jar for the Essenes, and the knife for the Zealots. A brief description of each icon is provided on the back of the timeline. You should also identify the mosaic icon from the synagogue floor with a menorah at its center. This represents the "liturgy of hope" rehearsed daily in anticipation of the coming Messiah.

Tiberius Julius Caesar rules as Roman emperor

We move closer at last toward Jesus' public ministry with four final developments that prepare the stage of history for the fullness of time. First, there is a new emperor in Rome. Tiberius Julius Caesar rules as Roman emperor from AD 14-37. He is the adopted stepson of Augustus. Although a gifted general, Tiberius reluctantly agrees to the role of emperor and prefers others to act on his behalf. In AD 19, he expels the Jewish community from Rome over false accusations from his advisers. In AD 26, he removes himself to the island of Capri and leaves the government in the hands of the Praetorian

Prefect Sejanus. Sejanus is outspoken in his hatred of the Jewish community and influences the appointment of Pontius Pilate as procurator of Judea. Tiberius will hold imperial power and authority during Jesus' public ministry. The silver denarius about which Jesus asks: "Whose likeness is this?" bears the face of Tiberius Caesar (Matt. 22:19-21). The Roman historical tradition remembers Tiberius as "the saddest of men." He will leave the empire with an extraordinary surplus of three billion coins. He will die in AD 37 at the age of seventy-eight, probably completely unaware of Jesus Christ, the Son of God, and his everlasting kingdom.

The city of Tiberius is built by Herod Antipas

The second development is a new capital city in Galilee. We have seen above that Herod Antipas rules as tetrarch of Galilee and Perea. Following the example of his father Herod the Great, Antipas seeks to honor his Roman patron with cities and public buildings. He elevates Bethsaida to the rank of a city and gives it the name "Julia" after the daughter of Tiberius. In AD 20, he builds a new city along the shore of the Sea of Galilee and names it Tiberias after the emperor. He adds an ornate palace and Roman stadium. However, he builds over an ancient burial ground, and thus devout Israelites declare the city ritually impure. Antipas settles the city with a mixed population of Jews, Gentiles, and freed slaves. He mints coins with the name Tiberias written in Greek within a laurel wreath. All official dates are calculated from the founding of the city. Even the Sea of Galilee was renamed the "Sea of Tiberias" (John 6:1; 21:1). Jesus will walk along these shores and call his first disciples in this region. In Galilee of the Gentiles, the people who walk in darkness will soon see a great light (Matt. 4:15-16; cf. Isa. 9:1-2).

Paul educated in Jerusalem under Gamaliel the elder

The third development is a new student in Jerusalem. Although originating from Tarsus in Cilicia, Saul (later Paul) is sent to receive a rabbinic education at the feet of Gamaliel, the grandson of Hillel, and one of the leading sages of his generation (Acts 22:3). Gamaliel serves as president of the Sanhedrin and receives the honorific title *Rabban* ("our Rabbi"). He is remembered for giving priority to the role of a teacher and proposing a number of ordinances aimed at improving the status of women. Even Herod Agrippa would consult

Gamaliel on religious questions. In Acts 5:34-40, Gamaliel intervenes on behalf of the early followers of Jesus and prevents the execution of the apostles. He counsels the Sanhedrin: "Keep away from these men and let them alone, for if this plan or this undertaking is of man, it will fail; but if it is of God, you will not be able to overthrow them. You might even be found opposing God!" (Acts 5:38-39). As a young man at this time, Paul learns the hope of Israel from Gamaliel. He awaits the promises of God and one day will come to believe that "all the promises of God find their Yes" in Jesus Christ (2 Cor. 1:20).

Pontius Pilate governs as procurator of Judea

The fourth development is a new Roman governor in Judea. Pontius Pilate serves as the fifth Roman governor from AD 26-36. He directs all aspects of the Roman administration from the governor's residence in Caesarea. Like most governors of Judea, Pilate displays tremendous disrespect for Israel's customs and often provokes conflict. At the very beginning of his term, he secretly brings Roman military standards bearing the image of Caesar into Jerusalem at night. Great crowds surround his residence in Caesarea and petition that the standards be removed. Pilate orders his soldiers to execute those who will not accept the images. The people fall to the ground and expose their necks, claiming that they would rather be killed than transgress God's law. Astonished at the intensity of their devotion, Pilate relents and orders the removal of the standards. Pilate later confiscates funds from the Jerusalem Temple to build an aqueduct in Jerusalem. He rejects the appeal of Jerusalem leadership and sends soldiers into the crowds to beat the people with clubs. Many perish from the blows and others are trampled to death. Luke also reports certain "Galileans whose blood Pilate had mingled with their sacrifices" (Luke 13:1). Pilate would maintain his rule through bribery, insults and outrage. He would conduct executions without trial and carry out judgments with brutality. As Roman governor, Pontius Pilate will preside at the trial of Jesus.

Our survey of the various political and religious groups has set the scene for the public ministry of Jesus. There is an atmosphere of unparalleled expectation in Israel. God has spoken great and precious promises. The kingdom of God will come. The promised Messiah, the Son of David will reign in righteousness. The messianic herald will appear and call people to repentance right before the arrival of the Lord himself. The moment is at hand for God to act—the fullness of time has now arrived.

The word of the Lord comes to John in the wilderness

As we return to the gospels, the narrative takes a breathtaking turn. This is how Luke tells the story:

> In the fifteenth year of the reign of Tiberius Caesar, Pontius Pilate being governor of Judea, and Herod being tetrarch of Galilee, and his brother Philip tetrarch of the region of Ituraea and Trachonitis, and Lysanias tetrarch of Abilene, during the high priesthood of Annas and Caiaphas, the word of God came to John the son of Zechariah in the wilderness. (Luke 3:1-2)

Luke lists a series of overlapping rulers in order to locate this momentous event in history. He follows the pattern of ancient historians since there was no universal system of dating. You should be familiar now with these names. The fifteenth year of Tiberius is AD 29. Pilate is the governor. Herod Antipas is the tetrarch of Galilee. Philip rules the northern territories. A certain Lysanias rules a small kingdom near Mount Hermon in the north. Annas and Caiaphas are high priests. The exact moment in time is made absolutely clear. History converges to this particular moment. All of these temporal phrases direct our attention to the most significant statement of all—*the word of God came to John in the wilderness*. After four hundred years without a prophetic voice, the living God speaks to his people once again.

John's baptism of repentance: "prepare the way of the Lord"

John begins his prophetic ministry by preaching a baptism of repentance for the forgiveness of sin in preparation for the arrival of the Lord himself. All four gospel writers identify John as the messianic herald in the wilderness, as the prophet Isaiah had announced (Matt. 3:3; Mark 1:2-3; Luke 3:4-6; John 1:23); John is the "voice of one crying in the wilderness: 'Prepare the way of the Lord, make his paths straight. Every valley shall be filled, and every mountain and hill shall be made low, and the crooked shall become straight, and the rough places shall become level ways, and all flesh shall see the salvation of God'" (Luke 3:4-6; cf. Isa. 40:3-5). The prophetic imagery compares the day of salvation to a second Exodus when the LORD God would stretch out his mighty hand "a second time" and create a highway of redemption (Isa. 11:11, 16; 19:23; 35:8; 62:10; Jer. 31:21). God had announced through Malachi that his people needed to repent before the return of the Lord himself (Mal. 3:1-12). This is how the promised restoration had unfolded in Deuteronomy and at the end of the Old Testament in Malachi (Deut. 30:1-14; Mal. 4:5-6). When John was born, his father Zechariah had been filled with the Holy Spirit and prophesied:

> You, child, will be called the prophet of the Most High; for you will go before the Lord to prepare his ways, to give knowledge of salvation to his people in the forgiveness of their sins, because of the tender mercy of our God, whereby the sunrise shall visit us from on high to give light to those who sit in darkness and in the shadow of death, to guide our feet into the way of peace. (Luke 1:76-79)

Great crowds from Jerusalem, Judea, and beyond the Jordan receive John's baptism of repentance, confessing their sins (Matt. 3:5-6). John warns the people that they must prepare their hearts for the coming day of the LORD. This will be a day of wrath and judgment for sin. He urges the people that their repentance must be visible and sincere. He warns them against presuming that participation in the kingdom of God is a birthright (Matt. 3:9). He emphasizes that the day of the LORD will come like a refiner's fire and that they must be prepared for his appearance (Matt. 3:10; cf. Mal. 3:2). John prepares God's people by proclaiming their need for repentance, which was symbolized in baptism:

> I baptize you with water for repentance, but he who is coming after me is mightier than I, whose sandals I am not worthy to carry. He will baptize you with the Holy Spirit and fire. His winnowing fork is in his hand, and he will clear his threshing floor and gather his wheat into the barn, but the chaff he will burn with unquenchable fire. (Matt. 3:11-12)

John's ministry consistently points to the one who would come after him: "He who comes after me ranks before me, because he was before me" (John 1:15). He openly confesses: "I am not the Christ, but I have been sent before him" (John 3:28). Despite the unique role God has assigned to John, he considers himself "a friend of bridegroom" (John 3:29). He rejoices to hear the voice of the groom. He offers himself in dedicated service of the one who is to come. His joy is made complete in knowing: "He must increase, but I must decrease" (John 3:30).

John is the Elijah who was to come

John the Baptist appears in the wilderness dressed like Elijah the prophet. Matthew records that "John wore a garment of camel's hair and a leather belt around his waist, and his food was locusts and wild honey" (Matt. 3:4; cf. 2 Kgs. 1:8; Mark 1:6). Just as Elijah's prophetic ministry had sought repentance (1 Kgs. 18), so too does the Elijah who was to come. The imagery of Malachi should not be understood literally, as though Elijah the Tishbite would physically return to earth (1 Kgs. 17:1). The unusual departure of Elijah from the earth in the divine chariot in 2 Kgs. 2:11 prompted some to speculate of his literal return. To counter this expectation, John states that he is not Elijah the Tishbite (John 1:21). Indeed, he is John, the son of Zechariah. Yet Jesus will identify John as the promised Elijah who is to come:

> Truly, I say to you, among those born of women there has arisen no one greater than John the Baptist. Yet the one who is least in the kingdom of heaven is greater than he. From the days of John the Baptist until now the kingdom of heaven has suffered violence, and the violent take it by force. For all the Prophets and the Law prophesied until John, and if you are willing to accept it, he is Elijah who is to come. (Matt. 11:11-14)

New Testament timeline

You may want to take a few moments to locate the picture of John on the timeline, along with the description of him on the back of the timeline. John the Baptist called for a baptism of repentance in the wilderness to prepare for the imminent arrival of the Messiah (Isa. 40:1-3; Matt. 3:1-12). Jesus calls him the Elijah who was to come (Matt. 11:14; cf. Mal. 4:5-6).

Jesus is baptized, filled with the Spirit, and declared Son of God

One day as John is baptizing, Jesus approaches the waters. When John sees Jesus, he announces his identity and saving mission: "Behold, the Lamb of God, who takes away the sin of the world!" (John 1:29). Jesus is the sin-bearing Lamb who bears our griefs and carries our sorrows (Isa. 53:4). The Lord will lay upon him the iniquity of us all (Isa. 53:6). There is no other solution to the plight of humanity than Jesus Christ, the Lamb of God. For this saving accomplishment he is forever praised (Rev. 5:6-10). Nothing should stir our own hearts like the atoning sacrifice of Christ. John feels his own inadequacy in the presence of Christ. He tries to prevent Jesus' request for baptism, with the profound recognition that he himself needs to be baptized by Jesus (Matt. 3:14). Nevertheless, even though Jesus is without sin, he answers that he must be baptized in order "to fulfill all righteousness" (Matt. 3:15).

Immediately after Jesus is baptized, the heavens are opened and the Spirit of God descends upon him like a dove (Matt. 3:16; cf. Isa. 42:1). The voice of the Father is heard in affirmation of his beloved Son now revealed to Israel: "This is my beloved Son, with whom I am well pleased" (Matt. 3:16-17; cf. Ps. 2:6-7). Father, Son, and Holy Spirit appear together as the prayer of Isaiah is finally answered that God would "rend the heavens and come down" (Isa. 64:1). Indeed, "from of old no one has heard or perceived by the ear, no eye has seen a God besides you, who acts for those who wait for him" (Isa. 64:4). The Lord had told John that the one upon whom you see the Spirit descend and remain, this is he who baptizes with the Holy Spirit (John 1:33). John witnesses these remarkable events. He hears the voice from heaven. He solemnly testifies that "this is the Son of God" (John 1:34).

Jesus is tempted by the devil in the wilderness and triumphs

The Holy Spirit leads Jesus into the wilderness to be tempted by the devil (Luke 4:1). Devil means "accuser" in Greek (the term Satan means the same in Hebrew). The devil is a fallen angel, that ancient serpent who accuses humanity of their sinfulness before God (Rev. 12:9-10). He is cursed in Gen. 3:14 for having deceived Adam and Eve to eat from the prohibited tree. In the very next verse, the LORD first announces the gospel — that one of Eve's descendants would utterly defeat the serpent (Gen. 3:15). This epic confrontation now begins in the wilderness.

Like Moses and Elijah, Jesus fasts for forty days (Luke 4:1-2; cf. Exod. 34:28; 1 Kgs. 19:8). Jesus is tempted by the devil with the same temptations that had been offered to Adam and Eve in the Garden of Eden and to Israel in the wilderness. The devil incites Jesus to doubt the word of God, to test the character of God, and to grasp for the kingdoms of all the earth—something that God had already granted Jesus. Unlike Adam in the Garden of Eden (Gen. 3), Jesus triumphs over the devil in perfect obedience to the Father (Matt. 4:1-11). The devil tempts him: "If you are the Son of God, command these stones to become loaves of bread." Jesus answers with Deut. 8:3: "Man does not live by bread alone, but by every word that comes from the mouth of God." Jesus refuses to doubt God's Word. The devil tempts Jesus again: "If you are the Son of God, throw yourself down, for it is written, 'He will command his angels concerning you, and 'On their hands they will bear you up, lest you strike your foot against a stone.'" Jesus answers with Ps. 91:11-12: "You shall not put the Lord your God to the test." Jesus refuses to test the character of God. The devil finally tempts him with all the kingdoms of the world: "All these I will give you, if you will fall down and worship me." Jesus answers with Deut. 6:13: "You shall worship the Lord your God and him only shall you serve." Jesus knows that the kingdoms of this world already belong to him (Ps. 2:8; Dan. 7:13-14; Rev. 11:15).

We have now come to the end of MESSIAH Part 1. I would encourage you to review the New Testament timeline up to this point near the lower section of the first column. We have celebrated the advent of Jesus, the promised Messiah, the Son of David, the son of Abraham. His birth signals the end of the exile and the return of the divine presence. The nations stream toward him in adoration. He is the one who brings peace to the world. We have seen that Israel suffers the birth pangs of the Messiah during the interval of time before Jesus' public ministry. Great suffering causes God's people to eagerly await the fulfillment of his promises. The Word of the living God comes to John as the messianic herald crying out in the wilderness: "prepare the way of the Lord." Jesus is baptized with the divine declaration that he is God's beloved Son. As the Son of God endowed with the Spirit, Jesus triumphs over the temptations of the devil. Even though offered the kingdoms of the world, Jesus comes to establish the *kingdom of God*. The devil will be cast out. Those in bondage will be set free. We are now ready to hear Jesus proclaim the gospel of the kingdom. The time is fulfilled and the kingdom of God is at hand.

Chapter 3
MESSIAH Part 2

Jesus proclaims the gospel of the kingdom

THE PERIOD OF MESSIAH continues with Jesus' climactic proclamation about the arrival of the kingdom of God, which is represented on the timeline by the blue crown. The expectation of the kingdom of God is a deep prophetic theme (Zech. 14:9). The LORD promised his people that after the sequence of four earthly kingdoms, the kingdom of God would come. The everlasting reign of the Son of Man would be revealed (Dan. 2; 7). God has prepared the stage of history and the hearts of humanity for his beloved Son. After defeating the devil in the wilderness, Jesus begins his public ministry with the stunning proclamation: "The time is fulfilled, and the kingdom of God is at hand; repent and believe in the gospel" (Mark 1:15). Jesus' royal announcement must have caused the hearts of those who heard him to burst with joy (Isa. 66:14; Zeph. 3:14; John 3:29). The arrival of the kingdom of God is the central theme of Jesus' preaching, the point of his parables, and the accomplishment of his death and resurrection.

The preaching of Jesus always calls for a response to repent and believe. Repentance is turning away from sin. Belief is turning toward God. Moses had announced that repentance would mark the beginning of Israel's restoration after the covenant curses had come upon them for their sin. While in exile, they would return to the Lord in repentance, for God had promised to restore his people (Deut. 30:1-4; cf. Lev. 26:40). Daniel prayed in humble confession to usher in the return from exile (Dan. 9). Ezra led God's people in national repentance after leading a partial return (Ezra 9; Neh. 8-9). At the close of the Old Testament, Malachi called Israel to return to God in repentance. John the Baptist has just called God's people to express their repentance in baptism before the coming of the Lord himself. As Jesus announces the arrival of the kingdom, he invites his hearers to believe in him (Mark 5:36; John 6:29; 14:1). He has been sent forth into the world from the Father's love. He will give his life as a ransom for many. All who believe in Jesus Christ, the Son of God, will have eternal life "for God so loved the world, that he gave his only Son, that whoever believes in him should not perish but have eternal life" (John 3:16).

Jesus calls disciples to follow him

As Jesus proclaims the gospel of the kingdom, he invites people to follow him. The compelling call of Jesus often comes with just two words: "Follow me!" (Matt. 4:19; 8:22; 9:9; Mark 8:34; Luke 18:22; John 1:43; 21:22). Jesus describes his followers in the gospels as "students" or "learners." The Greek word is *mathetes,* but it is through the Latin translation *discipuli* ("students") that we derive the English word "disciples." Jesus becomes their teacher or "Rabbi" (John 1:38). His followers must learn to walk in his ways, to understand his interpretation of the Scriptures, and to grasp the meaning of his death and resurrection. Jesus' disciples eventually pattern their entire way of living after him, as those who are called to take up their cross and follow him (Matt. 16:24-25; cf. 1 Cor 11:1; Phil 2:5; 1 Thess. 1:6).

Jesus gathers twelve disciples and designates them as apostles (Matt. 10:1-4; Mark 3:13-19; Luke 6:12-16). These include Simon (whom Jesus called "Peter," meaning "rock") and his brother Andrew; James (lit. "Jacob"), the son of Zebedee, and his brother John; Philip and Bartholomew (also called Nathaniel); Thomas (also called Didymus, meaning "twin") and Matthew (also called Levi); James (lit. "Jacob"), son of Alphaeus, and Thaddeus (also called Judah); Simon the zealot and Judas Iscariot who betrayed him. With the number twelve, Jesus signifies the restoration of the twelve ancestral tribes. Later, we read of a group of seventy disciples who are sent out to proclaim the kingdom of God (Luke 10:1). Seventy is often used in Scripture as a way of representing all the nations (Gen. 10). Throughout the gospel narratives, the reader is given access to the pattern of discipleship that leads the followers of Jesus from unbelief to belief. The gospel writers do not conceal the weaknesses, failures, and temptations of the twelve. All of them, except for Judas Iscariot who betrayed Jesus, will give their lives in the cause of global mission claiming that Jesus, who was crucified, is alive.

Jesus preaches the Sermon on the Mount

Jesus calls his disciples up on a mountain and begins to teach them (Matt. 5-7). This portion of Jesus' teaching is known as the Sermon on the Mount. Matthew sets the scene by recalling the time when the voice of God was heard from the mountain of Sinai. Jesus confers upon his disciples the blessings of the kingdom with divine authority. He defines the community of God around himself and grants to his followers the eschatological blessings of the kingdom (Matt. 5:3-10). Jesus describes them as the "salt of the earth" and the "light of the world." These expressions are used to describe the role of Israel in the Old Testament (Lev. 2:13; Num. 18:19; 2 Chron. 13:5; Isa. 60:1-3). The followers of Jesus preserve the world and shine forth the light of Christ to the world.

Jesus explains the life of the kingdom as one of consecrated obedience. His followers are to reflect the knowledge of God in their lives to the surrounding world. Remember that "knowing God" characterizes the new covenant community (Jer. 31:34). Jesus continues with a programmatic statement: "Do not think that I have come to abolish the Law or the Prophets; I have not come to abolish them but to fulfill them. For truly, I say to you, until heaven and earth pass away, not an iota, not a dot, will pass from the Law until all is accomplished" (Matt. 5:17-18). Jesus does not come to reject the Old Testament but to fulfill it. He warns his disciples against any who would weaken the commandment of God and teach others to do the same. He is explicitly concerned with the way the scribes and Pharisees are interpreting the text of Scripture. He warns against a formal obedience that misses the heart of God. Some Christian interpreters over the centuries sadly avoid the plain sense of Jesus' instruction in the Sermon on the Mount. Some find Jesus' teaching so convicting that they propose Jesus' intention is only to convict us of our sin in order that we might turn to him in repentance. Others describe Jesus' teaching as so high that it is only relevant for the new creation. Instead, we ought to genuinely embrace how Jesus describes the life of the kingdom. Real human life is found when we turn away from sin and learn to walk in God's ways. This will prove our lasting joy as we reflect our Father's glory in the world (Matt. 5:16).

Jesus calls all of his disciples to the life of the kingdom. He first does this by expounding the meaning of six passages of Scripture dealing with murder, adultery, divorce, oaths, punishment, and love for one's enemies. Jesus teaches in his own name and by his own authority as the Author of Scripture. His exposition reveals the meaning of the commandments and guards against a disobedience that flows out of a sinful heart (Matt. 15:18). His teaching contrasts an important interpretive principle among the Pharisees: "To build a fence around the Torah," which means drawing the line of obedience further back from the commandment in order to guard against potential disobedience (Exod. 19:23). Instead of moving further back, Jesus moves his disciples further in toward the intention of the commandment.

Jesus teaches that murder begins with anger and urges his disciples to be known for taking initiative in reconciliation (Matt. 5:21-26; cf. Exod. 20:13). Jesus teaches that adultery begins with a lustful glance and urges his disciples to be known for an exacting pursuit of holiness (Matt. 5:27-30; cf. Exod. 20:14). Jesus permits divorce only on the grounds of marital unfaithfulness and urges his disciples to be known for their devoted love for one another (Matt. 5:31-32; cf. Deut. 24:1-4; Eph. 5:25-28). Jesus teaches that oaths are to be kept and urges his disciples to be people whose word can be trusted (Matt. 5:33-37; cf. Lev. 19:12). Jesus teaches his disciples that the *lex talionis* (the law that required a penalty equal to the crime) is a safeguard against the escalation of violence and revenge. He urges his disciples to be known as a community that disarms aggression by the consistent practice of non-violence (Matt. 5:38-42; cf. Exod. 21:24). Jesus teaches that loving your neighbor includes your enemy and urges his disciples to pray for those who persecute them (Matt. 5:43-47; cf. Lev. 19:18). Jesus summarizes the life of the kingdom with the exhortation: "Be perfect, as your heavenly Father is perfect" (Matt. 5:48). This same language is used to describe key Old Testament figures, such as Noah, Abraham, and Job, who were "blameless" (Gen. 6:9; 17:1; Job 1:1). This language applies to an unblemished sacrifice (Lev. 1:3), and it echoes Israel's calling: "You shall be holy, for I the LORD your God am holy" (Lev. 19:2).

In Matt. 6, Jesus warns his disciples against the danger of hypocrisy. In Greek theater, an actor is called a "hypocrite." Jesus warns his disciples against any form of pretending to be someone that they are not. Jesus teaches them to care for the needy, and to pray and fast in a way that is not obvious to others. He teaches them to beware of seeking the public praise of others and the manifold temptations of the public stage (Matt. 6:1-17). Within this section, Jesus repeatedly promises that their heavenly Father will reward and care for those who seek him first (Matt. 6:4, 18, 33).

Jesus teaches his disciples how to pray in Matt. 6:9-13. The Lord's Prayer is profound. It provides us with both words and a structure to pray. Jesus invites us to call upon God as our heavenly Father (Isa. 64:8). Our first request is that God would act in such as way that would cause his name to be regarded as holy in the world (Isa. 6:3). We ask that his kingdom come (Zech. 14:9). We ask that his will be done in this world just as in heaven (Ps. 103:21). Then, and only then, we move to our own personal requests. We ask for a daily provision of bread. We live in daily dependence upon the Lord, just like the daily provision of manna in the wilderness (Exod. 16:4). We ask for forgiveness of our "debts," referring to our covenantal obligations toward God. Luke's version of the Lord's Prayer uses the word "sins" (Luke 11:4). Both ideas are important. We need forgiveness for what we should have done but did not. We also need forgiveness for what we have done but should not. We ask that the Lord would not lead us into the power of temptation, but rescue us from the power of the evil one. Some translations render this expression with the abstract noun "deliver us from evil" (ESV, KJV). Other versions understand "evil" as a personal reference to the evil one, namely, the serpent (NIV, NRSV). In Matt. 13:19, this same expression clearly describes "the evil one." The Lord's Prayer ends with the declaration that the kingdom, power, and glory belong to God.

In Matt. 7, Jesus warns his disciples against using their relationship with him as an opportunity to judge others. Instead, he urges them to be demanding of themselves and gracious toward others. At the same time, they are to guard that which is sacred against those who show no regard for his words. Jesus instructs his disciples into a vital and ongoing relationship in which they can ask, seek, and knock in anticipation of receiving good gifts from their heavenly Father (Matt. 7:7-11). Jesus then summarizes the Law and the Prophets by saying "whatever you wish that others would do to you, do also to them" (Matt. 7:12).

The Sermon on the Mount concludes with three urgent parables. Like all of Jesus' parables, they require the hearer to make a decision by presenting a set of opposing alternatives. The first parable contrasts a wide and narrow gate (Matt. 7:13). The wide gate leads to destruction and is well traveled. The narrow gate leads to life and only a few find it. The second parable contrasts a good and bad tree (Matt. 7:15-23). The fruit of the trees reveals a person's real identity. Those merely pretending to know Christ are exposed, cut down, and burned. The third parable contrasts the wise and foolish builder (Matt. 7:24-28). Only those who hear the words of Jesus and put them into practice will survive the rising storm of judgment. Matthew records that those who hear the preaching of Jesus are astonished at his teaching, "for he was teaching them as one who had authority, and not as their scribes" (Matt. 7:29). Jesus teaches in his own name, unlike the rabbinic practice of transmitting teaching in the name of one's teacher. Jesus interprets the Scripture, speaking as though he wrote it. He redefines the people of God around himself, conferring the blessings of the kingdom of God upon his disciples. Astonishment seems a fitting response.

Jesus demonstrates the kingdom with signs

Throughout his public ministry, Jesus demonstrates the reality of the kingdom of God with visible actions (Matt. 4:23-24; Mark 1:39; John 2:11). These actions confirm Jesus' proclamation of the gospel that the time is fulfilled and the kingdom of God is at hand (Mark 1:14-15). They also call forth belief in the person of Jesus as the promised Messiah. Three major types of actions characterize his ministry: healings, casting out of demons, and prophetic signs. It is important for us to listen carefully to the interpretation that Jesus himself gives for each of these actions.

Jesus heals: "Tell John what you see and hear" (Matt. 11; Isa. 35)

The gospels record numerous examples of the healing ministry of Jesus. He touches a leper and makes him clean (Matt. 8:1-4; Mark 1:40-44; Luke 5:12-14); he heals the son of a Roman centurion with his spoken word (Matt. 8:5-13; Luke 7:1-10); he touches Peter's mother-in-law and her fever leaves (Matt.

8:14-17; Mark 1:30-31; Luke 4:38-39); he heals a paralytic man, a woman with an issue of blood, and raises a young girl from the dead (Matt. 9:1-26); he opens the eyes of the blind (Matt. 9:27-31; 20:29-34; John 9:1-41); he heals a crippled man (John 5:1-15); he causes the mute to speak (Matt. 9:32-33); and he raises Lazarus from the dead (John 11:1-44).

Jesus provides the interpretation of his healings in Matt. 11. John the Baptist is in prison for his critique of Herod Antipas' unlawful marriage. He sends his disciples to ask Jesus: "Are you the one who is to come, or shall we look for another?" (Matt. 11:3). This is not a question of doubt, but a question seeking assurance. John is asking Jesus to confirm that he is in fact the promised Messiah. Jesus answers: "Go and tell John what you hear and see: the blind receive their sight and the lame walk, lepers are cleansed and the deaf hear, and the dead are raised up, and the poor have good news preached to them" (Matt. 11:4-5). John has asked if Jesus is the Messiah. Jesus replies with a list of his healings. How does this answer John's question? Like most New Testament questions, the answer lies in connection with the Old Testament. Jesus' reply is in fact a quotation from Isa. 35:3-6:

> Strengthen the weak hands, and make firm the feeble knees. Say to those who have an anxious heart, "Be strong; fear not! Behold, your God will come with vengeance, with the recompense of God. He will come and save you." Then the eyes of the blind shall be opened, and the ears of the deaf unstopped; then shall the lame man leap like a deer, and the tongue of the mute sing for joy.

You will remember from our study of the Old Testament that Isaiah was commissioned as a prophet to a people who had become blind, deaf, and lame through their idolatry (Isa. 6). The Lord had promised that one day he would come with salvation. On that day, eyes and ears would be opened and God's people would sing for joy of Yahweh's salvation (Isa. 12). Jesus' reply to John affirms that this time is now fulfilled. The healings of Jesus confirm the reality that the kingdom of God has arrived and that Jesus is the King of the kingdom of God. Jesus' reply flows out of Scripture and is a moving way to answer John: "Yes! I am the one who was to come!"

New Testament timeline

You will notice on the timeline a picture of a blind man who has recovered his sight. This picture is taken directly from the Old Testament, recalling the prophet Isaiah who announced that Israel was spiritually blind and deaf due to their idolatry. The Servant of the LORD would bring sight to the blind and open the ears of the deaf. When Jesus quotes Isa. 35 to interpret his healings, he reveals that he is the promised Servant and that the day of God's salvation has now arrived.

Jesus casts out demons: "The kingdom of God has come" (Matt. 12)

The gospels frequently include the casting out of demons as an important aspect of Jesus' public ministry. Mark reports that Jesus "went throughout all Galilee, preaching in their synagogues and casting out demons" (Mark 1:39). Matthew records: "they brought to him many who were oppressed by demons, and he cast out the spirits with a word" (Matt 8:16). Luke relates that wherever Jesus proclaimed the kingdom, "demons also came out of many, crying, 'You are the Son of God!'" (Luke 4:41). Jesus provides the interpretation of his casting out of demons in Matt. 12. When Jesus had driven out a demon from a man, the people were astonished at his authority. They rightly ask if he is the Messiah: "Can this be the Son of David?" (Matt. 12:23). At the same time, the religious leaders condemn Jesus and propose that he is driving out demons by the power of Beelzebul, the prince of demons. Jesus explains that such a theory is impossible, for every kingdom divided against itself cannot stand. Instead, Jesus says: "If it is by the Spirit of God that I cast out demons, then the kingdom of God has come upon you" (Matt. 12:28). Jesus interprets the casting out of demons as evidence that the kingdom of God has come. He is the divine warrior rescuing those whom the devil has held hostage. He makes this explicit in the next verse: "How can someone enter a strong man's house and plunder his goods, unless he first binds the strong man? Then indeed he may plunder his house" (Matt. 12:29). In Luke's account, Jesus explains that when "a strong man, fully armed, guards his own palace, his goods are safe; but when one stronger than he attacks him and overcomes him, he takes away his armor in which he trusted and divides his spoil" (Luke 11:21-22). Jesus Christ is the "stronger man." He is a warrior, mighty to save (Exod. 15:3; Deut. 1:30; Neh. 4:20; Isa. 63:1-5; Rev. 19:11). He has come to defeat the devil (Heb 2:14-15; 1 John 3:8). The casting out of demons demonstrates that his kingdom has come!

Jesus' prophetic signs: "This is the Prophet who is to come!" (John 6)

The gospels record a number of prophetic signs that reveal Jesus' power and confirm his identity as messianic king. Jesus turns water into wine, signifying that the messianic banquet is here (John 2:1-11; cf. Isa. 25:6-9). Jesus calms a raging storm and his disciples marvel: "What sort of man is this, that even winds and sea obey him?" (Matt. 8:23-27; cf. Exod. 15; Mark 4:36-41; Luke 8:22-25; John 6:16-22). Jesus signals that the temple will be destroyed and that he will rebuild it in himself (John 2:12-22). He will be the dwelling of God and the place of prayer where all nations will gather in praise (Isa. 11:10; 56:7; Matt. 21:13).

Jesus provides the interpretation of his prophetic signs in John 6. Jesus feeds a vast multitude in the wilderness around the time of the Passover. All four of the gospel writers mention this sign (Matt. 14:13-21; Mark 6:30-44; Luke 9:10-17; John 6:1-14). The setting of the Passover is important. Jesus deliberately chooses this moment in the calendar that marks the Exodus from Egypt through Moses. Jesus miraculously feeds several thousand people with five loaves and two fish. The response of the people is striking: "When the people saw the sign that he had done, they said, 'This is indeed the Prophet who is to come into the world!'" (John 6:14). This fulfills the Lord's promise to raise up a prophet like Moses once again. God would put *his words* in his mouth. The prophet will speak all that God commands him (Deut. 18:15, 18). Those who do not heed the prophet like Moses will be held to account (Deut. 18:19). The people recognize Jesus' action as a prophetic sign and they rightly confess that he is "the Prophet who is to come into the world!" (John 6:14).

New Testament timeline

The picture of loaves and fish represents Jesus' prophetic signs that reveal his glory (John 2:11). Providing food in the wilderness causes many to recognize Jesus as a second Moses, the Prophet who was to come (John 6:14; cf. Deut. 18:15).

Jesus announces the kingdom in parables (Matt. 13)

Throughout the gospel narratives, Jesus announces the kingdom of God in parables. The gospels record more than forty parables of Jesus. Parables are not moralistic stories like Aesop's fables. They are not earthly metaphors to illustrate spiritual truths. Parables are a prophetic way of speaking rooted in the Old Testament. Nathan's parable to David is an important example (2 Sam. 12). Nathan tells a parable about a rich man who stole a poor man's sheep. The parable reveals David's sin and calls forth repentance. Other examples include Isaiah's parable of the vineyard (Isa. 5) and Ezekiel's parable of the unfaithful woman (Ezek. 16). A parable invites the hearer inside the story and requires a response of faith. Parables are dramatic confrontations. They produce a change in the hearer. Jesus' parables usually have a binary structure: there are two different people, two different ways, or two contrasting pictures. However, there is only one desired response. The parables of Jesus consistently invite the hearers to repent and believe in him. Jesus' parables reveal his identity and announce the arrival of his kingdom in the world. At the end of every parable, we should always ask two questions: "Who is Jesus Christ revealed to be in this parable?" and "What is required of us in response?"

Matthew, Mark, and Luke include Jesus' parable of the sower (Matt. 13:3-8; Mark 4:3-8; Luke 8:5-8). The parable is represented on the New Testament timeline with the open hand of Jesus sowing seed. It is a fitting entrance to the parables:

> A sower went out to sow. And as he sowed, some seeds fell along the path, and the birds came and devoured them. Other seeds fell on rocky ground, where they did not have much soil, and immediately they sprang up, since they had no depth of soil, but when the sun rose they were scorched. And since they had no root, they withered away. Other seeds fell among thorns, and the thorns grew up and choked them. Other seeds fell on good soil and produced grain, some a hundredfold, some sixty, some thirty. (Matt. 13:3-8)

The parable captures our attention with the image of one who is sowing seed. Some of the seed falls along a path, others upon rocky ground, still others among thorns. All of these seeds perish. Some of the seed, however, falls on good soil and produces an astonishingly bountiful harvest. What is the point of this parable? Thankfully, Jesus provides the interpretation in Matt. 13:18-23. The seed refers to the word of the kingdom. We see immediately that the parables are ways of announcing the kingdom of God. The seed on the path is devoured by the evil. The seed on rocky ground withers under persecution. The seed among thorns is choked by the cares of the world and the deceitfulness of riches. All of these seeds perish and are unfruitful. Only the seed on good soil flourishes. This is the one who hears the word of the kingdom and understands it. The parable reveals that there are three ways to die, but only one way to live.

Who is Jesus Christ revealed to be in the parable? He is the sower of the word of the kingdom. Jesus fulfills the prophetic imagery of Isa. 55. God's people are invited to seek the Lord, return to him, and incline their ear that they may live. His word will burst forth in fruitfulness in their lives as sin's curse is uprooted and joy breaks forth:

> For as the rain and the snow come down from heaven and do not return there but water the earth, making it bring forth and sprout, giving seed to the sower and bread to the eater, so shall my word be that goes out from my mouth; it shall not return to me empty, but it shall accomplish that which I purpose, and shall succeed in the thing for which I sent it. (Isa. 55:10-11)

What is required of us in response to God's word? We are to receive the word of the kingdom from Jesus Christ. The time is fulfilled. The kingdom of God is at hand. Repentance and faith are required of us. Like Jesus' prophetic signs, the parables announce the central proclamation of Jesus (Mark 1:14-15; cf. Dan. 2:44). There is a great urgency to our response, for Jesus echoes Isa. 6 with the refrain "he who has ears, let him hear" (Matt. 13:9). All who do not receive the word of Christ will perish in unbelief.

New Testament timeline

You should locate the picture of a hand dropping seeds on the timeline, which signifies Jesus' parable of the sower (Mark 4). Jesus' parables dramatically announce the kingdom of God and call for a response of faith in him as messianic King. The imagery of Jesus' parables is drawn from the Old Testament.

Invitation to believe and receive forgiveness (Luke 14)

Many of Jesus' parables end with an invitation to believe in him and to receive forgiveness. The need for repentance and belief is necessary for all. In Luke 14, Jesus eats in the home of a prominent Pharisee. A man enters who is critically ill. Jesus asks his host if it is lawful to heal on the Sabbath. In rabbinic Judaism, no work can be done, nor is any change of status allowed for a person on the Sabbath. Jesus' hosts are silent as he takes hold of the man and heals him. Again his hosts are silent. Jesus then offers a set of three parables aimed at the heart of his hosts. All three parables are set in the context of a banquet.

The first parable of a wedding banquet creates great tension for his hosts with the warning toward those who take a seat of honor, yet they are required to step down when a person of greater honor arrives (Luke 14:8-11). Who is Jesus revealed to be? He is the most distinguished guest in their midst. The second parable warns of the danger of inviting only one's friends to dinner. Jesus teaches his hosts to invite the poor, crippled, lame, and blind to participate in the banquet, emphasizing that the kingdom of God is open to all. One of the guests grasps Jesus' meaning when he bursts out: "Blessed is everyone who will eat bread in the kingdom of God!" (Luke 14:15). The third parable relates the story of a man who has prepared a great banquet. He sends his servants to his intended guests, who announce that all is prepared. The hearers offer pathetic excuses for why they cannot attend: a purchased field must be viewed, a team of purchased oxen must be tested, or a new bride must be appeased. The parable ends with the master sending his servant to "go out quickly to the streets and lanes of the city, and bring in the poor and crippled and blind and lame" (Luke 14:21). Those outside are invited inside while those originally invited inside are now outside. In this parable, Jesus is revealed to be the one inviting the poor, blind, and lame to the messianic banquet of God for all peoples (Isa. 25:6-9; 35:1-4; 61:1-3). The time is now fulfilled. The kingdom of God is at hand. What is required of us in response?

As with the other parables, Jesus' hearers are invited to repent and believe in him—all who do will find forgiveness.

Warnings of judgment and promises of life

Many of Jesus' parables end with warnings of judgment and promises of life. The parable of the weeds depicts a man who sowed good seed in his field but his enemy sowed it with weeds (Matt. 13:24-30, 36-43). As harvest approaches, servants are sent to gather the weeds and bind them to be burned. Then, the wheat is gathered into the barn. Jesus interprets the parable by identifying himself as the man who sows the seed. The field is the world. The time of harvest is the close of the age. Jesus will send his angels to gather the wicked for judgment where "there will be weeping and gnashing of teeth," but the righteous will "shine like the sun in the kingdom of their Father" (Matt. 13:42-43; cf. Dan. 12:2-3). A similar warning is made at the end of the parable of the fishing net (Matt. 13:47-50), the improperly dressed man at the wedding banquet (Matt. 22:2-14), the wise and foolish servants (Matt. 24:45-51), and the three servants entrusted with talents (Matt. 25:14-30). There is great urgency to respond in faith to the parables of Jesus.

Jesus' parables fulfill the Old Testament

Jesus draws his imagery largely from the Old Testament to signify the fulfillment of what God had promised. It is also important to notice that Jesus often retells the entire Old Testament narrative in order to bring the narrative to a climax in himself. This is usually marked by an explicit quotation or clear allusion to an Old Testament passage. We see this in the parable of the vineyard (Matt. 21:33-44). Jesus retells the history of Israel by echoing the parable of the vineyard in Isa. 5. He reminds his hearers of the master who plants a vineyard, takes great care with it, and leases it to tenants. As the harvest approaches, he sends his servants to get his fruit. The tenants beat the servants, kill another, and stone another. These servants are the Old Testament prophets (cf. Amos 3:7). Finally, the master sends his very own son (Matt. 21:37). The tenants seize the son, throw him out of the vineyard, and kill him. Jesus asks his hearers: "When therefore the owner of the vineyard comes, what will he do to those tenants?" (Mat 21:40). They answer: "He will put those wretches to a miserable death and let out the vineyard to other tenants who will give him the fruits in their seasons" (Matt. 21:41). Jesus ends the retelling of the Old Testament narrative by revealing himself as the rejected son who becomes the cornerstone: "Have you never read in the Scriptures: 'The stone that the builders rejected has become the cornerstone; this was the Lord's doing, and it is marvelous in our eyes?'" (Matt. 21:42; cf. Ps. 118:22-23).

New Testament timeline

The parable of the vineyard is represented on the timeline by a cluster of grapes, which recalls Jesus' teaching that God's people are to bear fruit of righteousness for the world. Israel is likened to a vineyard that God planted (Isa. 5). Jesus retells the Old Testament narrative, bringing it to a climax in his death and resurrection (Matt. 20-21).

Rising opposition to Jesus' preaching about the kingdom

Jesus asserts a number of decisive claims in his public ministry. The kingdom of God is at hand. He is the promised messianic King. He is Son of God and Son of Man. Jesus demonstrates the kingdom with prophetic signs. He announces the kingdom in parables. He urgently calls for repentance and faith in him from all who hear his voice. Though great crowds are drawn to him, even from the surrounding countries, opposition to Jesus continues to grow. This opposition focuses on his claim of divine authority, his apparent disregard of the Sabbath, and his pattern of welcoming sinners and recovering the lost. We will consider each of these in turn.

Jesus' authority: "Who can forgive but God alone?" (Matt. 9:1-8)

The gospel writers emphasize that Jesus teaches and acts with the authority of God himself. The authority of Jesus' teaching produces astonishment in those who hear him (Matt. 7:28-29). Soldiers of rank recognize the superior authority that he commands (Matt. 8:9). His disciples marvel that even the wind and sea obey him (Matt. 8:27). The ultimate expression of his divine authority appears in his authority to forgive sins. On one occasion, people bring a paralytic lying on a bed to Jesus (Matt. 9; cf. Mark 2; Luke 5). When Jesus sees their faith, he says to the paralytic: "Take heart, my son; your sins

are forgiven" (Matt. 9:2). The religious leaders hear these words as blasphemous, as they reason among themselves: "Who can forgive sins but God
alone?" (Luke 5:21). Knowing their thoughts, Jesus asks whether it is easier
to pronounce forgiveness or to say "Rise and walk"? (It would be easier to say
a person is forgiven since such words cannot be visibly confirmed). Jesus answers their silence by healing the paralytic. This healing is further evidence
that they may "know that the Son of Man has authority on earth to forgive
sins" (Matt. 9:6). When the crowds witness the healing, they are in awe and
glorify God for granting Jesus such authority.

"The Son of Man is Lord of the Sabbath" (Matt. 12)

Jesus further reveals his identity as the divine Son of God in claiming to be
Lord of the Sabbath. God creates the Sabbath day to guard the freedom of
weekly worship. Israel alone would celebrate one day of rest per week to imitate their Creator and remember their Redeemer (Exod. 20:11; Deut. 5:15).
Failure to observe the Sabbath was one of the specific causes of the exile
(Ezek. 20). Scribes and Pharisees devoted careful attention to describe what
could and could not be done on the Sabbath. They taught that if all Israel
faithfully kept the Sabbath even once, then the Messiah would come. They
reasoned that only God continued his unique work of providence, sustaining
the universe, and providing for his people without violating the Sabbath.
God's own works do not break the Sabbath since the entire universe is God's
domain. God's provision of sufficient food for his people is included within
the Sabbath command and allows for the seventh day of rest (Exod. 16:29).
Jesus' actions on the Sabbath provoke rising opposition because they are the
actions of God himself. Jesus provides food for his disciples on the Sabbath.
When rebuked, Jesus openly declares: "the Son of Man is Lord of the Sabbath" (Matt. 12:8). Jesus even heals on the Sabbath and affirms his divine
authority to do so. Jesus' actions on the Sabbath reveal that he is equal with
God (John 5:16, 18).

Jesus welcomes sinners and recovers the lost (Luke 15)

Jesus' public ministry welcomes those who are regarded as outcasts and sinners. He demonstrates the divine capacity to hate sin and yet love the sinner.
Those who knew that they needed forgiveness were drawn to him. Jesus

announces forgiveness of sins to tax collectors and prostitutes, to the self-righteous and to the self-conscious. He signals their reconciliation to God and restoration into the community through the joy of shared table fellow-ship. Jesus is repeatedly accused of being "a glutton and a drunkard, a friend of tax collectors and sinners!" (Luke 7:34). When asked why he eats with tax collectors and sinners, Jesus replies: "Those who are well have no need of a physician, but those who are sick," and emphasizes that he has come "not to call the righteous, but sinners" (Matt. 9:12-13). Jesus invokes the imagery of the messianic banquet as further confirmation that the kingdom of God has come.

Jesus' actions produce grumbling, complaints, and rising opposition from religious leaders. In response, Jesus tells a set of three parables to reveal his joy in recovering the lost and his call to others to join in the celebration (Luke 15). All three parables share the same plot line and final summons. The third and climactic parable is perhaps the most famous of all, the parable of the prodigal son (Luke 15:11-32). The first parable describes a shepherd who has lost one from among his one hundred sheep. Something of value is lost and a costly search begins. The shepherd goes after his lost sheep until he finds it. He places his sheep upon his shoulders and returns home. In the end, he gathers the community for a public celebration and announces: "Rejoice with me, for I have found my sheep that was lost!" (Luke 15:6).

The second parable increases the value, for in this story a woman loses one out of ten coins. Silver coins were rare in village life and this sum prob-ably represents her dowry or life savings. Again, something of value is lost and a costly search begins. The woman lights a lamp, sweeps the house and searches diligently until she finds it. In the end, she too gathers the commu-nity for a public celebration: "Rejoice with me, for I have found the coin that I had lost!" (Luke 15:9). Jesus interprets both of these parables with reference to the joy in heaven over one sinner who repents, one lost person who has been found.

The third parable increases the value to the extreme. Instead of one out of a hundred, or one out of ten, one out of two is lost. More than a sheep or a coin, a child is lost. Jesus does not describe how the sheep or the coin was lost, but the loss of a child requires explanation. A man had two sons and the younger son had requested his share of the property while his father was still living. Such a request insults the father with the wish that he were dead. There was no legal provision at the time of Jesus for such a request. Astonishingly, the father gives his son the inheritance. The younger son quickly converts his assets into cash, deepening the insult to the father. He leaves the village and goes into a far country where he squanders his property in reckless, prodigal living. When his resources are exhausted, a severe famine comes and he is among the first to feel need. He hires himself out to citizen of that country. It is a polite custom in the Middle East to get rid of someone by offering them work that they would certainly refuse. The man offers the son the role of feeding pigs. Remarkably, this lost son agrees, for he looks longingly at the pods that the pigs are eating. The pods are taken from the carob shrub; its branches are full of thorns and yield small, bitter black berries as their only fruit. In sheer desperation, the son longs to eat the pods from this shrub. When the son is close to dying, he conceives of a plan for his survival. He knows that his father's servants have food to eat, so he decides to return to his father. He knows his sinfulness, and considers that he is no longer worthy to be called a son. He will seek the status of a hired servant in order to stay alive.

The scene shifts to the father, whose eyes have never stopped scanning the horizon for his lost son. The father's love is reminiscent of the God of the Old Testament, who relentlessly pursues his wayward son Israel. The father is the first to see his son while he is still a long way off. The father is moved with compassion. He does something that no man of status does publicly—he runs. Bearing the insult and shame of his son's sinfulness, he races to embrace him and kisses him. The son begins his prepared speech, but the father interrupts him with the lavish summons: "Bring quickly the best robe, and put it on him, and put a ring on his hand, and shoes on his feet. And bring the fattened calf and kill it, and let us eat and celebrate. For this my son was dead, and is alive again; he was lost, and is found!" (Luke 15:22-24). Like the previous two parables, something of great value had been lost, and a costly search begins. In the end, the recovery of the lost son gathers the community for a public celebration. Jesus' parable takes a surprising turn when the older son refuses to join the celebration. We discover that the older son is lost as well. For the second time in a single day, the father bears the insult of his son. He goes out and searches for him. He pleads with him to share his father's joy, and explains to his son: "It was fitting to celebrate and be glad, for this your brother was dead, and is alive; he was lost, and is found" (15:32). Who is Jesus revealed to be? He is one who comes to seek and save the lost. What is required of us in response? We are to rejoice with him. Our highest joy, our deepest celebration at home and in church should be the recovery of the lost.

Peter confesses Jesus as Messiah, Son of God

In the midst of rising opposition, Jesus withdraws with his disciples to the northern region of Caesarea Philippi. This is the territory of Herod's son Philip who built a city to honor Caesar Augustus as *divi filius* ("son of a god"). Far from Jerusalem, some twenty-five miles north of the Sea of Galilee, Jesus asks his disciples: "Who do people say that I am?" (Mark 8:27). The disciples offer the various opinions of the crowds: some say he is John the Baptist, others say Elijah, and others one of the prophets. Each of these responses is attested. Herod the tetrarch of Galilee heard about Jesus' miracles and concluded that he was John the Baptist brought back from the dead (Matt. 14:1-2). Others listened to Jesus' preaching and believed that Jesus was the promised Elijah who would call people to repentance before the arrival of the Lord himself (Mal. 3:1; 4:5-6). Others saw Jesus' prophetic signs and considered that Jesus was like one of the great prophets of old (John 6:14). None of these answers is sufficient.

Jesus then turns to his own disciples who have followed him for nearly three years. They have lived with him, eaten with him, listened to him, and prayed with him. He now asks them: "Who do *you* say that I am?" (Mark 8:29). Peter steps forward and solemnly confesses: "You are the Christ, the Son of the living God" (Matt. 16:16). Peter's confession comes through the gracious work of the Father. His confession marks a turning point in the narratives of Matthew, Mark, and Luke. The gospel writers have not only come to believe in Jesus themselves, but they are writing that others may come to the truth about Jesus and believe (Luke 1:1-4; John 19:35; 20:30-31; 21:24). At this climactic moment in the gospel narratives, Jesus is openly acknowledged as the promised Messiah.

Each of us should pause for a moment to answer Jesus' question: "Who do you say that I am?" If you have not yet believed that Jesus is the Messiah and that he has authority to forgive your sins, I would encourage you to ask

God to open your eyes that you might see Jesus and respond to him with faith. You may even want to turn to the prayer at the end of this study guide. If you have already come to know Jesus, it is important to build your life upon his teaching and fully embrace what it means to follow him.

Jesus teaches that the Messiah must suffer, die, and be raised

After Peter's great confession of faith, Jesus devotes most of his time to his disciples. He must explain to them the meaning of his messiahship. He strictly charges them to tell no one that he is the Messiah. They are not yet ready for global missions. They do not yet understand the gospel of Jesus Christ crucified. Jesus begins to show his disciples that as Messiah "he must go to Jerusalem and suffer many things from the elders and chief priests and scribes, and be killed, and on the third day be raised" (Matt. 16:21). Peter, who moments earlier had been praised, struggles to grasp God's plan of redemption. He responds: "Lord, this shall never happen to you!" (Matt. 16:22). Jesus rebukes him as a voice of Satan who would seek any means of averting the cross. The cross of Christ will defeat the accusation of the enemy and justify the ungodly by faith. Jesus now resolutely sets his face to Jerusalem in perfect obedience to the Father. He sets this pattern for his disciples to follow: "If anyone would come after me, let him deny himself and take up his cross and follow me. For whoever would save his life will lose it, but whoever loses his life for my sake will find it" (Matt. 16:24-25).

Jesus is transfigured: Moses and Elijah discuss his Exodus

As Jesus journeys toward Jerusalem, he takes his closest companions, Peter, James, and John up to a high mountain by themselves (Matt. 17; Mark 9; Luke 9). Jesus is transfigured before them. His face shines with divine glory like the sun (Exod. 34:29-30; Num. 6:25; Ps. 80:3; Dan. 9:17). His clothes are white like bright light (Ps. 104:2; Ezek. 1:27-28). Jesus is seen with the radiant glory that he possessed before the world began (John 17:5; Heb. 1:2-3). Moses and Elijah appear and talk with Jesus. Luke describes the substance of their conversation in that they spoke of "his departure, which he was about to accomplish at Jerusalem" (Luke 9:31). The word that Luke chooses here is, literally, "his exodus." Jesus has come forth from the Father, full of grace and power, to lead the promised second Exodus (Isa. 11:11; 40:1-5). As the disciples gaze in wonder, the Father confirms the true identity of Jesus: "This is my beloved Son with whom I am well pleased; listen to him!" (Matt. 17:5; cf. Isa. 42:1; Matt. 3:17). The picture of Moses parting the sea on the timeline represents the transfiguration, as Moses and Elijah discuss Jesus' "Exodus."

Jesus expounds the kingdom: "The last are first and the first are last"

Jesus expounds the kingdom to his disciples as they approach Jerusalem. He warns them against ambition and redefines greatness as childlike humility (Matt. 18:1-6). He teaches the disciples about the absolute necessity of forgiveness and the unfathomable depths of divine mercy for the worst of sinners (Matt.18:15-35). He loves a rich young man enough to ask him to separate from his attachment to wealth so that he might find eternal life in following Christ (Matt. 19:16-30). His parable of the workers in the vineyard reveals that no man holds God in his debt. Divine love is generous and grants full wages to all who enter the vineyard, even at the last hour. Jesus' incarnation and steady movement toward the cross humbles us to believe that in his kingdom "the last will be first, and the first last" (Matt. 20:16).

Jesus' hour to be glorified has come (John 12)

Jesus came into the world in order to die. In dying, he would complete a life of perfect obedience to the Father; he would make atonement for the sin of the world; he would defeat sin, death, and hell forever. Death on a Roman cross was designed to produce shame, humiliation, and maximum suffering. According to the New Testament, Jesus' death on the cross will result in glory, honor, and eternal praise (Rev. 5:11-14). John's gospel holds us in suspense throughout with the timing of Jesus' *hour*. In John 2:4, Jesus tells his mother Mary at the wedding in Cana, "My hour has not yet come." In John 7:30 and 8:20, the temple authorities are not able to arrest Jesus because "his hour had not yet come." As Jesus arrives in Jerusalem at the beginning of his passion, he openly declares: "The hour has come for the Son of Man to be glorified" (John 12:23). Jesus announces that it is for this purpose of dying that he has come into the world. His death will bear much fruit (John 12:24; cf. Gen. 1:28). When he is lifted up on a cross, he will draw all people to himself (John 12:32). In and through his death and resurrection, the Father will glorify the Son (John 17:1).

Jesus enters Jerusalem as Son of David on Palm Sunday

All four of the gospel writers describe Jesus' dramatic public entrance into the Jerusalem on Palm Sunday (Matt. 21:1-11; Mark 11:1-10; Luke 19:28-44; John 12:12-16). He acts with great intentionality to enact the fulfillment of Zech. 9:9-10. The Lord had promised exiled Israel that her true king would return. Just as David had left Jerusalem upon a donkey during the revolt of Absalom, the son of David would return to Zion in the same way (2 Sam. 16:1-2). The donkey was a royal mount in antiquity and identified the legitimate ruler of a city (Gen. 49:10-11; Judg. 10:4; 12:14). The coming Son of David would be the righteous king, bearing salvation. Upon his arrival, he would remove confidence in human weapons of war and establish his rule to the ends of the earth (Pss. 20:6-9; 33:16-18; 72:8). Zechariah had proclaimed that his coming would summon our highest joy:

> Rejoice greatly, O daughter of Zion! Shout aloud, O daughter of Jerusalem! Behold, your king is coming to you; righteous and having salvation is he, humble and mounted on a donkey, on a colt, the foal of a donkey. I will cut off the chariot from Ephraim and the war horse from Jerusalem; and the battle bow shall be cut off, and he shall speak peace to the nations; his rule shall be from sea to sea, and from the River to the ends of the earth. (Zech. 9:9-10)

After instructing his disciples, Jesus enters the city riding upon a donkey and so publicly identifies himself as Zion's true king. The crowds recognize the imagery and rejoice. They wave palm branches as symbols of victory and shout: "Hosanna to the Son of David! Blessed is he who comes in the name of the Lord! Hosanna in the highest!" (Matt. 21:9). The term *Hosanna* is the Hebrew imperative "Save us LORD!" and is quoted from Ps. 118:25. Although some of the religious leaders rebuke the crowds, Jesus replies: "I tell you, if these were silent, the very stones would cry out" (Luke 19:40).

New Testament timeline

The picture of a man riding on a donkey is taken directly from the Old Testament and recalls Zechariah's prophecy that the Son of David would return in this manner (Zech. 9:9-10). Jesus' entry into Jerusalem upon a donkey signi-fies that he is the promised Messiah and thus Zion's true king (Matt. 21:1-9).

Jesus teaches publicly in the temple courts

Upon his arrival in Jerusalem, Jesus teaches publicly in the temple courts (Matt. 21-23). He drives out the moneychangers and all who seek an unlawful profit from the temple worship. He quotes from the prophet Isaiah that "my house shall be called a house of prayer for all peoples" (Isa. 56:7). Jesus heals the blind and lame, and he welcomes children to him. He engages in a public confrontation with Israel's teachers who question his authority. Jesus tells a series of prophetic parables which contend for the heart of the nation. The parable of the two sons in the vineyard warns against the pretense of obedi-ence and urges the necessity of repentance and faith in Christ (Matt. 21:28-32). The parable of the tenants retells the narrative of the Old Testament and brings it to a climax in the arrival of the son, the heir of the vineyard who must be received (Matt. 21:33-44; cf. Isa. 5). The parable of the wedding ban-quet announces the messianic banquet of the son and warns of the imminent disaster facing any who would dishonor and insult him by refusing to appear in wedding garments.

The Pharisees try to trap Jesus over the question of paying taxes to Caesar as he is handed a coin bearing the image of Tiberius. Jesus wisely replies: "Render to Caesar the things that are Caesar's, and to God the things that are God's" (Matt. 22:21). In other words, give Caesar his taxes, but give glory, honor, and praise to God and his Messiah! The Sadducees try to trap Jesus over the question of the resurrection which he answers from Exod. 3:6. He critiques them for their failure to know the Scripture and the power of God. A leading Pharisee asks Jesus which is the greatest commandment of the Torah. Jesus replies that the entire will of God hangs upon these two commandments, namely, to love God with all that we are and to love our neighbor as ourselves (Matt. 22:36-40; cf. Lev. 19:18; Deut. 6:5). Jesus then asks a question regarding the identity of the Son of David, as described in Ps. 110. This Psalm is one of the most quoted Old Testament passages in the New Testament; it recalls that David had been given a vision of the glory of the messianic king. Although the king would be "the son of David" in his humanity, David praises him in the Psalm as "my Lord." Jesus asks how the

Messiah can be both the son of David and David's Lord. Jesus' question is yet another invitation to believe in him. His opponents remain silent. Jesus responds with a series of covenantal judgments against Israel's religious leaders for their hypocrisy and failure to recognize the time of God's visitation (Matt. 23:1-39; cf. Luke 19:44).

Jesus teaches about the end of the age and his glorious return

As Jesus leaves the temple courts, his disciples call his attention to the beautiful buildings of the Herodian Temple Mount. Jesus replies: "There will not be left here one stone upon another that will not be thrown down" (Mark 13:2), prophesying the destruction of the temple in AD 70. Jesus then gathers his disciples upon the Mount of Olives and teaches them about the end of the age and his own glorious return. This section of Jesus' teaching is referred to as the Olivet Discourse (Matt. 24-25; Mark 13-14; Luke 21). Jesus teaches his disciples that they will bear witness to him amidst a violent, deceptive, and hostile world. He invokes the image of the messianic birth pangs to depict the reality of physical suffering and spiritual persecution. His disciples will be hated by all nations because of him, yet he assures them: "This gospel of the kingdom will be proclaimed throughout the whole world as a testimony to all nations, and then the end will come" (Matt. 24:14). This is the only chronological promise regarding the timing of Christ's glorious return and second coming. Jesus confirms that all nations will hear the gospel and that people from around the globe will believe and be saved.

Jesus instructs his disciples about the imminent destruction coming against Jerusalem within a generation (Matt. 24:15). He quotes from Dan. 9:27 regarding the "abomination of desolation" to depict a coming desecration of the city. This will take place in AD 70 at the hands of the Roman general Titus, as we will see later in our study. Jesus instructs his disciples to flee the city in advance of the destruction. They must not bind themselves to any national cause but live in the world as citizens of his everlasting kingdom. They are to serve as ambassadors of his inaugurated kingdom and proclaim the gospel to all peoples: Jews and Romans, Greeks and barbarians, Asians, Africans, and Europeans. They must not become distracted with the political upheavals of this world and the relentless human quest for power. They must be watchful, faithful, and fully engaged in the task of global mission. The faithful servant will be about his master's business when he returns (Matt. 24:46).

Jesus finishes the Olivet Discourse with a series of parables that inspire faithfulness in action. The parable of the ten virgins urges the disciples to keep their lamps burning and warns against complacency (Matt. 25:1-13; cf. Rev. 2:5). The parable of the talents stirs the believing community to dedicated service and warns against hiding the treasure of the gospel (Matt. 25:14-30). The parable of the sheep and the goats depicts an awesome scene of final judgment (Matt. 25:31-46). All nations are gathered before Jesus Christ in glory. He will divide them like a shepherd divides sheep from goats. Those who have expressed their love for him with compassion and faithfulness in the world will be received forever. Those who have not will be judged with an eternal punishment.

Jesus celebrates the Passover/Last Supper with his disciples

As Jesus' final hour approaches, he gathers his disciples to celebrate the Passover. He tells them that he has earnestly desired "to eat this Passover with you before I suffer. For I tell you I will not eat it until it is fulfilled in the kingdom of God" (Luke 22:15-16). As the Passover meal is being served, Jesus astonishes his disciples by taking off his outer garment and wrapping a towel around his waist. He pours water into a basin and begins to wash his disciples' feet (John 13). The Lord of glory, the incarnate Son of God, takes the form of a servant. He admonishes his disciples: "If I then, your Lord and Teacher, have washed your feet, you also ought to wash one another's feet. For I have given you an example, that you also should do just as I have done to you" (John 13:14-15). Jesus issues a new commandment that "you love one another: just as I have loved you, you also are to love one another (John 13:34). Jesus' willingness to die demonstrates that "greater love has no one than this, that someone lay down his life for his friends" (John 15:13). Jesus now goes to prepare a place for the disciples. They too will be included in God's growing family, identified as the Father's house (John 14:1-6). He will build many rooms for them using the wood and nails of the cross.

As the Passover meal progresses, Jesus and his disciples recount God's great act of salvation in the Exodus (Exod. 12). They rehearse the plight of the Israelites during their four hundred years of slavery, and the birth of Moses as God's agent of redemption. They recall the escalating conflict between God and Pharaoh, the series of plagues, and the climactic final judgment of the firstborn. They remember the moment when God's people were redeemed by the blood of the Lamb and led into a covenant relationship with the living God.

At the climax of this sacred meal, Jesus reinterprets the central symbols of the Passover meal around himself. Luke records that Jesus "took bread, and when he had given thanks, he broke it and gave it to them, saying, 'This is my body, which is given for you. Do this in remembrance of me'" (Luke 22:19). The giving of Jesus' body is a specific reference to his death (John 3:16; Rom. 8:32; Gal. 2:20). He would be the Passover Lamb slaughtered for them. Jesus then takes "the cup after they had eaten, saying, 'This cup that is poured out for you is the new covenant in my blood'" (Luke 22:20). Unlike in the Old Testament, when the covenant was made with the blood of an animal, Jesus will inaugurate the new covenant through his *own* shed blood. The disciples must have wept to hear these words. It had been nearly six hundred years since the Lord had promised through Jeremiah that a new covenant would be made between God and his people, when God would remember their sins no more (Jer. 31:31-34). Jesus hands the cup to his disciples with the divine assurance that only he can offer: "Drink of it, all of you, for this is my blood of the covenant, which is poured out for many for the forgiveness of sins" (Matt. 26:27-28; cf. Isa. 53:11).

New Testament timeline

You may want to locate the picture of bread and wine on the timeline, which represents Jesus' last supper celebrated at Passover. Jesus interprets the central symbols of the meal as a second Exodus from the bondage of sin and identifies himself as the Lamb of God. He calls the bread "My body" and the wine "the cup of the new covenant in My blood" (Luke 22:20).

Jesus prays to the Father at Gethsemane – the disciples sleep

After celebrating the Passover, Jesus journeys to the Garden of Gethsemane on the Mount of Olives. He seeks intimate communion with the Father just prior to his crucifixion. He takes Peter, James, and John close to him as he begins to pray. His soul is in deep anguish as he contemplates the task before him. He holds in his hands the full cup of God's wrath against the sin of the world (Jer. 25:15-16; Rev. 16:19). It is a staggering moment in the story of redemption. Jesus prays: "Father, if you are willing, remove this cup from me. Nevertheless, not my will, but yours, be done" (Luke 22:42). Jesus approaches the cross in perfect obedience to the Father. It is God's will to crush him (Isa. 53:10). His death will crush the head of the serpent (Gen. 3:15). Forgiveness of sin is impossible without the shedding of blood (Heb. 9:22). Only God can bear the full weight of sin. Only man needs to be redeemed. Only Jesus Christ, fully God and fully man, could fulfill the mission for which he had been sent (John 3:16; Phil. 2:8; 1 John 4:9-10). Luke tells us "in an agony he prayed more earnestly; and his sweat became like great drops of blood falling down to the ground" (Luke 22:44). Under extreme distress, Jesus' capillaries burst and mix with his sweat. When he arises from prayer, he returns to his disciples and finds them fast asleep.

Jesus is betrayed, arrested, and tried – the disciples deny him

As Jesus stirs his disciples with a final warning against falling into temptation, Judas Iscariot appears with an armed crowd carrying clubs and swords. Judas betrays the Son of Man with a kiss. Peter strikes out with violence against Malchus, the high priest's servant, yet Jesus rebukes him and heals the servant. He poignantly asks: "Am I leading a rebellion, that you have come with swords and clubs?" (Luke 22:52 NIV). Jesus is innocent of all capital crimes. Nevertheless, "the band of soldiers and their captain and the officers of the Jews arrested Jesus and bound him" (John 18:12).

Jesus is brought during the night to Annas and then to Caiaphas the high priest to be tried before the Sanhedrin. False witnesses supply evidence for a religious crime worthy of death. The charge is made that Jesus speaks against the temple and even intends to destroy it (Matt. 26:61; cf. John 2:19). Throughout the initial proceedings, Jesus remains silent (Isa. 53:7). At last, the high priest confronts him directly on oath: "I adjure you by the living God, tell us if you are the Christ, the Son of God" (Matt. 26:63). This is a question of eternal importance. Heaven and hell hang in the balance on the answer to this question. Before the highest religious court of his day, Jesus is asked if he is the promised Messiah. He responds by quoting from the prophet Daniel: "From now on you will see the Son of Man seated at the right hand of Power and coming on the clouds of heaven" (Matt. 26:64; cf. Dan 7:13). In the context of first-century Israel and the full testimony of Scripture, Jesus answers the high priest's question in the clearest of terms. He is the promised Son of Man. He is the one who has been given "dominion and glory and a kingdom, that all peoples, nations, and languages should serve him; his dominion is an everlasting dominion, which shall not pass away, and his kingdom one that shall not be destroyed" (Dan. 7:14). At this response, the high priest tears his robes at words that would have been blasphemy had they not been true. The judgment of the Sanhedrin concurs: "He deserves death" (Matt. 26:66). They spit in Jesus' face and strike him with their fists (Matt. 26:67; cf. Isa. 50:6; John 18:23). While his master is falsely accused and beaten, Peter denies three times that he even knows him.

In the morning, Jesus is brought before the Roman governor Pontius Pilate, who possesses the power of the sword to execute capital crimes. Only crimes against the state and emperor could receive the horrific punishment of crucifixion. Jesus is accused of being "King of the Jews." He is presented as a threat to Roman order that Pilate was responsible to maintain. Pilate questions Jesus and asks him directly: "Are you the King of the Jews?" (John 18:33). Jesus answers Pilate that his kingdom is not of this world. Jesus' kingdom does not originate from this world; nor does it extend by the means of this world (see Dan. 2:34). Pilate hears Jesus' kingly claim but does not recognize the truth of Jesus' identity. Like many moderns, Pilate dismissively responds with the question: "What is truth?" (John 18:38).

Although Pilate makes an initial attempt to release Jesus and rebuff the religious leaders, his resolve crumbles under pressure. He offers to them Jesus or Barabbas, a man who had been convicted of rebellion. Yielding to their demand, he releases Barabbas (John 18:40). His wife sends him a warning not to judge "that righteous man," but Pilate washes his hands in impotence to decide (Matt. 27:19, 24). Although he rightly declares: "I find no guilt in him," Pilate hands Jesus over to be mocked, beaten, and flogged (John 19:6). Flogging serves as a prelude to crucifixion. Heavy blows are inflicted with leather straps interwoven with lead balls and sharp pieces of bone. Deep bodily bruises combine with slashing wounds for a devastating effect. Often the condemned person would die just from the flogging. Roman soldiers crowd around Jesus in the Praetorium. They twist together a crown of thorns and array him in a royal, purple robe. They put a reed in his right hand. They kneel before him, and mock him, saying, "Hail, King of the Jews!" They spit on him and take the reed and strike him on the head (Matt. 27:29-30; cf. 2 Sam. 7:14; Isa. 53:3-5).

Pilate brings Jesus out a final time. He vacillates again by inviting the chief priests to crucify Jesus, even though they have no authority to do so. They insist that Jesus must die on the religious charge of blasphemy for claiming to be the Son of God (John 19:7). This is language that Pilate understands and it terrifies him. He asks Jesus: "Where are you from?" (John 19:9). Agitated by Jesus' silence, he presses: "Do you not know that I have authority to release you and authority to crucify you?" (John 19:10). Jesus, knowing the Father's will, replies: "You would have no authority over me at all unless it had been given you from above" (John 19:11). Pilate collapses under the threat of his own position: "If you release this man, you are not Caesar's friend. Everyone who makes himself a king opposes Caesar" (John 19:12). He sits down on the judgment seat and condemns the Son of God to be crucified. This fulfills Jesus' word to his disciples: "See, we are going up to Jerusalem. And the Son of Man will be delivered over to the chief priests and scribes, and they will condemn him to death and deliver him over to the Gentiles to be mocked and flogged and crucified" (Matt. 20:18-19; cf. Mark 8:31; 9:31; 10:32-34; Luke 9:51).

Jesus is crucified by the will of God for the sin of the world (April AD 33)

Jesus is led outside the walls of the city to be crucified in a prominent public place. He is stripped of his garments and forced to carry the wooden crossbeam for his own execution. Already severely beaten and weakened from a loss of blood, an African pilgrim named Simon of Cyrene is forced to carry the crossbeam the rest of the way. Jesus is brought to a rocky outcrop called *Golgatha*, which in Aramaic means "the place of the Skull." The Latin word for skull is *calvaria* from which we derive the English word Calvary. Jewish tradition held that the skull of Adam was buried underneath this rocky hill. Jesus, the last Adam, now approaches this place to be crucified.

The Roman rhetorician Cicero describes crucifixion as the most "extreme form of punishment" (*summum supplicium*) and deems it beneath the dignity of a Roman citizen to even use the word "cross" (*crux*). The Jewish historian Josephus describes it as "the most wretched of deaths." Although forms of impalement are attested in Assyrian, Persian, and Greek sources, the Romans perfected crucifixion for maximum pain, suffering, and shame. The condemned person was pierced through the median nerve in the wrist with large iron nails. The person was attached to a crossbeam where every movement generated an excruciating, lightning-bolt of pain. The victim was then hoisted onto a fixed vertical beam as a third nail was driven through the feet. While hanging upon the cross, the crucified man would enter hypovolemic shock as the heart races and blood pressure drops. The person would become desperately thirsty from the loss of blood (John 19:28). After fluid collects in the membranes around the heart and lungs (John 19:34), crucifixion ends in an agonizingly slow death by asphyxiation, until the person could no longer lift his body to draw another breath (Luke 23:46). A victim's legs might be broken to expedite death.

Pilate affixes a title onto Jesus' cross to identify his name and crime: "Jesus of Nazareth, the King of the Jews" (John 19:19). We must fix our attention on the overpowering reality of this scene. Jesus, the promised Messiah, has come. As messianic King, he is delivered up to be crucified by the will of God for the sin of the world. While hanging upon the cross, he is despised, rejected, and mocked by those he came to save (Isa. 53:3-4). Darkness fills the sky from noon to 3 PM as the righteous fury of God's wrath is poured out against the sin he carries (Matt. 27:45; cf. Joel 2:31; Zeph. 1:15). Jesus cries out in soulful anguish as God's wrath against humanity's sin is fully satisfied (Matt. 27:46; cf. Ps. 22:1). Thirsting at the point of death, Jesus declares: "It is finished" (John 19:30; cf. John 17:4). He bows his head and breathes his last. The veil of the temple is torn from top to bottom. The earth shudders as a Roman centurion confesses: "Truly this man was the Son of God!" (Mark 15:39). Jesus' body is carefully removed from the cross. Joseph of Arimathea and Nicodemus wrap his body in linen. They supply seventy-five pounds of costly myrrh and aloe as a fitting burial for their king (John 19:39). His body is wrapped in linen and laid in a freshly hewn tomb. A massive stone is rolled over the entrance. Soldiers guard and seal the tomb, recalling his words: "After three days I will rise!" (Matt. 27:63).

Jesus is resurrected from the dead!

Early at the dawn of the first day of the week, we learn that Jesus' atoning sacrifice for humanity's sin has been accepted. The power of sin, death, and hell has been broken forever. The new creation has begun. Mary Magdalene, Mary (mother of James), and Salome (mother of James and John) bring spices to anoint the body of Jesus (Mark 16:1). They encounter a powerful earthquake as an angel of the Lord rolls back the stone from the tomb. The angel announces to these women the good news that Jesus has been resurrected from the dead: "Do not be afraid, for I know that you seek Jesus who was crucified. He is not here, for he has risen, as he said" (Matt. 28:5-6; cf. Matt. 12:40; 16:21; John 2:19). The resurrection of Jesus fulfills God's promise to David: "*I will raise up* your offspring after you, who shall come from your body, and I will establish his kingdom" (2 Sam. 7:12). Jesus later appears to the gathered disciples and declares *peace*—something that only his death could achieve (John 20:21). Jesus' death and resurrection are the decisive events in God's plan of redemption and the controlling idea of our CASKET EMPTY study. Christ's death and resurrection, according to the Scriptures, are the topics of first importance (1 Cor. 15:1-3). Here the biblical story reaches its fulfillment in Jesus (Luke 24:45-47).

New Testament timeline

Take a few moments to identify this crucial scene on the timeline, noting the centrality of the cross. The picture of three crosses is the cover image for the Old Testament, reminding us that the death of Jesus is the answer to the human plight of sin and death. Here on the New Testament timeline the cross marks the decisive moment in God's plan of redemption. The sun rises in brilliant glory to reveal that Jesus is resurrected from the dead early Sunday morning. His empty tomb is the beginning of the new creation.

Jesus promises the Holy Spirit

After his resurrection from the dead, Jesus promises the Holy Spirit to his disciples to empower them as his witnesses in the world. Remember that the pouring out of the Holy Spirit on all peoples is an important aspect of Israel's hope (Joel 2:28-29). In John 15:26-27, Jesus promises: "When the Helper comes, whom I will send to you from the Father, the Spirit of truth, who proceeds from the Father, he will bear witness about me. And you also will bear witness." In Luke 24:49, Jesus gives the instruction: "I am sending the promise of my Father upon you. But stay in the city until you are clothed with power from on high."

Jesus commands his followers: "Go and make disciples of all nations" (Matt. 28:19-20)

The period of MESSIAH ends as Jesus commands his followers to make disciples of all nations (Matt. 28:18-20; Mark 16:15; Luke 24:46-47; John 21:15). Jesus' great commission issues directly from his own authority and the accomplishment of his cross. His death and resurrection form the substance of the gospel. It is through Jesus Christ that the blessing of Abraham now includes all nations. All who believe are identified by the new covenant sign of baptism, as they confess their sins and faith in Christ. Discipleship takes place over time as new believers are taught to obey all that Jesus commands. His teaching leads to the renewal of God's image and real transformation of individuals, families, and societies. Jesus empowers this sacred responsibility with the promise of his own ongoing presence. The next period of our study reveals how God's plan of redemption through history is carried to the nations as the Holy Spirit is poured out upon the church at PENTECOST.

Chapter 4
PENTECOST Part 1

The period of PENTECOST simply explained

THE THIRD PERIOD of the New Testament is called PENTECOST because it marks the beginning of the global expansion of the kingdom of God, as the Holy Spirit is poured out upon the church at Pentecost. After Jesus' resurrection, he teaches his disciples for forty days about the kingdom and instructs them to wait in Jerusalem. He promises them that they will receive power when the Holy Spirit has come upon them, and they will be his witnesses in Jerusalem and in all Judea and Samaria, and to the end of the earth. Jesus is lifted up before them and ascends to the Father as exalted Lord. Two angels answer the awestruck disciples with the promise that Jesus will one day return with the same visible glory in the clouds of heaven.

When the day of Pentecost arrives, the exalted Jesus pours out the Holy Spirit upon all those gathered in his name. The divine presence rests upon the disciples, recalling the pillar of cloud and fire that led Israel out of Egypt, and the fiery divine presence on Mount Sinai. Jesus' disciples are empowered by the Holy Spirit to proclaim the mighty works of God in the native languages of the diverse nations assembled in Jerusalem for the Feast of Pentecost. This marks the beginning of God's global mission through the church. Peter preaches the first Christian sermon to interpret these momentous events. He proclaims that God has exalted Jesus, who was crucified as both Lord and Christ. He has poured out his Spirit upon all people, men and women, young and old, so that everyone who calls upon the name of the Lord will be saved. Three thousand people respond and are baptized into Christ. They receive forgiveness of sins, the gift of the Holy Spirit, and a place within the growing community of faith.

The period of PENTECOST follows the narrative structure of the book of Acts. Luke tells us that in his first book (the Gospel of Luke) he wrote about all that Jesus *began* to do and teach until he was taken up into heaven. In his second book, Acts, Luke presents all that Jesus *continues* to do in the world from his exalted place at the right hand of the Father. It is important to realize that the missionary expansion of the church takes place by the powerful, active, sovereign hand of Jesus Christ. Throughout his public ministry he proclaimed the arrival of the kingdom of God. He purchased the lives of men, women, and children from every nation with his death upon the cross. As exalted Lord, he now actively pursues them, graciously using his disciples empowered by the Holy Spirit to gather the harvest of the nations. All who believe in Christ are formed into local church communities as a visible expression of the body of Christ in the world; this is the beginning of a renewed humanity.

Luke devotes a significant portion of his narrative to early Christian preaching. The proclamation of Christ is set within the broader narrative of Scripture to show that God's plan of redemption through history has reached a decisive point in the death and resurrection of the Messiah. In him forgiveness of sins and adoption into God's family are offered to all peoples. The gospel creates new communities in Christ, comprised of believers from diverse nations and different social classes. Jews and Gentiles, Greeks and Romans, men and women, rich and poor abandon their idolatry and receive forgiveness, salvation, and new life in Christ. The gospel crosses cultural barriers in fulfillment of the prophetic vision that the whole earth will be filled with the knowledge of the glory of the LORD, as the waters cover the sea.

The key people for PENTECOST are Peter, Stephen, James, Paul, Barnabas, Silas, Priscilla, Aquila, and Luke. Important Roman leaders whose lives intersect with this period are the emperors Caligula (AD 37-41), Claudius (AD 41-54), and Nero (AD 54-68) and the procurators Felix and Festus. Important Jewish leaders are Herod Agrippa I (AD 41-44) and Herod Agrippa II (AD 48-70).

New Testament timeline

As we learn about the period of PENTECOST, it is important for you to locate the picture of a fiery cloud that represents this period. The fiery cloud stands for God's own divine presence in the person of the Holy Spirit. This icon recalls an important element from our entire CASKET EMPTY study. The Holy Spirit was present in the opening verse of Scripture, hovering over the waters of creation (Gen. 1:1-2). Humanity was made alive by the divine presence (Gen. 2:7). Yet you will remember that the cloud of the divine presence that filled the tabernacle and temple had departed due to Israel's sin (Exod. 40:34; 1 Kgs. 8:11; Ezek. 9-11). God had promised that his presence would one day return to create new life for God's people and cause them to walk in his ways (Ezek. 36:26-27). In Jesus Christ, the divine presence has returned and Immanuel has come (Matt. 1:22-23). Now, the exalted Jesus pours out the Holy Spirit upon all peoples, men and women, young and old, rich and poor in order to fulfill God's promise (Acts 2:1-21; cf. Joel 2:28-29). The Holy Spirit is God's personal, empowering presence filling all who believe for lives of righteousness, mission, and service (Acts 1:8; Rom. 8; 1 Cor. 6:19; cf. Isa. 49:6; Heb. 2:4).

The two columns in the period of PENTECOST on the timeline follow the broad chronology presented in the book of Acts. Within this progression of time, you should notice that the twenty-one letters of the New Testament are located in their chronological setting. The New Testament letters are color-coded to help you remember them. James and Jude, brothers of Jesus, write to the church in Jerusalem. Their letters are brown for their earthy, concrete exhortation to practical discipleship (Jas. 1:27; Jude 1:20-21). The thirteen letters of Paul are red for his emphasis on Christ's atoning blood to justify the ungodly by faith (Rom. 3:23-25; Eph. 2:13; Col. 1:20). The letters of Peter are green for his final imperative to "shepherd the flock" under your care (1 Pet. 5:2; John 21:15-17). The letter of Hebrews is blue for its emphasis on Christ as our great high priest (Heb. 1:1-4; 4:14; 8:1). The letters of John are yellow for his declaration that "God is light" and believers are to "walk in the light" of Christ (1 John 1:5-7; 2:8-10).

Roadmap to the chapter

As you read through this chapter, you will notice that Luke uses a geographical outline to show how the exalted Jesus extends his kingdom, beginning in Jerusalem (Acts 1-7), then into Judea and Samaria (Acts 8-12), and finally, to the ends of the earth (Acts 13-28). These are the bold headings on the New Testament timeline for the period of PENTECOST. Summarizing statements below each heading describe the missionary activity, persons, and journeys that the Lord uses to claim each new territory and people. Jesus empowers his disciples to pray, preach, teach, send, and give. Some suffer, even giving their lives, yet all are called to rejoice as the gospel of Christ moves out into a waiting and needy world. The two chapters on the period of PENTECOST will progress through the narrative of Acts, with Part 1 concluding with the Jerusalem Council (Acts 15), and Part 2 tracing the missionary expansion into Europe and continuing until the gospel is proclaimed in Rome (Acts 28). We will give particular attention to how early Christian preaching includes many of the developing themes of our CASKET EMPTY study. Additional Bible references are given throughout the chapter. You will benefit from reading these verses along with this study guide.

God pours out His Holy Spirit upon the Church

The bold heading at the top of the column identifies God's major redemptive activity during the period of PENTECOST. The Feast of Pentecost was counted fifty days from the Exodus from Egypt (Lev. 23:16). It was remembered as the moment when Israel reached the base of Mount Sinai where God descended in visible, fiery glory. God spoke from the mountain to reveal his will. God's presence set Israel apart from the nations and called them to be a kingdom of priests and a holy nation in the midst of the world (Exod. 19:5-6; 40:34-38). The pouring out of the Holy Spirit upon the church now expands God's redemptive purpose into all the earth. God had promised that one day he would pour out his Spirit upon all humanity (Joel 2:28-29). The gathered church, both Jews and Gentiles, is made holy by the presence of the Holy Spirit. God reveals his missionary purpose and commissions the church as his witnesses into all the earth (Isa. 43:10-12; Acts 1:8). Filled with the presence and power of the Spirit, the church proclaims the gospel of Jesus Christ from Jerusalem to the ends of the earth (Isa. 2:1-4; Mic. 4:1-4; Luke 24:47-49).

Jesus tells his disciples: "You will be my witnesses in Jerusalem and in all Judea and Samaria, and to the ends of the earth" (Acts 1:8)

Jesus taught his disciples for forty days after his resurrection from the dead. He spoke to them about the kingdom of God. He instructed them to remain in Jerusalem for the gift of the promised Holy Spirit (Luke 24:49; John 15:26-27; cf. Joel 2:28-29). In Acts 1:6, the disciples ask Jesus: "Lord, will you at this time restore the kingdom to Israel?" Jesus redirects their question to a humble trust in the Father's will, authority, and timing. He then commissions his followers with Israel's missionary vocation as witnesses of the one true and saving God. Through the prophet Isaiah the LORD declares: "You are my witnesses . . . and my servant whom I have chosen, that you may know and believe me and understand that I am he. Before me no god was formed, nor shall there be any after me. I, I am the LORD, and besides me there is no savior" (Isa. 43:10-11). In Isa. 49:6, the Servant of the Lord comes to restore Israel and give the light of salvation to all nations. The LORD reveals his purpose to the Servant: "It is too light a thing that you should be my servant to raise up the tribes of Jacob and to bring back the preserved of Israel; I will make you as a light for the nations, that my salvation may reach to the end of the earth." We have seen that Jesus is the promised Messiah, the Servant of the Lord spoken of by the prophet Isaiah, who has restored God's people through his death and resurrection (Matt. 8:17; cf. Isa. 53:4, 7, 9; 61:1-2; Mark 15:5; Luke 4:16-21; John 19:38). In him the restoration of Israel has been accomplished and now salvation is proclaimed to all nations. With this missionary purpose in view, Jesus promises his disciples "you will receive power when the Holy Spirit has come upon you, and you will be my witnesses in Jerusalem and in all Judea and Samaria, and to the end of the earth" (Acts 1:8). God's plan to bless the nations will be taken up by Jesus' disciples, as the Holy Spirit empowers them to proclaim the gospel to all nations.

Jesus ascends to the Father as exalted Lord

After confirming his identity as messianic king, Jesus ascends to the Father as exalted Lord. He is lifted up before his disciples in the cloud of the divine presence. He returns to the Father with the glory he had before the world began (John 17:5). He approaches as Son of Man to whom all nations have been given (cf. Ps. 2:8; Dan. 7:13-14; Matt. 28:18-20). He arrives as the faithful Son of God who has completed the work that the Father sent him to accomplish (John 17:4). Jesus is the Savior and Redeemer; salvation is found in his name alone (Acts 2:21; 4:12; cf. Isa. 43:3, 10-11; 44:6; 45:21-25). His exaltation reveals him as sovereign LORD at whose name every knee should bow (Isa. 45:23; Phil. 2:8-11). Having made purification for sins, Jesus sits enthroned "at the right hand of the Majesty on high" (Heb. 1:3). Psalm 110:1-2 celebrates the enthronement of the messianic king as the LORD proclaims: "Sit at my right hand, until I make your enemies your footstool. The LORD sends forth from Zion your mighty scepter. Rule in the midst of your enemies!" Jesus Christ is now seated at the right hand of the Father (Acts 2:33-36; Heb. 1:13; cf. Ps. 110:1-2). He is extending his sovereign rule among all peoples on a daily basis. Every day approximately 174,000 people commit their lives to Christ for the first time throughout the world. At Pentecost, Jesus will signal his sovereign claim over all nations.

The Holy Spirit is poured out upon the nations at Pentecost

Jesus' first action as exalted Lord is to pour out the Holy Spirit upon the nations at the Feast of Pentecost:

> When the day of Pentecost arrived, they were all together in one place. And suddenly there came from heaven a sound like a mighty rushing wind, and it filled the entire house where they were sitting. And divided tongues as of fire appeared to them and rested on each one of them. And they were all filled with the Holy Spirit and began to speak in other tongues [languages] as the Spirit gave them utterance. (Acts 2:1-4)

The day of Pentecost celebrates when Israel reached Mount Sinai on the first day of the third month, fifty days after the Exodus from Egypt (Exod. 19:1). God had descended in visible glory and fire. God's word had been revealed. Those assembled at the base of the mountain were called to be witnesses of God's mighty acts. In the Bible, this event is remembered as the Festival of Weeks. In the Greek translation, this festival is called Pentecost ("fifty") as this festival is celebrated fifty days after Passover.

Jesus acts with divine intentionality to pour out the Holy Spirit on this very day. A rushing wind comes from heaven and fills the house. The gathered disciples see what seems to be tongues or flames of fire resting on each member of the believing community. There are about 120 people gathered in an upper room. They are filled with the fiery presence of God, yet remarkably, they are not consumed. Instead, they begin to speak in other languages (the Greek word for "tongue" means "language"). They announce "the mighty works of God" (Acts 2:11). As the nations stand in wonder asking what this means, Peter proclaims that the pouring out of the Holy Spirit upon all nations fulfills the hope of Israel spoken through the prophet Joel:

> And in the last days it shall be, God declares, that I will pour out my Spirit on all flesh, and your sons and your daughters shall prophesy, and your young men shall see visions, and your old men shall dream dreams; even on my male servants and female servants in those days I will pour out my Spirit, and they shall prophesy. And I will show wonders in the heavens above and signs on the earth below, blood, and fire, and vapor of smoke; the sun shall be turned to darkness and the moon to blood, before the day of the Lord comes, the great and magnificent day. And it shall come to pass that everyone who calls upon the name of the Lord shall be saved. (Acts 2:17-21; cf. Joel 2:28-32)

Luke emphasizes that there were people from every nation under heaven gathered at this pilgrimage feast (Acts 2:5). There were Parthians, Medes, and Elamites, representing Asia. There were residents of Mesopotamia, Judea, Cappadocia, Pontus, and Asia Minor, representing the Middle East. There were people from Egypt and parts of Libya near Cyrene, representing Africa. There were visitors from Rome, representing Europe. There were Cretans and Arabs, representing the islands and nomadic regions. Jesus' first act as exalted Lord declares that all the earth belongs to him. Believers in Christ are his witnesses to the ends of the earth. Jesus had promised that all authority in heaven and on earth had been given to him (Matt. 28:18-20). Pause for a moment to consider the encouraging reality that all authority in the entire universe belongs to Jesus Christ. What does Jesus do with his authority over the entire world? He authorizes his disciples to make disciples of all nations.

The exalted Jesus extends His kingdom in Jerusalem (Acts 1-7)

Acts 1-7 describes how the exalted Jesus extends his kingdom in Jerusalem. Jesus uses preaching to herald the gospel of Christ, as his death and resurrection are proclaimed by those empowered by the Spirit. Those who respond in faith to the word being proclaimed form the first Christian community. The believing community gathers in devotion to the apostles' teaching; they share in meals, communion, and prayer (Acts 2:42). Early Christian ministry grows through preaching, healings, and compassionate care of widows and the poor. Significant numbers of people respond and are added to the church in Jerusalem. Jesus also uses persecution to deepen their commitment and to provide further opportunity for witness. The first martyr, Stephen, proclaims Jesus as Messiah and is stoned. His death, like the death of Christ, will only cause the kingdom of God to grow.

More than ten thousand in Jerusalem believe!

Jesus Christ extends his kingdom in Jerusalem with miraculous results. The first Christian sermon preached by Peter in response to the event of Pentecost yields a great harvest of souls. In Acts 2:41 we read that "those who received his word were baptized, and there were added that day about three thousand souls." In Acts 2:47 we read: "the Lord added to their number day by day those who were being saved." In Acts 4:4 we read that "many of those who had heard the word believed, and the number of the men came to about five thousand." Luke counts the Christian community here by heads of families and so we conclude that the total number of believers, including women and children, had already grown to more than ten thousand. In Acts 6:7 we read that "the word of God continued to increase, and the number of the disciples multiplied greatly in Jerusalem, and a great many of the priests became obedient to the faith." This expression is particularly moving as Luke uses the same two verbs that occur in the Greek translation of Gen. 1:28 "to increase" and "to multiply." The word of God in Christ fulfills the original purpose of humanity. How beautiful it is also that a great number of Israel's priests become believers in Christ! Many who knew the Scripture well and officiated at the altar recognize the Lamb of God who takes away the sin of the world. The response in Jerusalem represents at least twenty-five percent of the inhabitants of the city. Jesus' word is effective and aims to gather an innumerable multitude of Jews and Gentiles to the praise of his glorious grace (Gen. 12:3; Eph. 1:11-14; Rev. 7:1-12).

What God had foretold about Christ He has fulfilled (Acts 3)

Early Christian preaching, like the ministry of Jesus himself, emphasizes the fulfillment of God's promise in Christ. The life, death, resurrection, and exaltation of the Messiah means that the "latter days" or "end times" have begun (Mark 1:15; 1 Cor. 10:11). The kingdom of God has arrived. Atonement for sin has been made. The new creation has dawned. Jesus is the promised Messiah and exalted Lord. All who believe in him receive forgiveness of sins. They are adopted as children of promise and sealed with the Holy Spirit. Peter's Pentecost sermon interprets the pouring out of the Spirit as the fulfillment of God's promise in Joel 2:28-29. Through the death and resurrection of the Messiah, God's promise has now come true. Peter rehearses Jesus' public ministry and miracles. In a key verse for CASKET EMPTY, he testifies that Jesus' death on the cross and resurrection from the dead was "according to the definite plan and foreknowledge of God" (Acts 2:23; cf. Isa. 53:10). Death could not hold the Author of life. Jesus has been raised and exalted at the right hand of God (Ps. 16:8-11; 110:1-2). He is the one who pours out the Holy Spirit (Acts 2:33). Many who hear respond with repentance and faith in Christ. They publicly identify themselves with Christ in baptism, receiving forgiveness of sins and the promise of the Spirit (Acts 2:37-39).

Christians gather regularly in the temple courts (Acts 2:46; 3:11). There they proclaim that what God had foretold about Christ has been fulfilled. Peter declares that Jesus fulfills the hope of Israel: "What God foretold by the mouth of all the prophets, that his Christ would suffer, he thus fulfilled" (Act 3:18). Peter preaches that they should "repent" and "return" so that their sins may be blotted out (Acts 3:19). Peter recalls from Deuteronomy what Moses had announced, that the Lord God would "raise up for you a prophet like me" from among their brothers and that they were to "listen to him in whatever he tells you" (Acts 3:22; cf. Deut. 18:15, 18-19). Peter recognizes that Jesus is the promised prophet. Peter continues to recall the covenant that God had made with their forefathers when he promised "And in your offspring shall all the families of the earth be blessed" (Acts 3:25; cf. Gen. 12:3). Take a few moments to read Peter's sermon and let God's word stir your own heart and soul with the fulfillment of God's plan of redemption in Christ.

Stephen proclaims Jesus as Messiah and is stoned

Early Christian preaching not only results in people coming to faith, but it evokes opposition in those who hear the word being proclaimed. Faithful ministry always includes persecution and suffering. Peter and John are arrested for "proclaiming in Jesus the resurrection from the dead" (Acts 4:2). The sovereign Lord brings Peter back to the high priest's courtyard, the very place where he had denied Jesus three times. Peter, now filled with the Holy Spirit, testifies that God raised Jesus from the dead and he is alive. Jesus is the rejected stone that has now become the cornerstone (Acts 4:11; cf. Ps. 118:22). Jesus is the only name under heaven "by which we must be saved" (Acts 4:12).

The apostles are later imprisoned and brought before the Sanhedrin. Gamaliel, the teacher of the apostle Paul, restrains the court on the analogy of history. He cites the examples of Theudas, a zealot who led a rebellion, and Judas of Galilee, who instigated a revolt during the census of Quirinius (Acts 5:36-37; Josephus, *Ant.* 18.1-6). Both men "claimed to be someone," but when they were killed their followers dispersed. Gamaliel reasons like a rabbinic sage that Jesus too has "claimed to be someone," but has been killed. He wisely concludes: "If this plan or this undertaking is of man, it will fail; but if it is of God, you will not be able to overthrow them. You might even be found opposing God!" (Acts 5:38-39). The apostles are spared, though beaten with rods and ordered not to speak in the name of Jesus (Acts 5:40; cf. 2 Cor. 11:24). In spite of this warning, they leave "rejoicing that they were counted worthy to suffer dishonor for the name. And every day, in the temple and from house to house, they did not cease teaching and preaching Jesus as the Christ" (Acts 5:41-42; cf. Matt. 5:11-12; Mark 13:9).

Persecution reaches new depths with the death of Stephen in Acts 6-7, which is dated to approximately AD 34. Stephen is introduced as part of the solution to early Christian growing pains. Greek speaking widows were being overlooked in the daily distribution of food. The disciples choose seven leaders to oversee this ministry. All seven (Philip, Procorus, Nicanor, Timon, Parmenas, and Nicolas) have very Greek names. There is an important lesson for ministry here that should not be overlooked. When a need exists in the context of ministry, people who are closest to the need should be empowered to provide the solution. These leaders are called "deacons" and were known to be full of the Spirit and wisdom (Acts 6:3). Raising up additional leadership causes the word of God to increase and multiply (Acts 6:7).

As the word of God increases, persecution intensifies. Stephen not only serves the Greek speaking widows, but he also testifies at Greek speaking synagogues and to other diaspora Jews from Cyrene, Alexandria, Cilicia, and Asia (Acts 6:9). He receives the same accusations that were leveled against Jesus: blasphemy against God, the Torah, and the temple (Acts 6:11-14). As in the trial of Jesus, the high priest asks Stephen: "Are these things so?" (Acts 7:1; cf. Matt. 26:61-62). Stephen defends his faith in Christ by a moving retelling of the Old Testament narrative (Acts 7). He draws attention to how God's people have often missed those whom God has appointed to save them. He begins with God's call to Abraham, Isaac, and Jacob. He continues with Joseph, who was rejected by his brothers, though God had sent him to preserve his family from famine. He tells of Moses, who was rejected, though God had appointed him as redeemer (7:35). He reminds his kinsmen of what Moses had promised: "God will raise up for you a prophet like me from your brothers" (Acts 7:37; cf. Deut. 18:15). He warns the people against rejecting the prophets who "announced beforehand the coming of the Righteous One" (Acts 7:52). Stephen boldly concludes that the promised, righteous one is Jesus the Messiah, whom God has sent to save.

Stephen's speech enrages his accusers. Filled with the Holy Spirit, he looks up calmly and sees the glory of the Father and Jesus the Son. He declares: "Behold, I see the heavens opened, and the Son of Man standing at the right hand of God" (Acts 7:56; cf. Dan. 7:13). Stephen is dragged out of the city to be stoned. Stoning was a religious execution according to Old Testament law, especially for blasphemy (Lev. 24:14-16; Deut. 17:7). This is what happens to Stephen, yet he dies in conscious imitation of Christ. As his accusers are stoning him, he prays: "Lord Jesus, receive my spirit" (Acts 7:59; cf. Luke 23:46). Falling to his knees, he cries out: "Lord, do not hold this sin against them" (Acts 7:60; cf. Luke 23:34). Stephen's death is not in vain. Luke tells us that the witnesses "laid down their garments at the feet of a young man named Saul" who "approved of his execution" (Acts 7:58; 8:1). This zealous persecutor will soon be commissioned as an apostle to the nations under Jesus' sovereign hand.

The exalted Jesus extends His kingdom in Judaea and Samaria (Acts 8-12)

Acts 8-12 recounts how the exalted Jesus extends his kingdom into all Judea and Samaria. Stephen's death sparks a great persecution against the church in Jerusalem (Acts 8:1). Persecution, however, fuels the missionary expansion of the church as believers are scattered throughout Judea and Samaria "preaching the word" (Acts 8:4). Martyrdom uniquely testifies to the death and resurrection of Christ. Suffering often precedes great movements of revival. It breaks demonic strongholds over entire people groups. There have been more martyrdoms in the past one hundred years than in all previous centuries combined. May these deaths enflame the hearts of Christians today with renewed devotion. May we experience what Tertullian, a second century Christian leader in Africa, grew to realize, that the blood of the martyrs is seed for the growing church.

Amidst this persecution, God uses Philip to herald the gospel of Christ in the city of Samaria (Acts 8:5). Herod had rebuilt the city and named it Sebaste (Greek for "Augustus"). He honored his patron with a large temple, stadium, and forum. A monumental street led into the city with three hundred marble columns. You may recall from our study of the Old Testament that Samaria was the capital of the idolatrous northern kingdom; it had been resettled with foreigners after the Assyrians had defeated it in 722 BC (2 Kgs. 17:24-34). As a result, the Samaritans were viewed as a mixed race. The Samaritans built a rival temple on Mount Gerizim and established their own ancestral priesthood. John Hyrcanus had destroyed this temple in 128 BC, thereby sealing the deep rift between Jews and Samaritans reflected in the gospels (John 4:9). Tensions between Jews and Samaritans escalated throughout the first century. In AD 7, a group of Samaritans desecrated the Jerusalem Temple by scattering human bones during the Passover (Josephus, *Ant.* 18.29-30). On another occasion, a group of Galilean pilgrims were massacred on their way to Jerusalem (Josephus, *Ant.* 20.118). Jesus now sends one of his own disciples to reconcile these traditional enemies and claim them for himself.

Jesus uses Phillip to announce the gospel as people are healed and set free from demonic power (Acts 8:6-7; cf. Matt. 4:24). Even a prominent Samaritan sorcerer named Simon appears to believe in Christ. Sorcery and magic are strictly forbidden for God's people, because they live in covenant relationship with a God who has revealed his will (Lev. 20:6-7). Hundreds of magical incantations on papyri have been preserved from antiquity. They reveal how magic was practiced for a fee, with the goal of securing things such as: a woman's love, a winning horse race, a curse upon one's enemy, or becoming invisible for a day! When the Jerusalem church leadership hears the remarkable news that Samaria has received the gospel, they publicly send Peter and John to pray for them. There could be no reconciliation of traditional enemies in secret. The apostles lay their hands upon these new believers as brothers in Christ and the Holy Spirit comes upon all of them (Acts 8:17), recalling what took place at Pentecost. Simon, the sorcerer, reveals his feigned conversion when he seeks to obtain the power of the Spirit through money. Philip urges him to "repent, therefore, of this wickedness of yours, and pray to the Lord that, if possible, the intent of your heart may be forgiven you" (Acts 8:22). Simon neither repents nor prays. Although Luke says nothing more, early Christian writings describe Simon as descending further into darkness. He makes increasingly blasphemous claims about himself and begins a heretical sect based on astrological speculation and sexual immorality. Nevertheless, the word of Christ extends further as believers preach "the gospel to many villages of the Samaritans" (Acts 8:25).

The exalted Jesus also uses Philip to reach a God-fearing Ethiopian eunuch on his way home from celebrating a festival in Jerusalem. This man served as an important official in charge of the Ethiopian queen's treasury (Acts 8:27). As Philip approaches, he hears the man reading from the prophet Isaiah: "Like a sheep he was led to the slaughter and like a lamb before its shearer is silent, so he opens not his mouth. In his humiliation justice was denied him. Who can describe his generation? For his life is taken away from the earth" (Isaiah 53:7-8). The eunuch asks Philip a critical question: "About whom, I ask you, does the prophet say this, about himself or about someone else?" (Acts 8:34). Beginning from this precious text, Philip tells him the "good news about Jesus" (Acts 8:35). The eunuch is baptized as a full member of the new covenant community of all nations. The word of God through Isaiah is fulfilled, that the time of restoration would include eunuchs and foreigners being incorporated into the people of God (Isa 56:3-5). At this time God's temple would be called a "house of prayer for all peoples" (Isa 56:7). What a wonderful testimony to the work of God when this Ethiopian eunuch becomes part of the people of God through faith! His baptism in Christ heralds another key moment in God's plan of redemption for all peoples.

Paul is commissioned as an apostle to the nations (Acts 9)

The exalted Jesus not only reconciles traditional enemies and includes foreigners, but he has the power to transform a zealous persecutor of the church into an apostle of the nations. Saul of Tarsus was born into a devout, diaspora Jewish family in the province of Cilicia around AD 5. He was a Roman citizen by birth; his father probably received Roman citizenship in the aftermath of Pompey's campaigns (Acts 22:28). Like many diaspora Jews, he had both a Hebrew name *Shaul* ("Saul"), and a phonetically similar Roman name *Paulus* ("small"). Around age fifteen he was sent to Jerusalem to receive a rabbinic education at the feet of the leading sage Gamaliel (Acts 22:3). Saul was a zealous student who distinguished himself among his peers. He devoted himself to the sect of the Pharisees and learned both written and oral Torah. He later describes himself at this time as "extremely zealous" for the traditions of his fathers (Gal. 1:14). Although his teacher was remembered for his moderation and tact, Saul's religious zeal could erupt in violence against foreigners or those he considered to be apostate Jews. He viewed the nations of the world as steeped in idolatry; their only hope to escape God's coming judgment was conversion. Full converts were marked with ritual circumcision and were taught to walk in the ways of Torah (Gen. 17:12-14; Lev. 18:2-5). Saul understood Israel as God's chosen people, descendants of Abraham. He knew from Scripture, tradition, and liturgy that "all Israel would have a portion in the world to come." Saul recognized that Israel alone had received the Torah and had known the revealed will of God. Israel's relationship to the world was to be "a guide to the blind, a light to those who are in darkness, an instructor of the foolish, a teacher of children" (Rom. 2:19-20). Saul believed and prayed for the hope of Israel; he longed for the coming kingdom of God. He anticipated that the LORD would send a redeemer in fulfillment of his ancient promise. Israel would be vindicated and the nations judged.

Saul became outraged by the early Christian confession that Jesus of Nazareth was the promised Messiah. Jesus had been condemned to death by Israel's religious leaders for blasphemy against God, Torah, and temple. Jesus had been publicly crucified under Roman law. His death on a cross was scandalous and meant that Jesus died under God's curse (Deut. 21:23). Jesus' followers, calling themselves "the Way," were leading Israel astray and must be stopped. After consenting to the stoning of Stephen, Saul obtained letters from the high priest Caiaphas, authorizing him to arrest the followers of Jesus in Damascus and bring them as prisoners to Jerusalem (Acts 9:1). He set out for Damascus (some 150 miles away) in his late twenties, full of confidence, sure of his opinions, eager to return to Jerusalem with honor. All of this would soon change.

As he approached the city of Damascus, suddenly a light from heaven flashed around him. Falling to the ground, he heard a voice saying to him: "Saul, Saul, why are you persecuting me?" Paul responds, "Who are you, Lord?" The Lord answers, "I am Jesus, whom you are persecuting" (Acts 9:4-5). Jesus now pronounces the divine name "I AM" and speaks as one who is alive. The heavenly glory of the risen Jesus blinds Saul. He is led by the hand into Damascus where he fasts for three days. Jesus appears to him again in a vision and then sends a disciple named Ananias to pray that Saul might receive his sight. In Acts 9:15-16, Jesus calms Ananias' fear by revealing his sovereign design: "Go, for he is a chosen instrument of mine to carry my name before the Gentiles and kings and the children of Israel. For I will show him how much he must suffer for the sake of my name." The zealous persecutor of the church is transformed into an apostle to the nations. He will bear the name of Jesus to nations, rulers, and his own kinsmen. His ministry will involve tremendous personal suffering. Such affliction will authenticate his testimony and maintain his close dependence upon Christ (2 Cor. 11:24-28). With courageous obedience, Ananias places his hands on Saul and says: "Brother Saul, the Lord Jesus who appeared to you on the road by which you came has sent me so that you may regain your sight and be filled with the Holy Spirit" (Acts 9:17). Immediately, something like scales falls from his eyes, and he regains his sight. Saul is publicly baptized into Christ and begins to preach in the synagogues that Jesus is the Messiah, the Son of God (Acts 9:20-22).

Peter visits the Roman Cornelius who believes (Acts 10-11)

The exalted Jesus continues to extend his kingdom throughout Judea as Peter is sent to visit a Roman centurion named Cornelius and his family (Acts 10-11). Cornelius was a professional soldier who served with the Italian Cohort based in Caesarea. This cohort was founded in AD 9 and was comprised of Roman citizens from Italy. Three surviving inscriptions locate this unit in the province of Syria during the first century. Luke tells us that Cornelius was a "God-fearer" (Acts 10:2). This was a technical term for Gentiles who were drawn to worship the God of Israel. They attended synagogue services, prayed to the living God, and honored the high ethical teaching of Scripture. However, they did not become full converts by undergoing ritual circumcision. Upon full conversion, proselytes adopted the distinctive Torah lifestyle, which included the practice of kosher dietary laws, Sabbath observance, and the Jewish festival calendar. Full converts became identified with "the house of Israel" and separated themselves from their previous ethnic identity. God-fearers, like Cornelius and his family, stood in between two worlds. It is important for us to remember that many from among the nations were attracted to the God of Israel.

In Acts 10 an angel appears to Cornelius in a heavenly vision; this God-fearing man receives the vision at the time of afternoon prayer (3 PM). He is to summon a man named Simon Peter from Joppa, almost forty miles away. At noon the following day, Peter also receives a heavenly vision. He sees a large sheet descending from heaven with all kinds of animals, reptiles, and birds. A voice from heaven tells him: "Rise, Peter; kill and eat!" (Acts 10:13). Peter protests that he has never eaten anything impure or unclean (see Lev. 11:1-47). The Lord speaks from heaven: "What God has made clean, do not call common" (Acts 10:15). The exalted Jesus declares all foods clean. The dietary laws that had kept Israel separate from the idolatrous nations no longer define the covenant community. This is a momentous heavenly decree. As Peter struggles to grasp the implications of what he has just heard, the Holy Spirit tells him to go with three men who have just arrived from Cornelius "for I have sent them" (Acts 10:20). When Peter arrives in Caesarea, Cornelius and his extended household are gathered together: "We are all here in the presence of God to hear all that you have been commanded by the Lord" (Acts 10:33). The Holy Spirit had prepared the people to receive the word that will be given by Peter, as he preaches the good news of Jesus Christ.

Peter's sermon: everyone who believes in Jesus receives forgiveness (Acts 10)

Peter proclaims to Cornelius' family the good news that God has sent Jesus as Israel's Messiah and that he is Lord of all. His presentation of the gospel contains many of the major themes of our CASKET EMPTY study. All of the prophets bear witness to the coming Messiah. Jesus' public ministry demonstrates that he is the Messiah. Through his death and resurrection, God's promises are now fulfilled. Jesus had commanded his followers "to preach to the people and to testify that he is the one appointed by God to be judge of the living and the dead" (Acts 10:42). Peter's sermon reaches a climax with the assertion that "everyone who believes in him receives forgiveness of sins through his name" (Acts 10:43). This is the language of the new covenant promise: "I will forgive their iniquity, and I will remember their sin no more" (Jer. 31:34). Peter announces God's intention to include the nations within the people of God. Faith in Jesus Christ and his atoning death brings the Gentiles into the covenant community, with baptism as the covenant sign. All who believe receive the Holy Spirit and are full members of the people of God. As Peter speaks these words, the Holy Spirit falls upon Cornelius and all who hear (Acts 10:44). The circumcised believers are astonished that Gentiles receive the Holy Spirit "just as we have" (Acts 10:47). Cornelius and his extended household are baptized in the name of Jesus Christ, as God's promise of the gospel to Abraham bears fruit (see Gen. 12:3; Gal. 3:8, 16).

The inclusion of the nations within the covenant community is a decisive movement forward in fulfillment of God's plan of redemption through history. It is a radical and defining moment for the early church. Some struggled to embrace this new reality (Acts 11:2-3). The growing church would need wisdom, humility, and practical compromise on both sides to realize the full implication of God's purpose in the gospel (Acts 15). Jews and Gentiles are united through faith in Christ (Acts 11:18). Both confess the same need for Christ's atoning death. Both must place their new identity in Christ before their ethnicity. Romans viewed themselves from a place of cultural dominance as rulers of the world. Now they publicly identify themselves as believers in Jesus, the Jewish Messiah, who is Savior of the world. Israelites viewed themselves from a place of religious superiority over the world. Now they publicly identify themselves as believers in Jesus, who died for the sin of the world, including their own. In humility, both groups repent and find forgiveness at the cross of Christ. Their shared identity in Christ will call forth a new name, as the disciples are called *Christianoi* ("Christ-ians") by the surrounding society (Acts 11:26). The visible unity of the early church shines brightly against the backdrop of an increasingly volatile relationship between Jews and Gentiles in the first century. You may want to take a few moments to locate Antioch on the New Testament timeline's map, along with the accompanying summary statement "Disciples first called Christians" (Acts 11:26) that recalls this event.

Caligula rules as Roman emperor (AD 37-41)

The inclusion of the nations through faith in Christ offers a compelling alternative to the counterfeit vision of imperial power in Rome. The proclamation of Jesus as Savior and Lord offers real hope to an increasingly decadent pagan world. The corruption and immorality of Roman society is further exposed during the rule of the Roman emperor Caligula (AD 37-41). Gaius Julius Caesar Augustus Germanicus was born in AD 12. He was given the nickname Caligula ("little boots") for dressing in a child's military uniform while his father campaigned in Germany. In AD 37, Caligula is hailed emperor after the death of Tiberius. His reign begins with benevolence as he sponsors gladiatorial games and public works. He even transports a large Egyptian obelisk and installs it at the center of a new racetrack. This obelisk still stands in front of the Vatican in Rome today.

During his second year in power, Caligula's personality dramatically changes. His sexual immorality becomes extreme. His projects increasingly aim at personal fame. He builds a floating bridge across the Bay of Baiae to surpass the feat of Xerxes crossing the Hellespont. He kills his opponents at random and on one occasion commands that an entire section of the crowd be thrown into the arena because he was bored. He appears publicly dressed as various gods and demigods. He even begins to refer to himself as "god" and signs public documents with the name Jupiter.

In AD 40, Caligula demands that a golden statue of himself be placed in the Jerusalem Temple to punish the Jews for refusing to honor him as god. Massive protests and petitions erupt throughout Israel. Thousands of people surround the governor's palace in Caesarea, preferring to be slain rather than have the temple defiled. The Roman governor of Syria, Publius Petronius, courageously defies the imperial decree in order to save countless lives. Caligula responds with a letter that Petronius be put to death for delaying the emperor's decree. However, in God's providence, those who carry Caligula's letter are caught in a storm and detained at sea for three months. Meanwhile, couriers who bring the news of Caligula's assassination in early AD 41 have a good voyage. Petronius hears about Caligula's death just before the warrant for his own death arrives, thereby enabling him to survive the ordeal. The rule of Caligula stirs us to faithful witness, even when the culture around us unravels and grows violently opposed to Christ.

Herod Agrippa I rules as king in Israel (AD 41-44)

The early Christian proclamation that Jesus is the promised Messiah fulfills the hope of Israel. Many in Israel, however, seek hope in a religious nationalism that excludes the nations. Christian preachers who unite Jews and Gentiles through faith in Jesus provoke violent opposition. Herod Agrippa I, the grandson of Herod the Great, comes to power at this time. Agrippa was born in 11 BC. He received an elite education in Rome, and lives an extravagant lifestyle, accumulating extraordinary debts. His uncle, Herod Antipas, intervenes and provides him with a modest income and position of authority in his capital of Tiberius in Galilee. After a dispute with his uncle, Agrippa flees to Rome to seek the favor of the young Caligula. He is overheard one day expressing his wish that Tiberius would soon die so that Caligula might rule in his place. Tiberius is informed and casts Agrippa in prison. When Caligula does become emperor, Agrippa is released. He is given a golden chain equal in weight to the iron one he had worn in prison. The Senate declares him king of the northern territories. After Caligula's assassination, Agrippa helps to ensure that Claudius becomes the new emperor. As a reward, Claudius gives him the additional territories of Judea and Samaria. In AD 41, just a few years into the period of PENTECOST, Herod Agrippa I suddenly and almost unimaginably becomes one of the most powerful kings in the east. He rules over a kingdom almost equal to that of Herod the Great. Swollen with pride, he issues coins with the Greek inscription: "The Great King Agrippa, Friend of Caesar." His coins also bear his own image, something that no Jewish ruler had ever done.

Like his grandfather Herod the Great, Agrippa courts favor with both his Roman patrons and his Jewish subjects. He builds large public works to honor Caesar and begins construction on a massive defensive wall to protect the north side of Jerusalem. To display his piety, Agrippa brings the offering of first fruits to the temple in Jerusalem and dedicates the golden chain given to him by Caligula. He is handed a Torah scroll and reads the king's portion in Hebrew. When he reaches the line: "One from among your brothers you shall set as king over you. You may not put a foreigner over you" (Deut. 17:15), his eyes flood with tears. The religious leadership of Jerusalem replies: "Do not fear Agrippa, you are our brother!" Agrippa curries favor with the religious leaders by persecuting the church (Acts 12:1-3). This outbreak of persecution results in the death of James and the imprisonment of Peter.

James is beheaded and Peter is imprisoned (Acts 12)

During this time of persecution, Herod Agrippa arrests James (the brother of John) and puts him to death with the sword (Acts 12:1-2). During the Feast of Unleavened Bread, he arrests Peter, intending to bring him out for public trial after the Passover (Acts 12:3-4). Facing certain death, we can understand why the church offers earnest prayer for Peter's release (Acts 12:5). The night before Peter is to stand trial, an angel of the Lord suddenly appears to him and leads him out of prison. Peter is reunited with the church and his life is spared (Acts 12:6-11). He will one day die a martyr's death, but only after the full course of his earthly ministry is complete (John 21:18-19; 2 Pet. 1:14).

After executing the prison guards deemed responsible for Peter's escape, Agrippa travels to Caesarea to celebrate games in honor of the new Roman emperor Claudius. Herod enters the stadium in royal robes, takes his seat upon the throne, and delivers an oration to the crowds. As the morning rays of the sun reflect off his resplendent silver garments (Josephus, *Ant.* 19.343-345), the people shout: "The voice of a god, and not of a man!" (Acts

12:22). Luke records that "immediately an angel of the Lord struck him down, because he did not give God the glory, and he was eaten by worms and breathed his last" (Acts 12:23). Josephus also attests to Herod's sudden death with violent intensity (Josephus, *Ant.* 19.346-350). We are reminded that those who mock the living God and persecute the body of Christ will not endure. Jesus promises that the power of hell would not prevail against the church (Matt. 16:18). In the midst of persecution, "the word of God increased and multiplied" (Acts 12:24; Gen. 1:28).

Claudius rules as Roman emperor (AD 41-54)

Claudius is appointed as the new Roman emperor in AD 41. He is first mentioned in the New Testament when Paul is still in Antioch (Acts 11:25-28). Claudius will rule over the Roman world throughout Paul's first two missionary journeys. After Herod Agrippa's sudden death (see Acts 12:20-23), Claudius appoints Cuspius Fadus (AD 44-46) and then Tiberius Julius Alexander (AD 46-48) as Roman procurators of Judea. Tiberius is the nephew of the Jewish philosopher Philo, although he abandons his ancestral faith to gain Roman political power. The return of direct Roman rule through governors heightens tensions between Jews and Romans in Israel.

Throughout his reign, Claudius tries to increase the size of the Roman Empire. He celebrates a triumph for the conquest of Britain. He builds a massive aqueduct for the growing population of Rome. He conducts a census and reports that the growing empire now includes 5,984,072 free, adult male Roman citizens (women, children, slaves, and non-citizens are not counted). He celebrates the 800th anniversary of the founding of Rome with public spectacles and gladiatorial games. Claudius actively promotes the meaning of Roman identity and the proper form of state religion. He does not allow men of foreign birth to use Roman names. He revitalizes the traditional Roman practice of divination. He grows especially concerned over the spread of non-Roman religious ideas and practices.

The expanding missionary witness of the church during the reign of Claudius presents a direct challenge to the Roman world. You will remember the prophetic image from Daniel that it is the stone cut without human hands that becomes "a great mountain and filled the whole earth" (Dan. 2:35). This promise will be fulfilled as the church continues to proclaim the gospel to the end of the earth. All who believe are received into the everlasting kingdom of the Son of Man (Dan. 7:13-14). His kingdom will stand forever.

Paul and Barnabas visit Jerusalem for famine relief

During the early reign of Claudius, a series of poor harvests produce severe food shortages throughout the Roman Empire. The early Christian prophet Agabus had predicted this by the Holy Spirit (Acts 11:28). The famine is acutely felt throughout Judea, and so the Christian community in Antioch resolves to send famine relief. They send their sacrificial gift through Barnabas and Saul as a demonstration of their unity and support for the church in Judea (Acts 11:29; Gal. 2:1, 10). Their gift is indicated on the New Testament timeline with the three stalks of wheat under "famine relief." We are now ready to locate our first New Testament letter in the narrative of Acts.

James writes a letter to the dispersed church (c. AD 45)

During this period, James, the brother of Jesus (not to be confused with James, the brother of John, who has just been killed by Agrippa; see Acts 12:2), writes the earliest letter of the New Testament. He is the leader of the church in Jerusalem (see Acts 12:17; 15:13-21). His letter is given the approximate date of AD 45, just before Paul's first missionary journey that begins in AD 46 (cf. Acts 13). Although we will explore the content of the New Testament letters in more depth in the chapters devoted to TEACHING, we want to locate the letters in their chronological setting in the period of PENTECOST. James writes a letter addressed to all Israel (Jas. 1:1). He urges faithfulness in times of persecution and trial. He calls believers to be hearers and doers of the word of God (Jas. 1:22-24; cf. Matt. 7:24). He emphasizes works of mercy toward the vulnerable and cautions against friendship with the world. He knows that the Christian community has been attacked by those "who blaspheme the honorable name by which you were called" (Jas. 2:7). He has heard the slander of those who misrepresent justification by faith as if it were a license for sin. He defends the church as those who "fulfill the royal law according to the Scripture, 'You shall love your neighbor as yourself'" (Jas. 2:8; cf. Lev. 19:18). For James, genuine faith is expressed in deeds of compassion that cause God's name to be praised (Jas. 2:14-17). The Christian community should be united in godliness, wisdom, lack of favoritism, patience in affliction, and dedicated prayer for one another in the midst of a hostile world. Inspired by the Holy Spirit, James helps to define Christian identity during this formative period of the early church.

The exalted Jesus extends His kingdom to the ends of the earth (Acts 13-28)

The kingdom of God continues to advance as the exalted Jesus extends his kingdom to the ends of the earth (Acts 13-28). Beginning in Acts 13, Luke focuses on how Christ uses Paul and his companions to proclaim the gospel in an expanding sphere of global witness to the "end of the earth" (Acts 1:8; cf. Isa. 49:6). This will be accomplished through a series of missionary journeys that cross cultural barriers to bring Christ to the nations. You will remember that the resurrected Jesus had commissioned Paul as "a chosen instrument of mine to carry my name before the Gentiles and kings and the children of Israel" (Acts 9:15). Paul's early missionary activity had taken place in Damascus, Arabia, and his home province of Cilicia (Acts 9:19; Gal. 1:17). After believers from Cyprus and Cyrene in North Africa shared Christ with Greeks at Antioch, Barnabas brought Paul to the city where he taught the growing community of Jewish and Gentile believers for a year (Acts 11:20-26). We have seen that in Antioch these believers are first identified by a new name, "Christians," given to them by the surrounding society. The name "Christ-*ian*" reflects the Greek noun formation pattern used to describe a distinct ethnic group, the citizens of a particular country, or the followers of a certain person. Examples in the New Testament abound such as Galat-*ians*, Thessalon-*ians*, Parth-*ians*, Pamphyl-*ians*, Jud-*eans*, Rom-*ans*, or Herod-*ians*. Those who observe the followers of Jesus conclude that despite their diverse ethnic, geographical, or political views, the one thing that they shared in common was Christ. Faith in Jesus Christ defines the people; his kingdom is their place of citizenship; he is their leader above all—they are thus rightly identified as Christ-*ians*.

First missionary journey: Paul and Barnabas are sent from Antioch (AD 46-48)

Paul and Barnabas are sent out from Antioch on their first missionary journey (Acts 13). Antioch was the third largest city in the Roman Empire after Alexandria and Rome, with a population of over 500,000. The city was founded in approximately 300 BC by Alexander's general Seleucus and was named after his son. Antioch was built at the base of Mount Silpius on the Orontes River, around three hundred miles north of Jerusalem and twenty miles inland from the Mediterranean Sea. To distinguish it from the other fifteen cities named Antioch built by Seleucus, it was known as Antioch on the Orontes or Antioch the Beautiful (it is simply called Antioch in Acts 13:1, not to be confused with Pisidian Antioch in Acts 13:14). The city boasted of having all the civic institutions of Roman life: temples, theaters, and a hippodrome for horse racing. An impressive street lined with columns traversed the city from the northeast to the southwest. The marble paved street was two miles long and ninety feet wide with porticoes on each side. 3,200 marble columns supported the porticoes with vaulted stone roofs at each intersection. Antioch was also home to a large Jewish population of at least 65,000, including a large number of God-fearing Greeks.

The growing Christian community in Antioch contains Jews and Gentiles. Luke introduces a vibrant picture of shared leadership in that "there were in the church at Antioch prophets and teachers, Barnabas, Simeon who was called Niger, Lucius of Cyrene, Manaen a member of the court of Herod the tetrarch, and Saul" (Acts 13:1). Barnabas is a Levite from Cyprus, whose Aramaic name means "son of exhortation or encouragement." Simeon, whose Hebrew name recalls the tribal patriarch, is called "Niger" meaning "black" or "dark skinned" in Latin; he probably originates from Africa. Lucius is a native of Cyrene in North Africa, whose Latin name means "light." Manaen reflects the Hebrew Menahem meaning "comforter." He had grown up with Herod Antipas in Rome as part of an upper class family. Lastly, we hear of Saul, whose Hebrew name recalls Israel's first king, but whose Roman name Paul ("Small") conceals the large role that Christ had appointed for him.

While the church gathers for worship, the Holy Spirit makes known God's sovereign will: "Set apart for me Barnabas and Saul for the work to which I have called them" (Acts 13:2). To be set apart means to be holy, to belong to God, reserved for his use in the world. This language is used in the Old Testament of Israel (Lev. 20:26), the priesthood (Num. 8:11), and individual prophets like Jeremiah (Jer. 1:5). Paul never forgot this moment of consecration; years later he introduces himself as "Paul, a servant of Christ Jesus, called to be an apostle, *set apart for the gospel of God*" (Rom. 1:1; cf. Gal. 1:15). The particular work to which they are called is to extend the gospel to the nations. After fasting and prayer, the church of Antioch lays hands on the missionary team, together with Barnabas' young cousin John Mark, and commissions them for the work of God (Acts 13:3-5).

New Testament timeline

You may want to locate the picture of a ship on the timeline. This picture represents the launching of global mission to share God's redemption in Christ Jesus with all peoples of the world. Antioch is marked as the first sending church for Paul's mission to the nations (Acts 13).

The journey to Cyprus, Galatia, Pisidian Antioch, Iconium, Lystra and Derbe

Paul, Barnabas, and John Mark set sail for the island of Cyprus, some ninety miles from the coast. Barnabas is a native of Cyprus, and after arriving there, they proclaim Christ in the synagogues at Salamis. They continue across the island to Paphos, the new capital and seat of the Roman governor Sergius Paulus. They find that the governor employs a Jewish sorcerer named Elymas ("Dreamer" in Aramaic) in his court. Romans were very superstitious about planning public affairs and often paid people to read omens and predict auspicious days for state activities. When Sergius Paulus desires to hear the word of Christ, however, Elymas tries to turn him away. We hear Paul speak for the first time in Acts within a ministry setting. Full of the Holy Spirit, his words mark a spiritual power encounter as he stares at Elymas and says: "You son of the devil, you enemy of all righteousness, full of all deceit and villainy, will you not stop making crooked the straight paths of the Lord? And now, behold, the hand of the Lord is upon you, and you will be blind and unable to see the sun for a time" (Acts 13:10-11). As Elymas is struck blind, Sergius Paulus' eyes are opened to believe in Christ. On their first missionary journey, Jesus converts the Roman governor (Acts 13:12). This is a wonderful beginning of all that Christ will accomplish through his consecrated servants.

Paul, Barnabas, and Mark continue north, astonished at the power of Jesus Christ at work in their midst. They sail from Paphos toward the coast of Asia Minor and arrive at Perga in the Roman province of Pamphylia. As they approach the shore, the towering peaks of the Taurus Mountains, nearly 12,300 feet high, rise before them. Upon seeing the mountains, Christ inflames Paul's missionary zeal to cross over them into utterly unreached territory. The vast interior province of Galatia lay beyond those mountains, which could only be crossed on foot. Barnabas too is willing to go. Young John Mark, however, is overwhelmed and returns to Jerusalem. John Mark's departure later opens a rift between Paul and Barnabas, but their ultimate reconciliation forms a moving subplot in the New Testament (Acts 15:39; Col. 4:10; 2 Tim. 4:11).

Paul and Barnabas cross the mountains and reach Pisidian Antioch after ten days. We hear Paul preaching here for the first time in Acts 13:16-41 as he addresses his kinsmen and the God-fearers attending the synagogue. His sermon rehearses God's plan of redemption through history that has now reached a decisive point in the Messiah. Many of the key ideas of our entire CASKET EMPTY study can be found here. Paul begins by summarizing the narrative of the Old Testament (Acts 13:17-23). The God of creation had graciously chosen Abraham and his descendants. He multiplied them in Egypt and brought them out with an uplifted arm to enter into a covenant with them on Mount Sinai. He gave them the land of Canaan as an inheritance. He led his people during the period of kings and promised David an everlasting kingship (2 Sam. 7:16). Even after the exile, God raised expectations that one of David's descendants would be raised up as messianic king.

In his sermon Paul testifies that Jesus is the promised Messiah (Acts 13:24-31). God had sent John the Baptist to prepare the people for his coming salvation. Jesus fulfilled the words of the prophets in his public ministry, and even in his death on the cross, for he was crucified according to "all that was written of him" (Acts 13:29). He was laid in a tomb, but God raised him from the dead. He appeared to those who "are now his witnesses" (Acts 13:31). Paul's sermon reaches a climax with the declaration that "we bring you the good news that what God promised to the fathers, this he has fulfilled to us their children by raising Jesus" (Acts 13:32-33; cf. Ps. 2:7; 16:10; Isa. 55:3).

Paul ends with a crucial formulation that we translate very literally, that in Christ "forgiveness of sins is announced to you, and from all the things which you were not able in the Law of Moses to be justified, in him everyone who believes is justified" (Acts 13:38-39). This is the first explicit New Testament formulation of justification by faith in Christ. Paul makes the stunning claim that forgiveness—for both Jews and Gentiles—is based solely in Christ's atoning, sacrificial death. He confesses that Israel's narrative history, and even his own personal story, has not left them right with God. Instead, they too need God's promised forgiveness that has come about in Christ. Paul recognizes, therefore, that the new covenant community is open to the nations, solely on the basis of faith in Christ. In him, *everyone who believes is justified.* The theological statements that are presented here for the first time will be extremely important for understanding Paul's entire ministry. Justification by faith in Christ alone will have profound implications for the identity of the early Christian community and the shape of Christian mission.

Paul receives a mixed reaction to his preaching about Christ. Some Jews and God-fearers believe. Some of his Israelite kinsmen, however, are filled with zeal for their ancestral traditions and begin to contradict and revile Paul (Acts 13:45, 50). When the Gentiles hear that they are full members of the covenant community through faith in Christ, they begin "rejoicing and glorifying the word of the Lord, and as many as were appointed to eternal life believed" (Acts 13:48-49; cf. Isa. 49:6). This marks an important point in the narrative as the gospel proclamation includes the nations (Acts 13:46-47). Paul's calling to the Gentiles echoes his conversion and recalls the great prophetic hope that God's Servant would bring "light to the Gentiles" (Acts 9:15; cf. Isa. 42:6; 49:6).

Driven forward by persecution, the first missionary journey continues east along the Via Sebaste to the city of Iconium, ninety miles away. They spend time preaching in the synagogues, but flee to the Roman city of Lystra, eighteen miles away, after being threatened with the religious execution of stoning. In Lystra, Paul and Barnabas encounter a totally unreached pagan audience. After Jesus authenticates their preaching by healing a crippled man through them, the Lycaonian natives try to offer bull sacrifices to Barnabas and Paul, thinking they were the gods Zeus and Hermes. The missionaries plead with the people to "turn from these vain things to a living God, who made the heaven and the earth" (Acts 14:15). The free gift of salvation in Christ provokes further controversy among zealous Israelites who drag Paul outside the city and stone him (Acts 14:19). He would later include this among his sufferings for the gospel (2 Cor. 11:25). Paul gladly fills up his portion of Christ's afflictions in the world and willingly bears in his body the marks of Christ (Gal. 6:17; Col. 1:24). Yet Jesus sovereignly preserves Paul's life that he might finish the course set before him (2 Tim. 4:7). For the present, in spite of persecution, he continues on to Derbe, sixty miles southwest, where he "preached the gospel to that city and ... made many disciples" (Acts 14:21).

Many Gentiles believe in "Christ who gave himself for our sins"

Barnabas and Paul return to Antioch to report all that God had done through them and how God "had opened a door of faith to the Gentiles" (Acts 14:27). The inclusion of the nations is a vital part of God's plan of redemption (Gen. 12:3; 49:10; Isa. 11:10; 49:6; Dan. 7:14). On this point, there is no disagreement. However, what was required of the Gentiles who were turning to God does produce a significant conflict. Some Jewish believers argue that since the covenant sign of circumcision has been practiced for almost two thousand years, Gentiles who believe in the Jewish Messiah should also receive this sign. Moreover, they reason that Gentile believers should fully embrace the Torah lifestyle that the covenant community has kept for centuries, including the dietary laws, Sabbath observance, and the festival calendar. Besides, in an increasingly volatile atmosphere between Jews and Gentiles, the Christian church should stand with Israel and not against her. Following such reasoning, "some men came down from Judea and were teaching the brothers, 'Unless you are circumcised according to the custom of Moses, you cannot be saved'" (Acts 15:1). Theological conflict, though painful, often clarifies the gospel and can produce a lasting unity among believers. Christ accomplishes these ends through Paul's letter to the Galatians and the decision of the Apostolic Council in Jerusalem (Acts 15).

Paul writes GALATIANS (c. AD 48)

Paul's first letter, Galatians, is written at this time. It is given the approximate date of AD 48, since it was written prior to the Council in Jerusalem dated to AD 49 (cf. Acts 15). Paul writes to the early Christian communities throughout the province of Galatia. He introduces his letter by emphasizing the finished work of Christ "who gave himself for our sins to deliver us from the present evil age, according to the will of our God and Father" (Gal. 1:4). He is unswerving in his proclamation that there is no other gospel than the death and resurrection of Jesus the Messiah. Faith in Christ alone justifies the ungodly—both in Israel and among the nations. All who believe in him are declared right in God's sight by virtue of his atoning death (Gal. 3:13). Those who believe in Christ receive forgiveness and are adopted as sons and daughters. They are full members of Abraham's family by faith in Christ. They are heirs of God's promise and sealed with the Holy Spirit (Gal. 3:26-4:7). Paul reasons that if justification had been available through the Torah, then Christ died for nothing (Gal. 2:21). He admonishes the Galatians that in Christ "neither circumcision counts for anything, nor uncircumcision, but a new creation" (Gal. 6:15). We will return to this letter in the period of TEACHING, but for now, this summary will help you understand the significance of Paul's first letter during this formative period of the early church.

The Apostolic Council in Jerusalem accepts Gentile believers (Acts 15)

The status of Gentiles believers, and especially, what they were required to do as part of the new covenant community, becomes a central issue in the early church. The first large gathering of Christian leadership takes place in Jerusalem in AD 49 to resolve this issue. As we consider what is accomplished at this time, we are reminded that the exalted Jesus even works through committee meetings! When Paul and Barnabas report all that God has done in the conversion of the Gentiles, some believers who belong to the Pharisees reason that it is necessary to circumcise them and to instruct them to keep the Torah (Acts 15:4-5). After much debate, Peter recounts his experience with Cornelius and his family, who had heard the word of the gospel and had believed. God had confirmed that they had been fully accepted into the covenant community by giving them the Holy Spirit, the same Holy Spirit that had come upon them at Pentecost. Peter testifies that the Lord "made no distinction between us and them, having cleansed their hearts by faith" (Acts 15:9). He reasons that the church should not place "a yoke on the neck of the disciples that neither our fathers nor we have been able to bear" (Acts 15:10). In first century Judaism, full conversion to a Torah life was often described as "taking on the yoke of the kingdom." Although Peter had buckled under social pressure from Jerusalem earlier in Antioch (Gal. 2:11-21), he now takes his stand to defend the full acceptance of the Gentiles because "we believe that we will be saved through the grace of the Lord Jesus, just as they will" (Acts 15:11).

After Barnabas and Paul relate what God had done among the Gentiles, James, the brother of Jesus and leader of the Jerusalem church, speaks openly to all. He recognizes that the inclusion of the Gentiles is part of what God had purposed all along, quoting Amos 9:11-12: "After this I will return, and I will rebuild the tent of David that has fallen; I will rebuild its ruins, and I will restore it, that the remnant of mankind may seek the Lord, and all the Gentiles who are called by my name, says the Lord" (Acts 15:16-18). James proposes a compromise to protect the visible unity of the body of Christ. Jewish believers must not demand circumcision and a full Torah life for new Gentile believers in Christ. Such a requirement would obscure the accomplishment of the cross and disobey the explicit command of the risen Jesus who declares all foods clean. However, Gentile believers must abstain from practices that are repulsive to fellow Jewish believers and actions that would discredit the church. He concludes that Gentile believers must avoid idolatry and sexual immorality, as well as meat that had been strangled and from blood. The Apostolic Council in Jerusalem formally accepts Gentile believers by faith in Christ alone. This momentous decision is communicated in letters sent through Paul and Barnabas and addressed to "the brothers who are of the Gentiles" (Acts 15:23). This Council confirms that both Jews and Gentiles are one covenant community through faith in Jesus Christ. The picture of a rolled-up letter represents this key event, recalling that letters communicating the decision of the Council are sent to churches.

Claudius expels Jews from Rome due to riots over "Chrestus"

As we continue to follow the missionary witness of the early church, it is important to remember that the exalted Jesus uses countless others, whose names are known to him, to spread the gospel across the Roman Empire. The same year that Paul begins his second missionary journey in AD 49, the Roman historian Suetonius records that the emperor Claudius expelled the Jews from Rome, since they had been making disturbances "at the instigation of *Chrestus.*" Remember that the Hebrew word *Messiah* is rendered in Greek as *Christos.* These names sound the same in Latin. Suetonius thus provides us with important primary evidence for the far-reaching witness of Christians at this time. The exalted Jesus will use the edict of Claudius to move his servants into the places where he has called them (see Acts 18:2).

We have now completed Part 1 of the period of PENTECOST. We have followed the missionary witness of the church empowered by the Holy Spirit, as the exalted Jesus extends his kingdom in Jerusalem (Acts 1-7), then in Judea and Samaria (Acts 8-12), and beyond as Paul and Barnabas are sent out from Antioch (Acts 13). We have been introduced to the letter written by James. We have heard Paul's first sermon and seen the effective preaching of the gospel of Jesus Christ, which results in both Jews and Gentiles believing and being incorporated into the people of God. Amidst the growth of the church, issues arise regarding the status of Gentiles and what they were required to do as part of the new covenant community. Paul addresses these matters in his letter to the Galatians, emphasizing that Jews and Gentiles are united through faith in Christ. The Apostolic Council in Jerusalem makes the important decision to accept Gentile believers by faith in Christ alone. This marks a significant movement forward in God's plan of redemption as the nations are incorporated into the people of God by faith. Part 1 of PENTECOST concludes with this key decision in place. The proclamation of the gospel to the ends of the earth is now on the horizon as Paul and Silas are poised to preach the gospel in Europe.

Chapter 5
PENTECOST Part 2

Second missionary journey: Paul and Silas are sent into Europe (AD 49-52)
WE BEGIN PART 2 of PENTECOST with Paul's second missionary journey, which Luke records in Acts 15:36-18:22. This next movement in the expansion of God's kingdom takes place as Paul and Silas preach the gospel in Europe. After an initial disagreement with Barnabas over John Mark, Paul chooses Silas as his ministry partner. Notice how early Christian leaders follow Jesus' own example of sending out ministry in teams (Luke 10:1). Ministry without dedicated partnership can be discouraging, dangerous, and unfruitful. However, mutual gifts exercised in humility can result in great advancement of Christ's kingdom. God has such plans for this second missionary journey. Paul will be joined by some of his closest long-term ministry partners, like Timothy, Luke, Aquila, and Priscilla. Together they will cross the Hellespont into Europe. Unlike like Xerxes centuries before, they will not arrive at the head of an army forcibly recruited from subject peoples for the glory of man. They will come with the royal proclamation of the Lord Jesus Christ, who willingly died to redeem all nations for the glory of God.

The journey to Lystra, Troas, Philippi, Thessalonica, Berea, Athens, and Corinth

After strengthening the churches in Cilicia, Paul and Silas return to Lystra where they meet a young disciple named Timothy, who was probably in his early twenties (Acts 16:1). His mother was a Jewish Christian, but his father was an unbelieving Greek. Timothy is considered ethnically Jewish, following the practice of tracing descent through the mother. Paul wants to bring Timothy with him as part of the missionary team. Paul has Timothy circumcised in order to prevent any unnecessary offense to his kinsmen. He feels free to accommodate Jewish sensitivity in this case, precisely because Timothy is Jewish. To flagrantly disregard circumcision in Timothy's case would overstate Paul's theological position and weaken his missionary cause. At the same time, Paul resolutely refuses circumcision for Gentiles like Titus, for he had already been received as a full member of the covenant community by faith in Christ. Paul and his companions travel throughout the region of Phyrgia and Galatia, gladly delivering the decision of the Apostolic Council in Jerusalem and proclaiming the gospel of Christ.

The exalted Jesus directs their movements toward the far western coast until they arrive at Troas, near the site of ancient Troy. During the night, Paul receives clear direction through a vision from God. He sees a man of Macedonia urging him: "Come over to Macedonia and help us" (Acts 16:9). Luke records that in response to the vision "immediately we sought to go on into Macedonia, concluding that God had called us to preach the gospel to them" (Acts 16:10). This verse marks an important change to the first person plural in the Acts narrative ("*we* sought"). Luke, the beloved physician, has now joined the missionary team at Troas and relates what follows from the perspective of an eyewitness.

They cross a major cultural divide into Europe and proceed to Philippi, a leading city of Macedonia and a Roman colony. The city was resettled with military veterans after the famous victory of Octavian and Anthony over Cassius and Brutus. Philippi maintained close communication with Rome through a major road called the Via Egnatia, which links the city across Greece to the Adriatic coast and then to Italy. When Paul and Silas arrive, they look for a synagogue, but find only a small group of women who had gathered for prayer near the riverside on the Sabbath. Never despise what the Lord Jesus can accomplish in small gatherings. Many dedicated servants of Christ have been evangelized in settings that look insignificant to human eyes. Such is the beginning of the church in Philippi. Luke records three precious openings for the gospel of Christ. One of the women at the river, Lydia, a wealthy merchant in purple cloth from Thyatira, was a God-fearer. The Lord opens her heart to the gospel and she is baptized with her entire household, which would include family members and workers (Acts 16:14-15).

The acts of the exalted Jesus continue in Philippi. Paul frees a slave girl "in the name of Jesus" from a spirit of divination. Jesus rescues both the wealthy and the destitute. Instead of rejoicing at her freedom from demonic oppression, her owners seize Paul and Silas and bring them to the city magistrates with the charge: "these men are Jews, and they are disturbing our city. They advocate customs that are not lawful for us as Romans to accept or practice" (Acts 16:20-21). Paul and Silas are beaten with rods and imprisoned. While they are praying and singing hymns to God around midnight, suddenly there is a great earthquake. The doors of the prison open, and everyone's bonds unfasten. The jailer draws his sword and is about to kill himself, supposing that the prisoners have escaped, yet this becomes the very moment of his conversion. After Paul cries out: "Do not harm yourself, for we are all here" (Acts 16:28), the jailer asks: "What must I do to be saved?" (Acts 16:30). The answer rings clear: "Believe in the Lord Jesus, and you will be saved, you and your household" (Acts 16:31). Upon hearing the words of the gospel, the jailer believes! Paul and Silas then share the word of Christ with "all who were in his house" (Acts 16:32). The jailer's entire household believes and experiences the sign of baptism, signifying their new life in Christ. This remarkable beginning of Christ's kingdom in Europe stays with Paul as a lasting source of encouragement and joy. The church at Philippi would remain in gospel partnership with him throughout his entire ministry (Phil. 1:3-5).

The missionary team leaves Philippi and travels west across northern Greece along the Via Egnatia. They arrive in Thessalonica, the capital of Macedonia with a population of around 200,000, including a large Jewish population. As was his custom, Paul first visits the synagogue. For three successive Sabbath days, he is invited to preach. The content of his message reflects the central theme of our CASKET EMPTY study, as Luke tells us: "He reasoned with them from the Scriptures, explaining and proving that it was necessary for the Christ to suffer and to rise from the dead, and saying, 'This Jesus, whom I proclaim to you, is the Christ'" (Acts 17:2-3). The verb "reasoned" is used in Judaism to describe the act of biblical interpretation. Paul read the great narrative of God's redemptive plan in Scripture. He understood that the center of the biblical story was the death and resurrection of the Messiah. He gloriously announces that Jesus is Israel's promised Messiah. All who turn to him in faith will find forgiveness and new life. A number of people are persuaded, including Jews, God-fearing Greeks, and several prominent women (Acts 17:4).

However, others from among his kinsmen become zealous for their ancestral traditions (Acts 17:5; cf. Gal. 1:14). They gather a crowd from the market place. They rush to the house of Jason, who had become a believer in Christ, to search for Paul and Silas. They drag them before the city officials with the charge: "These men who have turned the world upside down have come here also, and Jason has received them, and they are all acting against the decrees of Caesar, saying that there is another king, Jesus" (Acts 17:6-7). This charge of inciting rebellion is serious, potentially being perceived as a capital crime. It echoes the same charge that the Jerusalem leadership made against Jesus (Luke 23:1-2; John 18:33-37). Despite the intensity of the societal conflict, the exalted Jesus establishes his church in Thessalonica. Paul would later write to them with affection: "You yourselves know, brothers, that our coming to you was not in vain. But though we had already suffered and been shamefully treated at Philippi, as you know, we had boldness in our God to declare to you the gospel of God in the midst of much conflict" (1 Thess. 2:1-2). We are reminded again that the proclamation of the gospel is not without conflict, but such conflict will not thwart the establishment of Christ's kingdom.

The missionary team quietly leaves Thessalonica at night and travels to Berea, a small town twelve miles south of the Via Egnatia. Even after such persecution, they do not remain silent but enter the synagogue where the Jewish community "received the word with all eagerness, examining the Scriptures daily to see if these things were so" (Acts 17:11). Many from the synagogue believe in Christ, together with a number of prominent Greek women and men (Acts 17:12). This calm is soon broken as some members of the Jewish community arrive from Thessalonica and stir the crowds against Paul. Some of the new believers escort Paul to the coast where he sails around the tip of Attica to Athens. Silas and Timothy remain in Berea with instructions to join Paul in Athens as soon as possible.

The scene of Saul the Pharisee, now Paul the apostle of Christ, wandering around the streets of Athens alone is a powerful picture. You may remember from chapter one in this study guide that Athens was the cultural epicenter of the classical world. Athens was distinguished in art, literature, and philosophy. Her golden age had never been equaled. The superiority of Greek religion and thought was openly acknowledged and adopted into Roman life. A well-known Roman poet named Horace famously stated that although Rome had conquered the Greeks militarily, Greece had conquered Rome *culturally*. While the classical tradition contains much that can be admired, Paul's Jewish theological worldview sees the pagan world as ignorant of God and trapped in idolatry. The conflict of these worldviews is evident throughout the city. Altars and statues depicting the Olympian gods adorn every street. Their appearance stands in dramatic contrast to the God of Israel, who could not be represented by human hands. Their immorality cannot be compared to the Holy One of Israel. Paul's spirit becomes "provoked within him as he saw that the city was full of idols" (Acts 17:16). Paul arrives in Athens, however, not only as a Jew, but as an apostle of Jesus Christ. He believes that the God of Israel has acted to fulfill his ancient promises and that he is now calling all nations to himself. So Paul begins to reason in the synagogues with Jews and God-fearers, as well as in the public marketplace with those he encounters there.

In the marketplace Paul meets a group of Epicurean and Stoic philosophers (Acts 17:18). These are the two leading philosophical schools of the first century. They espouse radically different accounts of humanity and hold different views of the kind of wisdom necessary to solve human problems. It is helpful to learn briefly about each group so that we can better understand the dialogue that follows. The Epicureans are named after their founder Epicurus. They believe that truth lies within human beings. People should trust in their own perceptions and intuitions. They should look to nature and imitate the behavioral patterns of animals. Epicurus' school is located in a garden. Their founder teaches that the summit of happiness was pleasure, which is understood as the absence of pain. Human beings are merely made of atoms. When people die, their bodies simply decompose. The gods do not exist and an afterlife should not be feared. Belief in gods only causes unnecessary anxiety, they reason. Epicurus summarizes his philosophical prescription for humanity in what is known as the "four-fold pharmacy," paraphrased as follows: "Don't fear god. Don't worry about death. What is good is easy to obtain. What is terrible is easy to endure." Take these four pills and your troubles will be solved!

The Stoics, on the other hand, are founded by Zeno of Citium. They are named after the portico (*stoa*) in which they taught. They believe that truth is all around us. The universe is governed by a wise, powerful, and rational god. Human beings are "like god" in their ability to reason. People should not trust their perceptions and intuitions, but rather train their minds to recognize the good. People often make erroneous judgments of what is good; these false judgments arouse passions within. Such passions produce an inordinate desire for pleasure or an irrational fear of pain. The truly wise man, completely governed by reason, will control his passions to achieve happiness. He will be totally unmoved by the circumstances of life. The Stoics make great advances in the areas of formal logic, poetry, and language to train their adherents into the good life. Paul's proclamation of Christ in Athens will address these competing worldviews with the redemptive narrative of Scripture.

Paul's marketplace conversation first prompts scornful criticism over his perceived inability with the Greek language; his teaching then draws the dangerous accusation that he is introducing new gods into the city (Acts 17:18). Socrates had earlier been tried and executed for corrupting the youth of Athens and introducing new deities. Paul is brought before the Council of the Areopagus ("Mars Hill") to defend himself. Here on a rocky outcrop with the Parthenon looming directly behind him, Jesus supplies Paul with the words to say (cf. Matt. 10:19-20).

Paul begins by affirming that the people of Athens are thoroughly devout. Indeed, they even have an altar with the inscription "To the unknown god" (Acts 17:23). This God whom they revere as unknown, Paul now proclaims from the testimony of Scripture. Paul's speech reflects a deeply biblical understanding of God's revelation and his purpose for humanity. He is the creator God who made the world and everything in it. As Lord of heaven and earth, he "does not live in temples made by man, nor is he served by human hands, as though he needed anything, since he himself gives to all mankind life and breath and everything" (Acts 17:24-25; cf. Gen. 1-2). This is a remarkably courageous statement to make with the Parthenon, housing the towering gold and ivory statue of Athena, the patron goddess of the city, immediately behind him. Paul continues that not only is God the creator of the world, he is the creator of all humanity. From one man God made "every nation of mankind to live on all the face of the earth, having determined allotted periods and the boundaries of their dwelling place" (Acts 17:26; cf. Gen. 1-11; Deut. 32:8). Paul's teaching removes the possibility of any ethnic pride, which stands as a great barrier to the gospel among his Greek audience. The Greeks he addresses believe that their ancestors had sprung up from the ground in Greece and that the most beautiful place in the world belongs to them. Instead, Paul explains that God has determined their place and time in order that all might seek after him (Acts 17:27; cf. Deut. 4:29; Isa. 55:6; Amos 9:12; Zech. 8:22).

Paul bridges the chasm of worldviews with his audience by finding redemptive analogies among the Greek poets. He quotes the Cretan Epimenides, who wrote that Zeus was not dead but alive and that "in him we live and move and have our being." He cites the Stoic Cleanthes' *Hymn to Zeus* that "we are God's offspring." However, he concludes by warning them that "we ought not to think that the divine being is like gold or silver or stone, an image formed by the art and imagination of man" (Acts 17:29). Paul's speech cuts into the heart of the Athenians' cultural self-perception as a learned people when he says: "the times of ignorance God overlooked, but now he commands all people everywhere to repent" (Acts 17:30). Few visitors had ever called the Athenians ignorant! Paul courageously charges that sin and idolatry in all forms, even based on ignorance, require repentance. God's righteous judgment is certain (Pss. 96; 98; Isa. 63). It will be carried out through God's appointed Son of Man (Dan. 7:13-14), whom God has raised from the dead.

When the Greeks hear of the resurrection, the conversation abruptly ends. Some mock Paul for an idea that most Greeks at the time considered absurd. Aeschylus had long ago asserted: "Dead people don't rise!" Others, however, are intrigued and want to hear more at another time. As Paul walks out from their midst, he turns to see that several people join him and believe. The Lord opens the heart of Dionysius (a member of the Areopagus Council), a woman named Damaris, and several others with them (Acts 17:34).

Paul leaves Athens and travels south some thirty-six miles to Corinth, the capital of the Roman province of Achaia (Acts 18). The city had been destroyed by the Romans in 146 BC and re-founded by Julius Caesar as a colony. The Corinth of Paul's day became a bustling new city, burgeoning with a rapid influx of resources, settled veterans, and a growing population. Yet Corinth also had reputation as a decadent city of commerce, vice, and immorality. For Paul, it was a long way from home, the farthest place he had yet traveled. It must have seemed overwhelming. He would later write that he came to Corinth "in weakness and in fear and much trembling" (1 Cor. 2:3). The exalted Jesus encourages Paul by sending Aquila and his wife Priscilla to help him. They had recently left Rome due to the edict of Claudius mentioned above. They share the same trade as tentmakers and begin to work together. This couple will become long-term partners and remain among his closest friends in ministry (1 Cor. 16:19; cf. Rom. 16:3; 2 Tim. 4:19).

Strengthened by such support, Paul begins to reason in the synagogues with Jews and God-fearing Greeks. After Silas and Timothy arrive from Macedonia, Paul devotes himself to preaching that "the Christ was Jesus" (Acts 18:5). After being expelled from the synagogue, he enters the house next door, owned by a God-fearer named Titius Justus. Crispus, the ruler of the synagogue at Corinth, comes to believe in the Lord and is baptized along with many others (Acts 18:8; cf. 1 Cor. 1:14). In Acts 18:9-10, Jesus directs Paul to remain in Corinth by appearing to him in a vision: "Do not be afraid, but go on speaking and do not be silent, for I am with you, and no one will attack you to harm you, for I have many in this city who are my people." With the promise of a great harvest, Paul remains in Corinth for a year and six months.

Paul's missionary success among Jews and Gentiles eventually produces conflict with some members of the Jewish community. He is brought before Gallio, the Roman proconsul of Achaia. Gallio was the younger brother of the Stoic philosopher Seneca and was known for his mild temperament. A surviving inscription records that Gallio served as proconsul from AD 51-52, providing a key date for the chronology of Paul's life and missionary journeys. Paul is accused by his kinsmen for "persuading people to worship God contrary to the law" (Acts 18:13). Gallio, however, finds this charge outside the scope of his competency and dismisses the case. He does not consider Paul's proclamation about Christ a vicious crime, but rather "a matter of questions about words and names and your own law" (18:15). Paul's accusers turn on the new synagogue ruler Sosthenes for failing to achieve Paul's condemnation before the tribunal. The next time we hear of Sosthenes, he too has become a believer and brother in Christ (1 Cor. 1:1).

New Testament timeline

Before continuing with Paul's ministry in Corinth, you may want to locate Athens and Corinth on the timeline's map, as it will help you to gain a sense of the distance Paul has traveled in order to proclaim the gospel of Christ. You will also notice a picture of the Parthenon on the timeline, which represents an enduring symbol of the classical world. Dedicated to the goddess Athena, the Parthenon housed a forty-foot statute of her made of ivory, silver, and gold. This will help you to recall Paul's courageous address to the Athenians with the Parthenon directly behind him (Acts 17).

Greeks, Romans, and Jews believe in Christ

While in Corinth, Paul and his missionary team see great numbers of Greeks, Romans, and Jews believe in Christ. The exalted Jesus is at work in the world, claiming men, women, and children from diverse nations as part of God's family. This is in accord with God's ancient promise and eternal purpose (Gen. 12:3; Rev. 7:9-10). In Christ, Abraham's descendants shine forth like the innumerable stars (Gen. 15:5). These new believers are gathering together for worship and learning to walk in God's ways. It is important to remember that for Paul, conversion is just the beginning. New believers are discipled in order that their new life in Christ might be fully formed (Gal. 4:19). Following the instructions of Jesus, new converts are marked through public baptism and then taught to obey all that he had commanded (Matt. 28:19-20).

The gospel confronts idolatry and creates new communities in Christ

As Christ is proclaimed across cultures, the gospel confronts idolatry in various forms. Paul's missionary journeys have brought him into direct contact with diverse forms of paganism. Like Israel's prophets in the Old Testament, early Christian missionaries call people to turn "from idols to serve the living and true God" (1 Thess. 1:9). New believers are justified by faith in Christ's atoning death. They are adopted as full members of God's redeemed people. Forgiven, cleansed, and freed from idolatry, they are filled with the Holy Spirit. The Spirit empowers lives of fruitful obedience and supplies generous gifts to build up the new communities in Christ. This fulfills the prophetic hope of Ezekiel, when God had promised that he would one day cleanse his people from idolatry. He would remove their heart of stone and give them a heart of flesh. He would put his Spirit within them and cause them to walk in his ways (Ezek. 36:25-27). These new communities will require patient instruction so that they reach full maturity in Christ.

Paul writes 1-2 THESSALONIANS (c. AD 51-52)

We will explore the New Testament letters in more detail in the period of TEACHING, but it is important to see their purpose within the historical narrative of Acts. Paul's letters advance his goal of discipleship and the formation of Christian identity. Paul writes 1-2 Thessalonians from Corinth near the end of his second missionary journey around AD 51-52. He writes to encourage the gathered believers in the city of Thessalonica. Both letters are sent from "Paul, Silas, and Timothy" (1 Thess. 1:1; 2 Thess. 1:1). Despite his abrupt departure and prolonged absence from Thessalonica (Acts 17:10-14), he continued to hold them in his prayers. When he could endure it no longer, he sent Timothy to find out about their faith. He wants them to know that the report of their steadfast faith in Christ despite persecution is providing an example to others. He reminds them of the practical implications of their conversion and the importance of the instructions they had received about how to walk and please God. He writes: "this is the will of God, your sanctification: that you abstain from sexual immorality; that each one of you know how to control his own body in holiness and honor, not in the passion of lust like the Gentiles who do not know God ... for God has not called us for impurity, but in holiness" (1 Thess. 4:3-7). Paul generously applies Israel's calling to "be holy for I am holy" (Lev. 19:2) to the gathered Christian community. He encourages them that their new life in Messiah Jesus will win the respect of unbelievers and prepare them for the glorious return of Christ himself.

After staying in Corinth for eighteen months and teaching the word of God (Acts 18:11), Paul and his missionary team vow to return with a report of praise. Paul cuts his hair in Cenchreae to fulfill a Nazirite vow of special consecration to God (Acts 18:18; cf. Num. 6:1-5). He leaves Priscilla and Aquila along the way in Ephesus. After landing in Caesarea, he first goes up to visit the church in Jerusalem. He then visits Antioch to encourage the church with the good news of all that they had seen Christ accomplish through them (Acts 18:22).

Third missionary journey: Paul strengthens the churches and remains in Ephesus (AD 52-57)

We now turn to the third missionary journey. As God continues to extend his kingdom in the world, Paul and his companions are sent from Antioch to strengthen newly planted churches and to open a new work in the strategic city of Ephesus. Luke records this narrative in Acts 18:23-20:3. Although we usually imagine Paul moving from place to place almost daily, Jesus often directs him to remain in a particular location for an extended period of time. Such will be the case in Ephesus, for Paul will preach in this city for three years in order to establish a gospel movement that radiates out from the city to reach the entire region (Acts 20:31). The third missionary journey also confirms Paul's deep commitment to discipleship. During his time in Ephesus, Paul corresponds with the growing church at Corinth and labors toward their mature Christian formation (1 Cor. 14:20).

The journey to Galatia, Ephesus, Philippi, Macedonia, Illyricum, and Corinth

Luke records the route of Paul's vast third missionary journey rather succinctly, even though it takes place over five years (AD 52-57). In Acts 18:23, we read that after spending some time in Antioch, he "departed and went from one place to the next through the region of Galatia and Phrygia, strengthening all the disciples." In Acts 19:1, we read that Paul then travels through "the inland country," reaching Ephesus after a month-long journey of some five hundred miles. After three years of ministry in Ephesus, Paul sets out for Philippi and Macedonia to strengthen the churches and even break new ground. In Acts 20:1-2, we read that Paul departed for Macedonia, traveling "through those regions" and giving "much encouragement." This portion of his journey probably lasted eighteen months, during which time he later references ministry all the way to Illyricum on the western coast of Greece (Rom. 15:19). Eventually, Paul arrives in Corinth in January AD 57 where he spends three critical months preparing to follow Christ to the "end of the earth" (see Acts 1:8).

Paul stays in Ephesus for three years

When Paul reached Ephesus in the fall of AD 52 (Acts 19:1), he entered a bustling metropolis of 250,000 inhabitants enclosed by a five mile wall. The city was built at the mouth of the Cayster River and served as the major port of the province of Asia. A long colonnaded street led to the city center with a civic theater that could hold 25,000 people. Ephesus was renowned as the cult center and guardian of Artemis, goddess of hunting, fertility, and patron deity of the city. You will notice a picture on the timeline of the goddess Artemis next to Paul's third missionary journey under PENTECOST, which will remind you of the challenge of idolatry at Ephesus. The Temple of Artemis housed her multi-breasted image, which devotees claim to have fallen from heaven (Acts 19:36). The temple was the largest Greek building in the world at the time, more than twice the size of the Parthenon, with 127 columns each sixty feet high. The temple was considered one of the Seven Wonders of the Ancient World; it employs a large number of priestesses known as "honey bees" and castrated priests called "drones." Ephesus also had a reputation for magic and the occult. The phrase "Ephesian writings" was used in antiquity to describe documents that contain various incantations and spells. Despite such deep cultural barriers and imposing idolatry, Paul was most impressed in Ephesus by how Jesus had opened "a wide door for effective work" (1 Cor. 16:9).

Following his usual pattern, Paul goes first to the synagogue and begins to reason from Scripture about the arrival of the kingdom of God (Acts 19:8). God does extraordinary work through Paul, who performs miracles and casts out demons in the name of the Lord Jesus. The spiritual authority of Jesus leads many to abandon their idolatry and occult practices. Luke describes a moving scene of genuine repentance as "many of those who were now believers came, confessing and divulging their practices. And a number of those who had practiced magic arts brought their books together and burned them in the sight of all. And they counted the value of them and found it came to fifty thousand pieces of silver" (Acts 19:18-19). The gospel of Christ continues to confront idolatry and set captives free. In fulfillment of God's promise to fill the earth with the knowledge of the glory of the Lord like the waters cover the sea, "the word of the Lord continued to increase and prevail mightily" (Acts 19:20; cf. Isa. 11:9).

Suffering and opposition from Jews and Greeks

Some members of the Jewish community at Ephesus begin to publicly malign "the Way" (Acts 19:9; cf. Isa. 40:3; John 14:6). We are reminded that the life of Christ, including his suffering, will be reproduced in authentic gospel ministry. The most dramatic opposition to the Christian witness at this time, however, comes from the pagan community. Paul's preaching about Jesus Christ comes as a frontal assault against the idolatrous worship of Artemis. Luke describes the resulting opposition as "no small disturbance concerning the Way" (Acts 19:23). Those who prosper through idolatry and the degradation of the image of God in humanity always resent the restoration of that image in Christ. A wave of opposition arises from the guild of silversmiths who benefited from selling images of Artemis. Their leader, Demetrius, rightly understood Paul's preaching about Christ to claim that "gods made with hands are not gods" (Acts 19:26; cf. Isa. 44:9-20; Acts 17:29). Demonic power can only parody the reality of God. The incarnation of Christ exposes the myth of Artemis' descent from heaven. New birth through Christ reveals the misguided devotion to Artemis for protection at birth. The glory of Christ's everlasting kingdom silences the petty civic pride that shouts: "Great is Artemis of the Ephesians!" (Acts 19:28). Alternative religious beliefs cannot compare to the truth of the gospel in Jesus Christ.

Daily lectures in the hall of Tyrannus

Although Paul is opposed by some of the Ephesian Jewish community, a surprising venue is opened for the public proclamation of the gospel. Luke records that Paul began "reasoning daily" in the lecture hall of Tyrannus (Acts 19:9). The Latin term *Tyrannus* means Tyrant; it might have been a nickname given to the teacher by his students! Nevertheless, Jesus tames the heart of this tyrant to open his school for the cause of Christ. An early Greek manuscript variant records Paul's daily hours of instruction as 11 AM to 4 PM. During the peak heat of the day, Paul taught five hours a day for two years, more than three thousand hours. Over these many hours of teaching, Paul set forth "the unsearchable riches of Christ" (Eph. 3:8). As a result, "all the residents of Asia heard the word of the Lord, both Jews and Greeks" (Acts 19:10). The Lord uses Paul's daily lectures in the school of Tyrannus to establish a flourishing Christian community and a gospel movement in Ephesus that would even result in churches being planted in neighboring cities (Col. 1:7). We are reminded here that thorough teaching of the Scriptures is central to the Christian faith. The Word of God is powerful and it will accomplish what God has purposed (Isa. 55:11; Matt. 13:3-8).

Paul declares "the whole counsel of God" (Acts 20:27)

Paul's extensive teaching ministry in Ephesus reveals his commitment to individual conversion and community formation. The preaching of the gospel requires a personal response of repentance and belief. New believers then need the full counsel of Scripture over time to reach maturity in Christ. Christian preachers often present the gospel as a simple transaction where faith in Christ yields forgiveness of sins and eternal life in heaven. Paul's preaching and his letters, however, show that he understood the gospel as the beginning of an entirely new life in Christ. This new life required patient instruction in the Old and New Testament Scriptures and living examples to follow. Paul carries out his sacred responsibility to declare "the whole counsel of God" (Acts 20:27). This is an important phrase for our CASKET EMPTY study. Paul makes the intentional effort over time to communicate God's full redemptive plan to his hearers. Mature Christian discipleship requires instruction in the whole Bible. Without deep roots in God's great redemptive story that begins in Genesis and ends in Revelation, new believers are vulnerable to false teaching. They are easily exploited by self-centered ministries that are based on personal charisma and ego. Paul later warns the Ephesians of such dangers (Acts 20:28-30). Like Samuel before him, Paul conducts his ministry with personal integrity, diligent labor, and financial sacrifice (Acts 20:33-35; cf. 1 Sam. 12:3). Paul's teaching directs people "to God and to the word of his grace, which is able to build you up and to give you the inheritance among all those who are sanctified" (Acts 20:32). His preaching, letters, and own example reveal that transformation into Christ-likeness takes place over time through strong teaching rooted in the whole counsel of God's word.

Paul writes 1-2 CORINTHIANS (c. AD 52-56)

During Paul's extended missionary labor at Ephesus, he corresponds with the growing church at Corinth. This is the context for the two letters we know as 1-2 Corinthians. Couriers could cross the Aegean between Ephesus and Corinth in three or four days. Paul himself makes at least one brief personal visit (2 Cor. 2:1). Paul's Corinthian letters reveal the diverse challenges that new believers face in reaching Christian maturity. The young Corinthian church labors to reflect how Jews and Gentiles, rich and poor, men and women, are united together as a new community in Christ. They struggle with internal divisions, sexual immorality, and false teaching. They wrestle with the extent to which they should or should not participate in their surrounding culture. They even question Paul's authority over them, preferring teachers who seem more impressive in appearance, eloquence, and charisma. Yet Paul did not abandon the church at Corinth during her growing pains, even at great emotional cost. He would later write that the most difficult of all his suffering was "the daily pressure on me of my anxiety for the churches" (2 Cor. 11:28). He became their spiritual father and thus he admonishes them as his "beloved children" (1 Cor. 4:14-15). Paul sends Timothy and Titus to remind them of what they had learned from his own example of following Christ (1 Cor. 4:17; 11:1). These letters reveal Paul's detailed answers to their specific questions about marriage, spiritual gifts, and the nature of the resurrection. God will use the difficulties Paul faced at Corinth to birth some of the most moving passages in all of his letters, such as the surpassing excellence of love (1 Cor. 13), the treasure of Christ in jars of clay (2 Cor. 4), and the centrality of Christ's death and resurrection as the heart of the gospel (1 Cor. 15:1-11). Having written letters to the church at Corinth, Paul finally resolves to visit them again in person. He leaves Ephesus and sets out for Macedonia, stopping to encourage the growing churches in Philippi and Thessalonica along the way (Acts 20:2-3). He finally reaches Corinth in January AD 57.

Paul remains in Corinth for three months and looks toward "the ends of the earth"

Upon arriving at Corinth, Paul finds that the letters the Holy Spirit inspired him to write had proven effective. He returns to a restored and reconciled community that has received his rebuke in love. He is refreshed by the Corinthian church and now contemplates where Christ is calling him next. This provides a critical pause in Paul's ministry over the next three months (Acts 20:3). He has served Jesus Christ for nearly twenty-five years in an expanding circle of witness to his Israelite kinsmen and the nations of the world. Christ has brought him over great distances of land, sea, and culture. He has seen the Lord open the hearts of fellow Jews and idolatrous Gentiles to newness of life in Christ. He has experienced Christ's sustaining power in his own life and knows that Jesus Christ could be trusted in any and all of life's circumstances.

Paul knows from Scripture that the dominion of the messianic king would extend to the ends of the earth (Pss. 2:8; 72:8; Isa. 49:6). The glad obedience of all peoples and nations rightly belongs to him (Dan. 7:13-14). Those living upon distant shores and islands stood eagerly waiting for him (Isa. 42:4). His suffering would make "the many" to be reckoned as righteous (Isa. 53:11-12). In joyful response, the tribute of the nations would be brought to his feet (Gen. 49:10; Isa. 60:1-11). The Holy Spirit now stirs Paul to reach the uttermost limit of the world with the gospel of Christ. Paul therefore purposes to go up to Jerusalem with the following goal in view: "After I have been there, I must also see Rome" (Acts 19:21). From Rome, he will look even further toward the western extremity of the Mediterranean Sea, the Roman province of *Hispania*, which we know today as Spain.

He knows that a vibrant Christian community is already flourishing in Rome, probably established through the witness of returning Pentecost pilgrims (Acts 2:10). Paul has heard the good report of their faith in Christ. Over the years, he has developed personal friendships with many whom he knew by name and who were serving Christ there. Although Paul did not plant the church in Rome, he realizes that he would need their support in order to reach his missionary object of proclaiming Christ to "the ends of the earth" (Acts 1:8). He would need their prayers, gifts, and partnership. He would also need them to embrace his presentation of the gospel and vision of the church, that Jews and Gentiles are justified and united by faith in Christ. Therefore, with his preaching and teaching freshly clarified by hundreds of sermons and thousands of lectures, Paul introduces himself and his ministry to the church in Rome with a letter. The letter is dictated to Tertius in the spring of AD 57, during Paul's three-month stay at Corinth. The letter is entrusted to the hands of a faithful woman named Phoebe, a deaconess in the church at the neighboring port of Cenchreae. This is the letter we know as Romans.

Paul writes ROMANS while at Corinth (AD 57)

Romans is Paul's most significant letter for several good reasons. It reflects the mature pattern of his preaching. It displays a full presentation of Paul's ministry vision. It contains his experienced response to common objections to the cross. It shows his pastoral approach to secondary issues, and ends with a moving portrait of the diverse worshiping church as the people of God. Romans is Paul's longest, and for many, his most profound letter. At the same time, it is important to remember that Romans is a missionary support letter, read publicly in just over an hour, and intended to be understood by all. Paul's self-understanding and ministry vision are encapsulated in his opening sentence, which in Greek extends from Romans 1:1-7. He introduces himself as "a servant of Christ Jesus, called to be an apostle, set apart for the gospel of God" (Rom. 1:1). He is the Messiah's servant, on his master's mission, like Israel's prophets of old. His mission is to announce God's gospel about his Son "which he promised beforehand through his prophets in the holy Scriptures" (Rom. 1:2). Paul's preaching about Christ is in fulfillment of the Scriptures, not in opposition to them. Jesus is the promised Son of David in his humanity and the exalted Son of God in his divinity (Rom. 1:4). Paul proclaims that through Christ's atoning death and enthroning resurrection "we have received grace and apostleship to bring about the obedience of faith for the sake of his name among all the nations" (Rom. 1:5). Paul's missionary labor is focused on the gospel, the good news about Jesus Christ, whose death secures grace for sinners and whose resurrection launches a global mission to claim all nations. Paul's ministry seeks personal conversion and real transformation into a community characterized by obedience (Rom. 1:6). He addresses the gathered church in Rome, comprised of Jews and Gentiles, as the people of

God. He describes all who belong to Jesus Christ with the precious heritage of Israel when he declares that they are loved by God and are called to be holy (Rom. 1:6-7; cf. Lev. 19:2; Deut. 7:6; Isa. 5:1).

Paul desires to visit the Roman Christians and reap a harvest among them as he has among other nations. He is eager to preach the gospel in Rome, for he considers himself obligated to all peoples and social classes. He is not ashamed of the gospel of Christ crucified because it is the power of God for salvation to everyone who believes, both Jews and Greeks. The good news of Christ's death and resurrection reveals the righteousness of God whereby sinful humanity, including both Jews and Gentiles, are justified by faith in Christ (Rom. 1:14-17). According to Paul, Jews and Gentiles alike stand under God's wrath and are declared righteous by faith in Christ's atoning death (Rom. 1:18-3:30). Justification by faith fulfills God's ancient promise to Abraham (Rom. 4) and leads believers to new life in Christ, the new Adam (Rom. 5). Believers now belong to Christ and are filled, empowered, and sanctified by the Holy Spirit (Rom. 6-8). This is in accordance with God's sovereign design and unfathomable wisdom to display his mercy upon all (Rom. 9-11). Through God's mercy, believers in Christ now present their bodies as living sacrifices, holy to the Lord, as God's renewed humanity on display in the church (Rom. 12-15). Paul summarizes his first twenty-five years in Christ's service with a single sentence: "I will not venture to speak of anything except what Christ has accomplished through me to bring the Gentiles to obedience—by word and deed, by the power of signs and wonders, by the power of the Spirit of God—so that from Jerusalem and all the way around to Illyricum I have fulfilled the ministry of the gospel of Christ" (Rom. 15:18-19). Paul writes that he now aspires to preach the gospel where Christ is still unknown in order to fulfill the promise of the prophet Isaiah, that "those who have never been told of him will see, and those who have never heard will understand" (Rom. 15:21; cf. Isa. 52:1). He intends to visit the Roman Christians while on his way to Spain, with the hope that they might approve of his ministry and support him on his way (Rom. 15:24). However, he first plans a visit to Jerusalem at Pentecost in order to present his priestly offering of the Gentiles with the prayer that all might find them acceptable before the Lord (Rom. 15:16).

Paul journeys to Jerusalem with offerings from the Gentiles (AD 57)
Paul sets out from Corinth toward Jerusalem in the spring of AD 57 (Acts 20:3). This trip to Jerusalem represents a significant moment in his life and service to Christ. This important journey is marked on the New Testament timeline with a boat directed *toward* Jerusalem. Paul has served the exalted Jesus in an expanding sphere of witness across many cultural lines for almost twenty-five years. He has seen Jews and Gentiles respond with faith in Christ and start a new life together in Christian community. Throughout his journeys, Paul has experienced persecution and suffering from two very different directions. From his Greco-Roman critics, Paul has been attacked as a narrow-minded, conservative Jew who proclaims a single God and Savior Jesus Christ. To pagans, Paul's preaching that Christ died to rescue an idolatrous, sinful humanity seems utterly foolish (Rom. 1:18-23; 1 Cor. 1:24). Paul's demand that the pagan world must repent, believe in Christ, and change their entire pattern of living often produces scorn. From his Jewish critics, Paul has been attacked as a dangerous, liberal theologian who freely welcomes pagans into the heritage of Israel without requiring a Torah life, including ritual circumcision, kosher dietary laws, and the festival calendar. To Jews, Paul's preaching that Christ died to rescue unfaithful Israel from the covenant curse seems completely scandalous (1 Cor. 1:24). Paul's demand that fellow Israelites must repent, believe in Christ, and change their entire pattern of living often provokes hostility.

For Paul, the gospel confronts both an overconfident pagan society and a proud, religious nationalism with the Lordship of Christ. He believes that the gathered Christian church, comprised of believing Jews and Gentiles, represents the beginning of God's new humanity in Christ (Gal. 3:28; Eph. 2:15-16; Col. 3:10-11). This new humanity requires pagans to embrace a new heritage, found in Israel's God and sacred Scriptures. It requires ethnic Israelites to embrace a new family, as believing Gentiles are received as brothers and sisters in Christ. Paul intends to display the reality of God's new humanity in Christ at the feast of Pentecost in Jerusalem.

With this in view, Paul gathers representative believers from every geographical area of his ministry so far. We find their names listed in Acts 20:4. Sopater, son of Pyrrhus, is from Berea in central Greece. Aristarchus and Secundus are from Thessalonica in northern Greece. Gaius is from Derbe in the province of Lycaonia near Galatia. Timothy is a Jew from Lystra, who joined Paul during his second missionary journey and became like a son to him. Tychicus and Trophimus are from Ephesus in the province of Asia. They both have very Greek names and became Christians during Paul's third missionary journey. Together with Luke, these eight men of very diverse backgrounds journey to Jerusalem as brothers in Christ, the visible fruit of Paul's ministry.

They will not appear before the Lord empty-handed (cf. Deut. 16:16). They carry with them a substantial offering for those in need among the church in Jerusalem. Paul and Barnabas had earlier brought a contribution to Jerusalem from the Christian community at Antioch during a time of famine (Acts 11:28-30; Gal. 2:1, 10). During the course of his missionary journeys, Paul instructs predominantly Gentile Christian communities to collect a regular offering for Jewish believers in Jerusalem (1 Cor. 16:1-4; 2 Cor. 8-9). He realizes the special significance of Gentile Christians expressing such solidarity with Jewish Christians across ethnic lines. He may have even understood this offering as the tribute of the nations streaming to Zion in fulfillment of the prophetic hope (Ps. 72:10; Isa. 2:3). Paul reports that his missionary churches were pleased "to make some contribution for the poor among the saints at Jerusalem ... and indeed they owe it to them. For if the Gentiles have come to share in their spiritual blessings, they ought also to be of service to them in material blessings" (Rom. 15:26-27). Paul earnestly desires believing Jews in Jerusalem to receive the Gentile believers who are traveling with him as brothers. At the same time, he earnestly desires believing Gentiles to identify themselves with the believing Jewish community as their brothers. Paul hopes that both the men and the money will be warmly received. He knows the potential that one or both might be rejected in the increasingly tense atmosphere of the city. Together, they approach the city with Paul's prayer that "my service for Jerusalem may be acceptable to the saints" (Rom. 15:31).

Paul is received by the Jerusalem church but arrested in the temple (Acts 21)

When Paul and his companions arrive in Jerusalem for Pentecost, they quietly stay at the house of Mnason, a Hellenistic Jewish believer from Cyprus (Acts 21:15-16). Shortly thereafter, they meet with the broader church where the brothers receive them gladly (Acts 21:17). The following day Paul meets privately with James and the leadership of the Jerusalem church. He tells them in vivid detail about all that God has done among the nations through his ministry with the result that when they "heard it, they glorified God" (Acts 21:20). The Jerusalem leaders embrace Paul's companions as brothers and receive their offering as grateful support for their local ministry. Their conversation must have lasted for many hours. Saul, the zealous Pharisee, now Paul, the devoted apostle, has returned. Lives are being changed by the gospel of Christ. There are even further horizons and peoples to reach.

The Jerusalem leaders, however, know firsthand that the Christian community, and Paul in particular, face powerful opposition. Many Jews, even some who had become believers, have spoken against the Christian community for their generous stance on Gentile inclusion and weak position on the role of Torah. They have heard the slanderous misrepresentation of Paul's ministry as teaching "all the Jews who are among the Gentiles to forsake Moses, telling them not to circumcise their children or walk according to our customs" (Acts 21:21). As a result, the Jerusalem leaders suggest that Paul show his solidarity with Jewish believers by participating in a Nazirite vow (see Num. 6:1-21). They ask Paul to ritually purify himself together with four other men, pay the cost of their offering, and notify the priests in the temple. Seven days were required for ritual purification. Afterward, their heads would be shaved at the altar. A sin offering and burnt offering would be made for each to complete their vow. Paul readily agrees to this symbolic gesture, consistent with his overall position on secondary issues (Rom. 14; 1 Cor. 9:20-23).

When the seven days are almost complete, Paul enters the Jerusalem Temple. He has come up to Jerusalem "in the priestly service of the gospel of God, so that the offering of the Gentiles may be acceptable, sanctified by the Holy Spirit" (Rom. 15:16). Passing through the outer courts, he reaches the low dividing wall that separates the Court of the Gentiles from the Court of Israel. This low partition, just over four feet high, is made of ornately carved stone. Inscriptions in Greek and Latin are set at regular intervals "declaring the law of ritual purity that no foreigner should go within the sanctuary" (Josephus, *War* 5:193-94; *Ant.* 15.417). Two of these inscriptions have been found with the warning: "No foreigner is allowed to enter within the balustrade surrounding the sanctuary and the court. Whoever is caught will be personally responsible for his ensuing death."

Paul believes that Jesus' death has removed this division between Jews and Gentiles and that all people now have access to the God of Israel through faith in Christ (Rom. 5:2; Eph. 2:18; 3:2). Nevertheless, he would have been compelled, even reluctantly, to leave his Gentile companions for the moment at the dividing line, lest they be publicly attacked. As Paul enters the sanctuary to fulfill his vow, certain Jews from Asia who had come up for Pentecost recognize him. They had seen Trophimus the Ephesian with him and wrongfully assume that Paul had brought him beyond the dividing wall. They stir the swelling pilgrimage crowd crying out: "Men of Israel, help! This is the man who is teaching everyone everywhere against the people and the law and this place. Moreover, he even brought Greeks into the temple and has defiled this holy place!" (Acts 21:28). Paul is forcibly dragged out of the sanctuary and the temple gates are closed. The Roman commander sends in troops to calm the volatile situation. He arrests Paul, binds him with chains, and brings him into the Antonia Fortress, the military tower rising over the northwest corner of the Temple Mount. As Paul is being pulled into the barracks, he asks for permission to address his people. The Roman commander, surprised to hear Paul speaking Greek, asks him: "Are you not the Egyptian, then, who recently stirred up a revolt and led the four thousand men of the Assassins out into the wilderness?" (Acts 21:38). Paul denies the implied accusation that he is a cause of civil unrest and receives permission to address the swelling pilgrimage crowds from the elevated fortress.

Paul testifies before Pentecost pilgrims, the Sanhedrin, and Felix (Acts 22-24)

Paul speaks to his kinsmen in Hebrew, calming them with the language of their heart. Hebrew was still spoken in Judea throughout the first century, although Aramaic was spoken in Galilee and in the north. Paul identifies with his listeners by reminding them: "I am a Jew, born in Tarsus in Cilicia, but brought up in this city, educated at the feet of Gamaliel according to the strict manner of the law of our fathers, being zealous for God as all of you are this day" (Acts 22:3). He rehearses his own persecution of the early followers of Jesus (Acts 22:4-5). Then, he tells of the decisive moment in his life: "As I was on my way and drew near to Damascus, about noon a great light from heaven suddenly shone around me. And I fell to the ground and heard a voice saying to me, 'Saul, Saul, why are you persecuting me?' And I answered, 'Who are you, Lord?' And he said to me, 'I am Jesus of Nazareth, whom you are persecuting'" (Acts 22:6-7). He who had been a zealous guide to the blind was blinded by the glory of the resurrected Jesus Christ. Paul emphasizes that his ministry has come from "the God of our fathers," who has appointed him to know his will, to see the Righteous One, and to hear his voice (Acts 22:14). Though already a devout Israelite, Paul confesses his commitment to Christ with public baptism, signifying the forgiveness of his sins (Acts 22:16). Paul tells the people that he had come up to Jerusalem previously with an eagerness to testify of their Messiah but had been warned they would not receive him. The Lord, therefore, had sent him far away to the Gentiles (Acts 22:21). At the word "Gentiles," the pilgrimage throng turns violently against Paul. The inclusion of the Gentiles into the people of God was the decisive issue, yet their inclusion was the distinctive note of Paul's missionary labor in Christ (Rom. 15:5-12; Eph. 3:4-7). This would remain a sharp dividing line for many zealous Israelites, since they did not recognize that the time for "the fullness of the Gentiles had come" (Rom. 11:25).

The following day, the Roman commander brings Paul before the Sanhedrin, the highest religious court comprised of Sadducees and Pharisees. Paul addresses the council as "brothers" and testifies that he has lived his life "before God in all good conscience up to this day" (Acts 23:1). The term that Paul uses for "live" is a technical term used to describe the duties of a faithful citizen. Paul views himself as a faithful member of the covenant community by believing in Christ. The confidence of his expression explains the violent reaction of the high priest, Ananias, who commands those nearby to strike Paul. A tense exchange follows. Paul accuses Ananias of hypocrisy for rendering judgment by Torah while violating the requirement of Torah: "You shall do no injustice in court" (Lev. 19:15). Paul in turn is accused of violating the Torah: "You shall not revile God, nor curse a ruler of your people" (Exod. 22:28). Paul realizes that this parlay of accusations only escalates the tension. He therefore draws attention to the most crucial issue at hand: "Brothers, I am a Pharisee, a son of Pharisees. It is with respect to the hope and the resurrection of the dead that I am on trial" (Acts 23:6). Paul believes that the resurrection from the dead has begun with Jesus the Messiah. You will recall that a great theological disagreement existed between the Pharisees and Sadducees over the bodily resurrection. Paul's assertion ignites this simmering debate within the assembled council. In the uproar, some of the Pharisees stand up in Paul's defense and assert: "We find nothing wrong in this man. What if a spirit or an angel spoke to him?" (Acts 23:9). Paul is rushed out of the council, as the dissension turns violent, and is returned to the Antonia Fortress. The exalted Lord Jesus stands close by him the following night in a dream and promises: "Take courage, for as you have testified to the facts about me in Jerusalem, so you must testify also in Rome" (Acts 23:11).

After learning of a plot against Paul's life, the Roman commander, Claudius Lysias, transfers Paul to Caesarea at night under a heavily armed guard. He refers Paul's case to the Roman procurator of Judea, Antonius Felix. Felix was a freedman who had been appointed by the emperor Claudius five years earlier in AD 52. The Roman historian Tacitus reports that Felix "held the power of a tyrant with the disposition of a slave." Josephus describes him as a man disposed to act unjustly. Five days later, the high priest Ananias comes down from Jerusalem to Caesarea with some of the elders and a trained rhetorician named Tertullus, who serves as public prosecutor. They label Paul a public menace and set forth three charges against him: first, he stirs up riots among Jews everywhere; second, he is a ringleader of the Nazarene sect; and third, he is a desecrator of the temple (Acts 24:5). Paul responds to each of these charges in a moving defense. To the first charge, he denies ever having the intention to stir up crowds in either the temple or synagogue. To the second charge, he refuses to consider the early Christian community as a sect, but rather the fulfillment of the hope of Israel: "This I confess to you, that according to the Way, which they call a sect, I worship the God of our fathers, believing everything laid down by the Law and written in the Prophets, having a hope in God, which these men themselves accept, that there will be a resurrection of both the just and the unjust" (Acts 24:14-15). To the third charge, he rejects the accusation of defiling the temple and insists that he was present in a state of ritual purity "to bring alms to my nation and to present offerings" (Acts 24:17). Paul restates the central issue, then and now: "It is with respect to the resurrection of the dead that I am on trial before you this day" (Acts 24:21).

Paul is imprisoned in Caesarea for "the hope of Israel" (AD 57-59)

Felix refuses to decide the case and Paul remains imprisoned in Caesarea for two years (Acts 24:27). Throughout this period, Paul's friends visit and attend to his needs. Felix, along with his young Jewish wife Drusilla (daughter of Herod Agrippa I), often sends for Paul to converse with him in hope of receiving a bribe to release him. On such occasions, Paul's consistent message is about faith in Christ (Acts 24:24). Paul reasons from Scripture about "righteousness and self-control and the coming judgment" (Acts 24:25). From Paul's letters, we know that he understands righteousness as the righteousness of God revealed in the atoning death of Christ (Rom. 3:21-25). Self-control is the fruit of the indwelling Holy Spirit, who empowers Christian discipleship in fulfillment of the Torah (Gal. 5:22-23). The coming judgment is Christ's visible return in glory, when the whole world will appear before his judgment seat (2 Cor. 5:10). When Paul reaches the topic of judgment, Felix, like many modern people, ends the conversation. It is of particular importance for our study to see how Paul presents faith in Christ as the fulfillment of the biblical story. He believes that the hope of Israel has come true in the death and resurrection of Jesus the Messiah. This is indeed the center of the biblical story and the dominant idea for our CASKET EMPTY study together. For Paul, all of God's promises are "Yes" in Christ, atonement for sin has been made, and the new creation has begun. The time for sharing this good news is at hand and Paul sees himself as Christ's ambassador to the world (2 Cor. 5:20; Eph. 6:20).

Paul's journey and witness to Rome, Caesarea, Sidon, Crete, Malta, Rome (Acts 25-28)

The Holy Spirit had long stirred Paul to bear witness for Christ in Rome (Acts 19:21). Paul had purposed to visit the thriving Christian community in the city en route to further missionary witness in Spain (Rom. 15:24-28). He had written them a moving letter, Romans, to explain his understanding of the gospel and its implications for ministry and for the church. By Christ's sovereign hand, the time has come for Paul's journey to Rome. As we will see, his journey begins from a prison cell inside Herod's palace in Caesarea (Acts 25-26). Christ will bring him to Sidon, past Cyprus, then Cilicia and the coastal provinces of his earlier missionary journeys. He will stop in Crete, the great island remembered as the birthplace of Zeus. Christ will preserve Paul's life through a devastating shipwreck, finally landing safely at Malta (Acts 27). From there, he will reach the coast of Italy and eventually Rome. Paul will arrive in the city as Christ's "ambassador in chains" (Eph. 6:20; cf. Acts 28). While in Rome, Paul will openly share Christ with all who visit him. He will write more than half of his letters during this period. New converts will be made, even within the imperial household, for Paul will declare that although he is bound with chains, "the word of God is not bound" (2 Tim. 2:9).

Paul appeals to Nero before Festus and Herod Agrippa II (Acts 25-26)

As we follow Paul's imprisonment in Rome, it is important to set the scene. Antonius Felix, the Roman procurator of Judea, is recalled to Rome in AD 59/60 for mishandling riots over citizenship rights between the Jewish and Gentile communities in Caesarea. The emperor Nero replaces him with Porcius Festus, who had no direct experience in Jewish affairs. Three days after arriving in office, Festus visits Jerusalem. The chief priests inform him of their accusations against Paul and request that he be transferred back to Jerusalem for trial. Paul repeatedly declares his innocence before Festus, stating that he has committed no offense against the Torah, temple, or Caesar (Acts 25:8). Paul recognizes that a transfer to Jerusalem would almost certainly lead to his death. Therefore, he courageously invokes the right of all Roman citizens to have his case heard before Caesar in Rome. Festus must have replied with a measure of relief: "To Caesar you have appealed; to Caesar you shall go" (Acts 25:12).

Yet Festus was uncertain how to report the specific charge against Paul. He receives a state visit from the Jewish King Agrippa II, along with his sister Bernice, at which time he had hoped to clarify Paul's case. In a fascinating comment, Festus reports that the only thing he was able to determine was that the Jerusalem leaders had certain points of dispute with Paul "about their own religion and about a certain Jesus, who was dead, but whom Paul asserted to be alive" (Acts 25:19). Festus convenes an assembly in the palace auditorium. Agrippa and Bernice enter with great pomp together with high-ranking military officers and prominent citizens dressed in expensive garments and full regalia. Paul is brought into the room in chains and invited to speak for himself. Paul's moving defense before Agrippa focuses on the hope of Israel, which he believes has been realized in Christ: "I stand here on trial because of my hope in the promise made by God to our fathers, to which our twelve tribes hope to attain, as they earnestly worship night and day" (Acts 26:6-7). Agrippa knows about the hope of Israel. He knows from Scripture that God would act again. The kingdom of God would come, the Son of Man would appear, and the Son of David would sit upon his throne. Atonement for sin would be provided and a new covenant established forever. The Holy Spirit would be poured out upon all humanity and the blessing of Abraham would reach all nations. There would be a resurrection from the dead and then a final judgment and a new creation. These are the Old Testament promises we have learned in the period of EXPECTATIONS.

Paul knows the hope of Israel as well, but he is certain that this hope has been fulfilled in the life, death, and resurrection of Jesus the Messiah. Paul rehearses his pre-conversion rage against the name of Jesus and his violent persecution against those who appeared to make blasphemous claims about him (Acts 26:9-11). Yet everything changed when Paul encountered a heavenly vision of the exalted Jesus (Acts 26:12-15). The resurrected Jesus commissioned him as a servant to open the eyes of his own people and to turn the nations from darkness to light by faith in Christ (Acts 26:16-18; cf. Isa. 35:5; 42:7). Paul solemnly confesses that he has not disobeyed the heavenly vision of Christ. He has testified in Jerusalem, Judea, and to the Gentiles that all must turn to God in repentance. He boldly declares that the death and resurrection of Christ is the fulfillment of God's redemptive plan for humanity:

> Therefore, O King Agrippa, I was not disobedient to the heavenly vision, but declared first to those in Damascus, then in Jerusalem and throughout all the region of Judea, and also to the Gentiles, that they should repent and turn to God, performing deeds in keeping with their repentance. For this reason the Jews seized me in the temple and tried to kill me. To this day I have had the help that comes from God, and so I stand here testifying both to small and great, saying nothing but what the prophets and Moses said would come to pass: that the

Christ must suffer and that, by being the first to rise from the dead, he would proclaim light both to our people and to the Gentiles. (Acts 26:19-23)

Paul's defense produces diverse reactions. Festus interrupts Paul with the derisive charge that his great learning has led him to insanity. Paul replies that his words are in fact true and reasonable. Agrippa, however, appears to open his heart for a moment when he asks: "In a short time would you persuade me to be a Christian?" (Acts 26:28). Paul replies that whether in a short time or long "I would to God that not only you but also all who hear me this day might become such as I am—except for these chains" (Acts 26:29).

Festus honors Paul's appeal to Caesar and sends him to Rome in the custody of a centurion named Julius, who is a member of the elite Augustan Cohort. Luke and Aristarchus travel with him (Acts 27:2). They stop in Sidon on the Phoenician coast where Paul is refreshed by his friends. As they sail to the south of Cyprus due to heavy winds, Paul must have recalled all that Christ had accomplished during the first missionary journey. As they continue along the coast of Asia Minor, past Cilicia and Pamphylia, Paul must have remembered his family and all those whom Christ had claimed during his second and third missionary journeys. At Myra they board a large Alexandrian cargo ship bound for Italy. Against the rising northerly winds that end the summer sailing season, they struggle to reach Cnidus and are forced to seek shelter along the southern coast of Crete in a small harbor called Fair Havens. Luke tells us that the open sailing season had ended, because the fast for the Day of Atonement (which was on October 5th in AD 59) had already passed (Acts 27:9). The ship's captain, encouraged by a gentle south wind, attempts to reach the deeper western harbor at Phoenix. As they sail closely along the Cretan coast, "a wind of hurricane force" comes rushing down the slopes of Mount Ida (Acts 27:14). The ship is violently driven across the open sea. After three days, they jettison the ship's cargo and tackle. Pummeled by the raging storm and without sun or stars for navigation, the sailors abandon hope. In the midst of the storm, the Lord appears to Paul with the promise: "Do not be afraid, Paul; you must stand before Caesar. And behold, God has granted you all those who sail with you" (Acts 27:24). Paul encourages the men that although the ship would be destroyed, their lives would be spared.

They run aground on the island of Malta where all 276 souls are spared. They winter there for three months and set sail for Rome in the spring, aboard another Alexandrian cargo ship with the twin gods, Castor and Pollux, as figureheads (Acts 28:11).

They sail ninety miles north to Syracuse, an ancient Greek colony on the island of Sicily. They continue to Rhegium at the southern end of the straits of Messina. They cross the Bay of Naples with Mount Vesuvius looming in the distance and reach Puteoli, the deep port of Rome where heavy cargo was unloaded. There they find a small group of Christians. They stay with them for seven days and then continue on foot along the famous Via Appia toward Rome, a journey of nearly 120 miles. When they reach the post station called the Forum of Appius, still forty miles from the city, we finally learn about the original reception of Romans, Paul's missionary letter to the church in Rome. Members of the Christian community there hear that Paul has reached the shore of Italy, and they rush out to meet him. His letter had been read and understood. Their support and affection for him were assured. It must have been a deeply emotional scene about which Luke records: "On seeing them, Paul thanked God and took courage" (Acts 28:15).

Paul is in chains because of the hope of Israel (Acts 28)

Paul arrives in the heart of the Roman Empire in AD 60. Rome was a vast metropolis of over one million inhabitants, the largest city in the world at that time. The size and scale of Roman architecture communicated imperial ambition and authority. Paul enters the city through the Porta Capena in the Severan wall, built in the fourth century BC. He passes the aqueduct recently finished under Claudius with towering arches 110 feet high. He walks past Nero's sprawling racetrack, the *Circus Maximus*, which had seating for 250,000. He sees the imperial palaces and temples built upon the Palatine Hill. Following the Sacred Way, he passes through the Roman Forum, which was the civic center of the city where Rome's returning armies marched in triumphal procession. He sees the elevated platform from which public speeches were made. He passes by the golden milestone, which marked the beginning of all roads and recorded the distances from Rome to the major cities of the empire. He sees the Capitoline Hill, crowned with the ornate Temple of Jupiter Optimus Maximus, the religious epicenter of the Roman world dedicated to the gods, Jupiter, Juno, and Minerva. Finally, he is led to the Praetorian Barracks on the northeast of the city. Here Julius reports to the commanding officer, delivering Paul and the documents that specify the charges against him. Paul is allowed to live nearby in one of the apartments "with the soldier that guarded him" (Acts 28:16), while he awaits his trial before Nero.

Following a pattern he developed throughout his missionary life, Paul first seeks an audience with the Jewish community of the city. It is important for us to remember that Paul never stops trying to reach his own people with the good news that Israel's Messiah has come. He addresses them as brothers and testifies that he has done "nothing against our people or the customs of our fathers" (Acts 28:17). He is not guilty of any crime deserving death. He states his purpose in meeting with them in the clearest of terms: "It is because of the hope of Israel that I am wearing this chain" (Acts 28:20). From morning till evening, Paul reasons with them from the Scriptures "testifying to the kingdom of God and trying to convince them about Jesus both from the Law of Moses and from the Prophets" (Acts 28:23). Like almost every preaching moment, then and now, some are persuaded, while others refuse to believe. Paul urges his kinsmen with a strong warning from Isa. 6:9-10 against their unbelief. Following his pattern, he then turns his attention to the Gentiles in confident hope that some of them have been appointed to eternal life (Acts 28:28; cf. Acts 13:38). Paul stays in Rome for two years and welcomes "all who came to him, proclaiming the kingdom of God and teaching about the Lord Jesus Christ with all boldness and without hindrance" (Acts 28:30-31).

Luke's inspired narrative of Acts ends with Paul's open proclamation of Christ in Rome. Many have wished over the centuries that the Holy Spirit had moved Luke to write a third volume in the series. However, God wisely chose a fitting place to close this portion of the narrative. The word of Christ continues to spread throughout the world. God's redemptive purpose extends even further through the faithful witness of countless others. Paul's imprisonment in Rome actually serves to advance the gospel (see Phil. 1:12). The word of Christ reaches the imperial guard and even members of Caesar's own household (see Phil. 4:22).

Paul writes EPHESIANS, PHILIPPIANS, COLOSSIANS, and PHILEMON (c. AD 60-62)

Paul not only teaches about the Lord Jesus while imprisoned in Rome, he writes about him. The Holy Spirit inspires Paul to write letters to the Christian communities in Ephesus, Philippi, and Colossae, together with a personal letter addressed to Philemon, Apphia, and Archippus and the church that meets in their home. These are the letters we know as Ephesians, Philippians, Colossians, and Philemon. Each of these letters makes explicit reference to Paul's imprisonment, and together they are referred to as the Prison Epistles (Eph. 3:1; 4:1; Phil. 1:14; Col. 4:3, 10; Phlm. 1:1). You will notice on the timeline a picture of chains, which represents Paul's imprisonment in Rome. Despite Paul's affliction, these letters reveal his consistent life of prayer, profound joy in Christ, and enduring affection for the body of Christ. He urges believers to walk worthy of their calling and to stand firmly united in Christ (Eph. 4:1; Phil. 1:27; Col. 3:15). They are to imitate Christ in all things (Eph. 5:1; Phil. 2:5-11). They are to be on guard against false teachers and press on toward full maturity in Christ (Eph. 4:14-20; Phil. 3:2-15; Col. 2:8-23). He thanks Christ for their partnership in the gospel and requests prayer for boldness in witness and a favorable outcome at his trial.

Paul is released for ministry in Spain and imprisoned again

Paul later writes that at his first defense "the Lord stood by me and strengthened me ... so I was rescued from the lion's mouth" (2 Tim. 4:16-17). Several early Christian sources affirm that Paul is released for further ministry in Spain and later imprisoned again in Rome a second time. During this second imprisonment, the Holy Spirit inspires Paul to write his final letters to trusted co-laborers for the gospel. They will serve the exalted Jesus among the next generation of Christian leadership. These are the letters that we know as 1-2 Timothy and Titus.

Paul writes 1-2 TIMOTHY and TITUS (c. AD 63-65)

Paul's letters to Timothy and Titus are filled with mature pastoral wisdom and tender affection for future leaders of the church. These three letters are known as the Pastoral Epistles. Paul teaches these church leaders the importance of godly character and the priority of the preached word of God (1 Tim. 3; 2 Tim. 4:2; Tit. 2:1). He reminds them that the central theme of the gospel is "Jesus Christ, risen from the dead, the offspring of David" (2 Tim. 2:8). He emphasizes that their greatest, most effective, and inexhaustible teaching resource is the whole counsel of God's word for "all Scripture is breathed out by God and profitable for teaching" (2 Tim. 3:16).

As we conclude the period of PENTECOST, it is important to note that the final years of Paul's life and the remaining New Testament letters will be presented in the period of TEACHING, since we will be discussing the content of each letter in more detail in the next few chapters. Our focus in PENTECOST has been on the narrative of Acts, but there will be some overlap as we move into the next period. Before continuing with the period of TEACHING, I would encourage you to read through the book of Acts if you have not already done so. My prayer for you is that the historical account of all that Jesus continues to do through the church will encourage your heart and embolden your own witness. Jesus has promised his disciples: "you will receive power when the Holy Spirit has come upon you, and you will be my witnesses in Jerusalem and in all Judea and Samaria, and to the end of the earth" (Acts 1:8). May we be fervent in our witness, empowered by his Spirit, and may the name of Jesus be exalted in the still unreached peoples of our world today.

Chapter 6
TEACHING Part 1

The period of TEACHING simply explained

THE FOURTH PERIOD of the New Testament is called TEACHING because it represents the time in redemptive history when God commissions his people to teach the gospel to the nations. Teaching is an essential aspect of global mission. Jesus has instructed his followers to make disciples, baptizing them and teaching them to obey all of his commands. This sacred task fulfills the prophetic imagery of Isaiah, when all the nations of the world would stream toward the living God in order that they might be taught his ways.

Through the empowering presence of the Holy Spirit, Christians share the good news about Jesus Christ in an expanding geographical sphere of witness. Christian communities are established in urban centers and then spread into surrounding regions. After churches are planted, Christian leaders provide additional teaching through letters. Twenty-one of the twenty-seven New Testament books are letters sent to early Christian communities, so that they might be instructed on matters of doctrine and how to live as followers of Jesus. These letters are sometimes called epistles, which is the Greek word for "letter." All of the authors of the New Testament letters are Israelites who became followers of Jesus. Their letters to Christian communities have helped to define Christian faith and theology from the apostolic age until the present. These authors draw richly from the Old Testament, the teachings of Jesus, and their own testimony of what God is doing in the newly formed Christian communities. These New Testament letters are the divinely inspired biblical books for the period of TEACHING.

The period of TEACHING has significant overlap with the period of PENTECOST. Both periods cover the missionary expansion of the church under the Lordship of the exalted Jesus. In PENTECOST, the focus has been on the book of Acts. The letters were included by name and were located chronologically within the narrative of Acts. In the period of TEACHING, the focus is on the content of the letters. Each letter is placed on the timeline's map according to the location of the original recipient of each letter. For example, Paul writes Romans during his stay in Corinth. However, the letter is placed on the timeline's map in Rome rather than in Corinth, since the original recipients of the letter reside in Rome. Each letter on the map is in red to remind us that Christ's blood was shed for our transgression. Each letter has a key phrase in yellow summarizing the main teaching of the letter. Yellow reminds us that the resurrection of Christ is the beginning of God's new creation. Although there are different authors, circumstances, and audiences of the New Testament letters, these two colors emphasize the unity of early Christian teaching about the death and resurrection of the Messiah as the center of the biblical story.

In published editions of the Bible, it is important to notice that the New Testament letters are arranged according to author and descending length. According to their canonical order, Paul's thirteen letters are listed first, beginning with Romans since it is the longest, and concluding with Philemon since it is the shortest. Hebrews is placed next due to an early association with Paul or one of his disciples. James, Peter, John, and Jude complete the letters using similar criteria. This practice reflects the Greek publishing convention according to literary genre, author, and size. For the period of TEACHING, however, we will follow the chronological arrangement of the letters under the period of PENTECOST to reinforce the learning objectives of our CASKET EMPTY study.

A helpful way to remember the broad chronology of the New Testament letters is as follows: James and Jude are brothers of Jesus writing to the church in Jerusalem (all conveniently starting with the letter J: James, Jude, brothers of Jesus, Jerusalem). These function almost like chronological bookends for the New Testament letters. For Paul's letters, you may want to memorize them this way: on Paul's *first* missionary journey he writes *one* letter (Galatians). On his *second* missionary journey he writes *two* letters (1-2 Thessalonians). On Paul's *third* missionary journey he writes *three* letters (1-2 Corinthians and Romans). After his *fourth* journey as a prisoner to Rome he writes *four* letters under house arrest awaiting trial (Ephesians, Philippians, Colossians, and Philemon). These letters are called the Prison Epistles. Near the end of his life he writes *three* last letters to the next generation of Christian pastors (1-2 Timothy and Titus). These letters are known as the Pastoral Epistles. This gives a total of thirteen letters written by Paul. Finally, there are seven more letters written to strengthen the churches. These letters are known as the General Epistles and include Hebrews, 1-2 Peter, Jude, and 1-3 John.

As the teaching of Christ spreads out into the world, political tension between Rome and Jerusalem continues to escalate. The Jewish War erupts in AD 66 as religious nationalism and imperial ambition forcefully collide. This conflict of worldviews leads to the devastating destruction of the Jerusalem Temple in AD 70 and the expression of dehumanizing power in Rome. This significant event is marked on the lower right-hand corner of the New Testament timeline under TEACHING, with the picture of the temple in flames. In the midst of such upheaval, the kingdom of God continues to expand as the gospel is proclaimed to all nations. Jews and Gentiles are justified by faith in Christ and taught to walk in his ways together. The gathered Christian church boldly reflects God's renewed humanity to a sinful, broken, and violent world. Persecution will produce perseverance. False teaching will motivate faithful instruction. Societal conflict will reveal the gospel of peace.

The key dates for the period of TEACHING are AD 33 and AD 95. AD 33 marks the time when Jesus commissions his followers to teach the nations after his resurrection. This means that in this chapter we will retrace the storyline of Acts, yet our emphasis will be on the content of the letters. Additional dates for individual letters will be provided throughout this chapter. AD 95 represents the approximate time of the last of the New Testament letters. The key people for this period are the authors of the New Testament letters, namely, James, Paul, Peter, John, and Jude. Roman emperors who rule during this period are Claudius (AD 41-54), Nero (AD 54-68), Vespasian (AD 69-79), and his son Titus (AD 79-81).

New Testament timeline

As we learn about the period of TEACHING, it is important for you to locate the picture of a scroll on the timeline, which represents this period. Jesus has commissioned his disciples as teachers of the nations (Matt. 28:20; 1 Tim. 2:7; 2 Tim. 1:11; cf. Isa. 2:3). The New Testament letters are sent to early Christian communities in an expanding sphere of witness to the truth that is in Jesus (Eph. 4:21). These letters are divinely inspired instruction for living as God's people in the world. The scroll reminds us of a Torah scroll. The word *Torah* means "instruction" or "teaching" given by God to his people in the Old Testament (Exod. 24:12; Pss. 19:7; 119:18; Isa. 2:3; 8:16; 42:4; Jer. 31:33). The teaching mission of the church includes the New Testament as well. The structure of Christian theology is the fulfillment of the hope of Israel that has begun in Christ. One out of every ten verses in the New Testament is a quotation or clear allusion to the Old Testament. This reminds us of the importance of the Old Testament in the biblical narrative. God's plan of redemption through history must be communicated through the Old and New Testaments in order to present everyone "mature in Christ" (Col. 1:28).

Roadmap to the chapter

As you read through this chapter, I would encourage you to keep the New Testament timeline in front of you. It will be beneficial for you to locate each letter on the map, so that you will be able to grasp visually the expansive movement of early Christian mission. Allow this map to stir your own heart to join God's mission in the world today. This period of TEACHING has been written in three parts and will cover all twenty-one letters of the New Testament. Part 1 surveys the seven letters written during the period covered in the book of Acts. This will include James, and Paul's letters during his three missionary journeys, namely, Galatians, 1-2 Thessalonians, 1-2 Corinthians, and Romans. Part 2 will also survey seven letters: the four letters written during the period of Paul's Roman imprisonment plus his last three letters written to Timothy and Titus. This will include the Prison Epistles: Ephesians, Philippians, Colossians, Philemon and the Pastoral Epistles: 1-2 Timothy and Titus. Part 3 will survey the seven remaining New Testament letters, known as the

General Epistles. These letters are written to strengthen the church in the midst of persecution, false teaching, and societal conflict. This will include 1-2 Peter, Hebrews, Jude, and 1-3 John. At the end of Part 3, we will summarize the key beliefs that unite Christian teaching.

God commissions His people to teach the Gospel to the nations

The bold heading at the top of the timeline under TEACHING identifies God's major redemptive activity during this period. A map of the greater Mediterranean world unfolds the scale of early Christian mission. The map is presented in rich color to signify the renewal of life and creation in the world under the Lordship of Christ (Gen. 1:28; Isa. 65:17; 2 Cor. 5:17; Gal. 6:15). The blue waters of the sea satisfy the eye with the fulfillment of the prophetic promise that "the earth will be filled with the knowledge of the glory of the LORD as the waters cover the sea" (Hab. 2:14; cf. Isa. 11:9). The borders of the map have been carefully chosen to include the movement of the gospel into Africa, Asia, Europe, and beyond. The dominion of Jesus the Messiah extends even to the distant shores and islands of the world (Pss. 2:8; 22:27; 72:8-11; Isa. 11:11; 52:10). There is a key in the lower-left corner of the map. This key identifies seven beliefs that form the essential TEACHING of the New Testament letters. We will conclude the period of TEACHING by summarizing these seven key beliefs.

As we begin our survey the New Testament letters, it is important to underscore at the outset that the role of Christians as teachers of the world is an enduring responsibility. The core curriculum is the Scripture of both the Old and New Testament. Learning is required of all disciples, not just pastors and teachers. Preaching is established to proclaim and apply the Word of God. Christian education of children, youth, and adults is a vital aspect of church ministry. Seminaries, Bible colleges. and training institutes are essential to support Christian scholarship. There will always be rival curriculums. Even religious people will clamor for topics other than the Word of God. Cultural figures or popular entertainers will claim that the role of teaching the world belongs to them. Despite all such claims, God has commissioned *his people* to teach the gospel to the nations.

JAMES, the brother of Jesus, to the church of Jerusalem (c. AD 45)

James is the earliest of the New Testament letters, written by James, the brother of Jesus. Although Jesus' brothers did not believe in him at first (John 7:5), James came to believe after seeing Jesus resurrected from the dead (1 Cor. 15:7). James became a leader of the church in Jerusalem (Acts 15). In the Greek text, the author's name is *Iacobos,* reflecting the patriarch Jacob. The Latin form of the name *Iacombus* became simplified into English as James. You should have already located James on the timeline under the period of PENTECOST, as this will help you place the letter in the storyline of Acts. You will also notice that James is placed on the timeline's map in Jerusalem, since the recipients of the letter reside there. James writes his letter around AD 45, at a time of hardship due to famine and societal persecution after the brief but violent reign of Herod Agrippa I (AD 41-44). You should be familiar with the rule of Herod Agrippa I from our earlier section on PENTECOST. You may want to review that section, along with the challenges facing the church during the rule of the emperor Claudius (AD 41-54). Although he is Jesus' earthly brother, James introduces himself as "a servant of God and of the Lord Jesus Christ" (Jas. 1.1). He addresses "the twelve tribes in the Dispersion" (Jas. 1:1). This expression signals that he has the entire community in view.

James begins by encouraging believers to persevere during times of trial and to remain faithful to Christ (Jas. 1:2-8). He urges them to "count it all joy, my brothers, when you meet trials of various kinds, for you know that the testing of your faith produces steadfastness" (Jas. 1:2-3). Christians in Jerusalem face intense opposition from their Israelite kinsmen and from the surrounding pagan world. They are pressured to join with zealous nationals or to compromise with pagan culture. They could also be enticed by their own desires into sin that only leads to death. For those who stand the test, James promises "the crown of life, which God has promised to those who love him" (Jas. 1:12).

James is profoundly shaped by the wisdom and ethics of Scripture. There are also more than twenty clear allusions to the Sermon on the Mount in his letter (Jas. 1:4, cf. Matt. 5:48; Jas. 1:5, cf. Matt. 7:7-11; Jas. 1:22, cf. Matt. 7:24-27, etc.). Both the Old Testament and the words of Jesus are cited as divinely inspired teaching. Throughout his letter, James calls believers to put their faith in Christ into action. His practical appeal can be observed even on a linguistic level. There are nearly fifty imperatives in the letter's 108 verses. James wants believers to "be doers of the word, and not hearers only" (Jas. 1:22). Believers have been brought forth "by the word of truth" (Jas. 1:18), which should be understood as the gospel message. They have received "the implanted word," which uproots the power of sin and leads to new growth in righteousness (Jas. 1:21). They are not to be a "hearer who forgets but a doer who acts" (Jas. 1:25). The royal law of Scripture is fulfilled in them: "You shall love your neighbor as yourself" (Jas. 2:8; cf. Lev. 19:18; Matt. 5:17). This imagery fulfills the prophetic hope that the new covenant community will be characterized by obedience (Jer. 31:34). James teaches that faith without works is dead (Jas. 2:14-26). Genuine faith comes to expression in observable actions that cause God to be glorified. James cites two Old Testament examples to support this: Abraham, when he offered up Isaac in obedience to God (Jas. 2:21-24; cf. Gen. 22:1-18; Heb. 11:17-19), and Rahab, the prostitute, when she acted in faith to aid God's people (Jas. 2:25-26; cf. Josh. 2:1-24; Heb. 11:31). James' teaching on works does not contradict Paul's later emphasis that "by grace you have been saved through faith ... not a result of works" (Eph. 2:8-9). Both authors agree that salvation is a gift of God's grace through faith in Christ. Both agree that works are not the basis of salvation, but the result of saving faith. As Paul himself immediately adds, "for we are his workmanship, created in Christ Jesus for good works, which God prepared beforehand, that we should walk in them" (Eph. 2:10).

James urges Christians to show the love of God in Christ by caring for the poor and vulnerable. Widows and orphans are the particular object of God's fatherly care (Jas. 1:27; cf. Deut. 10:18; 15:4-11; Ps. 68:5-6; Isa. 1:17; Jer. 7:5-7). The poor are to receive equal honor in the family of faith. The Christian community is to "show no partiality as you hold the faith in our Lord Jesus Christ" (Jas. 2:1). Believers are to display the character of God in an increasingly tense cultural environment. They must exercise restraint in their speech. They must maintain a unified witness and guard against any form of arrogance, jealousy, or selfish ambition. They are to display the wisdom of God in their life together, in contrast to violent religious nationalism on the one hand, and arrogant Roman imperialism on the other. The believing community calls everyone to faith in Christ and to display God's wisdom which is "first pure, then peaceable, gentle, open to reason, full of mercy and good fruits, impartial and sincere" (Jas. 3:17).

James cautions believers against a friendship with the world that would compromise their faith and witness (Jas. 4:4). They are to distance themselves from worldly passions and pleasures in order to remain dedicated to God. He warns them against trusting in the vanity of riches, defrauding workers for personal gain, and living in luxury and self-indulgence (Jas. 5:1-5). He closes his letter with an exhortation to pray for one another. He promises that God will answer with healing, forgiveness, and even the restoration of a wandering brother (Jas. 5:13-20).

Our summarizing statement for James on the timeline's map is "Put faith in Christ into action," with the following key verse: "Be doers of the word, and not hearers only" (Jas. 1:22). Being "doers of the word" is especially important when we live in a world filled with conflict. The Christian community presents an alternative vision of life according to God's wisdom. Truth is observed in action. You may recall that Jesus' Sermon on the Mount had ended with the promise: "Everyone then who hears these words of mine and does them will be like a wise man who built his house on the rock" (Matt. 7:24). The letter of James strongly emboldens us to do the same.

GALATIANS, written by Paul to the churches of Galatia (c. AD 48)

Our next New Testament letter is Galatians. This is Paul's first letter, written at the conclusion of his first missionary journey (AD 46-48). You may want to locate Galatians on the timeline's map so that you gain a sense of the vast geographical area included in the Roman province of Galatia. Paul and Barnabas had seen Christ's power throughout their missionary witness in the synagogues and cities of Galatia. When Paul proclaimed the gospel, Jews and Gentiles responded with faith in Christ (Acts 13-14). Paul's own experience on the Damascus road confirmed that both Jews and Gentiles stand in need of God's forgiveness. No one is righteous in God's sight, whether from good works or from works of the law ("deeds of Torah"). Christ's death on the cross has provided atonement for sin. Therefore, all who believe in Christ are justified ("declared right before God"). Faith in Christ defines the new covenant community. God confirmed this reality by filling new believers with the Holy Spirit (Acts 13:52; cf. Gal. 3:1-3).

The recognition that believing Gentiles are full members of God's covenant family by faith in Christ had life-changing and practical implications for Paul and these new believers. He did not compel Gentile converts to receive the old covenant sign of circumcision; nor did he require them to follow the dietary laws or to observe the festival calendar that had set Israel apart from the nations. Paul's theological position produced violent opposition from some of his kinsmen in Galatia. Some believing Jews even came down from Jerusalem, teaching that new Gentile believers must be circumcised and taught to live by Torah (Acts 15:1, 5). It is important to understand why they might have held such a view. These Jewish believers in Christ were motivated by their reading of Scripture, the weight of tradition, and the threat of persecution from their zealous kinsmen in Israel. They also sensed that Paul was offering to Gentiles all of the benefits of being incorporated into Israel without any of the costs. The infant churches of Galatia became unsettled and confused. For Paul, this teaching obscures the accomplishment of Christ's death and denies the necessity of the gospel for all. In response, he writes his impassioned first letter to the Galatians from Antioch in Syria around AD 48, shortly before the Jerusalem Council (Acts 15).

Paul begins his letter by asserting his authority as "an apostle—not from men nor through man, but through Jesus Christ and God the Father, who raised him from the dead" (Gal. 1:1). He does not stand alone, but with "all the brothers who are with me" (Gal. 1:2). He greets the churches of Galatia with his distinctive expression: "Grace to you and peace from God our Father and the Lord Jesus Christ" (Gal. 1:3). Paul joins together the customary Greek ("grace") and Hebrew ("peace") greetings within a unified theological confession of God the Father and the Lord Jesus Christ. He highlights the absolute uniqueness of Christ as the one "who gave himself for our sins to deliver us from the present evil age, according to the will of our God and Father" (Gal. 1:4). He is astonished that the Galatians are so quickly deserting "him who called you in the grace of Christ and are turning to a different gospel" (Gal. 1:6). He concludes with an imprecatory oath upon any who would preach another gospel (Gal. 1:9). Paul's thought in the letter to the Galatians develops primarily as a defense of the gospel. Chapters 1-2 describe Paul's own experience of the gospel. Chapters 3-4 appeal to the Galatians' experience of the gospel. Chapters 5-6 conclude with an exhortation to stand firm and live out the gospel of Christ in the power of the Spirit.

Paul begins with his own conversion (Gal. 1:10-24). Although he had been a violent persecutor of the church and zealous for his ancestral traditions, he testifies that God, "who had set me apart before I was born, and who called me by his grace, was pleased to reveal his Son to me" (Gal. 1:15-16). Paul received the gospel from the exalted Jesus who called him to carry his name to the nations (Acts 9:15; 13:46-47; 26:17-18). His preaching, therefore, did not depend on any human authority but on Christ's call. He explains to the Galatians that his understanding of the gospel had been recognized and affirmed by the leadership of the Jerusalem church during his visit to bring famine relief (Gal. 2:1-10). Peter, James, and John did not compel the Gentile Titus to be circumcised. Instead, they affirmed that God's grace had been upon Paul's ministry, so they gave him the right hand of fellowship (Gal. 2:9).

Paul ends his own experience of the gospel by recalling his conflict with Peter in Antioch (Gal. 2:11-21). Peter had been eating together with new Gentile believers in Christ (Gal. 2:12; cf. Acts 10). However, when certain men had come down from James in Jerusalem, Peter "separated himself, fearing the circumcision party. And the rest of the Jews acted hypocritically along with him" (Gal. 2:12-13). Paul saw that such conduct was a denial of the gospel. He confronted Peter in public: "If you, though a Jew, live like a Gentile and not like a Jew, how can you force the Gentiles to live like Jews?" (Gal. 2:14). Peter must have blushed with shame. Paul did not leave his brother exposed, but quickly adds his own personal testimony in the first person plural: "We ourselves are Jews by birth and not Gentile sinners; yet we know that a person is not justified by works of the law but through faith in Jesus Christ, so we also have believed in Christ Jesus" (Gal. 2:15-16). Paul affirms that no one stands righteous before God on the basis of works of the law. The gospel reveals that Jews are sinners in need of forgiveness through Christ crucified, just like the

Gentiles. Paul ends his personal experience with a memorable formulation of new life in Christ:

> I have been crucified with Christ. It is no longer I who live, but Christ who lives in me. And the life I now live in the flesh I live by faith in the Son of God, who loved me and gave himself for me. I do not nullify the grace of God, for if righteousness were through the law, then Christ died for no purpose. (Gal. 2:20-21)

Paul then appeals to the Galatians' own experience of the gospel. He begins with their conversion (Gal. 3:1-5) and asks with alarm: "Who has bewitched you?" (Gal. 3:1). They had been taught clearly about Christ crucified for their sins. They had received the Holy Spirit as confirmation of their adoption into God's family. Paul asks: "Did you receive the Spirit by works of the law or by hearing with faith? ... Having begun by the Spirit, are you now being perfected by the flesh?" (Gal. 3:2-3). These questions introduce two contrasting pairs that are vital for understanding Paul's letters. "Works of the law" (lit. "deeds of Torah") are contrasted with "hearing with faith." Similarly, the term "flesh" is contrasted with the "Spirit." The particular "works of the law" highlighted in this passage are circumcision and the dietary laws. Such observances had defined the covenant community in Israel as separate from the pagan world for millennia (Gen. 17:9-14; Lev. 20:26). Paul contends that the new covenant community is defined by faith in Christ and comprised of believing Jews and Gentiles, who are no longer separated but have become one in Christ. This new covenant community is not distinguished by the flesh of ethnicity or race, but by the indwelling presence of the Holy Spirit.

Paul reasons from Scripture that what the Galatians have experienced is God's own plan of redemption and the fulfillment of his ancient promise to Abraham. In our study of the Old Testament we learned that Abraham was justified by faith as a gift (Gen. 15:6; cf. Gal. 3:6). Paul emphasizes that Abraham was declared righteous before God by faith, prior to receiving the sign of circumcision and before the law was given at Mount Sinai. Abraham is an important figure in God's redemptive plan because he receives the gracious gift of justification by faith apart from works of the law. He becomes the model, therefore, for one who is justified by faith. God had in fact promised to bless all the families of the earth "along with Abraham, the man of faith" (Gal. 3:8-9; cf. Gen. 12:3; 22:18). Paul recognizes that in this way God proclaimed the gospel beforehand to Abraham. He therefore urges the Galatians: "It is those of faith who are the sons of Abraham" (Gal. 3:7). All who believe in Christ experience the promised blessing of God and are full members of God's people by faith.

Paul emphasizes the priority of this blessing upon Abraham. He explains that even though God had graciously given the law to Abraham's descendants, the law does not become the means of obtaining God's promise (Gal. 3:17-18). He knows from Scripture and his own life that Israel's experience under the law had actually brought them under God's wrath. The law had pronounced the covenant curse on anyone who did not abide by "all things written in the Book of the Law, and do them" (Gal. 3:10; cf. Deut. 27:26; Jer. 11:3-12). Israel had disobeyed God's commandments and was removed from the land into exile by divine discipline. Paul teaches that Israel's own history demonstrates that justification does not come through the law (Gal. 2:16; cf. Rom. 3:20, 28). Instead of boasting in the law (Gal. 3:12; cf. Lev. 18:5), the righteous must live by faith in God's promise just like Abraham (Gal. 3:11; cf. Hab. 2:4).

Paul explains further that God's solution for Israel's disobedience and the curse that results is found in the crucified Messiah: "Christ redeemed us from the curse of the law by becoming a curse for us—for it is written, 'Cursed is everyone who is hanged on a tree'—so that in Christ Jesus the blessing of Abraham might come to the Gentiles, so that we might receive the promised Spirit through faith" (Gal. 3:13-14). Paul teaches the Galatians that the solution to Israel's disobedience and theirs is found at the cross, when Jesus hangs on a "tree" (Gal. 3:13; cf. Deut. 21:23; Acts 5:30; 10:39; 1 Pet. 2:24). Jesus absorbs God's wrath in place of the guilty and obtains forgiveness of sins for all who believe. The cross secures redemption from the curse of the law so that God's blessing to Abraham might extend to the nations (Gal. 3:14). Jesus is the "seed" of Abraham through whom the promise has been fulfilled (Gal. 3:16, 19; cf. Gen. 18:18; 26:4). Therefore, all who believe in Christ, both Jews and Gentiles, are one people of God, part of Abraham's family of faith. He powerfully concludes: "If you are Christ's, then you are Abraham's offspring, heirs according to promise" (Gal. 3:29; cf. Rom. 9:6-8).

All who believe in Christ receive full adoption as God sends forth "the Spirit of his Son into our hearts, crying 'Abba! Father'" (Gal. 4:4-6).

Galatians ends with a stirring exhortation to stand firm and live out the gospel in the power of the Spirit (Gal. 5:1). Paul warns his readers with irony not to submit to a yoke of slavery. He testifies that those who receive circumcision would be "severed from Christ" (Gal. 5:4). At the same time, he exhorts the Galatians not to use their freedom in Christ to indulge their flesh (Gal. 5:13). Paul strongly contrasts the works of the flesh with the fruit of the Spirit (Gal. 5:16-23). Believers must crucify the flesh with its passions and desires in order to live by the Spirit (Gal. 5:24-25). The fruitful new covenant community fulfills the Torah in the power of the Spirit by faith working through love (Gal. 5:6, 14; 6:8; cf. Jer. 31:33-34; Ezek. 36:27; Rom. 8:4). Paul affirms at the end that in Christ, "neither circumcision counts for anything, nor uncircumcision, but a new creation" (Gal. 6:15).

Our summarizing statement for Galatians on the timeline's map is "No other gospel than Christ," with the following key verse: "If we or an angel from heaven should preach to you a gospel contrary to the one we preached to you, let him be accursed" (Gal. 1:8). We must guard against anything that would obscure or relativize the person and work of Christ. The accomplishment of his death is complete. His resurrection marks the beginning of the new creation. Nothing can be supplemented without diminishing the gospel. Taking our stand on the gospel means that repentance and faith are required for everyone, whether indifferent pagans or the culturally religious. Entering into the new covenant community is a public act that creates new relationships in Christ. There are no private paths to following Christ that would exempt us from persecution or suffering. Instead, new covenant believers, both Jews and Gentiles, experience God's plan of redemption in Christ as they are filled with the Holy Spirit and walk in his ways together.

1-2 THESSALONIANS, written by Paul to the church at Thessalonica (c. AD 51-52)

We now turn to consider Paul's letters written on his second missionary journey. 1-2 Thessalonians are the two letters written by Paul near the end of his journey into Europe (AD 49-52). It would be helpful for you to locate

1-2 Thessalonians on the timeline's map. You should notice the great distance between Thessalonica and Jerusalem. The missionary expansion of the church fulfills Jesus' promise in Acts 1:8. When Paul had first arrived at Thessalonica (Acts 17), the city was the capital of the Roman province of Macedonia with a population of around 200,000. Paul was invited to preach in the synagogue. He reasoned from Scripture that the Messiah had to suffer and be raised from the dead, and claimed "this Jesus whom I proclaim to you is the Christ" (Acts 17:3). Many Jews, God-fearing Greeks, and several prominent women responded with faith (Acts 17:4). Others became zealous for their ancestral traditions and accused the missionaries of "acting against the decrees of Caesar, saying that there is another king, Jesus" (Acts 17:7). Despite intense opposition, Jesus established his church in Thessalonica. Paul and his companions, however, were forced suddenly to leave the city. They traveled south into central Greece, praying that the new Thessalonian believers would stand firm in Christ.

When they reached Athens, Paul sends Timothy to visit them "when I could bear it no longer, I sent to learn about your faith, for fear that somehow the tempter had tempted you and our labor would be in vain" (1 Thess. 3:5). After rejoining Paul in Corinth, Timothy brings "the good news of your faith and love" (1 Thess. 3:6). Paul is greatly comforted by news of the Thessalonians' strong faith in Christ and he confesses: "Now we live, if you are standing fast in the Lord" (1 Thess. 3:8). At the same time, Timothy shares specific questions and pastoral concerns that the young church in Thessalonica now faces. In response, Paul, Timothy, and Silas send two letters, known as 1-2 Thessalonians, to encourage their faith and provide further instruction on living for Christ.

After the greeting of grace and peace from God the Father and the Lord Jesus Christ, Paul opens with thanksgiving to God for "your work of faith and labor of love and steadfastness of hope in our Lord Jesus Christ" (1 Thess. 1:3). This is the first occurrence of the triad of virtues: faith, love, and hope that Paul uses to summarize the Christian life. Faith in Jesus Christ defines the community, love is the outward expression of faith in action, and hope is the future orientation of believers in anticipation of Christ's glorious return. Paul graciously applies Israel's language of election (being "chosen") to the entire believing community (1 Thess. 1:4), indicating that Jews and Gentiles are one in Christ. The Holy Spirit confirms their election and adoption (1 Thess. 1:5). By the power of the Spirit, the Thessalonian believers "became imitators of us and of the Lord," so that they have become an example to all the believers in Macedonia and Achaia (1 Thess. 1:6-7). The Thessalonian believers have "turned to God from idols," now serving the living and true God (1 Thess. 1:9). Their new life together anticipates the glorious return of "his Son from heaven, whom he raised from the dead, Jesus who delivers us from the wrath to come" (1 Thess. 1:10).

The letter continues with a moving description of authentic gospel ministry (1 Thess. 2-3). Paul and his co-workers declared the gospel in the midst of much conflict. They appealed to them without impure motives, greed, or vainglory (1 Thess. 2:3-6). He recalls that they "were gentle among you, like a nursing mother taking care of her own children" (1 Thess. 2:7). They were affectionate, ready to share not only the gospel of God, but also their own lives. They worked hard to support themselves and not burden the growing community. Paul also compares their ministry to a father's care, saying, "Like a father with his children, we exhorted each one of you and encouraged you and charged you to walk in a manner worthy of God, who calls you into his own kingdom and glory" (1 Thess. 2:11-12). Though suddenly torn away, the missionaries longed to see the believers at Thessalonica and further instruct them in their new faith in Christ (1 Thess. 2:17; 3:10). Until that day, they pray that "the Lord make you increase and abound in love for one another and for all, as we do for you, so that he may establish your hearts blameless in holiness before our God and Father, at the coming of our Lord Jesus with all his saints" (1 Thess. 3:12-13).

1 Thessalonians ends with a series of exhortations on living for Christ. Believers are urged "to walk and to please God" (1 Thess. 4:1). This language reflects the Hebrew idiom "to walk with God," used of Enoch, Noah, Abraham, and Isaac (Gen. 5:22-24; 6:9; 17:1; 48:15). Paul reminds the Thessalonian believers that their new life in Christ connects them with a new heritage, a new community, and an entirely new pattern of living. After their conversion, the will of God is for their holiness (1 Thess. 4:3). Paul applies God's command in the Old Testament, "You shall be holy, for I the

LORD your God am holy" (Lev. 19:2), to the new covenant community. Their new relationship with a holy God means abstaining from sexual immorality and passionate lust, in contrast with the nations who do not know God (1 Thess. 4:3-5; cf. Lev. 18). Their new relationships with one another should be characterized by brotherly love, revealing that they have been taught by God (1 Thess. 4:9; cf. Isa. 54:13).

Finally, Paul instructs the Thessalonians about the certainty of Christian hope in Christ's return. Apparently some members of the new community had died; Paul gives instructions so that the church might not grieve as those without hope (1 Thess. 4:13). He reassures them that Jesus died and rose again, and he will bring with him those who have fallen asleep when he returns. The Lord will descend from heaven and the dead in Christ will rise first. Then, those who are still alive will join them in the clouds of divine glory to greet their returning Lord (1 Thess. 4:14-17). The imagery depicts the arrival of a great dignitary to a city. Loyal inhabitants would rush out in advance to meet him and then accompany him into the city. Believers are to encourage one another with this hope. They are to conduct themselves in faith, love, and hope, knowing they are not destined for wrath but for salvation (1 Thess. 5:5-9). The letter ends with a series of imperatives and with the prayer that "the God of peace himself sanctify you completely, and may your whole spirit and soul and body be kept blameless at the coming of our Lord Jesus Christ" (1 Thess. 5:23).

2 Thessalonians is written shortly after the first letter had been written. In his second letter, Paul continues many principal ideas from his first letter (2 Thess. 2:15). Paul and his missionary companions thank God because the Thessalonians' faith in Christ and love for one another is growing (2 Thess. 1:3). They have remained steadfast in the face of persecutions and afflictions, with eager anticipation of seeing Christ "when he comes on that day to be glorified in his saints, and to be marveled at among all who have believed" (2 Thess. 1:10). The biblical teaching about the return of Christ requires patient instruction. Remember that Israel was the only people group in the ancient world who believed in a bodily resurrection from the dead (see Isa. 25:8-9; Ezek. 37; Dan. 12:1-2). The Greco-Roman world held no such belief, offering only Plato's disembodied, eternal soul or Epicurus' body decomposing in the ground. A common gravestone inscription in the Roman Empire

was, "I was not, I was, I am not, I care not" (*non fui, fui, non sum, non curo*). In Scripture, the hope of resurrection is connected with the return from exile and the day of the Lord. Thessalonian believers were exposed to false teaching that claimed that the day of the Lord had already come. Paul, Timothy, and Silas warn that such teaching does not come from them. There will be a great increase in lawlessness, wickedness, and deception before Christ's glorious return (2 Thess. 2:3-12). In stark contrast, the Thessalonian Christians are chosen and beloved by God. They are "the firstfruits to be saved through sanctification by the Spirit and belief in the truth" (2 Thess. 2:13). They have been called through the gospel to obtain the glory of the Lord Jesus Christ. They must "stand firm and hold to the traditions that you were taught by us" (2 Thess. 2:15; cf. 2 Thess. 3:6). The dictated letter ends with a greeting written with Paul's own hand, probably in large letters with his distinctive script (2 Thess. 3:17; cf. Gal. 6:11). As with all of his letters, Paul's closing words echo his introduction by restating the unique treasure of the Christian community: "The grace of our Lord Jesus Christ be with you all" (2 Thess. 3:18).

Our summarizing statement for 1-2 Thessalonians on the timeline's map is "Live for Christ's return," with the following key verse: "Now may the God of peace himself sanctify you completely, and may your whole spirit and soul and body be kept blameless at the coming of our Lord Jesus Christ" (1 Thess. 5:23). The young church in Thessalonica experienced true conversion when they responded to the gospel with faith in Christ. Their faith was demonstrated in their new love for God and for one another. They remained steadfast in the midst of persecution and affliction, sustained by the hope of Christ's return. They are encouraged now to live in pursuit of holiness while spreading the gospel in anticipation of seeing Christ face-to-face. Paul's inspired letters continue to teach all who read them today.

1-2 CORINTHIANS, written by Paul to the church at Corinth (c. AD 55-56)

We now turn to consider the letters written by Paul on his third missionary journey (AD 52-57). 1-2 Corinthians are the two letters written to the church in Corinth by Paul and Sosthenes (1 Cor. 1:1), and by Paul and Timothy (2 Cor. 1:1). These two letters were written while Paul was in Ephesus (1 Corinthians), and later in Macedonia (2 Corinthians). You should locate Corinth on the timeline's map. You may recall that Paul had first arrived in Corinth toward the end of his second missionary journey after his intense visit to Athens (Acts 18:1-11). Corinth was overwhelming and utterly unreached with the gospel. The city had an established reputation as a commercial city of wealth, immorality, and idolatry. Yet Jesus had established his church there, and he had even told Paul in a vision that he had many people in the city (Acts 18:10). Paul remained in Corinth for a year and a half (AD 50-52), working closely with Aquila and Priscilla, Silas and Timothy, Crispus and Sosthenes (Acts 18:1-11). Over this time, the new community of believing Jews and Gentiles became very dear to him. Paul was intimately aware of the cultural and spiritual challenges facing these new believers.

After a brief return to Antioch, Paul began his third missionary journey and remained in Ephesus for three years (Acts 20:31). While in Ephesus, Paul exchanges a series of letters with the Corinthian church whom he loved. He had learned about divisions and immorality that were affecting the church (1 Cor. 1:10-11). The church was divided over spiritual leadership and the implications of the gospel for discipleship and Christian community. Paul wrote a letter that the church should not treat sexual immorality lightly, since such conduct discredits the gospel (1 Cor. 5:9; cf. 1 Thess. 4:3; 2 Thess. 3:6, 14). The Corinthians sent a letter in reply to Paul with several specific questions (1 Cor. 7:1). The letter was delivered by Stephanas, Fortunatus, and Achaicus (1 Cor. 16:17). Paul then writes the letter that we call 1 Corinthians (c. AD 55), to answer their questions and make a strong appeal for unity in Christ.

1 Corinthians opens as Paul affirms that he is an apostle of Christ Jesus by the will of God (1 Cor. 1:1). He writes in unity with his brother Sosthenes, who had served as the ruler of the synagogue in Corinth (Acts 18:17). Together they address the church in Corinth as those made holy in Christ and called to be holy (1 Cor. 1:2; cf. Exod. 19:6; Lev. 19:2; Isa. 62:12). Paul's opening thanksgiving reflects the key New Testament beliefs that unite early Christian mission and teaching (1 Cor. 1:4-9). Paul holds the conviction that Jesus is the Messiah, Christ the Lord. The Corinthians have been justified by faith. The Holy Spirit and his gifts are present in power. Jews and Gentiles are one in Christ through the gospel, and together they are called into the fellowship of Jesus Christ their Lord (1 Cor. 1:9). The obedience of faith among the nations is demonstrated in their speech, knowledge, and conduct. As living sacrifices

holy to the LORD, they are sustained to the end, and are guiltless before God. The return of Christ in glory as Judge orients the new community forward as they await "the day of our Lord Jesus Christ" (1 Cor. 1:8).

Paul raises one of his primary concerns by appealing to the Corinthians "that all of you agree, and that there be no divisions among you, but that you be united in the same mind and the same judgment" (1 Cor. 1:10). Paul develops this concern for unity with rhetorical skill. Paul humbles himself before his beloved congregation, and makes the bold assertion that effective preaching rests on the power of the gospel, not on the eloquence of the speaker (1 Cor. 1:17). He reminds them that the cross of Christ appears as folly, yet it is the power of God for salvation (1 Cor. 1:18). He points out that not one of them is wise, powerful, or of noble birth, but God has chosen the weak, the lowly, and despised to reveal Christ in order that all boasting might be in him alone (1 Cor. 1:26-31; cf. Jer. 9:23-24). Paul wishes that they were full of the Spirit, but finds them thinking and acting according to the flesh (1 Cor. 3:1). They are full of jealousy, strife, and immorality, and yet somehow they are proud! He concludes with a series of questions: "Do you not know that the unrighteous will not inherit the kingdom of God?" (1 Cor. 6:9). "Do you not know that your bodies are members of Christ?" (1 Cor. 6:15). "Do you not know that your body is a temple of the Holy Spirit?" (1 Cor. 6:19). He forcefully concludes: "You are not your own, for you were bought with a price. So glorify God in your body" (1 Cor. 6:19-20).

In the remaining sections of his letter, Paul addresses the topics about which the Corinthians had written (1 Cor. 7:1). He systematically addresses their key issues in an effort to unite the church in Christ. He responds to their questions about marriage (1 Cor. 7), food sacrificed to idols (1 Cor. 8-10), unity in worship and the Lord's Supper (1 Cor. 11), spiritual gifts (1 Cor. 12-14), the resurrection (1 Cor. 15), and the regular collection of money to support the work of Christ (1 Cor. 16). These practical topics affect the character, life, and witness of the local church in the world. Regarding marriage, Paul instructs the Corinthians to fidelity in their marriages and to avoid divorce. At the same time, he endorses singleness as a genuine expression of following Jesus. He reminds them that marriage is a powerful witness to the gospel in an immoral age. Regarding food sacrificed to idols, Paul urges the Corinthians to abandon all associations with idolatry: "You cannot drink the cup of the Lord and the cup of demons. You cannot partake of the table of the Lord and the table of demons" (1 Cor. 10:21). Some of the Corinthian Christians apparently felt free to continue their participation in pagan ritual meals and were causing others to stumble. Paul does allow food sold in the marketplace to be eaten. He also teaches them to eat whatever is set before them by an unbeliever if it allows them the opportunity of sharing the gospel over a meal (1 Cor. 10:25-28). He tells them to prefer others more than to exercise their rights. He admonishes them that "whatever you do, do all to the glory of God" (1 Cor. 10:31). Regarding the Lord's Supper, he instructs the church to come together in unity as they "proclaim the Lord's death until he comes" (1 Cor. 11:17-34). Regarding spiritual gifts, he explains that they are to be exercised in love, so that the church is built up (1 Cor. 12-14).

Regarding the resurrection, Paul views the death and resurrection of Christ as a matter of first importance for the gospel (1 Cor. 15:3-4). Without Christ's resurrection, believers remain in their sins and have believed in vain (1 Cor. 15:17-19). Christ's resurrection marks the beginning of God's new creation and reveals Christ as Lord; it provides the example and guarantee of a future resurrection for all believers (1 Cor. 15:20-21). Paul encourages the church, affirming that in Christ believers will be clothed with immortality and inherit an everlasting kingdom when death is swallowed up in victory (1 Cor. 15:50-58). Believers gather on Sunday, the first day of the week, in remembrance of Christ's resurrection (1 Cor. 16:2). Lastly, regarding the regular collection of money, Paul instructs them to take a weekly collection (1 Cor. 16:1). This collection advances global mission and reinforces the unity of the body of Christ. The letter concludes with a final exhortation to stand firm, followed by personal greetings from sister churches and fellow believers (1 Cor. 16:12-20). Paul appends a greeting written with his own hand, confirming his love for them in Christ (1 Cor. 16:24).

2 Corinthians is written approximately one year later in AD 56 from Macedonia, after Paul had left Ephesus with the resolve to visit the Corinthians in person (Acts 20:1; cf. 2 Cor. 2:13). This is a deeply emotional letter in which Paul defends the authenticity and character of true ministry. During Paul's prolonged absence, the church at Corinth had become attracted to certain "super-apostles" who offered discipleship without suffering and who appeared more impressive than Paul in their appearance, speech, and pedi-

gree (2 Cor. 11:5; 12:11). These "false apostles" boasted about their eloquence and ministry technique. They appear to boast in their Hebraic ancestry and knowledge of Scripture (2 Cor. 11:22). Paul had made a brief, painful visit after writing 1 Corinthians (2 Cor. 2:1). Now he plans to visit them for the third time (2 Cor. 13:1). He writes 2 Corinthians in advance of his visit in hope that they might repent of their folly and embrace Christ's death and resurrection as the controlling vision of their life together.

Paul begins by thanking the "God of all comfort, who comforts us in all our afflictions" (2 Cor. 1:3-4). Genuine ministers experience trial, affliction, and suffering in the cause of Christ. Paul hopes that the Corinthians would not despise, but embrace Christ's sufferings so that they might experience Christ's comfort. He distances himself from ministry impostors by "the testimony of our conscience, that we behaved in the world with simplicity and godly sincerity" (2 Cor. 1:12). He cites his own conduct in that "we are not, like so many, peddlers of God's word, but as men of sincerity" (2 Cor. 2:17). He asserts: "We have renounced disgraceful, underhanded ways. We refuse to practice cunning or to tamper with God's word, but by the open statement of the truth we would commend ourselves to everyone's conscience in the sight of God" (2 Cor. 4:2). Paul boasts that the gospel treasure is placed in "jars of clay, to show that the surpassing power belongs to God and not to us" (2 Cor. 4:7). Real ministry is compelled by the love of Christ "that those who live might no longer live for themselves but for him who for their sake died and was raised" (2 Cor. 5:14-15). Paul urges the Corinthians to be reconciled to God in Christ and to receive his true ambassadors (2 Cor. 5:16-21). He warns them against evaluating spiritual leaders from a human point of view. Christ and his genuine followers are recognized by suffering and vindication, dying and being raised, sorrowful yet always rejoicing, as poor yet making many rich, as having nothing yet possessing everything (2 Cor. 6:1-13). He calls the Corinthians to repentance and holiness (2 Cor. 7), and encourages them to give generously in the relief of the saints, not for Paul's personal benefit but for the cause of global mission (2 Cor. 8:4). He warns them against those who seek to enrich themselves by ministry and boast only in their successes. Paul boasts in his weakness "so that the power of Christ may rest upon me. For the sake of Christ, then, I am content with weaknesses, insults, hardships, persecutions, and calamities. For when I am weak, then I am strong" (2 Cor. 12:9-10). His emotional letter ends with an appeal for the Corinthians to examine themselves and aim for restoration (2 Cor. 13:5, 11). Paul closes with personal greetings and his prayer that "the grace of the Lord Jesus Christ and the love of God and the fellowship of the Holy Spirit be with you all" (2 Cor. 13:14). Despite the painful urgency and agonized tone, the Spirit of God uses this letter to humble the proud, young church. Paul will shortly be reconciled with the Corinthians upon his arrival in the city in AD 57. From there and with their support, he will journey to Jerusalem, Rome, and Spain.

Our summarizing statement for 1-2 Corinthians on the timeline's map is an emphatic "Do all for the glory of Christ," with the following key verse: "Whether you eat or drink, or whatever you do, do all to the glory of God" (1 Cor. 10:31). Paul's letters to the growing church at Corinth reveal the powerful temptations of worldliness, division, and spiritual pride that can devastate the church. Paul's letters point relentlessly toward Christ and his crucifixion as the controlling paradigm of spiritual leadership and genuine discipleship. Authentic ministry advances by the preaching of the gospel of Christ crucified. Godly leadership relies upon the power of the Spirit, with an attitude of humility, rather than the techniques of man. Enduring commitment to local congregations presses through dark times of difficulty into the bright light of sanctification where new mission is born.

ROMANS, written by Paul to the church in Rome (AD 57)

We now turn to Paul's third letter written near the end of his third missionary journey. When Paul returns to Corinth in January AD 57, he finds a community that has received his rebuke in love. Over the next three months (Acts 20:3), Paul is supported, refreshed, and encouraged by the Corinthian church. Paul has served the exalted Jesus for nearly twenty-five years in an expanding witness across great distances and cultural divides. He has grown familiar with common objections to Christian faith and the challenges of communicating the gospel to all kinds of people. He has seen the Lord open the hearts of fellow Jews and idolatrous Gentiles to new life in Christ. He has become intimately aware of the challenges facing new believers as they learn a new way of life together in holiness. He also knows that the church would face persecution from the surrounding society, and false teaching from those who misunderstood the implications of the gospel. He has clarified his preaching and teaching in hundreds of sermons and thousands of lectures in Ephesus. He has deepened his conviction that the church is God's renewed humanity in Christ through his recent experience with the Corinthians.

At this important juncture in his ministry, Paul, probably in his early fifties, begins to contemplate even more distant shores. He desires to preach where Christ remains yet unknown (Rom. 15:20-21; cf. Isa. 52:15). He longs to herald the arrival of the Messiah to the coastlands that stood waiting for him (cf. Pss. 2:8; 72:8; Isa. 42:4; 49:6). He first resolves to display the fruit of his ministry in person through the offering of the Gentiles in Jerusalem at Pentecost (Rom. 15:16, 25). He then hopes to reach the uttermost limit of the western Mediterranean world, the Roman province *Hispania*, which we know today as Spain. To accomplish such a mission, he would need the support of the Christian community in the imperial capital of Rome (Rom. 15:24). He would need them to embrace his presentation of the gospel and vision of the church comprised of Jews and Gentiles united through faith in Christ. Therefore, in advance of his personal visit, Paul introduces himself and his gospel ministry with a letter. This letter, which we call Romans, is dictated to Tertius and entrusted for delivery into the hands of a faithful woman named Phoebe, who holds the office of deacon in the neighboring church of Cenchreae (Rom. 16:1, 22).

Romans is Paul's longest letter and his most complete statement of the Christian gospel. Paul's divinely inspired presentation of the gospel in Romans has influenced Christian faith, theology, and preaching beyond our ability to measure. Paul identifies himself as "set apart for the gospel of God" (Rom. 1:1; cf. Acts 13:2). He affirms that the gospel had been "promised beforehand through his prophets in the holy Scriptures" (Rom 1:2). The gospel is about God's Son, Jesus Christ our Lord, "who was descended from David according to the flesh and was declared to be the Son of God in power according to the Spirit of holiness by his resurrection from the dead" (Rom. 1:3-4). The gospel of Jesus Christ offers grace and apostleship "to bring about the obedience of faith for the sake of his name among all the nations" (Rom. 1:5). God's good news about his Son contains grace and mission, justification and sanctification, the salvation of humanity and the glory of God. In a programmatic statement for Romans, Paul confesses:

> I am under obligation both to Greeks and to barbarians, both to the wise and to the foolish. So I am eager to preach the gospel to you also who are in Rome. For I am not ashamed of the gospel, for it is the power of God for salvation to everyone who believes, to the Jew first and also to the Greek. For in it the righteousness of God is revealed from faith for faith. (Rom. 1:14-17)

Paul considers himself under sacred obligation to all people, cultured and uncultured, wise and foolish. He stands eager to preach the gospel in Rome. The Roman orator Cicero described crucifixion as so shameful that the very word "cross" (*crux*) should never be associated with a Roman citizen, but far removed from even his thoughts, eyes, and ears. The apostle Paul feels no shame over the gospel of Christ crucified. He knows that the gospel is God's power for salvation. This is true for everyone who believes, whether Jews or Gentiles. The gospel is God's power for salvation to all who believe because the righteousness of God is revealed by faith at the cross of Christ. Paul's thought in Romans develops the principal ideas and key terms expressed in these opening verses. The gospel of Christ's death and resurrection reveals the righteousness of God for sinful humanity. Jews and Gentiles are justified by faith through the atoning death of Christ. Together they are called into God's renewed humanity, sanctified by the Holy Spirit, empowered for the obedience of faith, and invited to join God's mission in the world.

Paul's first step in announcing the gospel is to expose the universal need for the gospel. In Rom. 1:18-3:20, the unrighteousness of all humanity—both Jews and Gentiles—provides the necessary context for recognizing the righteousness of God revealed at the cross. Paul begins by asserting that the righteous wrath of God is presently revealed against an unrighteous humanity (Rom. 1:18-32). Although clear evidence for God's power and nature are demonstrated in God's creation, people actively suppress such knowledge, failing to honor or even thank God. They have even exchanged the worship of the living God for idolatrous worship of mortal men, like deified emperors in Rome, or images of animals and reptiles, as seen in popular Egyptian religion of the time. Paul explains, therefore, that humans have exchanged the truth of God for a lie, reminiscent of humanity's original fall (Gen. 3). As a result, God has given humanity over to an unrestrained dishonoring of their bodies in all manner of sexual immorality. God has given them over to a debased mind that yields all varieties of evil practices and the inability to recognize and approve what is good. Human beings, made in the image of God, have become degraded, defaced and dishonored.

Many devout Israelites would have readily affirmed such condemnation of pagan idolatry and immorality. In Rom. 2, however, Paul condemns his own people, including himself. He writes that those who would judge others actually commit the same types of sin. Beginning in Rom. 2:17, he takes aim at Jewish religious pride in possessing the Torah and rehearses the reality of their disobedience to God's commands. He asks whether Jews are better than Gentiles, and humbly acknowledges "both Jews and Greeks are under sin" (Rom. 3:9). You may recall that Israel's central and pervasive problem in the Old Testament was idolatry (Exod. 32-34; Isa. 40-45; Jer. 2:11; 10:1-16, etc.). We have seen that Israel displays the human plight since Adam is in them. With the witness of the Old Testament, Paul realizes that none is righteous, not even one (Rom. 3:10-18; cf. Ps.14:1-3). Paul's reading of Scripture shows that Israel also rightly falls under God's righteous wrath, as seen in 586 BC when God's people were taken into exile for their disobedience to his commands (Jer. 11; Ezek. 18). Paul asserts, therefore, that no one will be justified in God's sight by works of the law, but rather, the law exposes sin in the human heart (Rom. 3:19-20). He forcefully concludes that the whole world is accountable to God (Rom. 3:19).

Against the dark plight of idolatrous pagans and disobedient Israelites, the bright light of the gospel shines forth (Rom. 3:21-5:21). The righteousness of God is now revealed "through faith in Jesus Christ for all who believe" (Rom. 3:22). Paul states emphatically that there is no distinction when it comes to sin and guilt before God: "All have sinned and fall short of (lit. "lack") the glory of God" (Rom. 3:23). Amidst the human plight of sin and loss of glory, God's solution is that all who believe "are justified by his grace as a gift, through the redemption that is Christ Jesus" (Rom. 3:24). Christ's redemption recalls the redemption from slavery in Egypt at the Exodus. His blood is like the blood of the Passover lamb, when God caused his wrath to "pass-over" his people. God put forward his Son as the atoning sacrifice for sin. He is the mercy seat, where God's wrath against sin is absorbed and forgiveness of sins is obtained (Rom. 3:25; cf. Exod. 25:17; Lev. 16:2). On the cross, the wrath of God is poured out on Christ, revealing God's public and righteous condemnation of sin. The death of Christ provides substitutionary atonement so that God "might be just and the justifier of the one who has faith in Jesus" (Rom. 3:26). Justification by faith is one of the greatest treasures of Christian theology. The ground near the cross is bloodstained, yet level. There is no room for boasting, except in Christ alone (Rom. 3:27; cf. Gal. 6:14). The work of Christ on the cross is necessary and complete for all who believe. It cannot be supplemented without being diminished. Here Jews and Gentiles alike are declared righteous by faith in Christ alone.

In Rom. 4, Paul turns to Israel's forefather Abraham to reveal God's consistent intention to justify the ungodly by faith (Rom. 4:1-5; cf. Gen. 15:6). In our study of the Old Testament we learned that Abraham, an ungodly man, was justified when he believed in God (Gen. 15:6). God had promised him many descendants, even though he was elderly and his wife was barren (Gen. 11:30; 18:11). Yet in spite of his circumstances, Abraham believed that God would perform what he had promised. He had "resurrection faith," being fully assured that God could bring life out of that which was dead (Rom. 4:18-21). God justifies Abraham as a gift of grace since the patriarch had not done any "works" to deserve or merit this verdict. Paul cites King David as another example of someone who had known the blessing of undeserved forgiveness, citing Ps. 32 (Rom. 4:6-8). These two Old Testament figures experience the grace of God. Paul presses further to announce that Abraham's promised descendants are those who share his faith, whether Jews or Gentiles, whether physically circumcised or uncircumcised (Rom. 4:11-12, 23-25). Believers are reckoned as Abraham's descendants, heirs of the world according to God's gracious promise. The inclusion of the nations by faith in Christ fulfills God's promise to Abraham, that he would be the father of "many nations" (Rom. 4:17; cf. Gen. 17:5).

Having been justified by faith, believers have "peace with God through our Lord Jesus Christ" (Rom. 5:1; cf. Isa. 53:5). God's presence and peace shine upon them (see Num. 6:24-26). They have obtained access to God and stand in his grace, united as his covenant people. Together believers rejoice in the hope of the glory of God as well as in their present sufferings, knowing that under God's sovereign hand they will produce endurance, character, and hope (Rom. 5:2-5; 8:28). God's love for his people has been forever demonstrated at the cross of Christ (Rom. 5:6-8), and they now boast in him alone (Rom. 5:11; cf. Gal. 6:14).

Paul's letter reaches an initial climax with an extended comparison of Adam and Christ (Rom. 5:12-21). Paul has in view the account of Adam in the garden, when the first man disobeyed God's command, resulting in death (Gen. 2-3). Since all human beings are descended from Adam, they, too, share in the reality of sin and death (Rom. 5:12-14; cf. Gen. 4:1-16; 5:1-32; 6:1-5). Paul recalls this story, noting that through one man sin entered the world, and death through sin (Rom. 5:12). He explains further that because all human beings have sinned, they share the human plight of death (Rom. 5:15; cf. Rom. 6:23). Yet Paul finds the solution to the human story in the second Adam: for just as Adam's disobedience leads to death, so Christ's obedience brings life (Rom. 5:17-19; cf. 1 Cor. 15:21-22); just as Adam's trespass leads to condemnation, so Christ's righteousness leads to justification. Paul summarizes this succinctly: "For as by the one man's disobedience the many were made sinners, so by the one man's obedience the many will be made righteous" (Rom. 5:19; cf. Isa. 53:11-12). Righteousness is offered as a gift—the guilty are acquitted through the atoning death of Jesus, who became obedient unto death, even death on a cross. Jesus is the solution to the human plight of sin, death, and the loss of glory, but his gift can only be received by faith. Paul himself has experienced this new life in Christ. He now rehearses all that Christ has accomplished for the believers in Rome to ensure that the gospel defines their new life in Christ as well.

In Rom. 6-8, Paul describes the new life of the gospel. Believers now belong to Christ and are filled, sanctified, and empowered by the Holy Spirit. These chapters reveal Paul's pastoral conviction that justification leads to sanctification, that conversion brings transformation into Christ-likeness. He has been slanderously accused of promoting sin by the gospel of grace. This charge he emphatically rejects (Rom. 6:1-2; cf. Rom. 3:8; Gal. 2:17). In reality, Paul believes that union with Christ means that a person's old life has been crucified with Christ (Rom. 6:6; cf. Gal. 2:20). This is true for former pagans (Rom. 6) and for devout Israelites (Rom. 7). All must consider themselves dead to sin and alive with Christ, so that they might walk in newness of life (Rom. 6:4). Believers are not to obey their passions, but to present their bodies as instruments for righteousness (Rom. 6:13, 19). They have been set free from sin in order to become slaves of God, leading to sanctification and eternal life (Rom. 6:22; cf. Lev. 18:2-5; 19:2; John 3:16; 1 Thess. 4:3). Paul reminds his Israelite kinsmen in Rome that they too are called to die to their former life that they might have new life in Christ (Rom. 7:1-6). He recalls that though they possessed the divinely inspired Torah, their lives had been characterized by sinful passions and disobedience just like the Gentiles; they too are now to walk in newness of life.

In a moving autobiographical section that echoes Israel's own plight, Paul describes his former inability to obey God's holy, righteous, and good law due to his own indwelling sin (Rom. 7:9-24). Like Paul himself, Israel without Christ stands condemned just like the nations. In God's redemptive purpose, the law did not make Israel alive, but revealed the greatness of her sinfulness and need for atonement (Rom. 7:13-14; cf. Gal. 2:21; 3:21). The solution to the wrath of God is found at the cross, for Paul pronounces: "There is therefore now no condemnation for those who are in Christ Jesus" (Rom. 8:1). God has sent his own Son to condemn sin in the flesh "in order that the righteous requirement of the law might be fulfilled in us, who walk not according to the flesh but according to the Spirit" (Rom. 8:4). This conclusion is of immense significance for Paul's understanding of the gospel. Believing Jews and Gentiles are justified by the atoning death of Christ and are sanctified together in newness of life by the Spirit. Indwelling sin is now replaced with the indwelling Spirit (Rom. 8:11). The presence of the Holy Spirit brings life, peace, and new obedience.

Paul uses the important term "debtors" to describe their religious obligations owed to God (Rom. 8:12). This term was used in Israel for the things that are owed to God or ought to be done in glad obedience (see Matt. 6:12). Believers are no longer obligated to their sinful human condition, but to the Spirit who confirms their adoption into God's family (Rom. 8:12-16). The Holy Spirit empowers them to walk in God's ways. Such transformation fulfills the divinely inspired expectations of Israel's prophets (Jer. 31:33-34; Ezek. 36:25-27). This breathtaking reality causes Paul to look forward to the full realization of God's redemptive purpose when "the creation itself will be set free from its bondage to corruption and obtain the freedom of the glory of the children of God" (Rom. 8:21). In anticipation of that glorious future, the Holy Spirit helps God's people in their weakness, redeems their suffering, and assures them that "all things work together for good, for those who are called according to his purpose" (Rom. 8:28). Paul is confident that neither "death nor life, nor angels nor rulers, nor things present nor things to come, nor powers, nor height nor depth, nor anything else in all creation, will be able to separate us from the love of God in Christ Jesus our Lord" (Rom. 8:38-39). These are powerful words of encouragement and hope for us today.

The triumphant joy at the end of Rom. 8 is met with a depth of sorrow at the beginning of Rom. 9. Paul has seen significant response to the gospel among Jews and Gentiles. Yet he writes that he has "great sorrow and unceasing anguish in my heart" over his kinsmen according to the flesh (Rom. 9:2). He strains the limits of language to wish that he might be accursed and cut off from Christ for their sake (Rom. 9:3; cf. Exod. 32:32). Here lies a longing for the conversion of those we love that many of us have known. In Rom. 9-11, Paul confirms the absolute necessity of the gospel for Israel and the nations. These chapters are not an excursus or an abstract discussion of election. Rather, they form an important continuation of Pauls' presentation of the gospel "to the Jew first and also to the Greek" (Rom. 1:16). They provide further access to the goal of his missionary labors and the theological convictions that supported them. For Paul, the sovereign purposes of God are fulfilled in the gathered church of Jews and Gentiles who share belief in Israel's Messiah, Jesus Christ. Israel needs faith in Christ and to make room in her heart for the ingathering of the nations. The nations need faith in Christ and to make room in their heart for a new heritage intimately connected with the God of Israel.

Paul never stopped trying to reach his own people. He affirms the great gifts that God had bestowed upon Israel (Rom. 9:4-5). They were entrusted with the very words of God (Rom. 3:2). They had been adopted as God's son (Rom. 9:4; cf. Exod. 4:22). They had experienced God's glory at the Red Sea (Exod. 15:6). They had been made God's covenant partner and received his law on Mount Sinai (Exod. 19-20). They had been given the divine worship of the tabernacle and temple (Exod. 25-40). Israel held the storyline of God's redemptive purpose for the world from the patriarchs to the promise of the Messiah. Yet Paul warns that Israel cannot presume upon such privileges as a birthright, for inherent in God's promise to Abraham was the reality that not all his biological children were considered his descendants. God had told Abraham that "through Isaac shall your offspring be named" (Rom. 9:6; cf. Gen. 21:12), indicating that Abraham's children were those born according to promise. Paul draws out the significance of this for the believers in Rome: "it is not the children of the flesh who are the children of God, but the children of the promise are counted as offspring" (Rom. 9:8). This is vividly confirmed in the case of Isaac and of Jacob, who both received God's undeserved mercy.

Next, he reminds his kinsmen that God's mercy is sovereign. Israel received grace at the golden calf rather than the judgment that Pharaoh's hardened heart received. Finite human beings should not question God's will or justice, but stand in awe of his mercy upon all who call upon him. This is true for both Jews and Gentiles who now call upon the living God through the gospel. The nations of the world have been adopted into God's people and declared righteous through faith in Christ (Rom. 9:24-26, 30; cf. Hos. 1:10; 2:23). Israel must concede her own sinfulness as well and receive forgiveness through faith in Christ.

Paul now focuses his attention on the centrality of Christ, stating that the goal of the law is indeed Christ (Rom. 10:4). Paul invokes the dramatic scene of covenant renewal promised in Deut. 30:1-15. The Lord had promised through Moses that after Israel had experienced the blessings and curses of the covenant, they would be restored once again. After the exile, they would return and obey God's voice. They would hear his word and receive it. Paul writes that God's word to his people is "the word of faith" that he now proclaims, namely, that "if you confess with your mouth that Jesus is Lord and believe in your heart that God raised him from the dead, you will be saved" (Rom. 10:8-9). God's great redemptive purpose is accomplished in the death and resurrection of Christ. Salvation comes through faith in Christ. Paul concludes with pathos that "there is no distinction between Jew and Greek ... for everyone who calls on the name of the Lord will be saved" (Rom. 10:12-13; cf. Joel 2:32). Paul's entire missionary labor seeks this end. Those who are sent must preach Christ so that those who hear might call upon his name and be saved (Rom. 10:14-17; cf. Acts 2:21; 4:12).

Paul concludes this section by turning his attention to the Gentile believers. He reminds them that God has not rejected Israel simply to make room for them. God continues to save a portion of Israelites by his sovereign grace, just as he has always done (Rom. 11:1-6). Israel has not stumbled beyond repentance. In fact, Gentile believers are part of God's own plan to draw ethic Israelites to faith in Christ. Paul says: "I magnify my ministry in order somehow to make my fellow Jews jealous, and thus save some of them" (Rom. 11:13-14). Paul warns Gentile converts against spiritual pride, especially as their numbers grow in the churches. They are like wild olive shoots grafted into a long established tree (Rom. 11:17). They must regard the root of the tree as holy and continue in their efforts to announce the gospel to the Jew first and also to the Greek. Jesus is the Savior of the world because he is the Messiah of Israel. The church needs the Old and New Testaments in order to understand and communicate God's plan of redemption through history. Paul declares the mystery of God's saving purpose in that "a partial hardening has come upon Israel, until the fullness of the Gentiles has come in. And in this way all Israel will be saved" (Rom. 11:25-26). This is in accordance with God's sovereign design and unfathomable wisdom to display his mercy upon all (Rom. 11:32). The sustained theological discourse of Rom. 1-11 rightly resolves into praise and worship "for from him and through him and to him are all things. To him be the glory forever. Amen" (Rom. 11:36).

In Romans 12:1-15:13, Paul explains how the gospel shapes the Christian community. Gospel truth leads to gospel transformation. Rom. 12:1-2 calls forth a dramatic renewal for those made in the image of God:

> I appeal to you therefore, brothers, by the mercies of God, to present your bodies as a living sacrifice, holy and acceptable to God, which is your spiritual worship. Do not be conformed to this world, but be transformed by the renewal of your mind, that by testing you may discern what is the will of God, what is good and acceptable and perfect.

The new life of the community grows in response to the mercy of God displayed in the gospel (Rom. 11:36). Believers offer themselves fully to God as living sacrifices, holy and belonging to God in a life of worship (Rom. 12:1). This is a complete and total reversal of humanity's situation apart from

Christ. In Rom. 1-3, the image of God in humanity had become degraded, defaced, and dishonored. The radiance of God's glory had been lost through sin (Rom. 3:23). Now, the image of God has been restored through the cross. The phrase translated "spiritual worship" (lit. "logical worship"), means that which is "appropriate" or "fitting" for human beings. The greatest expression of our humanity is to render praise to God. With this radical new beginning in view, the new covenant community presses onward toward total transformation. Believers no longer draw their life and logic, nor their belief and behavior, from the pattern of this world. They are being transformed with renewed minds that recognize and affirm the will of God (Rom. 12:2), thus replacing the depraved mind of fallen humanity (Rom. 1:32).

Paul continues in his letter to write about the diversity of spiritual gifts, which strengthen the body of Christ (Rom. 12:3-8). The new humanity is characterized by genuine love, brotherly affection, devoted service, joyful hope, patient endurance, dedicated prayer, care for the poor, and the constant refusal to repay evil with evil; these characteristics signal the reality that God's new creation has begun (Rom. 12:9-21). Christians are to honor those in authority and pay their taxes out of reverence for God's established earthly rulers (Rom. 13:1-7). New covenant believers are to love one another and thus fulfill the law (Rom. 13:8-10; cf. Lev. 19:18; Matt. 22:39; Gal. 5:14; Jas. 2:8). The community must maintain a gracious unity on debatable matters of secondary importance (Rom. 14). Paul encourages a generous posture among Jewish and Gentile believers regarding the dietary laws and Sabbath keeping. Although persuaded that all foods are clean, he instructs his readers to follow their conscience and "pursue what makes for peace" (Rom. 14:19). We have an obligation not to please ourselves, but rather "let each of us please his neighbor for his good, to build him up" (Rom. 15:2). Paul's goal is that "together you may with one voice glory the God and Father of our Lord Jesus Christ" (Rom. 15:6). Christ came to confirm God's promises to Israel and to gather the nations for his glory (Rom. 15:8-13; cf. Deut. 32:43; Pss. 18:49; 117:1; Isa. 11:10).

In Rom. 15:14-16:27, Paul concludes his letter by revealing his missionary aim to further the gospel among those who have not yet heard. He has labored "in the priestly service of the gospel of God, so that the offering of the Gentiles may be acceptable, sanctified by the Holy Spirit" (Rom. 15:16).

His first twenty-five years in Christ's service have brought him from Jerusalem all the way to Illyricum in the ministry of the gospel of Christ (Rom. 15:19). He now aspires to preach the gospel where Christ is still unknown in order to fulfill the promise of Isa. 52:15 that "those who have never been told of him will see, and those who have never heard will understand" (Rom. 15:21). After presenting the fruit of his ministry among the nations and their offering for the saints in Jerusalem, he plans to visit the Roman Christians on his way to Spain. He writes in hope that they might understand and approve his gospel ministry and that they may offer their prayers and full support (Rom. 15:24-32). His heart overflows with a list of twenty-seven ministry partners in Rome whom he wishes to greet by name (Rom. 16:3-16). This list of names should not be passed over too quickly. These names reflect God's new humanity on display in the church. There are Jews and Gentiles, men and women, freedmen and servants. All are laboring together for the gospel of Christ. Paul blesses his readers in confident praise "to him who is able to strengthen you according to my gospel and the preaching of Jesus Christ … to the only wise God be glory forevermore through Jesus Christ! Amen." (Rom. 16:25-27).

Our summarizing statement for Romans on the timeline's map is "The righteousness of God in Christ," with the following key verse: "I am not ashamed of the gospel … for in it the righteousness of God is revealed" (Rom. 1:16-17). Paul's letter to the Roman Christians focuses our attention on the righteousness of God revealed in the gospel. The gospel is God's good news about his Son Jesus Christ. Christ's death on the cross provides substitutionary atonement for all who believe. Believers are declared righteous by faith and made holy by the presence of the Holy Spirit. The Holy Spirit confirms our adoption into God's family and empowers our obedience as the church. The church displays God's renewed humanity. God's renewed humanity offer themselves in sacrificial service and join God's mission. God's mission in the world invites the support and participation of the Roman Christians as well as ours today.

As we conclude Part 1 of TEACHING, I would encourage you to read through the letters we have studied so far. It is a good habit to read through an entire letter in one sitting. It is also helpful to read through the letters in chronological sequence and to notice developing ideas and recurring themes.

We have heard the letter of James call the church to put faith in Christ into action. We have heard the letters written by Paul during his three missionary journeys: Galatians (first missionary journey), 1-2 Thessalonians (second missionary journey), and 1-2 Corinthians and Romans (third missionary journey). Galatians urges new believers that there is no other gospel than Christ. 1-2 Thessalonians addresses new Christians to pursue holiness and live for Christ's return. 1-2 Corinthians appeals for church unity, and answers the questions of discipleship with a call to do all for the glory of Christ. Romans presents the gospel of the righteousness of God in Christ for all who believe, in the hope that God's good news about his Son will reach the uttermost ends of the earth.

Chapter 7
TEACHING Part 2

Paul's remaining seven letters: the Prison Epistles and the Pastoral Epistles

PART 2 OF TEACHING will survey Paul's remaining seven letters, covering his four letters written during his Roman imprisonment, as well as his last three letters written to Timothy and Titus. These include the Prison Epistles: Ephesians, Philippians, Colossians, and Philemon, and the Pastoral Epistles: 1-2 Timothy and Titus. We ended TEACHING Part 1 with Paul in Corinth, having just written his letter to the Romans (AD 57). We rehearse only briefly here Paul's subsequent journey to Rome, since this portion of the Acts narrative has already been discussed in detail in the section under PENTECOST (Acts 20-28). After being in Corinth for three months, Paul reaches Jerusalem in time for Pentecost in AD 57. He plans to visit Rome and eventually proclaim Christ in Spain. Paul was aware that imprisonment and afflictions awaited him in the days ahead, for the Holy Spirit had testified that this would be the case (Acts 20:22-23). Yet his commitment to Christ and his calling are sure; he states boldly: "I do not account my life of any value nor as precious to myself, if only I may finish my course and the ministry that I received from the Lord Jesus, to testify to the gospel of the grace of God" (Acts 20:24). You will recall that Paul is arrested in the temple (Acts 21) and then imprisoned in Caesarea for two years (AD 57-59). Jesus protects Paul's life and allows him the opportunity to testify of faith in Christ before his own people, King Herod Agrippa II and his sister Bernice, as well as before the Roman procurators Felix and Festus (Acts 22-26; cf. Acts 9:15). As a Roman citizen, he invokes the right to have his case tried before Caesar himself (Acts 25:11). Paul journeys to Rome as an ambassador of Christ in chains. The Lord preserves his life through a perilous journey and terrifying shipwreck (Acts 27; cf. 2 Cor. 11:25-27). Paul arrives in Rome and is placed under house arrest. The gospel continues to spread as he shares Christ openly with all who visit him. The narrative of Acts ends with Paul in Rome for two years awaiting trial and "teaching about the Lord Jesus Christ with all boldness and without hindrance" (Acts 28:30-31).

While under house arrest in Rome (AD 60-62), the Holy Spirit inspires Paul to write letters to various churches and trusted co-laborers in Christ. The four letters of Ephesians, Philippians, Colossians, and Philemon all make explicit reference to Paul's imprisonment and are therefore called Prison Epistles (Eph. 3:1; 4:1; Phil. 1:14; Col. 4:3, 10; Phlm. 1:1) While awaiting trial before the increasingly unstable emperor Nero, Paul continues his teaching ministry through writing. He writes about the death and resurrection of Christ and the glorious calling of the church. After an initial release and second imprisonment in Rome, Paul writes three final letters to trusted future leaders, Timothy and Titus, known as the Pastoral Epistles (1-2 Timothy, Titus). This means that seven of Paul's thirteen letters are written during his final years. These letters contain the major themes of Paul's preaching: Jesus is Israel's promised Messiah; all who believe in him are justified by faith; and the church of all nations is sanctified by the Holy Spirit to reflect God's renewed humanity in Christ. These letters also reveal Paul's example of intercessory prayer for the church, his commitment to personal evangelism, even while in prison, and his earnest desire to support future leaders of the church. These letters provide the moving testimony of a man completely transformed by Jesus Christ. Saul, the zealous persecutor of the church, has become Paul, a consecrated servant of Christ, who has dedicated his life to proclaim the gospel for all nations.

Roadmap to the chapter

As we trace God's redemptive purpose through Paul's remaining letters, make sure that you have an open Bible nearby so that you can follow along. We will present the content of each letter and then provide a summarizing statement and key verse to help you remember their teaching about Christ. As we study together, take time to locate each letter on the timeline's map under TEACHING and allow God to stir your heart to join his mission in the world. The gospel is God's good news about his beloved Son for the entire world. This is good news worth sharing, no matter what the cost.

EPHESIANS, written by Paul to the church at Ephesus (c. AD 60-62)

Ephesians is the first of four letters written by Paul during his imprisonment in Rome (AD 60-62). Ephesus was an important city in Paul's third missionary journey (Acts 19). He remained at Ephesus for three years (Acts 20:31). The city was the fourth largest in the Roman Empire, with a population of around 250,000, including 10,000 Jews. The geographer Strabo described Ephesus as the greatest trading center west of the Taurus Mountains. The exalted Jesus had used Paul's preaching in the synagogues to draw Jews and Gentiles to faith in Christ, and Paul had lectured daily in the Hall of Tyrannus (Acts 19). The Ephesians had experienced miracles of healing; many had abandoned their magical arts (Acts 19:18-19), and attendance at the Temple of Artemis was in noticeable decline (Acts 19:23-41). Nevertheless, the young church faced familiar temptations of false teaching, division, and worldliness. Paul's letter to the Ephesians is a stirring restatement of God's eternal purpose in Christ and an exhortation to live out the unity of the church that is found in Christ. Since Paul is in prison, he entrusts the letter to Tychichus for delivery; it was probably circulated among the various churches in the province of Asia (Eph. 6:21-22).

Paul begins Ephesians by identifying himself as "an apostle of Christ Jesus by the will of God" and addresses the church at Ephesus as "saints" (lit. "holy ones"), who are faithful in Christ Jesus (Eph. 1:1). Paul generously applies here and in other letters the language of Israel's calling to the entire family of faith (Exod. 19:6; Lev. 19:2), underscoring their unity in the gospel. Paul offers an expanded blessing in praise for what God has accomplished in Christ (Eph. 1:3-14). His blessing is a single sentence in Greek and draws the hearer to the absolute centrality of life *in Christ*. Paul writes that *in Christ* God has blessed us with every spiritual blessing (Eph. 1:3). He has chosen us *in Christ* before the foundation of the world (Eph. 1:4). He planned our adoption as sons and daughters *through Jesus Christ* (Eph. 1:5). *In Christ* we have redemption and forgiveness according to the riches of his glorious grace (Eph. 1:6-7). *In Christ* the mystery of God's redemptive purpose has been revealed (Eph. 1:9). All things in heaven and on earth are united *in him* (Eph. 1:10). *In Christ* we share in God's promised inheritance (Eph. 1:11). *In Christ* we are sealed with the promised Holy Spirit who guarantees our inheritance until we acquire possession of it to the praise of his glory (Eph. 1:13-14). This is precisely where our CASKET EMPTY study has led us—*Jesus Christ* stands at the center of God's plan of redemption through history. His death and resurrection reveal God's saving purpose. His glorious design is breathtaking. Paul prays that God would give believers a spirit of wisdom and revelation to know the hope to which they have been called. He prays that they would experience God's great power in their life together as the church, the body of Christ in the world (Eph. 1:15-23).

Paul then describes the unity of the church in Christ (Eph. 2-3). His thought develops along the same lines as in his letter to the Romans. He begins by urging Gentile believers to remember that "you were dead in the trespasses and sins in which you once walked, following the course of this world, following the prince of the power of the air, the spirit that is now at work in the sons of disobedience" (Eph. 2:1-2; cf. Rom. 1). At the same time, he includes himself and fellow Jews by saying "we all once lived in the passions of our flesh, carrying out the desires of the body and the mind, and were by nature children of wrath, like the rest of mankind" (Eph. 2:3; cf. Rom 2-3). Despite the universal sinfulness of humanity, Paul resounds with praise for God's grace and mercy, which we have seen as the defining character of God in the Old Testament (Exod. 34:6). The mercy of God comes to climactic expression in the redemptive work of Christ: "But God, being rich in mercy, because of the great love with which he loved us, even when we were dead in our trespasses, made us alive together with Christ" (Eph. 2:4-5; cf. Rom. 3:21-26). This new life is found through Christ's death and resurrection. Paul reminds the believers at Ephesus that they have been saved by grace and through faith (Eph. 2:5, 8). Salvation is not their own doing, but it is "the gift of God, not a result of works, so that no one may boast" (Eph. 2:8-9; cf. Rom. 3:27).

Paul expounds upon the astounding accomplishment of the cross. He reminds Gentiles that at one time they had been separated from Christ, "alienated from the commonwealth of Israel and strangers to the covenants of promise, having no hope and without God in the world" (Eph. 2:11-12). However, Paul states boldly that in Christ Jesus those who were far off have been "brought near by the blood of Christ" (Eph. 2:13). He reassures the Ephesians that Jesus has brought peace and has "broken down in his flesh the dividing wall of hostility" (Eph. 2:14). The image of the temple must be kept in mind here. Paul had been arrested on the specific charge of bringing a Gentile past the dividing wall that separated the nations from the inner courts of the Jerusalem Temple (Acts 21). Yet Paul had recognized the staggering reality that Christ had broken down this dividing wall of hostility "in his flesh," that he might create in himself "one new man" in place of the two (Eph. 2:14). Peace has been accomplished in the death of Christ, and all now have "access in one Spirit to the Father" (Eph. 2:18). Paul writes, therefore, that all who believe "are no longer strangers and aliens," but rather, they have become "fellow citizens with the saints and members of the household of God, built on the foundation of the apostles and prophets, Christ Jesus himself being the cornerstone, in whom the whole structure, being joined together, grows into a holy temple in the Lord" (Eph. 2:19-21). What an amazing picture of the work accomplished by Christ! The gathered church of believing Jews and Gentiles is the growing mountain of the house of the Lord, the place of God's dwelling, the rock that would one day fill the earth (Eph. 2:22; cf. Isa. 2:1-4; Dan. 2:35, 44-45).

Paul's thought is deeply shaped by the Old Testament Scriptures. He sees that the mystery of God's redemptive purpose for all peoples has now been revealed in Christ. This mystery, which the Old Testament anticipated, is that "the Gentiles are fellow heirs, members of the same body, and partakers of the promise in Christ Jesus through the gospel" (Eph. 3:6). God's promise to bless the nations through Abraham's seed has been realized in Christ. Paul's calling was to preach to the Gentiles the "unsearchable riches of Christ," and to bring to light for all people what is the "plan of the mystery hidden for ages in God who created all things" (Eph. 3:8-9). The unity of the church thus displays the manifold wisdom of God to the rulers and authorities in the heavenly places (Eph. 3:10). The church fulfills God's eternal purpose "in Christ Jesus our Lord, in whom we have boldness and access with confidence through our faith in him" (Eph. 3:11-12). Paul's vision of God's new humanity in Christ is overwhelming and leads him directly into worship, prayer, and praise:

> For this reason I bow my knees before the Father, from whom every family in heaven and on earth is named, that according to the riches of his glory he may grant you to be strengthened with power through his Spirit in your inner being, so that Christ may dwell in your hearts through faith—that you, being rooted and grounded in love, may have strength to comprehend with all the saints what is the breadth and length and height and depth, and to know the love of Christ that surpasses knowledge, that you may be filled with all the fullness of God. (Eph. 3:14-19)

As you read Paul's words of praise, let the magnitude of who God is and what he has done for us in Christ stir your own heart. May the glorious vision of the church as the realization of God's redemptive purpose fill your heart with love for God and strengthen your resolve to serve him with your entire life.

In view of this glorious reality, Paul exhorts his readers to live out the unity of the church as God's renewed humanity in Christ (Eph. 4-6; cf. Romans 5-15). They are "to walk in a manner worthy of the calling" to which they have been called (Eph. 4:1). They are to bear "with one another in love, eager to maintain the unity of the Spirit in the bond of peace" (Eph. 4:2-3). Although there is one body, one Spirit, one hope, one Lord, one faith, one baptism, and one God and Father of all, there is a variety of gifts given to each one (Eph. 4:4-7; cf. 1 Cor. 12:4-11). Diverse gifts, especially the leadership roles of apostles, prophets, evangelists, shepherds and teachers, are given to equip God's people, so that they might accomplish the work of ministry. The goal is to build up the body of Christ, united in faith and full maturity (Eph. 4:11-13). Believers are "to grow up in every way into him who is the head, into Christ, from whom the whole body, joined and held together by every joint with which it is equipped, when each part is working properly, makes the body grow so that it builds itself up in love" (Eph. 4:15-16; cf. 1 Cor. 12-13). The centrality of Christ for the life of the church could not be more emphatically stated.

New believers are called to abandon their former way of life and embrace God's ways. They must no longer walk as the nations do, in the futility of their minds, hardness of heart, immorality, and impurity (Eph. 4:17-19; cf. Lev. 18:1-5; Rom. 1). Walking according to the pattern of the nations was Israel's ongoing problem in the Old Testament, but God's new creation in Christ enables his people to walk in newness of life. Paul exhorts them, therefore, to put off their old self and "be renewed" in their minds (Eph. 4:23; cf. Rom. 12:1-2). They are to put on the *new* self, "created after the likeness of God in true righteousness and holiness" (Eph. 4:24; cf. Rom. 6:4). This echoes the original creation story, when God made human beings in his image and likeness (Gen. 1:26); this image is being restored in Christ, who is the image of the invisible God. The first man, Adam, had brought sin and death to all humanity through his disobedience (Gen. 2-3; Rom. 5:12-21; 1 Cor. 15:21-22), yet Paul sees that God's renewed humanity is created *in Christ*. The transformed life of believers is evident in their control of anger, honest work, and holy speech (Eph. 4:26-31). They display the life of Christ by forgiving one another, as God in Christ has forgiven them (Eph. 4:32). They are to "be imitators of God, as beloved children" (Eph. 5:1; cf. Exod. 4:22). They are to "walk in love, as Christ loved us and gave himself up for us, a fragrant offering and sacrifice to God" (Eph. 5:2; cf. John 3:16; Rom. 5:8; 8:32). The verbs throughout this section are in the plural, indicating that such living can only be realized in community. This is the original intention of our heavenly Father (Gen. 1:28; Exod. 19:6; Isa. 11:9; Hab. 2:14), which is now being accomplished *in Christ*.

The new Christian life develops in sharp contrast to the behavior of a fallen world. Believers are to walk as "children of light," and as such, they are to take "no part in the unfruitful works of darkness" (Eph. 5:8, 11); they are to conduct themselves in wisdom, and thus Paul exhorts them not to be foolish, but to "understand what the will of the Lord is ... Do not get drunk with wine ... but be filled with the Spirit" (Eph. 5:17-18). God's renewed humanity prefers one another out of reverence for Christ (Eph. 5:21). Christ's example of humility and commitment to serve transforms all human relationships. Wives respect their husbands "as to the Lord" (Eph. 5:22-24). Husbands love their wives "as Christ loved the church and gave himself up for her" (Eph. 5:25-29). The marital union between a man and a woman offers a living, lifelong, parable of Christ's love for his bride, the church (Eph. 5:32-33). Children are to obey their parents "in the Lord" (Eph. 6:1), and parents are to bring up their children "in the discipline and instruction of the Lord" (Eph. 6:4). Servants obey those in authority "as servants of Christ, doing the will of God from the heart, rendering service with a good will as to the Lord" (Eph. 6:6-7). Those in authority do the same, knowing that they are accountable for their actions before God (Eph. 6:9).

Paul knows that the devil's scheme from the beginning has been to tempt and then accuse a disobedient humanity. How often the gospel has been discredited by the lives of those who claim to be in Christ! Paul is familiar with the terrain and tactics of spiritual battle. He also knows the way to victory: "Be strong in the Lord and in the strength of his might. Put on the whole armor of God, that you may be able to stand against the schemes of the devil" (Eph. 6:10-18). Perhaps looking at the Roman soldier who guards him, Paul depicts believers as outfitted with the belt of truth, the breastplate of righteousness, and shoes ready to carry the gospel. They hold the shield of faith to extinguish the devil's arrows. They wear the helmet of salvation and wield the sword of the Spirit, which is the Word of God. Their battle cry is the voice of prayer and supplication. They will prevail. No weapon formed against them will prosper. They stand firm on the gospel (Eph. 6:14; cf. Rom. 5:2; 1 Cor. 15:1). Paul concludes his letter with the blessing of grace and peace upon the church at Ephesus (Eph. 6:23-24).

Our summarizing statement for Ephesians on the timeline's map is "Unity in Christ," with the following key verse: "Maintain the unity of the Spirit in the bond of peace. There is one body and one Spirit ... one Lord, one faith, one baptism, one God and Father of all, who is over all" (Eph. 4:3-6). Paul's letter from prison to the growing church at Ephesus reveals the high calling of the church. God's eternal redemptive purpose has been accomplished in Christ and put on display to the entire cosmos in the church. Christ's atoning death on the cross has torn down the dividing wall of hostility and remade humanity as his living temple. God's renewed humanity, comprised of believing Jews and Gentiles, is called to walk worthy of the gospel. They must abandon their former way of life to embrace Christ. The example of Christ powerfully transforms all earthly relationships. Believers stand united against the devil's schemes. They stand firm in the gospel of peace that proclaims Christ to all nations.

PHILIPPIANS, written by Paul to the church at Philippi (c. AD 60-62)
Philippians is the second of four letters written by Paul during his imprisonment in Rome (AD 60-62). You may recall from the book of Acts that the church had been established at Philippi during Paul's second missionary journey (Acts 16). Paul had received a vision from God to go to Macedonia (Acts 16:9-10), where Lydia, a dealer in purple cloth, had become the first convert in Europe (Acts 16:14-15). Even Paul's imprisonment in the city had been used by God to reach the Philippian jailer and his family (Acts 16:20-34). The believers at Philippi became a source of lasting joy for Paul. They remained long-term partners in his ministry from the beginning, and they had often sent him financial support (Phil. 1:5; 4:15-16). The Philippian church had recently sent a gift for Paul's needs in prison through Epaphroditus (Phil. 2:25; 4:18). Paul now writes his letter to them with a heart full of gratitude. Even though in prison, Paul's letter exudes joy (Phil. 1:4; 1:18; 1:25; 2:2; 2:17-18; 2:28-29; 3:1; 4:1; 4:4; 4:10). He thanks the Philippians for their partnership and informs them that his imprisonment has advanced the gospel in some unexpected ways. He writes to strengthen their joy in the faith (Phil. 1:25), and to encourage their steadfast commitment to Christ (Phil. 2:5; 3:14-17).

Paul and Timothy write as servants of Christ Jesus, to all the saints who are at Philippi, along with the overseers and deacons (Phil. 1:1). Paul knows that the church prospers under shared, godly leadership. He made it a regular practice to train, empower, and entrust churches to dedicated servants. After his distinctive greeting, Paul's prayer for the Philippians reveals the theme of his letter (Phil. 1:3-11). His prayers are filled with joy, because of their "partnership in the gospel" (Phil. 1:5). He is confident that Christ will complete his good work among them. He holds them in his heart "for you are all partakers with me of grace, both in my imprisonment and in the defense and confirmation of the gospel" (Phil. 1:7). His prayer beautifully summarizes his hope "that your love may abound more and more, with knowledge and all discernment, so that you may approve what is excellent, and so be pure and blameless for the day of Christ, filled with the fruit of righteousness that comes through Jesus Christ, to the glory and praise of God" (Phil. 1:9-11).

Paul wants to update the Philippians about his own circumstances (Phil. 1:12-30). He wants them to know that his imprisonment has actually served to advance the gospel. The Philippians should be well-equipped to know that Jesus uses prison for his own purposes (Acts 16:23-33). Paul has witnessed to the Praetorian Guard, and even some members of Caesar's family have come to Christ (Phil. 1:13; 4:22). Other Christians have been emboldened by Paul's example to speak the word without fear (Phil. 1:14). Paul remains confident "that through your prayers and the help of the Spirit of Jesus Christ this will turn out for my deliverance" (Phil. 1:19). He knows that "to live is Christ, and to die is gain" (Phil. 1:21). Though he eagerly desires to be with Christ, he trusts that fruitful labor still remains. He is committed to their progress and joy in Christ and rejoices at seeing them again (Phil. 1:22-26). Until that day, he reminds them: "let your manner of life be worthy of the gospel of Christ, so that whether I come and see you or am absent, I may hear of you that you are standing firm in one spirit, with one mind striving side by side for the faith of the gospel and not frightened in anything by your opponents" (Phil. 1:27-28). Their commitment to Christ, despite opposition and persecution, is a sure testimony of their salvation. Christians represent an alternative kingdom in the midst of the world. As citizens of heaven on earth, believers in Christ serve the real King of the world and conduct their lives in hopeful anticipation of his personal and glorious return.

Paul instructs the church to be unified in their thinking and in their love, as they seek to imitate Christ (Phil. 2). He admonishes them to "do nothing from rivalry or conceit, but in humility count others more significant than yourselves" (Phil. 2:3). Above all, he invites them to imitate Christ, whose humility, obedience, and exaltation redefines greatness and sets the pattern for real human life:

> Have this mind among yourselves, which is yours in Christ Jesus, who, though he was in the form of God, did not count equality with God a thing to be grasped, but made himself nothing, taking the form of a servant, being born in the likeness of men. And being found in human form, he humbled himself by becoming obedient to the point of death, even death on a cross. Therefore God has highly exalted him and bestowed on him the name that is above every name, so that at

the name of Jesus every knee should bow, in heaven and on earth and under the earth, and every tongue confess that Jesus Christ is Lord, to the glory of God the Father. (Phil. 2:5-11; cf. Isa. 45:23)

This lofty poem of praise echoes the humility of the Servant of the Lord in Isa. 53 and provides the essential pattern of Christian discipleship (cf. Matt. 16:24; Luke 14:11; Rom. 6:5; 2 Cor. 4:8-18).

The Philippians likewise are to maintain a posture of humble obedience as they work out their salvation (Phil. 2:12). God is at work among them, birthing new desires and affections for Christ. Paul admonishes them to do all things without grumbling and to live as children of God, without blemish in the midst of a crooked generation (cf. Num. 14:27; Deut. 32:5; 1 Cor. 10:1-12). They shine as lights in the world, holding fast to the word of life (Phil. 2:13-16). They rejoice with Paul in the hope of future exaltation, even if their lives, like his, are to be poured out for others (Phil. 2:17). Paul commends Timothy and Epaphroditus as living examples of Christ-like service to others (Phil. 2:19-30).

Paul urges his beloved fellow believers to "rejoice in the Lord" (Phil. 3:1). He warns them once more against any person or teaching that would obscure the accomplishment of the cross. Throughout his ministry, Paul's most vocal critics came from his right. Many of his kinsmen resisted Paul's preaching that Israelites were as sinful as the rest of the world and needed repentance. Devout Israelites who had become believers struggled to accept the nations of the world as co-heirs solely on the basis of faith in Christ. Others insisted that the nations must be circumcised and taught the way of Torah (Acts 15:1-5; 2 Cor. 11:18-28; Gal. 3:1-3). Paul overturns this entire perspective, warning the Philippians against those who would teach any other way of salvation except faith in Christ. Paul boldly affirms: "We are the circumcision, who worship by the Spirit of God and glory in Christ Jesus and put no confidence in the flesh" (Phil. 3:3; cf. Deut. 10:16; 30:6; Jer. 4:4; Rom. 2:26-29). His own example reveals the surpassing worth of Christ when compared with boasting in any privilege or status before God. His religious pedigree cannot be eclipsed: he was "circumcised on the eighth day, of the people of Israel, of the tribe of Benjamin, a Hebrew of Hebrews; as to the law, a Pharisee; as to zeal, a persecutor of the church; as to righteousness under the law, blameless" (Phil. 3:5-6). Yet he counts all this as "loss for the sake of Christ. Indeed, I count everything as loss because of the surpassing worth of knowing Christ Jesus my Lord" (Phil. 3:7-8). Paul abandons all earthly pride in order that he might gain Christ and be found in him, "not having a righteousness of my own that comes from the law, but that which comes through faith in Christ" (Phil. 3:8-9). Paul presses on to know Christ and the power of his resurrection, to share his suffering and become like him in death (Phil. 3:10). He strains ahead "for the prize of the upward call of God in Christ Jesus" (Phil. 3:13-14). He urges them to think the same way and follow his example (Phil. 3:17). With tears flowing from his eyes, he warns that many "walk as enemies of the cross of Christ" (Phil. 3:18). They are fixed on certain foods, they boast in marks made on the body, and are concerned with earthly things (Phil. 3:19). Paul lifts his vision heavenward, believing that the new creation has already begun in Christ (cf. 2 Cor. 5:17; Gal. 6:15). Christ will surely return again, transforming us in full conformity with him who gloriously rules over all (Phil. 3:20-21).

In the final section of his letter, Paul exhorts the church to stand firm in the Lord (Phil. 4:1; cf. Rom. 5:2; 1 Cor. 15:1; Eph. 6:14). He exhorts the men and women who co-labor with him for the gospel to stay united (Phil. 4:2-3). Working together for the gospel, urges them: "Rejoice in the Lord always; again I will say, Rejoice!" (Phil. 4:4). Paul tenderly counsels them not to be anxious, but instead, they are to pray to God at all times with thanksgiving, letting their requests be made known (Phil. 4:6). He promises that "the peace of God, which surpasses all understanding" will guard their hearts and minds in Christ Jesus (Phil. 4:7). He calls them to fix their attention on "whatever is true, whatever is honorable, whatever is just, whatever is pure, whatever is lovely, whatever is commendable" and to practice "what you have learned and received and heard and seen in me" (Phil. 4:8-9). These teachings reflect the high calling of the church today.

Paul thanks the Philippians for their sacrificial gift, and he reveals the secret of contentment in all circumstances: "I can do all things through him who strengthens me" (Phil. 4:13). He concludes his letter with confident expectation that "God will supply every need of yours according to his riches in glory in Christ Jesus" (Phil. 4:19). Paul closes with joyful prison greetings from "the brothers who are with me," and from all the saints, "especially those of Caesar's household" (Phil. 4:21-22).

Our summarizing statement for Philippians on the timeline's map is "Joy in Christ," with the following key verse, "Rejoice in the Lord always; again I will say, Rejoice" (Phil. 4:4). Despite his imprisonment, Paul's letter overflows with joy. Paul experiences joy over their ongoing partnership with him in the gospel. His joy increases as the gospel spreads among all levels of society. Our joy likewise abounds in the surpassing greatness of knowing Christ and seeking to conform our entire life to his. Here we too find peace for anxiety, confidence instead of shame, and hope in place of fear.

COLOSSIANS, written by Paul to the church at Colossae (c. AD 60-62)

Colossians is the third of Paul's letters written from his Roman imprisonment. The exalted Jesus had established the church at Colossae through Epaphras, who had come to faith in Ephesus during the Paul's third missionary journey (AD 52-57). Epaphras had returned to his native city of Colossae, nearly one hundred miles away. He had proclaimed the gospel in Colossae and to the neighboring cities of Laodicea and Hierapolis (Col. 1:7; 4:12). This dedicated servant of Christ visits Paul in Rome to bring news of the new churches spreading along the cities of the Lycus River valley. Paul writes Colossians to encourage believers in their new life in Christ. The letter is entrusted to Tychichus, who travels with a fellow convert from Colossae named Onesimus (Col. 4:7-9).

Paul writes with authority as an apostle, together with Timothy who is with him in Rome (Col. 1:1). Paul addresses the church at Colossae as "saints and faithful brothers in Christ" (Col. 1:2). After his greeting of grace and peace, Paul shares his thanksgiving and prayer to God for them (Col. 1:3-14). He has heard about their faith in Christ, their love for Christ's people, and their hope in Christ's return. They have learned these truths in the gospel, which is bearing fruit and spreading throughout the world (cf. Acts 6:7; 19:10). Paul prays that they may be filled with the knowledge of his will "to walk in a manner worthy of the Lord, fully pleasing to him, bearing fruit in every good work and increasing in the knowledge of God" (Col. 1:10). He prays that they might be strengthened with power and joy, thanking the Father who has granted them a share in the inheritance with God's people in radiant glory (Col. 1:12). The Colossians have been rescued from the domain of darkness and transferred into the kingdom of God's beloved Son in whom they have redemption and forgiveness of sins (Col. 1:13-14). The supreme and glorious accomplishment of the cross leads Paul into praise and worship. He bursts into poetry when he considers the surpassing greatness of Jesus Christ, the eternal and incarnate Son of God, Creator, Redeemer, and preeminent Lord of the church:

> He is the image of the invisible God, the firstborn of all creation. For by him all things were created, in heaven and on earth, visible and invisible, whether thrones or dominions or rulers or authorities—all things were created through him and for him. And he is before all things, and in him all things hold together. And he is the head of the body, the church. He is the beginning, the firstborn from the dead, that in everything he might be preeminent. For in him all the fullness of God was pleased to dwell, and through him to reconcile to himself all things, whether on earth or in heaven, making peace by the blood of his cross. (Col. 1:15-20)

Paul here invites the believers at Colossae to reflect upon who Jesus is and his headship over the church. Jesus is to be preeminent over all things, including the church at Colossae.

Paul writes further that the Colossians were once alienated from God and hostile to him in mind and practice, but now they have been reconciled by Christ's atoning death and stand "holy and blameless and above reproach before him" (Col. 1:21-22; cf. Eph. 2:1-7). God's grace abounds to the nations in Christ. Paul knows that he is imprisoned for preaching the gospel for all peoples. He wants the Colossians to know that he rejoices in his sufferings for their sake, and in his flesh he is "filling up what is lacking in Christ's afflictions for the sake of his body, that is, the church" (Col. 1:24). Genuine ministry and all missionary expansion are authenticated through suffering. Paul again explains that the mystery of God's redemptive purpose has been accomplished in Christ. His saving will is now revealed to all nations, which is Christ in them, "the hope of glory" (Col. 1:26-27; cf. Eph. 3:1-12; Col. 2:2).

Paul therefore proclaims Christ and instructs the believers at Colossae, so that they might be mature in Christ (Col. 1:28).

Paul warns the Colossians against any teaching that would diminish Christ (Col. 2). Even though he has never seen them face-to-face, he is familiar with the challenges they will face. He points them to Christ and to his wisdom and knowledge (Col. 2:3). Paul cautions them against any who would deceive them with plausible arguments according to human tradition (Col. 2:4, 8; cf. Gal. 3:1). Such traditions are not according to Christ in whom "the whole fullness of deity dwells" and who "is the head of all rule and authority" (Col. 2:9-10). Paul's concerns become increasingly clear when he affirms that in Christ they were "circumcised with a circumcision made without hands" (Col. 2:11). The "circumcision of Christ" is identified as the new covenant sign of baptism (Col. 2:12; cf. Deut. 30:6; Rom. 2:29). The Colossians had been formerly dead in their trespasses and in their uncircumcision, but God had made them alive "together with him, having forgiven us all our trespasses" (Col. 2:13). Christ's atoning death has canceled the record of their debt when it was nailed to the cross (Col. 2:14). Christ has triumphed over all principalities and powers at the cross, and he has forever disarmed any accusation against God's people (Col. 1:15; cf. Gen. 3:15; Isa. 54:17; Matt. 12:29; Luke 10:18; Rom. 8:33-34).

Since believers are justified by faith in Christ and stand as full members of God's new covenant community, they must not allow any to condemn them over matters of food and drink, festivals, or Sabbath keeping (Col. 2:16; cf. Rom. 14:1-6). For Paul, the goal of the law is Christ. The law was a shadow of the good things to come; it was a guardian, protecting Israel until this time of maturity as sons (Col. 2:17; cf. Rom. 10:4; Gal. 3:24-26). Each of these metaphors values the role of the law, while pointing to the preeminence of Christ. Paul knows that neither rigorous spiritual disciplines, the law without the Spirit, nor human precepts have the power to restrain sin (Col. 2:18-23; cf. Rom. 7:1-11; Gal. 3:21). They are like "the elemental spirits of the world" to which believers have died (Col. 2:20; cf. Gal. 4:3, 9).

Paul urges the believers at Colossae to fix their attention on Christ. They have died and have been raised to new life in him. Note again the centrality of this resurrection imagery for our CASKET EMPTY study. They are to seek the things that are above, therefore, where Christ is exalted at the right hand of God. Christ will return, and they will appear with him in glory (Col. 3:1-4; cf. Phil. 3:14-21). As they focus their attention on the things above, they must "put to death" earthly passions, such as immorality and idolatry, which were part of their old life (Col. 3:5-7). As with his letter to the Ephesians, Paul exhorts them to "put off the old self with its practices" and to "put on the new self, which is being renewed in knowledge after the image of its creator" (Col. 3:9-10; cf. Rom. 12:1-2; 13:14; Eph. 4:22-24). God's renewed humanity means that "there is not Greek and Jew, circumcised and uncircumcised, barbarian, Scythian, slave, free; but Christ is all, and in all" (Col. 3:11). This has been a resounding theme throughout Paul's letters (Rom. 10:12; 15:9; 1 Cor. 12:13; 2 Cor. 5:16-17; Gal. 3:28; 5:6).

In contrast to their former way of life, believers are now clothed with Christ and are instructed to "put on" compassion, kindness, humility, meekness, and patience (Col. 3:12). They are to bear with one another and forgive, as the Lord has forgiven them (Col. 3:13). Above all, they are to put on love, which "binds everything together in perfect harmony" (Col. 3:14; cf. 1 Cor. 13). They are to teach, admonish, and sing together with thankfulness to God. Everything is to be done in the name of the Lord Jesus (Col. 3:15-17). Their relationships with one another, as husbands and wives, children and parents, employers and employees are to reflect their new identity in Christ (Col. 3:18-4:1; cf. Eph. 5:22-6:9). They are to remain steadfast in prayer, making the most of every opportunity to share Christ with others (Col. 4:2-6). It is clear from Paul's exhortations in the Prison Epistles that the church is to reflect the new humanity, which is being formed into the likeness of Christ.

Paul's letter to the Colossians ends with final greetings, with several names being given. The inclusion of these names reminds us that Paul always ministered in partnership with others. We often imagine him alone and may even wrongly embrace such a ministry vision for ourselves. Working with others in the cause of Christ will involve challenges, frustrations, and discouragements. However, Christ places those around us for our humility, sanctification, and growth in ministry. We need them. Paul's personal greeting advances a moving subplot in the New Testament regarding John Mark, the cousin of Barnabas. Almost fifteen years earlier, John had left Paul and Barnabas, overwhelmed by the scale of the Gentile mission (Acts 13:13). There had been a disagreement. Yet reconciliation has been made;

Mark is now with Paul in Rome. Paul writes, therefore, that if Mark comes to them, they are to welcome him (Col. 4:10). Here we learn of other believing Jews, like Justus, who is Paul's fellow worker for the kingdom, and Luke, the beloved physician (Col. 4:11, 14), who had been one of Paul's missionary companions. Paul adds a final greeting with his own hand, after dictating the letter to Timothy, a trusted co-laborer in Christ (Col. 1:1; 4:18).

Our summarizing statement for Colossians on the timeline's map is "New Life in Christ," with the following key verse: "When Christ who is your life appears, then you also will appear with him in glory" (Col 3:4). Modern readers, like the original audience here and in Romans, hear Paul's voice without ever having met him in person. Nevertheless, his divinely inspired letter addresses us all to embrace a new life in Christ. The church in Colossae also reminds us that God will use the people we teach to establish new outposts of his kingdom, as was the case with Epaphras, who first proclaimed the gospel at Colossae. The exponential increase of the gospel by the Holy Spirit through human agency reflects God's redemptive design from the very beginning.

PHILEMON, written by Paul to Philemon (c. AD 60-62)

Philemon is the last of Paul's Prison Epistles, addressed to "Philemon our beloved fellow worker and Apphia our sister and Archippus our fellow soldier, and the church in your house" (Phlm. 1:1-2). Like Epaphras, Philemon also apparently came to faith in Ephesus during Paul's third missionary journey (AD 52-57). He had returned to his native Colossae, where he and his wife Apphia hosted the church in their home. Philemon was a wealthy resident of Colossae who employed servants on his estate. One of his servants, named Onesimus, had fled for reasons unknown to us. By God's sovereign plan, the fugitive Onesimus came in contact with Paul in Rome and became a believer in Christ. Paul held great affection for Onesimus, treating him like a father would his son (Phlm. 1:10). He also saw how God had gifted Onesimus for Christian service. Paul even entrusted the delivery of his letter to the Colossians partly to him (Col. 4:9). At the same time, Paul knew that Philemon and Onesimus faced an important crossroad in their discipleship. Onesimus must return to his former owner and apologize for having fled. Philemon must receive him back with forgiveness as a brother in Christ. The letter of

Philemon is short, but profound; it aims to secure the reconciliation of these two men, that they might display the transforming power of the gospel.

Beginning with his customary greeting (Phlm. 1:3), Paul thanks God for Philemon and the report of his love and faith for Jesus and his people. He prays that the sharing of his faith may become effective and suggests that his letter provides just such an opportunity (Phlm. 1:6, 8). Paul could have given strict orders in his letters, but he prefers an appeal in love (Phlm. 1:8-9). This is a beautiful example for any who would initiate reconciliation between those in conflict. Paul appeals on behalf of Onesimus, his "child," with fatherly affection (Phlm. 1:10). The name Onesimus, which was a common name for a slave, means "useful" or "beneficial." In a clever play on the name, Paul points out that "formerly he was *useless* to you, but now he is indeed *useful* to you and to me" (Phlm. 1:11). Onesimus, once identified merely as a slave, has now become a valued servant of Christ. Paul sends Onesimus back to Philemon, with the hope that he would receive him back "no longer as a slave but more than a slave, as a beloved brother" (Phlm. 1:12-16). This is the profound reality of God's new humanity in Christ, where the slave stands with the master, as an equal member of God's family and a brother in Christ. Paul does not make such a remarkable request from a safe distance. He risks his own relationship with Philemon by asking: "If you consider me your partner, receive him as you would receive me" (Phlm. 1:17). He even assumes responsibility for financial restitution and any outstanding debt (Phlm. 1:18). He takes the stylus from Timothy to write with his own hand: "I will repay it." He then tactfully reminds Philemon that he is personally in his debt (Phlm. 1:19), recalling his conversion through Paul's ministry. He stirs Philemon even further: "Yes, brother, I want some *benefit* (meaning Onesimus) from you in the Lord. Refresh my heart in Christ" (Phlm. 1:20). Paul ends confident that Philemon will respond positively to his request (Phlm. 1:21), and asks him to prepare a guest room when Paul visits in person (Phlm. 1:22). In the meantime, Paul remains a prisoner in Rome. He sends greetings from Epaphras, who is now "my fellow prisoner in Christ Jesus," along with his fellow workers "Mark, Aristarchus, Demas, and Luke" (Phlm. 1:23).

Our summarizing statement for Philemon on the timeline's map is "Welcome your brother in Christ," with the following key verse: "Confident of your obedience, I write to you, knowing that you will do even more than

I say" (Phlm. 1:21). Paul's sweeping missionary labors always retained a human face. He believed that the gospel of Christ brings forgiveness, redemption, and personal transformation. In an intimate portrait of ministry, Paul's preaching converts a wealthy landowner and a fugitive slave. By God's providence, these lives are intimately connected. Paul calls both men forward into the implications of following Christ. Together they discover that Christ's death and resurrection have made them brothers. It would take the Western world almost nineteen centuries to catch up with Paul's request.

1-2 TIMOTHY, written by Paul to Timothy (c. AD 63-65)

According to Acts 28:30, Paul remained under house arrest in Rome for two years before his trial (AD 60-62). When his case was finally brought before Nero, Paul writes that "the Lord stood by me and strengthened me," rescuing him "from the lion's mouth" (2 Tim. 4:17). A number of early Christian sources indicate that Paul was released from prison after his initial trial and conducted ministry in Spain before being imprisoned again a second time in Rome (AD 63-65). During this later period, the Holy Spirit inspires Paul to write his final three letters to trusted co-laborers for the gospel. These letters are 1-2 Timothy and Titus; they are known as the Pastoral Epistles because Paul writes to the next generation of pastoral leaders. These letters are filled with pastoral wisdom and tender affection. Paul emphasizes the importance of godly character in leadership and the priority of the preached Word of God in faithful ministry (1 Tim. 3:1-13; 2 Tim. 4:2; Titus 2:1). He warns leaders against distraction, neglect, and division arising from false teaching. Instead, they must be diligent, devoted teachers of the truth that God has entrusted to the church (1 Tim. 2:4; 3:15; 2 Tim. 2:15; Titus 1:1). Their most effective and inexhaustible teaching resource is the whole counsel of God's word, for Paul affirms that all Scripture is "breathed out by God and profitable for teaching, for reproof, for correction, and for training in righteousness" (2 Tim. 3:16).

Paul writes two letters to Timothy, his beloved son in the faith (1 Tim. 1:1-2; 2 Tim. 1:1-2). You may recall from our study of Acts that Timothy had first joined Paul during his second missionary journey (Acts 16:1-3). The young Timothy was the son of an Israelite woman and a Greek father. He was highly regarded among the early believers who had commended him to join Paul's mission. This began a life-long mentorship and shared ministry in the gospel. Although much younger than Paul, Timothy proved faithful with important ministry assignments in Thessalonica, Corinth, and Philippi. When Paul had written to the church at Philippi while in prison, he had given the following words of commendation: "I have no one like him," and that "as a son with a father he has served with me in the gospel" (Phi. 2:19-22). Timothy is named as co-sender in six of Paul's letters (2 Cor. 1:1; Phil. 1:1; Col. 1:1; 1 Thess. 1:1; 2 Thess. 1:1; Phlm. 1:1). Paul describes him as "my fellow worker," "our brother," and "my true child in the faith" (Rom. 16:21; 2 Cor. 1:1; 1 Tim. 1:2).

After his initial release from Rome, Paul entrusts Timothy with leadership over the large church at Ephesus. Paul now writes his first letter to Timothy to encourage his faithfulness in such an important task. He instructs him to remain at Ephesus so that you might "charge certain persons not to teach any different doctrine" (1 Tim. 1:3). Paul had heard reports that many had become distracted with speculative teaching of "myths and endless genealogies" (1 Tim. 1:4). These are technical terms that refer to rabbinic teaching known as *Midrash Aggadah*, which was a major component of what came to be described as the Oral Torah. This vast body of material contains Scripture commentary, exemplary deeds of the sages, and apologetics toward the pagan world. Paul urges Timothy that certain people have wandered into vain discussions, "desiring to be teachers of the law" (1 Tim. 1:6-7). He reminds him that knowledge of the Torah does not make us righteous, but should help us to see our sin and our need for the gospel even more clearly (1 Tim. 1:8-11). Paul concludes this point with his own testimony: "though formerly I was a blasphemer, persecutor, and insolent opponent," yet he had received mercy and the "grace of our Lord overflowed" for him "with the faith and love that are in Christ Jesus" (1 Tim. 1:13-14). Rejecting any potential claims of privileged status, he praises God "that Christ Jesus came into the world to save sinners, of whom I am the foremost" (1 Tim. 1:15; cf. Rom. 7:14-8:4; Gal. 1:13-16; Phil. 3:4-9). The goal of the gospel is love flowing from a purified heart, a renewed conscience, and a sincere faith in Christ (1 Tim. 1:5, 18-19; cf. Rom. 13:10; Gal. 5:6).

Paul charges Timothy with instructions on orderly worship and leadership of the church. Prayers should be made for all, even the emperor, so that peaceable, quiet conditions might promote the teaching of the gospel to all nations (1 Tim. 2:1-7). Men should pray without disruptive arguing with one another (1 Tim. 2:8). Women should dress modestly, adorning themselves with godliness. Those who are disrupting the gathered congregation from listening attentively to the Word of God should learn quietly in a posture of respect (1 Tim. 2:9-12). Paul's overarching concern in this passage aims to foster a unified atmosphere so that the Word of God can be read, taught, and learned by all people, men and women (1 Tim. 2:1-7). He specifically warns here against arguing with one another or domineering over one another in a way that hinders the teaching of the gospel. Although believing Christians understand the application of this passage differently, all such discussions should reflect Paul's priority of the gospel, the diverse gifts of the Holy Spirit, and the unity of the church. Paul models for us a generous stance on secondary issues and the freedom in Christ not to exercise one's rights (Rom. 14; 1 Cor. 9:1-15). For Paul, since all people sin (1 Tim. 2:14; cf. Rom. 5:12-14; 1 Cor. 15:21-22), personal godliness is the main requirement for church leadership (1 Tim. 3:1-13). All who lead must be "above reproach" and "able to teach" (1 Tim. 3:2). They must show diligence and care for their own households. Leaders are likewise called to faithfulness "in the household of God, which is the church of the living God, a pillar and buttress of the truth" (1 Tim. 3:15).

Since false teachings abound, Paul admonishes Timothy to devote himself to "the public reading of Scripture, to exhortation, to teaching" (1 Tim. 4:13). He urges him to keep a "close watch on yourself and on the teaching" (1 Tim. 4:16). Timothy must not be intimidated by his own youthfulness, but set an example "in speech, in conduct, in love, in faith, in purity" (1 Tim. 4:12). His leadership should always be exercised with humility, teaching older men "as you would a father, younger men as brothers, older women as mothers, younger women as sisters" (1 Tim. 5:1-2). Those who share in church leadership are to be honored "especially those who labor in preaching and teaching" (1 Tim. 5:17). Paul stresses the importance of contentment with the ministry assigned by Christ, and warns against ambition, greed, and the love of money (1 Tim. 6:3-10). Paul charges Timothy to flee such things, fight the good fight, and take hold of eternal life (1 Tim. 6:11-12). At the conclusion of his letter, Paul stirs Timothy to "guard the deposit entrusted to you" (1 Tim. 6:20).

By the time Paul writes his second letter to Timothy, he is imprisoned again in Rome (2 Tim. 1:16; 2:9). He senses from the Lord that he is "already being poured out as a drink offering, and the time of my departure has come" (2 Tim. 4:6). With the end of his earthly life in sight, he writes a deeply personal letter to Timothy, addressing him as "my beloved child" (2 Tim. 1:2). Paul recognizes that God's redemptive purpose in the world will continue through the next generation of leaders. He exhorts Timothy to "fan into flame the gift of God, which is in you" and to not be afraid (2 Tim. 1:6-7). God's great purpose has been manifested "through the appearing of our Savior Christ Jesus, who abolished death and brought life and immortality to light through the gospel for which I was appointed a preacher and apostle and teacher" (2 Tim. 1:10-11).

With the reality of his own death in view, Paul urges Timothy to "follow the pattern of the sound words that you have heard from me, in the faith and love that are in Christ Jesus. By the Holy Spirit who dwells within us, guard the good deposit entrusted to you" (2 Tim. 1:13-14). Timothy must in turn share the gospel with those who will be able to teach others (2 Tim. 2:1-2). Like a good soldier of Christ Jesus, he must willingly share in suffering and not become distracted with civilian pursuits (2 Tim. 2:3-4). Like a noble athlete, he must compete by the rules to receive the crown (2 Tim. 2:5). Like a hard-working farmer, he will receive his share of the crops in due time (2 Tim. 2:6). He must present himself to God "as one approved, a worker who has no need to be ashamed, rightly handling the word of truth" (2 Tim. 2:15). He must not be surprised by difficulties, persecutions, or depth of sin among those whom he seeks to lead (2 Tim. 3:1-13). He must rely upon the sufficiency and power of the divinely inspired Word of God. These sacred writings make us "wise for salvation through faith in Christ Jesus" (2 Tim. 3:15). This exhortation to the young Timothy remains true for us today—priority must be given to the preaching of the Word.

As Paul's final days draw near, we are reminded that Paul has devoted himself to the preaching and teaching of God's word. He reaffirms the sufficiency of Scripture to Timothy when asserting that "all Scripture is breathed out by God and profitable for teaching, for reproof, for correction, and for training in righteousness, that the man of God may be competent, equipped for every good work" (2 Tim. 3:16-17). Therefore, Paul writes: "I charge you in the presence of God and of Christ Jesus, who is to judge the living and the dead, and by his appearing and his kingdom: preach the word; be ready in season and out of season; reprove, rebuke, and exhort, with complete patience and teaching" (2 Tim. 4:1-2).

Our summarizing statement for 1-2 Timothy on the timeline's map is "Preach the Word of Christ," with the key verse: "Preach the word; be ready in season and out of season; reprove, rebuke, and exhort, with complete patience and teaching" (2 Tim. 4:2). Paul has served Jesus Christ faithfully for more than thirty years. He has traveled vast distances, preached hundreds of sermons, and taught thousands of hours. He has seen countless conversions, new churches planted, and worked alongside men and women from diverse social classes and ethnic backgrounds in the cause of Christ. He also knows well the tactics and temptations of the enemy of our souls. His mature counsel to Timothy is as urgent then as it is today. Pastors and professors, missionaries and church planters, small group discussion leaders and Sunday school teachers must give their best attention to teaching the Word of God. God's glorious truth about his Son Jesus Christ has been entrusted to the church. God's people have been given the sacred responsibility of teaching the gospel to the nations.

TITUS, written by Paul to Titus (c. AD 63-65)

Paul's final letter to Titus was written during this period. Paul had first met Titus during his early missionary journeys (Gal. 2:1). Titus had come to Christ from a Gentile background. He was an important example of Paul's teaching that Gentiles were justified by faith, and as such, they should be treated as full members of God's covenant family apart from circumcision (Gal. 2:1, 3). Titus had become a faithful missionary companion and faithful co-laborer for Christ. Paul had entrusted Titus to deliver his painful letter to the Corinthian church; he had also been responsible for collecting their portion of the gift for the saints in Jerusalem (2 Cor. 2:3-4, 13; 7:6-16; 8:16-24). Paul had given Titus responsibility to establish godly leadership for the growing church in Crete (Titus 1:5). Paul's letter to Titus encourages him to accomplish this task with dedicated service.

Paul begins his letter with an extended opening greeting, recalling God's call upon his life. He identifies himself as a servant of God and an apostle of Jesus Christ, which is "for the sake of the faith of God's elect and their knowledge of the truth," which Paul affirms is in accordance with "godliness, in hope of eternal life, which God, who never lies, promised before the ages began and at the proper time manifested in his word through the preaching with which I have been entrusted by the command of God our Savior" (Titus 1:1-3; cf. Rom. 1:1-6). As Paul's final days draw near, Christ's call upon his life and the priority of preaching the word of God remain central. He writes to Titus with affection as "my true child in a common faith" (Titus 1:4). After the initial evangelization of Crete, Titus is directed to appoint leaders for the new churches in every city. As in 1-2 Timothy, personal godliness is the most significant qualification for church leadership (Titus 1:5-9; cf. 1 Tim. 3:1-6). Leaders are to be above reproach; they must "not be arrogant or quick-tempered or a drunkard or violent or greedy for gain, but hospitable, a lover of good, self-controlled, upright, holy, and disciplined" (Titus 1:7-8). They must hold firm to the word of God and be able "to give instruction in sound doctrine and also to rebuke those who contradict it" (Titus 1:9). Paul is again concerned about the misunderstanding of the gospel from "those of the circumcision party" who are upsetting "whole families" by their teaching (Titus 1:10-11). Paul uses the same technical terminology for Pharisaic traditions of the Oral Law that can obscure the accomplishment of the cross (Titus 1:13; cf. 1 Tim. 1:4; Titus 3:9). Titus is reminded that purity has been achieved through Christ's work (Titus 1:15).

Paul admonishes Titus to teach what accords with sound doctrine (Titus 2:1). He is to be an example of the good works that flow from justification by faith (Titus 2:7). Paul's theological vision of the church as God's renewed humanity in Christ reflects key themes of his entire ministry:

> The grace of God has appeared, bringing salvation for all people, training us to renounce ungodliness and worldly passions, and to live self-controlled, upright, and godly lives in the present age, waiting for our blessed hope, the appearing of the glory of our great God and Savior Jesus Christ, who gave himself for us to redeem us from all lawlessness and to purify for himself a people for his own possession who are zealous for good works. (Titus 2:11-14)

Paul urges Titus to declare these things, and to "exhort and rebuke with all authority" (Titus 2:15). He must call the church to obedience, so that God's people are ready for every good work (Titus 3:1). Paul rehearses the good news that has compelled his missionary service for decades:

> When the goodness and loving kindness of God our Savior appeared, he saved us, not because of works done by us in righteousness, but according to his own mercy, by the washing of regeneration and renewal of the Holy Spirit, whom he poured out on us richly through Jesus Christ our Savior, so that being justified by his grace we might become heirs according to the hope of eternal life. (Titus 3:4-7)

Paul affirms that these truths are indeed "excellent and profitable" for all people (Titus 3:8).

Our summarizing statement for Titus on the timeline's map is "Serve Christ our Savior," with the following key verse: "As for you, teach what accords with sound doctrine" (Titus 2:1). Paul calls Titus to dedicated service in the cause of Christ. New leaders must be identified in every city, among every people, and in every generation. They must be charged to herald the breathtaking gospel of God's grace in Christ. Jesus is our Savior who gave himself up for us. His blood has purified us. He has made us into a people for his own possession, zealous to display his glory in our lives. These great theological truths provide a lasting impression of Paul's life, conversion, and missionary labor. The death and resurrection of Christ changed his life. The love of Christ compelled his service. Jesus Christ continues to do the same for us today.

As we conclude Part 2 of TEACHING, I would encourage you to read through Paul's letters written from prison as well as those he sends to the next generation of Christian leaders. Allow the Word of God to saturate your own soul and lead you into praise. Take time to assess the patterns of your own discipleship. Ephesians provides an overwhelming vision of Jesus Christ and the extraordinary privilege of being incorporated into the church, his beloved bride. Philippians reveals the irrepressible joy that is found in Christ, no matter what our circumstances may be. Colossians reminds us that new life in Christ will grow, even through the work of others we may influence.

Philemon provides us with an intimate portrait of real ministry among real lives, even as the gospel proves that we are brothers. 1-2 Timothy call us to a courageous ministry based on the Word of God, even when we are tempted to be afraid of the challenges. Titus urges us to dedicated service unto Christ, even when the task seems great. Jesus Christ is our absolute sufficiency. He stands now as a banner for the nations and his resting place is glorious (Isa. 11:10). He has purposed that "the earth will be filled will the knowledge of the glory of the LORD as the waters cover the sea" (Hab. 2:14). Refresh your eyes with the sea of Christian mission on the New Testament timeline. Ask the Lord where he is calling you to serve.

Chapter 8
TEACHING Part 3

PART 3 OF TEACHING surveys the final seven New Testament letters, which include 1-2 Peter, Hebrews, Jude, and 1-3 John. These seven letters are sometimes called the General Epistles, since they were written to the church as a whole, or at least to a large geographical region. The Holy Spirit inspires the General Epistles to strengthen the church facing persecution, false teaching, and demonic power in an increasingly hostile world. It is important for us to remember that Christian teaching provokes persecution from two very different directions. On the one side, many religious Jews take offense at the cross and despise the inclusion of the nations. On the other side, many idolatrous pagans scorn the cross and refuse to glorify the God of Israel. The Christian community stands in the midst of these worlds with the teaching of Christ. God's people proclaim his death and resurrection according to the Scriptures. They offer forgiveness of sins for all who believe in his name. They invite all nations into the people of God as co-heirs with Christ. Christian teaching thus confronts both religious nationalism and Roman imperialism with the Lordship of Christ over all the earth. Under his sovereign hand, we will see that that societal persecution only causes the word of Christ to spread. We will discover that false teaching makes the distinctive light of the gospel to shine. We will realize that no power in heaven or on earth is able to prevail against the church, as the stone cut without human hands continues to fill the earth.

Roadmap to the chapter

As we trace God's redemptive purpose through the General Epistles, make sure that you have an open Bible nearby so that you can follow along. We will again present the content of the letters and then provide a summarizing statement and key verse for each letter to help you remember their teaching about Christ. Make sure that you locate each letter on the map of expanding Christian mission. Near the lower section of PENTECOST, you will also find the General Epistles as well as several key events that take place at this time, including the persecution of early Christian leaders and the outbreak of the Jewish War in AD 66, which leads to the destruction of the Jerusalem Temple in AD 70. We will integrate these headings into the narrative as we survey the General Epistles. The period of TEACHING will conclude with a summary of seven key beliefs that unify church teaching and compel Christian mission.

James, the brother of Jesus is executed in Jerusalem (AD 62)

The dramatic spread of Christian teaching continues to produce violent opposition in Israel. In early AD 62, the Roman governor Festus suddenly dies. You may recall that the apostle Paul had testified before him (Acts 25-26). Although Festus had not received his testimony about Christ, he had honored Paul's appeal to Caesar and had sent him as an imperial prisoner for trial in Rome (Acts 27-28). While Paul is imprisoned in Rome, the church also faces violent opposition in Jerusalem. During the short time before Festus' replacement arrives, the Jerusalem religious leadership moves violently against the church. A certain Ananus has recently been appointed high priest. He was a descendant of Annas, the father-in-law of Caiaphas, who had condemned Jesus and had ordered early Christian leaders not to speak or teach in his name (John 18:13, 24; Acts 4:6, 18). Ananus arrests James, the brother of Jesus, who had been leading the Christian community in Jerusalem for several decades. Annas also arrests some of James' closest companions and brings them before the Sanhedrin. Josephus reports that when Annas "had formed an accusation against them as breakers of the law, he delivered them to be stoned" (*Ant.* 20:200). James is brought before the people assembled for the Feast of Passover. He is commanded to rebuke those in Israel who openly confess that Jesus is the Messiah. Instead, James boldly testifies that Jesus is

Israel's promised Messiah, and that he is seated at the right hand of God and will come again in glory. As his accusers begin to stone him to death, James follows the example of Christ and prays: "Father, forgive them, for they know not what they do" (see Luke 23:34).

The great fire in Rome and persecution of Christians (AD 64)

Faithful Christian teaching also sparks persecution from imperial Rome, the very city where Paul is imprisoned. In AD 64, a great fire devastates the city. Three of Rome's central districts are destroyed. Rumors circulate that Nero set the fire to make room for his new palace. He responds by falsely accusing the Christian community for starting the blaze. He orders them to be burned alive as human torches to illuminate his evening parties at the imperial palace. This is the man to whom Paul has appealed and now awaits trial! The Roman historian Tacitus records that an immense multitude was convicted, not so much for the crime of setting fire to the city, but for "hatred against mankind." He names their founder as *"Christus,* who suffered the extreme penalty of crucifixion during the reign of Tiberius at the hand of the procurator Pontius Pilate." Although agreeing that Christians are criminals, he notes that the manner of their death stirred compassion in those who watched.

Several Roman writers fuel such persecution through popular slander. Their primary accusations against Christians are atheism, cannibalism, and incest. They attack Christians as atheists for not honoring the traditional gods or the deified emperors. They mock Christians as cannibals after hearing rumors that they "eat the body and drink the blood of their god." They slander Christians for their "love feasts" where everyone is called "brother and sister." Christianity appears to them as something dangerously new in a culture that values antiquity. They consider it un-Roman, a foreign superstition originating from a small corner of the empire. They label Christians in general as "haters of humanity," because they separate from the accepted pleasures and practices of Roman society to worship a crucified criminal whom they claim to be God.

Despite the intensity of persecution, the exalted Jesus protects the lives of many Christians. He grants others the privilege of suffering for the sake of his name. He also provides godly leadership and teaching to shepherd his beloved flock. The apostle Peter is also in Rome at this time. He has followed

Christ all the way from the shores of the Sea of Galilee to the heart of the Roman Empire. He has learned much about faithfulness to Christ when facing persecution, whether from fellow Israelites or the broader Roman world. The Holy Spirit now moves Peter to write two general letters from Rome to encourage the Christian community spreading throughout the world.

1-2 PETER, written by Peter to the dispersed church (c. AD 64-65)

1-2 Peter are the two letters written by the apostle Peter near the end of his earthly pilgrimage and service to Jesus Christ. 1 Peter is addressed to believers scattered across five provinces of Pontus, Galatia, Cappadocia, Asia, and Bithynia (1 Pet. 1:1). This vast area of 129,000 square miles had a population of around 8,500,000 in the first century. On the New Testament timeline, these provinces encompass the northern and western parts of modern day Turkey. The letters are sent from "Babylon," which is a veiled reference to Rome (1 Pet. 5:13; cf. Rev. 18:2). These letters are written in such an elevated Greek style that many have wondered how a Galilean fisherman could have authored them. Peter tells us that he wrote the letters with the help of Silvanus (also known as Silas), who had served alongside Paul (1 Pet. 5:12; cf. Acts 15:22; 16:19, 25). Peter writes as an eyewitness of Christ, bearing testimony that "this is the true grace of God" (1 Pet. 5:12, cf. 2 Pet. 1:16). He presents a moving vision of the church as God's chosen people, sprinkled by the blood of Christ, sanctified by the Spirit, and ready for obedience (1 Pet. 1:2). He encourages believers to stand firm in the face of persecution and to reject false teaching. By God's sovereign hand, such afflictions will only cause Christians to grow in godliness, as they await Christ's return with confidence (1 Pet. 1:6-9). Until that day, godly leaders must faithfully shepherd the flock of Christ until "the chief Shepherd appears" and then they will receive "the unfading crown of glory" (1 Pet. 5:4).

Jesus transforms Peter, the Galilean fisherman, into a dedicated servant leader. Writing in the very real context of increasing persecution and hostility, Peter speaks with urgency and calls the church to action. There are almost forty imperatives in these two letters. He admonishes his hearers that they are to prepare their minds for action, being "sober-minded" as they set their hope "fully on the grace that will be brought ... at the revelation of Jesus Christ" (1 Pet. 1:13). He tells them not to be conformed to the "passions of your former ignorance," but instead, they are to "be holy in all your conduct" (1 Pet. 1:14-15), which reminds us of Israel's calling (Lev. 19:2; Rom. 12:1-2). They have been ransomed "with the precious blood of Christ" and born again through "the living and abiding Word of God" (1 Pet. 1:19, 23; cf. John 1:12-13; 3:3). Therefore, they must long for the pure spiritual milk of God's word, so that they might grow up into salvation (1 Pet. 2:2). Together, like living stones, they are being "built up as a spiritual house, to be a holy priesthood, to offer spiritual sacrifices acceptable to God through Jesus Christ" (1 Pet. 2:5; cf. Eph. 2:19-22). Jesus himself is the stone that the builders rejected, which has become the cornerstone (1 Pet. 2:6-8; cf. Ps. 118:22; Isa. 8:14; 28:16). All who believe in Christ now share Israel's calling as "a chosen race, a royal priesthood, a holy nation, a people for his own possession" (1 Pet. 2:9; cf. Exod. 19:6; Deut. 7:6). In fulfillment of God's redemptive purpose, Peter reminds the Gentiles: "Once you were not a people, but now you are God's people; once you had not received mercy, but now you have received mercy" (1 Pet. 2:10; cf. Hos. 2:23; Rom. 9:25-26).

As God's people grow in godliness, they are to "abstain from the passions of the flesh which wage war against your soul" and "keep their conduct honorable" (1 Pet. 2:11-12). They "live as people who are free," yet they are now "servants of God" (1 Pet. 2:16; Exod. 8:20; 12:31). They follow the example of Christ "who bore our sins in his body on the tree, that we might die to sin and live to righteousness" (1 Pet. 2:21-24; cf. Isa. 53:5). Godliness is to be reflected in their marriage relationships, their love for one another, and their blessing upon those who persecute them (1 Pet. 3:1-12). Such actions win others to Christ (1 Pet. 3:1, 15-16). Believers must be "self-controlled and sober-minded" (1 Pet. 4:7; 5:7). Peter knows from experience that they must resist the devil, for "after you have suffered a little while, the God of all grace, who has called you to his eternal glory in Christ, will himself restore, confirm, strengthen, and establish you" (1 Pet. 5:9-10; Luke 22:31-34; John 21:7-18).

2 Peter was written a short time later and shares the same concerns as his first letter. Peter writes a final reminder to "make your calling and election sure" and urges believers to keep growing in holiness and godliness (2 Pet. 1:10; 1:3, 6-7; 3:11). He writes in full awareness "that the putting off of my body will be soon, as our Lord Jesus Christ made clear to me" (2 Pet. 1:14; see John 21:18-19). He testifies as an eyewitness of Christ's majesty,

remembering the unforgettable moment when God the Father spoke from heaven in an audible voice: "This is my beloved Son, with whom I am well pleased" (2 Pet. 1:17-18; cf. Matt. 17:5). Peter reminds the church that God's true prophets were inspired by the Holy Spirit and predicted both the sufferings of Christ and the glories to follow (2 Pet. 1:19-21; cf. Pet. 1:10-12). Just as false prophets led Israel astray, he warns them that false teachers will be among them, secretly bringing false teaching into the church (2 Pet. 2:1). False teaching always leads to ungodliness and the defacing of God's image (2 Pet. 2:10-21). False teachers offer sensual pleasures now, but their end will be destruction and judgment (2 Pet. 3:7). Believers must trust God's word and remain faithful as they await Christ's glorious return. The day of the Lord will come and the world will be refined by fire. Evil will be condemned forever. According to God's promise, believers will inherit "a new heavens and a new earth in which righteousness dwells" (2 Pet. 3:13; Isa. 65:17; 66:22).

Our summarizing statement for 1-2 Peter on the timeline's map is "Shepherd the flock of Christ," with the following key verse: "Shepherd the flock of God that is among you" (1 Pet. 5:2). Peter never forgot the moment when Jesus restored him. After having denied Jesus three times, Peter was asked three times: "Do you love me?" When Peter answered: "Yes, Lord," Jesus then commanded him: "Feed my sheep" (John 21:15-17). Peter spent the rest of his life in Christ's service as a faithful shepherd of Christ's flock. He instructs the next generation of leaders to do the same. They too must "shepherd the flock of God that is among you, exercising oversight, not under compulsion, but willingly, as God would have you; not for shameful gain, but eagerly; not domineering over those in your charge, but being examples to the flock" (1 Pet. 5:2-3). These letters provide our last words from the apostle Peter. He will soon be crucified in Rome. This will end Peter's earthly ministry, but he knows that when the chief Shepherd appears, all who believe will receive "the unfading crown of glory" (1 Pet. 5:4).

Paul is beheaded and Peter is crucified under Nero (c. AD 65)

The persecution against the church under Nero culminates in the death of Paul and Peter, apostles of the Lord Jesus Christ. Although the New Testament is silent as to the exact manner and place, several sources confirm that Paul is beheaded and Peter crucified upside down outside the city of Rome.

As a Roman citizen, Paul would have been exempt from the humiliation of the cross. As a member of a subject people, Peter would endure the cross of shame. Paul describes his imminent death as "a drink offering" upon the altar (2 Tim. 4:6; Exod. 29:40-41). Peter knows that his manner of death will fulfill Jesus' word (2 Pet. 1:14; John 21:18-19).

Although different in age, gifting, and personality, Peter and Paul share a great deal. Both men grew up as devout Jews. They heard, prayed, and read the Scriptures. They knew the hope of Israel. Both men were overwhelmed by their own sin when they first met Christ—Peter on the shores of Galilee and Paul on the road to Damascus (Luke 5:8; Acts 9:4-5). Both men found forgiveness through faith in Christ and were called to spend their lives in his service. Peter and Paul labored in many of the same fields in Jerusalem, Antioch, Asia Minor, and Rome. They discovered that Christ's love compels us. They realized that Christ's power is made perfect in our weakness. They found that Christ's life and death provide the pattern for their own (Phil. 3:17; 1 Pet. 2:21). Both share in Christ's sufferings, becoming like him in their death (Phi. 3:10). Both share in Christ's resurrection, becoming like him in glory (Phi. 3:11; Rev. 6:10).

The passing of significant Christian leaders gives us pause. We often realize just how important they have been in our lives, even at the mention of their name. Take a moment now to remember and thank Jesus Christ for those whom he has used to shape your life of faith. The lives of faithful leaders also inspire our own dedicated service to the Lord. The word of Christ must continue to spread throughout the world. He will raise up faithful teachers in every generation and in every place, even if their names are unknown to us. We will see this next in an extraordinary letter, which we call Hebrews.

HEBREWS, written to Jewish (Hebrew) Christians (c. AD 65).

The letter of Hebrews is unique. Whereas all of the other New Testament letters identify their author, the author of Hebrews remains uncertain. Most early readers recognized that the elevated literary style, method of argumentation, and rhetorical plan of Hebrews differs considerably from all of Paul's known writings. At the same time, Hebrews shares important theological ideas with Paul, such as Jesus Christ as the divine Son of God, the centrality of his death and resurrection, and the importance of faith. The personal greetings, including "our brother Timothy," are similar to those found at the end of Paul's letters (Heb. 13:17-25). Therefore, the most compelling view of authorship is someone closely associated with Paul's missionary team. The best suggestions are Barnabas, the Levite from Cyprus, an early companion of Paul (Acts 4:36; 13:2; 15:39); Silas (also known as Silvanus), who worked with Timothy and whose mastery of Greek is well attested (Acts 17:14-15; 1 Thess. 1:1; 1 Pet. 5:12); or perhaps best of all Apollos, "a native of Alexandria ... an eloquent man, competent in the Scriptures" (Acts 18:24; cf. 1 Cor. 3:5-6; 16:12), who powerfully showed the Jews from Scripture that Jesus was the Messiah (Acts 18:28).

The specific location of the audience of Hebrews is also uncertain. Scholars have suggested Rome, Jerusalem, or Alexandria as possible locations. Alexandria was home to a large Diaspora Jewish community, including Apollos (Acts 18:24). For our study, we have placed Hebrews near Alexandria on the New Testament timeline, near the famous lighthouse we learned about earlier in our study. The beam of light reflected by polished bronze mirrors on this lighthouse could be seen one hundred miles away, but for the writer of Hebrews, the radiant glory of Christ shines even further.

Although the author and location of Hebrews are uncertain, what is absolutely certain is that the author holds a breathtaking view of Jesus Christ. He describes the person of Christ and the Christian life with a remarkably vivid and rich vocabulary. There are 169 Greek words in Hebrews that do not occur elsewhere in the New Testament. The literary style of Hebrews is without equal in Scripture. The author was intimately acquainted with the Old Testament Scriptures, especially the Greek translation known as the Septuagint. He develops his entire discourse through scriptural exposition and application. There are thirty-one explicit scriptural citations and seventy-five clear allusions. His "word of exhortation" aims to encourage believers to remain faithful to Christ, even when facing persecution, imprisonment, and the plundering of their property (Heb. 13:22; cf. Heb. 10:32-39; 12:1-6). Some members of the believing community had apparently ceased meeting openly together as Christians, while others seemed in danger of returning to their ancestral customs for fear of reprisal (Heb. 10:25). All of this evidence, together with consistent descriptions of the Jerusalem Temple in the present tense, suggests a date around AD 65 prior to the destruction of the city in AD 70, which will be rehearsed later in this chapter.

The central thesis of Hebrews is that Jesus Christ is God's climactic word to his people. The opening sentence announces that the God who had spoken in many and various ways to our ancestors through the prophets has "in these last days ... spoken to us by his Son, whom he appointed the heir of all things, through whom also he created the world" (Heb. 1:1-2). Many translations begin verse 2 with "but" and introduce a contrast that is not in the original text. The author of Hebrews is not contrasting but actually emphasizing that the God whose voice we know from the Old Testament Scriptures has now spoken through his one and only Son. The Son is "the radiance of the glory of God and the exact imprint of his nature" (Heb. 1:3). If we want to know what God is like, we look to Jesus, the Son—for God now speaks to us through *him*. The writer emphasizes that the Son "upholds the universe by the word of his power," and that after making purification for sins, "he sat down at the right hand of the Majesty on high" (Heb. 1:3). The Son is superior to the angels, for "the name he has inherited is more excellent than theirs" (Heb. 1:4). The reality that God has spoken again stirs those who hear to listen well. Just as "God has spoken" is the main verb in the first sentence (Hebrews 1:1-4), the letter climaxes with the warning: "See that you do not refuse him who is speaking" (Heb. 12:25).

The rhetorical plan of Hebrews develops like a carefully constructed sermon. Through a series of seven scriptural expositions, the author presents the surpassing excellence of Jesus Christ as God's climactic Word. Each exposition leads to an exhortation to "hold fast our confession" of Christ (Heb. 4:14). Each Scriptural exposition also contains a warning of God's judgment against those who would draw back from their commitment to Christ (Heb. 2:1-4; 3:1, 12-14; 4:1, 14-16; 6:1, 18; 10:19-39; 12:1-3, 18-28).

First, the author presents the preeminence of the Son above the angels through a chain of seven Scripture citations (Heb. 1:5-2:4; citing Ps. 2:7; 2 Sam. 7:14; Deut. 32:43; Pss. 104:4; 45:6-7; 102:25-27; 110:1). The exhortation follows that the readers are to pay closer to attention to what they have heard, lest they drift from it. The writer recalls that the revelation of God's word on Mount Sinai was understood as having been accompanied by angels of the heavenly court (Heb. 2:1-3; cf. Deut. 33:2; Acts 7:53; Gal. 3:19). The author implies that none can safely remain indifferent to God's climactic word spoken in his Son.

Second, the author presents Jesus as the faithful representative of humanity, as described in Ps. 8 (Heb. 2:5-18). God had given humanity a unique status in creation, crowning them with glory and honor and giving them authority to rule over God's creation (Ps. 8; cf. Gen. 1:26-28). The author of Hebrews recalls this place of honor given to humanity, as those made "for a little while lower than the angels" and yet crowned with "glory and honor," with everything in subjection under them (Heb. 2:6-8; citing Ps. 8:4-6). The author of Hebrews draws our eyes now to behold Jesus, who is crowned with "glory and honor" through his incarnation, death, and resurrection (Heb. 2:7). Jesus is the exact representation of God's nature, and he is the one who brings "many sons to glory" (Heb. 2:10). Therefore, believers must keep their attention fixed upon Jesus, who is the author of our salvation and the high priest of our confession.

Third, the author explores the promised rest for the people of God with the key phrase "today if you hear his voice" from Ps. 95 (Heb. 3:1-4:13). He reminds his hearers that the Exodus generation perished in the wilderness due to their lack of faith (Num. 14). He warns them to take care and "exhort one another every day, as long as it is called 'today,' that none of you may be hardened by the deceitfulness of sin. For we have come to share in Christ, if indeed we hold our original confidence firm to the end" (Heb. 3:12-14). Believers are urged to enter Christ's Sabbath rest sincerely, since God's living and active word will reveal the truth of our confession (Heb. 4:11-13).

Fourth, the author interprets Christ as "a priest forever, after the order of Melchizedek" from Ps. 110 (Heb. 4:14-7:28). Christ's eternal high priestly ministry was carried out in the heavenly sanctuary of which the earthly is a copy (Heb. 4:14; 8:5; cf. Exod. 25:40). There he offered himself once for all time (Heb. 7:27). Through him we have forgiveness of sins and access to God's throne. Believers are warned about the spiritual danger of falling away from their confession. To do so would in effect be "crucifying once again the Son of God ... and holding him up to contempt" (Heb. 6:6). Though the writer issues a stern warning, he is sure that the believers will listen (Heb. 6:9). They will remain steadfast since Christ "always lives to make intercession for them" (Heb. 7:25).

Fifth, the author displays Christ as the mediator of the new covenant promised in Jer. 31 (Heb. 8:1-10:31). In our study of the Old Testament, we saw that the disobedience of God's people under the Mosaic covenant (also known as the *old* covenant), led to the judgment of exile (Jer. 11). The prophet Jeremiah had spoken about a future time when God would make a *new* covenant, unlike the old covenant, which Israel had broken. In the Old Testament, covenants were made (lit. "cut") by shedding the blood of an animal (cf. Gen. 15:7-21; Exod. 24:1-8). Christ inaugurates the new covenant with his *own* shed blood (Heb. 9:11-12; cf. Luke 22:20; 1 Cor. 11:25). His blood secures eternal redemption and purifies our conscience to serve the living God (Heb. 9:12-15). Christ's atoning death has enacted the new covenant that no longer requires the Levitical sacrifices. He offers himself once "for all time," thereby securing forgiveness and sanctification for us (Heb. 10:10, 14). Therefore, God's people are assured that they have confidence to enter "the holy places by the blood of Jesus, by the new and living way that he opened for us through the curtain, that is, through his flesh" (Heb. 10:19-20). Believers are again exhorted to "hold fast the confession of our hope without wavering" (Heb. 10:23). For those who have "spurned the Son of God," there is only a fearful expectation of judgment (Heb. 10:26-31).

Sixth, the author exalts Jesus as the ultimate example of persevering faith from Hab. 2 (Heb. 10:32-12:2). Believers "have need of endurance, so that when you have done the will of God you may receive what is promised" (Heb. 10:36). They must not shrink back but live by faith which is "the assurance of things hoped for, the conviction of things not seen" (Heb. 11:1). The author provides a sweeping view of Old Testament examples from Abel, Enoch, Noah, Abraham and Sarah, Isaac and Jacob, Moses and Joshua, Judges, and the prophets. This powerful chapter rehearses the great narrative of Scripture to spur persevering faith in the fulfillment of God's promise in Christ. Surrounded by a great cloud of witnesses, believers are to "run with endurance the race that is set before us" with eyes fixed upon Jesus, "the founder and perfecter of our faith, who for the joy that was set before him endured the cross, despising the shame, and is seated at the right hand of the throne of God" (Heb. 12:1-2).

Seventh, the author uses the example of Jesus to interpret persecution and hostility, as evidence of sonship from Prov. 3. Suffering is actually the divine discipline of our heavenly Father that will reap a great reward in the end. Our Father trains and disciplines those whom he loves. God always acts "for our good, that we may share his holiness" (Heb. 12:10). Though painful, God's discipline yields the "fruit of righteousness" for those who have been trained by it (Heb. 12:11). God's climatic theophany, the revelation of himself, has been spoken to us in Christ. Those who hear his voice cannot turn back. The writer bursts forth in a lofty description of the new reality for those who have faith in Christ:

> You have come to Mount Zion and to the city of the living God, the heavenly Jerusalem, and to innumerable angels in festal gathering, and to the assembly of the firstborn who are enrolled in heaven, and to God, the judge of all, and to the spirits of the righteous made perfect, and to Jesus, the mediator of a new covenant, and to the sprinkled blood that speaks a better word than the blood of Abel. (Heb. 12:22-24)

With this glorious hope in view, God's people are warned not to refuse "him who is speaking" to us in his Son (Heb. 12:25). Believers are reminded that they will not escape God's judgment if they reject the words that come from heaven itself (Heb. 12:25; cf. Heb. 1:1-2; 2:1-4). The letter closes with final exhortations and warnings followed by personal greetings (Heb. 13).

Our summarizing statement for Hebrews on the timeline's map is "Christ is above all," with the following key verse: "In these last days he has spoken to us by his Son, whom he appointed the heir of all things, through whom also he created the world" (Heb. 1:1-2). God's climactic word has been spoken in Christ. God's word to us in his Son inaugurates the promised "latter days" (Heb. 1:1; 6:5; 9:26; cf. Deut. 4:30; Isa. 2:2; Jer. 23:20; Dan. 2:28; Hos. 3:5; Mark 1:15; John 2:18; 1 Cor. 10:11; 1 Pet. 1:20). Jesus Christ sits enthroned above the angels. He represents the true humanity. He secures our promised rest. He intercedes as our great High Priest. He mediates the new covenant in his blood. He goes before us as our example of persevering faith. His suffering and exaltation reveal the path to glory. None can remain indifferent to him.

JUDE, written by Jude to the church in Jerusalem (c. AD 65)

We now turn to consider our next General Epistle. Jude is a short letter written by Jude, one of Jesus' brothers (see Matt. 13:55), to the church in

Jerusalem. Like James, Jude identifies himself as "a servant of Jesus Christ" (Jude 1:1). Although Jesus' earthly brothers did not initially believe in him (John 7:3-5), James and Jude were among those who had gathered at Pentecost (Acts 1:14), and they became leaders in the church (1 Cor. 9:5). Jude's reference to Jesus as "our only Master and Lord" (Jude 1:4), is a remarkable testimony that he had come to believe that Jesus, his (earthly) brother, was Israel's promised Messiah. Jude addresses "those who are called, beloved in God the Father and kept for Jesus Christ" (Jude 1:1). Although he intended to write about their common salvation, Jude found it necessary to urge his readers "to contend for the faith" (Jude 1:3). His short yet powerful letter exposes the lie of those teaching that the grace of God was in fact a license for sin. All early Christian leaders condemned such teaching as a fundamental misunderstanding of the gospel (Rom. 5:18; 6:1-15; 2 Pet. 2:1; 1 John 2:1).

Jude asserts that those who pervert the grace of God into sensuality will face judgment for denying Jesus, who is Master and Lord (Jude 1:4). He reasons from Scripture to confirm the fearful reality of God's righteous judgment. He cites the example of the Exodus generation who perished in unbelief (Jude 1:5; cf. Num. 14:11-12). He describes God's judgment upon angels who rebelled against his established authority (Jude 1:6; cf. 2 Pet. 2:4; Rev. 20:2; possible allusion to Gen. 6:1-4). Lastly, he points to God's judgment upon the sexual immorality of Sodom and Gomorrah as an example of personal conduct that provokes God's wrath (Jude 1:7; cf. Gen. 19:1-28).

Jude warns his readers that false teachers among them likewise "defile the flesh, reject authority, and blaspheme the glorious ones" (Jude 1:8). Their own appetites destroy them. Jude likens them to several key figures in the Old Testament who had walked contrary to God's ways (Jude 1:11; cf. Gen. 4; Num. 16; 22). With a set of vivid images, Jude likens those who pervert God's grace into sin as hidden reefs upon which ships crash, shepherds gorging themselves on the sheep, waterless clouds with no rain, uprooted trees with no fruit, wild waves casting up foam, and wandering stars in outer darkness (Jude 1:12-13). Jude warns of the certainty of God's judgment upon the ungodly (Jude 1:14-15), quoting from some well-known (non-canonical) literature of his day. Jude does not cite these works as having canonical authority, but rather, as illustrations similar to Paul's use of Greek poets (see Acts 17:28; 1 Cor. 15:33; Titus 1:12).

Believers should not be surprised by the presence of false teachers, which the apostles predicted would come in the latter days (Jude 1:17-18; cf. Acts 20:29-30; 1 Tim. 4:1-5; 2 Tim. 3:1-5; 2 Pet. 3:2-3). Rather, they must devote their best attention to building themselves up in the "most holy faith and praying in the Holy Spirit" (Jude 1:20). Jude admonishes them to keep themselves in the love of God, "waiting for the mercy of our Lord Jesus Christ that leads to eternal life" (Jude 1:21). They must be merciful on those who are afflicted with doubt and sin. They snatch others as out of the fire. They pursue holiness "without which no one will see the Lord" (Heb. 12:14; cf. Matt. 5:8; 1 Thess. 4:7). Jude closes in confident praise entrusting them "to him who is able to keep you from stumbling and to present you blameless before the presence of his glory with great joy, to the only God, our Savior, through Jesus Christ our Lord, be glory, majesty, dominion, and authority, before all time and now and forever. Amen" (Jude 1:24-25).

Our summarizing statement for Jude on the timeline's map is "Keep yourself for Christ," with the following key verse: "Contend for the faith that was once for all delivered to the saints" (Jude 1:3). Believers today must contend for the faith entrusted to them. We must recognize as false those who would pervert the grace of God into a license for sin. God has saved us by grace in order that we might live in holiness before him. God's judgment will be revealed against those who claim Christ as Savior and yet deny him as Lord. Believers live in confident assurance that Christ will keep us from falling and present us blameless before his glorious presence with great joy.

1-3 JOHN, written by the apostle John to the church (c. AD 65-95)

1-3 John are the last of the General Epistles. These three short letters are written by the apostle John toward the end of his life and ministry near Ephesus, although the exact date is unclear. We include these letters among the General Epistles, since no specific audience is named. John's letters were probably circulated among the Christian communities throughout the region of Asia Minor. The literary style closely resembles the Gospel of John, which the apostle John also wrote. John uses simple vocabulary and short sentences to convey lofty truths about Christ. John writes as an eyewitness of that "which we have heard, which we have seen with our eyes, which we looked upon and have touched with our hands, concerning the word of life" (1 John

1:1; cf. John 20:30-31; 21:24-25). As with his Gospel, John affirms that the Word took on flesh, revealing eternal life (1 John 1:2; John 1:14; 3:16; 17:3; 20:31). Just as Christ reveals the love of God, Christian community is defined by love for one another (1 John 3:11, 23; 4:7, 11-12; 2 John 1:5). John's letters are an enduring testimony of the beloved disciple to his beloved children in the faith.

John writes with the desire that "our joy may be complete" (1 John 1:4). He knows no greater joy than to hear that his children are walking in the truth (3 John 1:4). John affirms his message that "God is light, and in him is no darkness at all" (1 John 1:5). Believers have fellowship with one another as they walk in the light "and the blood of Jesus his Son cleanses us from all sin" (1 John 1:7). Those who claim to be without sin deceive themselves and make God a liar. Those who confess their sin find that they have an advocate with the Father, who is "Jesus Christ the righteous" (1 John 2:1). John makes the remarkable statement Christ is the atoning sacrifice "for our sins, and not for ours only but also for the sins of the whole world" (1 John 2:2; cf. John 3:16). Christian community exists in the world to bear witness of Christ's atoning death for the world.

For John, this means that believers are those who are born again from above (John 3:3). This new birth is evidenced by a new life of keeping his commandments (1 John 2:3; cf. Jer. 31:34). He writes, therefore, that whoever keeps God's word, that the love of God is perfected in them (1 John 2:5; cf. John 14:15). Believers must walk in truth, love, and imitation of Christ. They obey Jesus' new commandment "that you love one another: just as I have loved you" (John 13:34; cf. John 15:12; 1 John 2:7; 2 John 1:5). He warns his readers that they are not to love the world or the things in the world. He warns: "If anyone loves the world, the love of the Father is not in him. For all that is in the world—the desires of the flesh and the desires of the eyes and pride in possessions—is not from the Father but is from the world. And the world is passing away along with its desires, but whoever does the will of God abides forever" (1 John 2:15-17). Christian community exists in the love of Christ to reflect his love in a violent world.

John writes with urgency knowing that spiritual danger abounds in the latter days. He gives the strong warning that the spirit of the antichrist is recognized in those who deny that Jesus is the Christ (1 John 2:22; 4:1-3;

2 John 1:7). The Holy Spirit will always testify that Jesus is the Christ (John 15:26; 1 John 4:2; 5:6; cf. 1 Cor. 12:3). Those who deny the Son deny the Father, but whoever acknowledges the Son will know the Father (1 John 2:23; 4:15; 5:1; 2 John 1:9; cf. John 5:23). Believers must abide in Christ and the truth that they have received (1 John 2:24-25; cf. John 15:4). Their lives bear fruit in hopeful anticipation of Christ's coming again (1 John 2:28). When he appears, they shall behold him and be made like him (1 John 3:2). Christian community exists in the hope of Christ's return to warn an unwary world.

John declares that the Son of God appeared to destroy the works of the devil (1 John 3:8). Those who have been born of God walk in newness of life. They love one another in deed and truth (1 John 3:11, 16-18; 4:20-21). They overcome the world by God's love supremely manifested in the sending of his Son for our sins (1 John 4:4-12; 5:4-5). They testify that his beloved Son is the Savior of the world (1 John 4:14). They love because "he first loved us" (1 John 4:19). God himself testifies that Jesus is the Son of God, the promised Messiah, by giving eternal life to all who believe in him (1 John 5:9-13, 20). Christian community exists in the testimony of Christ as Savior to a needy world.

John's second brief letter is written "to the elect lady and her children" (2 John 1:1). This address may refer to a particular Christian woman and her family, or to the gathered local church personified as a woman (see Rev. 21:2, 9; 22:17). John rejoices to hear that they have been walking according to God's truth (2 John 1:4), and he again emphasizes Christ's new commandment "that we love one another" (2 John 1:5; cf. John 13:34). He warns against those who deny the coming of Jesus Christ in the flesh (2 John 1:7; cf. John 1:14). He encourages believers to abide in the teaching of Christ (2 John 1:9-10). His final greeting from "the children of your elect sister" seems to come from another local church (2 John 1:13).

John's third letter is written "to the beloved Gaius, whom I love in the truth" (3 John 1:1). Gaius was a common Roman name and may or may not be related to others with the same name in the New Testament (see Acts 19:29; 20:4; Rom. 16:23; 1 Cor. 1:14). John rejoices to hear that he has been walking according to God's truth (3 John 1:3). He thanks Gaius for his faithfulness in supporting Christian missionaries (3 John 1:7) and commends a certain Demetrius as faithful and worthy of full support (3 John 1:12). Yet

John warns Gaius about Diotrephes "who likes to put himself first" and refuses to support other faithful workers (3 John 1:9-10). Finally, John admonishes Gaius: "Beloved, do not imitate evil but imitate good" (3 John 1:11).

Our summarizing statement for 1-3 John on the timeline is "Love one another in Christ," with the following key verse: "Beloved, let us love one another, for love is from God, and whoever loves has been born of God and knows God" (1 John 4:7). The apostle John was overwhelmed by the love of God in Christ, and as such, he describes himself as beloved of Jesus. His writings emphasize that Jesus is the expression of God's love for the world (1 John 4:9; cf. John 3:16). This love caused Jesus to offer his life as an atoning sacrifice for our sins (1 John 2:12; 4:10). John recognizes that the Christian community lives in this love. They are called God's beloved (1 John 4:7; 3 John 1:2), and they know that "if God so loved us, we also ought to love one another" (1 John 4:11).

The Jewish War against Rome erupts in Caesarea (AD 66)

The Christian teaching to love one another takes on fresh urgency within the context of escalating tension between Jews and Romans. This conflict spirals violently into war during the corrupt rule of the Roman governor Gessius Florus (AD 64-66). The flashpoint for the war takes place in Caesarea during the summer of AD 66. The Jewish community had a synagogue next to a plot owned by a Greek. They had repeatedly tried to purchase the land, even at an inflated price. They finally offer Florus eight talents of silver, which he gladly accepts. As the Jewish community assembles on the following Sabbath, a Greek from Caesarea stands beside the entrance to the synagogue with a large earthen vessel over which he sacrifices birds. The Jewish community is infuriated at the insult, since sacrificing birds over an earthen vessel is the prescribed ritual for cleansing lepers (Lev. 14:2-9). Popular slander at the time accused Jews of being lepers who were driven out of Egypt because of their disease. Tempers flare and rioting ensues. When the Jewish leaders remind Florus of the eight talents, he arrests them and puts them into prison.

Violence spreads quickly to Jerusalem. As Florus plunders the city, Herod Agrippa II and his sister Bernice are unable to calm the situation. Zealots within Judaism attack the Roman garrison and seize the Herodian fortress at Masada. A young, zealous priest named Eleazar stops the daily sacrifices offered for Rome and the emperor in the Jerusalem Temple. This action declares Judea in open revolt with Rome. When the revolutionary faction within Judaism seizes control of Jerusalem, they assassinate the high priest Ananias, who had been loyal to Rome, and defeat the Roman garrison stationed in the city.

Cestius Gallus, the Roman legate of Syria, sets out from Antioch with the Twelfth Roman Legion to put down the revolt. In the fall of AD 66, he besieges Jerusalem and advances to the Temple Mount. Content that he has quieted the revolt, he unexpectedly withdraws. Jewish forces attack the retreating Roman army from the heights of Beth-Horon. Elated with success, they return to Jerusalem and prepare for war. Jewish leaders gather in the temple and appoint regional generals to conduct the war. Josephus, whom we have referenced throughout our study, is given command of Galilee. He fortifies the cities and raises a citizen army of 60,000 soldiers, 350 cavalry, and 4,500 mercenaries. He is twenty-nine years old.

When the Roman emperor Nero learns of Cestius' defeat, he appoints Vespasian to suppress the revolt in Judea. He is a career soldier whose grandfather had been a centurion and his father a customs official. He is fifty-seven years old. Vespasian dispatches his son Titus to bring up the famous Fifteenth Legion from Alexandria. He himself crosses the Hellespont and marches to Antioch at the head of two legions, the Fifth and the Tenth. As Vespasian moves south, the Roman camp swells in size as regional rulers supply archers, cavalry, and auxiliary soldiers.

In AD 67, Vespasian launches a campaign against Galilee. As Roman forces move into the countryside, Josephus laments: "Galilee from end to end became a scene of fire and blood" (*War* 3.63). Romans kill all who could bear arms and sell the others into slavery. The surrounding villages are burned. Josephus flees to the fortified city of Jotapata near Cana of Galilee and musters a spirited defense for forty-seven days. At the end of the siege, Josephus takes refuge in a deep cistern with forty leading citizens of the city. When their hiding place is betrayed, Vespasian urges them to surrender alive. The Jewish leaders know what Romans do with captured generals—they are paraded at the end of a Roman triumph and then executed to the roar of the crowds. Josephus' companions resolve to commit suicide by lot. In a moment of extreme duress that few of us can even imagine, Josephus gives himself up with this prayer to God: "I willingly surrender to the Romans that I may live; but I call upon you as witness that I go, not as a traitor, but as your servant" (*War* 3.354). After entering the Roman camp, Josephus requests a private audience with Vespasian. Alone with the Roman general and his son Titus, he predicts: "You, Vespasian will be Caesar and emperor, you and your son" (*War* 3.401). The Roman general must have been stunned. Vespasian retains Josephus as a prisoner at Caesarea for two years, like the apostle Paul ten years before. All in the Roman camp wonder about the truth of his prediction while Vespasian completes the conquest of Galilee and prepares for a final assault on Jerusalem.

The following year is known in Roman history as the "Year of Four Emperors," since four successive emperors rule in one year. Nero commits suicide on June 9, AD 68, and Galba, the Roman governor of Spain, is hailed as the new emperor at age seventy-three. After seven months, the Praetorian Guard assassinates Galba for failing to reward their loyalty. Otho, who had bribed them, is proclaimed emperor the same day. He commits suicide after three months. Meanwhile, German legions proclaim their governor Vitellius as new emperor and march to Italy. Vitellius quickly drives the empire toward bankruptcy and civil unrest. He is the fourth emperor in the "Year of Four Emperors." On July 1 AD 69, just over a year since Nero committed suicide, Roman legions in Judea hail Vespasian as emperor. He orders Josephus' chains to be cut and prepares for return to Rome. He leaves his son Titus, who is twenty-nine years old, to complete the assault on Jerusalem.

Inside the city walls, meanwhile, a civil war rages between three separate Jewish zealot factions. Jerusalem becomes an armed fortress. Titus surrounds the city with four legions and waits, as the zealot factions attack each other without restraint. Vast stores of food are burned. The area around the temple is defiled with the dead. As Jerusalem swells with Passover pilgrims in the spring of AD 70, zealot leaders close the gates of the city, trapping everyone inside.

You may recall that Jesus had prophesied this tumultuous event. When he was approaching Jerusalem on Palm Sunday, he wept over the city (Luke 19:41). He lamented that Jerusalem did not know the things that made for peace nor recognize the time of God's visitation (Luke 19:42, 44). He announced that its destruction was surely coming: "The days will come upon you, when your enemies will set up a barricade around you and surround you and hem you in on every side and tear you down to the ground, you and your children within you. And they will not leave one stone upon another" (Luke 19:43-44). He even warned his disciples: "When you see Jerusalem surrounded by armies, then know that its desolation has come near. Then let those who are in Judea flee to the mountains, and let those who are inside the city depart, and let not those who are out in the country enter it" (Luke 21:20-21). According to the early Christian historian Eusebius, the Christian community left Jerusalem just before the Roman siege, "having been commanded by a divine revelation given before the war." They would live to fight another day, in a different kind of war, under the banner of the Prince of Peace (Isa. 9:6; 2 Cor. 10:3; Eph. 6:10-18).

In May AD 70, Titus begins his assault against the walls of Jerusalem. He builds massive earthwork embankments. Roman catapults and ballistae launch large stones and iron spears against the ramparts and defenders. The situation inside the city becomes increasingly desperate as the terrifying sound of the battering ram pounds against the city wall. The outer wall collapses after fifteen days. A second inner wall is breached after five days. Only the towering Antonia Fortress, guarding the Temple Mount, and the sanctuary remain. Titus orders the Roman siege engines for a final assault. Josephus appeals to those inside to lay aside their arms and preserve the sanctuary. His father and mother, wife, and brother remain trapped inside the city as the horrors of the siege intensify. Those attempting to flee are executed. Others barter their entire possessions for a measure of grain. A woman driven mad with hunger roasts and eats her own child. Those who manage to escape the city are crucified in front of the walls at the rate of five hundred per day. Roman soldiers, out of boredom, hatred, and rage, amuse themselves by nailing prisoners in various positions on the crosses (Josephus, *War* 5.451).

On July 24, AD 70, Roman forces take the Antonia Fortress with fierce fighting and heavy losses on both sides. Titus orders the arduous task of building an access ramp to reach the north wall that protected the Temple Mount. On August 5, the daily sacrifices to God cease upon the altar. For six days, battering rams pound at the huge stones of Herod's monumental structure without success. Roman troops are forced to use scaling ladders, but the defenders above hurl down all who reach the top. Titus then orders the ornate gates surrounding the temple to be burned, and their silver overlays melt in flames. He holds a war council with six of his generals. Some advise him to destroy the Jerusalem Temple, while others counsel that such a structure would honor the Roman Empire. The following day, August 29 (the ninth of Ab in the Jewish calendar), the Romans launch a full assault at dawn. This was the very same day on which the Babylonian king Nebuchadnezzar had destroyed the Temple built by Solomon. In the midst of the ensuing violence, Josephus records:

> One of the soldiers, without awaiting any order and with no dread of so momentous a deed, but urged on by some supernatural force, snatched a blazing piece of wood and hurled the flaming brand through a low golden window that gave access, on the north side, to the rooms that surrounded the sanctuary. As the flames shot up, the Jews let out a shout of dismay for the sacred structure that they had constantly guarded with such devotion was vanishing before their eyes. (*War* 6.252-53)

Jerusalem is left utterly desolate, her treasures plundered, and her monuments destroyed (Matt. 23:36-38). One stone is not left upon another, just as Jesus had prophesied with tears would take place (Luke 19:44).

Total Roman victory in Judea is not achieved until the spring of AD 73. Only Masada (meaning "fortress") remained, overlooking the western shore of the Dead Sea with the last group of zealots, who had captured the fortress at the beginning of the war. Masada stands atop an elevated rock 1,300 feet high. Sheer cliffs plummet on all sides. The only path to the top was the "Snake Path," so-called for the twisting peril of the ascent. A fortified wall surrounds the summit with towers. Enormous cisterns of water and vast stores of food and weapons could supply nearly one thousand zealot fighters and their families for months.

The new Roman governor Flavius Silva faces a nearly impossible task, as he determines to conquer the seemingly impregnable fortress of Masada. His legions are surrounded by arid ground and the taunting glimmer of the Dead Sea, which provides neither food nor water. Silva sets up eight Roman camps around the base, the outline of which can still be seen today. He first surrounds Masada with a wall, as Titus had done in Jerusalem. Roman commanders notice that on the western side of the rock, an outcropping of boulders rises to within five hundred feet of the top. They build an enormous earthwork with slave labor. With extraordinary effort, Roman legions drag up an ironclad siege tower, nearly one hundred feet tall, with a battering ram to attack the summit. After the first wall is breached, the zealots inside quickly construct an earthen wall over wooden timbers. Silva orders the wooden framework to be burned. At first, the flames turn to engulf the Roman siege engine. When the wind suddenly shifts, the second wall is destroyed and Masada is left exposed to what would be a final morning attack.

Throughout the night, the zealots and their leader Eleazar ben Jair debate what they should do. They know at dawn they will be captured and their women and children will be sold into slavery. Their men will be forced to compete in bloody spectacles for Roman entertainment. Eleazar finally persuades the last defenders to take their own lives. Each man would write his name upon a broken piece of pottery. Lots would be drawn to select the men who would kill the others. Each man would first kill the members of his own family and then bare his own neck for the sword. Another drawing of lots would be held among the final ten to determine the order of the slain. The last man left alive would fall upon his own sword.

When the Romans burst into Masada the following morning, everything is quiet. Their war cry is met with deathly silence. Only an elderly woman emerges from an underground cistern accompanied by a younger woman and five small children. Their narrative of events seems unbelievable, yet it is quickly verified. The Romans find 960 bodies, each family lying together. Their mass suicide prevents the victors from deriving any pleasure from their triumph. The Roman troops are awestruck.

The lasting impact of the Jewish War can be seen in the diverse reactions of Jews, Romans, and Christians. The Jewish community reacts with deep lament and utter dismay. Josephus interprets the destruction of the city and the temple as divine discipline for the sin of the nation (*Ant.* 20.166). The rabbinic sage Eleazar ben Pedat laments the destruction as creating an iron wall of separation between God and Israel (cf. Ezek. 4:3). Denied access to the sanctuary that has now been destroyed, devout Jews study, mourn and pray. The destruction of the city awakens repentance in many who had not yet recognized the time of God's visitation in Jesus Christ. Others still wonder where atonement can be found, now that the temple lies in ruins.

The Romans react to the Jewish War with triumph. Masses of silver, gold, and ivory treasures are paraded through the streets of Rome. Huge movable stages, three or four stories high, with ornate tapestries depict the progress of the war. Most prominent among the spoils are those plundered from the Jerusalem Temple: a golden table weighing several talents, a menorah made of gold, and a copy of the Torah scroll. Vespasian and his sons lead the procession to the Temple of Jupiter Optimus Maximus on the Capitoline Hill. Here at the religious epicenter of the Roman world, Simon bar Gioras, the last defender of Jerusalem, is publicly executed to the acclamation of the crowds (Josephus, *War* 7.155).

Vespasian and his sons commemorate their victory on coins and in monumental architecture. Vespasian builds the Temple of Peace to display the treasures of the Jerusalem Temple. Domitian builds the Arch of Titus with the inscription: "To the divine Titus, son of the divine Vespasian," while the interior panels depict the plunder of Jerusalem. Their most impressive structure, however, is the Flavian Amphitheatre, later known as the Colosseum. This hulking building rises 157 feet tall with eighty entrances and seating for 50,000. A moveable canopy protects spectators from the sun. A vast network of underground tunnels suddenly releases animals and contestants, adding to the excitement. Titus dedicates the amphitheatre in AD 80 with one hundred days of gladiatorial games and public spectacles. Nine thousand animals and three thousand human beings, made in the image and likeness of God, are killed on the opening day. Thousands of Christians will bear witness to Christ on the sandy floor of this arena.

The Christian community reacts to the Jewish War by continuing to preach the gospel to all nations. They herald the good news to all the earth that the kingdom of God will never be destroyed. Atonement for sin has been made once for all time in Christ's final sacrifice upon a Roman cross. Jesus has been raised from the dead and now lives and reigns forever. He is the rejected stone who has become the precious cornerstone. He builds a living and enduring temple for all peoples, the church, where all who believe in him are "living stones" (1 Pet. 2:5).

Christian leaders spread out across the known world – Andrew to Europe, Thomas to India, John the beloved disciple to Ephesus in Asia. Together with countless others, they teach that Jesus died and rose again and "repentance and forgiveness of sins should be proclaimed in his name to all nations" (Luke 24:47). Christians offer forgiveness and new life to those devastated by war. Only the gospel can announce that Christ died for the violence born out of religious zeal. Only the gospel can proclaim that Christ died for the exploitation born out of idolatry. Only the gospel can provide a new identity and a new community together for all who believe in Christ. This is God's wisdom. This is lasting peace. This is God's renewed humanity on display in the church.

New Testament timeline

The importance of the Jewish War is indicated on the New Testament timeline under TEACHING. At the lower-right, you will see the icon of the Jerusalem Temple destroyed in AD 70. In the upper left, you will see the Flavian Amphitheatre, later known as the Colosseum, built with plundered funds from the Jerusalem Temple and dedicated in AD 80. In between these rival structures, Christian mission expands across our map as believers are made into a living temple with Christ as the cornerstone. The gathered church is God's dwelling place in the world. This is where the desire of all nations is found.

Key New Testament beliefs

As we conclude our survey of the New Testament letters, you will notice a key to the timeline's map on the lower-left corner under TEACHING. You will see a box labeled "Key New Testament Beliefs." These are seven key beliefs that compel Christian mission and unite Christian teaching, even in the midst of an increasingly hostile and violent world. These are the core convictions that inspire the New Testament authors, and they remain central to the church for all time. We have seen that persecution does not weaken these convictions, but only causes the church to grow strong. False teaching attempts to assail the church, but only makes the distinctive light of Christian beliefs to shine more brightly. Believers stand firm and communicate these truths with great urgency, knowing that no power in heaven or on earth is able to prevail against the church.

We should devote our primary teaching energy to communicate these key beliefs. We often take major truths of Christian teaching for granted and then give most of our attention to secondary divisions in the body of Christ. We should be generous with one another over secondary issues among believers, such as mode of baptism, preferred Bible translation, men and women in ministry, spiritual gifts, or millennial views. Diversity among committed believers in these areas should never obscure the radiant key New Testament beliefs that create and sustain Christian community. We will briefly summarize each of these beliefs since they are central to the TEACHING in the New Testament letters. As we have seen, followers of Jesus are willing to stake their lives on these key beliefs, being convinced that Jesus is Israel's promised Messiah and that he now reigns as exalted Lord at the right hand of God the Father. He is the stone cut without human hands that rises to fill the earth.

Jesus is the Messiah, Christ the Lord

The most important and distinguishing belief in the New Testament letters is the conviction that Jesus is Israel's promised Messiah. Jesus is the central figure throughout all of the New Testament letters. His name, Jesus, occurs 265 times in the twenty-one New Testament letters. The letters affirm with the gospels that Jesus is the promised Messiah of Israel (Matt. 16:16; John 20:31). We have noted that the combination of terms Jesus + Messiah (translated as Jesus Christ) forms the most compact confession of faith in the New Testament, and that the combined terms (Jesus Christ or Christ Jesus) occur over two hundred times in the New Testament letters. We have seen that the authors can hardly mention the name Jesus without affirming that he is the anointed King, the promised Son of David, and the reigning Son of God. The New Testament letters also emphasize that Jesus Christ is Lord. The noun "Lord" in the Greek translation of the Old Testament is regularly used for God. To call Jesus Christ "Lord" affirms his divinity, authority, and glory (Isa. 45:23; Rom. 10:9; Phil. 2:9-11). As Lord of the covenant and Lord of the world, Jesus calls forth the glad obedience of all peoples. The blue crown icon draws forward the Old Testament expectations of a promised Messiah that are now fulfilled in Christ.

Justification by faith in Christ

The second key New Testament belief we have discussed is justification by faith. The New Testament letters affirm that the death of Christ provides substitutionary atonement for the sin of the world. God's wrath against sin is fully satisfied by the willing offering of his beloved Son on the cross (Rom. 3:21-25; 1 John 2:2). The resurrection of Christ proclaims God's verdict that his offering for sin has been accepted, which is summarized in Paul's statement that God "made him to be sin who knew no sin, so that in him we might become the righteousness of God" (2 Cor. 5:21). We who are sinners are justified by faith in Christ alone (Eph. 2:8). Faith in Christ identifies God's new covenant people. The icon for justification by faith reminds us that salvation is a gift (Rom. 5:16). It also recalls Abraham, who was justified by faith, and who serves as a model for New Testament believers (Gen. 15:6; Rom. 4:3; Gal. 3:8)

Indwelling presence of the Holy Spirit

The third key New Testament belief is the presence of the Holy Spirit. The Old Testament prophets looked forward to the day when God would pour out his Spirit upon all peoples (Joel 2:28-29). There are 175 references to the Holy Spirit in the New Testament letters. Just as God's presence distinguished Israel from all other peoples, the presence of the Holy Spirit identifies the Christian community as the people of God (Exod. 33:15-16; Eph. 2:22). The Holy Spirit confirms our adoption into God's family in Christ (Gal. 4:6; Rom. 8:15). The Holy Spirit empowers our obedience to Christ (Rom. 8:11-14). The Holy Spirit teaches us to pray, provides joy in the midst of suffering, reveals Christ to others around us, convicts us of sin, unites us with the body of Christ, breathes out the Words of Scripture, and inspires our worship. The gifts of the Holy Spirit are to be used for building up the body of Christ (1 Cor. 12:7). They are God's own testimony to the truth of his Son (Heb. 2:4). The icon for the presence of the Holy Spirit is the fiery cloud of God's own presence (Exod. 19:9; Acts 2).

Jews and Gentiles are "one in Christ"

The fourth key New Testament belief we have seen throughout the New Testament letters is that Jew and Gentile are one in Christ. The Bible begins in Gen. 1 with the entire world in view. The sin of Adam brought condemnation to the world (Gen. 3; Rom. 5:12-21). God's redemptive plan begins with Abraham and Sarah, an idolatrous, barren couple saved by grace through faith (Gen. 12:1-3; 15:6). The God of glory reveals himself to them and promises them descendants like the stars (Gen. 15:5; Exod. 32:13; Deut. 1:10; 10:22). God promises that Abraham will be the father of "many nations" (Gen. 17:4-5). The New Testament letters teach that this promise is fulfilled in Christ: "If you are Christ's, then you are Abraham's offspring, heirs according to promise" (Gal. 3:28-29; Rom. 4:16-17). Both Jew and Gentile find forgiveness through Christ's death. Both Jew and Gentile find new life in Christ's resurrection. Together they become one people of God. Through the new covenant sign of baptism, "we were all baptized into one body, whether Jews or Greeks, whether slaves or free and we were all made to drink one Spirit" (1 Cor. 12:13). God's global intention, the great mystery now revealed in Christ, is that the Gentiles (nations of the world) are "fellow heirs, members of the same body, and partakers of the promise in Christ Jesus through the gospel" (Eph. 3:6). The authors of the New Testament letters exert much pastoral energy to work out this reality in the church. The icon for Jews and Gentiles becoming one in Christ are the descendants like the stars promised to Abraham.

Obedience of faith among the nations

The fifth key New Testament belief is obedience of faith among the nations. The opening sentence of Romans declares that through Jesus Christ "we have received grace and apostleship to bring about the obedience of faith for the sake of his name among all the nations" (Rom. 1:5-6; cf. Rom. 15:18; 16:25-27; Jude 24). Obedience is not an optional addition to Christian faith, but an essential feature of the new covenant (Jer. 31:31-34); the prophet Ezekiel had seen that obedience would be the result of the indwelling Spirit (Ezek. 36:26-27). Obedience grows out of genuine faith. Jesus said: "If you love me, you will keep my commandments" (John 14:15). Peter addresses Christians as God's chosen people "according to the foreknowledge of God the Father, in the sanctification of the Spirit, for obedience to Jesus Christ" (1 Pet. 1:2). Joyful obedience to Christ by the power of the Spirit brings pleasure and praise to God the Father. The New Testament letters repeatedly teach about the importance of walking according to God's ways. Such newness of life is possible only through the indwelling Holy Spirit. Transformation in Christ-likeness over time evidences the reality that God's renewed humanity has truly begun. The icon for the obedience of faith is Jeremiah's imagery of God's word written upon the heart.

Living sacrifices "holy to the LORD"

The sixth key New Testament belief is that Christians are called to be living sacrifices, "holy to the LORD." Holiness means being "set apart unto God" for his service in the world. Most of the New Testament letters address believers as "holy ones." Holiness means that believers are to reflect God's glory in every aspect of their lives. The language of "holy" is used in the Old Testament for prophets, priests, and sacrificial animals offered to God upon the altar (Exod. 28:36; 30:10; Lev. 11:44-45; Deut. 7:6; 14:2; Jer. 1:5). We have seen that the New Testament authors view themselves as those who have been "set apart for the gospel of God" (Rom. 1:1; 2 Tim. 2:21). They call believers to present their bodies as "living sacrifices, holy and acceptable to God" (Rom. 12:1; 1 Pet. 1:15-16). Such consecration will involve suffering, self-denial, and in some cases martyrdom for the cause of Christ (Col. 1:24). Such consecration also means living as a kingdom of priests who bring God to people and people to God (Exod. 19:6; 1 Pet. 2:9). Paul saw himself as a priest presenting the nations as an offering to God in worship (Rom. 15:16). He viewed his suffering as the pouring out of a drink offering to God (Phil. 2:17; 2 Tim. 4:6). All believers are called to imitate Jesus, our great high priest, who offered himself wholly unto God for the sake of the world (Phil. 2:5-11; Heb. 4:14). The icon of living sacrifices is the sacrificial altar, which burns continually before the Lord.

Return of Christ in glory as Judge

The seventh key New Testament belief is that Christ will return in glory as judge. We have seen throughout our study that the New Testament letters teach that the end times have begun with the incarnation, death, and resurrection of Jesus Christ (1 Cor. 10:11; 2 Tim. 3:1; Heb. 1:1-2; 2 Pet. 3:3; 1 John 2:18; Jude 1:18). Jesus is the firstborn from the dead, the firstfruits of the new creation (1 Cor. 15:20). The turning of the ages, which the prophets described as the "last days," has begun (Isa. 2:1; Hos. 3:5; Heb. 1:2). The time of gathering the nations is at hand. Christian mission is carried out with great urgency under the conviction that Christ will return again in glory as Judge (Acts 1:11; Phil. 3:20-21; 1 Thess. 1:10; Tit. 2:13). Christians call all people to repent and turn to Christ in faith, knowing that "all will appear before the judgment seat of Christ" (2 Cor. 5:10). This is underscored in the letter to the Hebrews: "Just as it is appointed for man to die once, and after that comes judgment, so Christ, having been offered once to bear the sins of many, will appear a second time, not to deal with sin but to save those who are eagerly waiting for him" (Heb. 9:27-28; cf. Phil. 3:20; 1 Thess. 1:10). Christ's return will bring history to God's appointed ending. Evil will be condemned. The dead will be raised to everlasting life. The righteous will be clothed with immortality. God will dwell with his people forever in a new heavens and new earth where righteousness dwells (2 Pet. 3:13). The icon for Christ's return in glory is the Ark of the Covenant, the throne of God before whom all will one day appear.

These seven key New Testament beliefs reflect "the glory of God in the face of Jesus Christ" (2 Cor. 4:6). Christians proclaim that Jesus is the Messiah, Christ the Lord. He fulfills the hope of Israel and he is the desire of all nations. All who believe are justified by faith in him alone. The indwelling presence of the Holy Spirit breathes new life into the dead, causing us to walk in God's ways. Jews and Gentiles are one in Christ and the gathered church is God's dwelling place in the world. The new covenant community is characterized by the obedience of faith. Pagans abandon their idols, forsaking plundered wealth and degrading entertainment. Zealots abandon their idols, confessing their own sin and making room in their hearts for all nations. Members of the Christian community dedicate themselves as living sacrifices, holy to the Lord. They serve Christ with full commitment as his consecrated servants in the world. They willingly fill up what remains of Christ's afflictions through suffering, witness, and even death. Christian mission is carried out with great urgency in certain hope of Christ's return in glory as Judge of the living and the dead. Faithful Christian teaching heals a violent and broken world and prepares us for what is yet to come.

We have come to the end of the period of TEACHING. We have seen in our study of the New Testament letters that teaching is an essential aspect of global mission and the life of the local church. As Christian communities are established, the Holy Spirit moves early Christian leaders to provide teaching through divinely inspired letters. Before beginning the next chapter, I would encourage you to read through the New Testament letters. As you read, refresh your own commitment to study and teach the Word of God. With so many competing voices and cultural distractions, diligent study and faithful teaching can take second place. Teaching is part of the great commission that Jesus gave to his disciples, and this is the responsibility of the church today. God's renewed humanity has begun in Christ. His wisdom shines brightly in the midst of a sinful, violent, and broken world. May God grant us grace and power to engage this sacred task. May all nations of the world stream toward the living God and be taught to walk in his ways. May faithful Christian witness overcome the challenges of societal persecution, false teaching, and demonic oppression. The everlasting kingdom of the Son of Man will prevail. We are now ready for the glorious ending of God's plan of redemption through history in our final period of YET-TO-COME.

Chapter 9
YET-TO-COME Part 1

The period of YET-TO-COME simply explained

THE PERIOD OF YET-TO-COME completes God's plan of redemption through history with a glorious vision of the ending. The New Testament announces the good news that God's ultimate purposes have truly begun in Christ. Jesus fulfills Israel's expectations of the Son of Man when he announces the arrival of the kingdom of God. His public ministry demonstrates the reality of the kingdom with healings, casting out of demons, and prophetic signs. His atoning death enacts the new covenant. His victory on the cross disarms principalities and powers. His resurrection dawns God's new creation. His ascension enthrones him as exalted Lord. With heavenly authority, Jesus commissions his people to teach the nations. He pours out the Holy Spirit to empower their witness. He gathers all nations into the church to display God's renewed humanity in Christ. We have explored these wonderful themes in our study of the New Testament so far.

At the same time, the New Testament also announces that the full realization of God's purposes are still YET-TO-COME. The kingdom of God grows among wheat and weeds. Church leaders are in the pains of labor until Christ is formed in the lives of their people. The church is a bride still being perfected. The kingdom of God suffers violence, and an unbelieving world persecutes the church. False teaching assails the church, which has been entrusted with God's truth. The end times have truly begun, and yet the spirit of the antichrist has gone out into the world. The kingdom of God is inaugurated but not fully consummated. An intense spiritual battle still remains.

The final book of the Bible encourages God's people with a "revelation" (Rev. 1:1). Note carefully that the word is singular, not plural. The term "revelation" means "to see behind the veil." The Greek word *apocalypsis* means the same thing. Revelation pulls back the veil and allows us to see a single, extended vision of God in the heavenly sanctuary. We see the Lord enthroned. He is worshiped in the beauty of holiness. He is surrounded by the heavenly host and an innumerable multitude of the redeemed from every nation. God is in control. His purposes will be fully accomplished in heaven and on earth.

The final book of the Bible is more specifically a "revelation of Jesus Christ" (Rev. 1:1). Revelation is not primarily a book about the "end times," but about Jesus Christ. God reveals Christ's present rule and future glory. This reality produces hope and strengthens our resolve in times of distress. Jesus is revealed as the exalted Son of Man and Lord of the church. He is worshiped in heaven and stands worthy to enact God's eternal purpose. He releases a measured wrath even as he gathers a people for himself. He triumphs in a spiritual battle over Satan's counterfeit kingdom. He will return in visible glory and final victory. He will condemn evil and create a new heavens and earth in which righteousness dwells. The New Jerusalem then descends like a bride adorned for her husband. In the end, we are drawn back to the very beginning of the Bible. God dwells in the midst of his people. Humanity made in his image has access to the tree of life. The Lamb who was slain for us is adored forever. He who testifies to these things says, "Surely I am coming soon." God's people respond in hope: "Amen. Come, Lord Jesus!" (Rev. 22:20).

It is important to remember that God gave the book of Revelation to make things *clear*. Christian readers are sometimes overwhelmed by the unfamiliar style of the book. Revelation is an example of apocalyptic writing. There are many examples of apocalyptic writing in antiquity, but only one in the New Testament. Apocalyptic writing reveals a heavenly perspective on this world. Such writings contain visions and make extensive use of symbolism. Apocalyptic writing answers the question: "Who is Lord over the world?" Those who read are challenged to respond to their world in light of the heavenly perspective revealed.

The heavenly perspective of Revelation is that God is in control. He sits enthroned today and is at work in the world gathering an innumerable multitude from every nation each and every day. His cause triumphs in the end no matter how things may appear at present. Believers are exhorted to faithful witness and patient endurance. They are warned against compromise with this world. They are assured of God's promises for all who conquer by being faithful to Christ. There is no reason for fear.

God gives this revelation of Jesus Christ to strengthen the church during a time of persecution and trial. The church represents God's alternative kingdom in the midst of a violent and hostile world. God's people display the present reality of God's new humanity in Christ. They extend the gospel to all nations in light of Christ's future return. This vision of Christ's present rule and future glory is "made known (lit. "signified") by sending his angel to his servant John" (Rev. 1:1). All of the symbols in Revelation are rooted in established biblical imagery, especially from the Old Testament. Many of the symbols are explicitly interpreted within the book. The symbolic imagery of Revelation should never be interpreted in way that would have been incomprehensible to the original audience. Our God does not speak in secret to conceal, but in the open to reveal.

The YET-TO-COME column on the New Testament timeline begins by setting the historical context and then follows the literary outline of Revelation. The key dates for this period are AD 95 and the Return of Christ. AD 95 represents the approximate date for Revelation. This was a time of persecution under the Roman emperor Domitian (AD 81-96), as we shall see shortly. The exact date for the Return of Christ is unknown to us by our Father's kindness and wisdom. Diverse interpretations among believers over the exact sequence of final events should never divide the church. Christians are the only people who believe that Jesus Christ will return again in visible glory as Lord of all. Every eye will see him. Every knee will bow before him. Every creature will worship and adore him. Our confident assurance in Christ's return should unite the church in common confession and shared hope.

New Testament timeline

The picture for YET-TO-COME is the New Jerusalem coming down from heaven. The tree of life is visible and accessible in the midst of the city. The tree of life picks up an important picture taken directly from the Old Testament timeline. The New Jerusalem reminds us that God's redemptive story for all people, which began in the Garden of Eden, ends with a city. The City of God comes down like a bride for her husband (Rev. 21:2). Inside the gate, the water of life flows from God's throne (Rev. 22:1-2). God and the Lamb have restored access to the tree of life. Testimony to Christ will extend forever from an innumerable multitude gathered from every nation. The blessing of God's presence, which had been lost in Eden, has now been restored forever (Gen. 2-3; Rev. 22).

Roadmap to the chapter

As you read through this chapter, I would encourage you to keep the New Testament timeline in front of you. Each point listed under YET-TO-COME will be discussed under a heading that reads the same as the points on the timeline. Additional Bible references are also given throughout the chapter. You will benefit greatly from reading these verses along with this study guide. Above all, keep your attention on Jesus Christ. In Revelation, you see him as he is right now. Grow confident in his power, authority, and saving activity in the world. Receive his loving rebuke and his promised reward. Allow the Holy Spirit to purify your imagination with the radiance of God's splendor. Turn your affections away from all counterfeit powers. Renew your commitment to Christ in light of his appearing. Trust his powerful grace even when the world seems to have the upper hand. Overcome by the blood of the Lamb and the word of your testimony. Follow the Lamb wherever he goes. Pray that he might use your life to help gather in the harvest of the nations.

God reveals the present rule and future glory of His Son

This bold heading at the top of the column identifies God's major redemptive activity during the period of YET-TO-COME. The book of Revelation reveals Christ's present rule and future glory. He is the one "who is and who was and who is to come" (Rev. 1:4). He is "the Alpha and the Omega, the first and the last, the beginning and the end" (Rev. 22:13). He rules today over the kings of the earth (Rev. 1:5; 11:17). He sits enthroned right now as exalted Lord of the church (Rev. 1-3). He is worshiped forever in heavenly glory as the Lamb who was slain (Rev. 4-5). He presently releases a measured wrath in the world, even as he gathers an innumerable multitude of the redeemed (Rev. 6-11). He daily wins the spiritual battle over the Serpent's counterfeit kingdom as the Accuser is thrown down (Rev. 12-15). At the same time, Christ will return again in future glory. Evil will be condemned. The false prophet will be silenced. The beast's exploitative rule will come to an end. The righteous reign of the Son of Man will endure forever (Rev. 17-20). The city of man will yield to the city of God (Rev. 21-22).

Believers share in Christ's present rule and future glory. He has loved them and freed them from their sins by his blood. He has made them "a kingdom, priests to his God and Father" (Rev. 1:6; cf. Exod. 19:6). They too "reign on the earth" (Rev. 5:10; 11:15). They are instruments in his hands as Christ gathers the nations to himself. At the same time, believers share "in the tribulation and the kingdom and the patient endurance that are in Jesus" (Rev. 1:9). They wage a spiritual battle "by the blood of the Lamb and by the word of their testimony" (Rev. 12:11). They must "follow the Lamb wherever he goes" (Rev. 14:4). All who overcome by faith in Christ will share his future glory. They will eat from the tree of life in the paradise of God (Rev. 2:7; cf. Gen. 2:9). They will be clothed in garments of glory (Rev. 3:5; cf. Exod. 28:2). They will have his name written upon them (Rev. 3:12; Exod. 28:36-38). They will receive everlasting life and reign with him forever (Rev. 3:21; cf. Exod. 15:18).

"Grace and peace from him who was, is, and who is yet to come" (Rev. 1:4)

The book of Revelation was first circulated among seven Christian communities in the Roman province of Asia Minor. There is a chain of communication from the Lord through his angel to John, and then to the churches. This divine revelation is given to the apostle John, who was an eyewitness of Jesus' earthly ministry (John 20:30-31; 21:24-25; 1 John 1:1). He is now given a heavenly vision of Jesus' present rule and future glory, as the fullness of God's redemptive plan is unveiled. John greets the churches with "grace ... and peace from him who is and who was and who is to come" (Rev. 1:4). The expression "grace and peace" recalls the distinctive Christian greeting we have seen in the New Testament letters. The identity of the Lord as the One who was, is, and is to come echoes the revelation of the divine name "I AM" given to Moses at the burning bush (Exod. 3:14). The form of the divine name emphasizes God's eternal existence, his covenant presence, and his future appearing. John also greets the churches from "the seven spirits who are before his throne" (Rev. 1:4). This is a figurative expression for the Holy Spirit who is active throughout the world. In the end, John greets the churches from "Jesus Christ the faithful witness, the firstborn of the dead, and the ruler of kings on earth" (Rev. 1:5). He is the one "who loves us and has freed us from our sins by his blood and made us a kingdom, priests to his God and Father" (Rev. 1:5-6). His glory and dominion are forever. He is coming again with divine glory, at which time the everlasting reign of the Son of Man will be fully revealed (Rev. 1:7; cf. Dan. 7:13).

John's greeting is Trinitarian in form. God is known as Father, Son, and Holy Spirit. The Christian life is lived in confident trust in the Lord God. He is unchanging in purpose, character, glory, and power. He is the Lord God Almighty who was, who is, and who is YET-TO-COME. The mention of his name throughout the book of Revelation is a recurring refrain to encourage the faithful (Rev. 1:4, 8; 4:8; 11:17; 15:3; 16:7, 14; 19:6, 15; 21:22).

Domitian rules as Roman emperor (AD 81-96)

The historical setting for the book of Revelation is toward the end of the first century AD. The early Christian leader Irenaeus writes in the second century AD that John saw Revelation near the end of Domitian's reign around AD 95. Domitian was born in AD 51 as the youngest son of Vespasian. He served as a teenager alongside his father during the Jewish War. He grew up in the shadow of his older brother Titus, who achieved military distinction through the destruction of Jerusalem and was even celebrated with a Roman triumph. After Vespasian becomes emperor, Titus shares tribunal power with his father as designated heir. He is named consul seven times and given command of the Praetorian Guard. Domitian, however, receives only honorary titles and civic priesthoods, but lacks any real power. When Titus succeeds Vespasian as emperor in AD 79, he is extremely popular with the Senate, military, and the Roman people. Despite the shock caused by the eruption of Mount Vesuvius in AD 79, Titus completes the Flavian Amphitheatre (later known as the Colosseum) in AD 80. He celebrates with one hundred days of gladiatorial games. Just after the games, Titus suddenly becomes ill and dies from a fever. His last words are that he had made "but one mistake in life." Domitian, who is suspected of plotting against his brother, is named emperor the following day.

Empire-wide persecution of Christians

The Flavian dynasty of Vespasian (AD 69-79), Titus (AD 79-81), and Domitian (AD 81-96) rose to power by the successful completion of the Jewish War (AD 66-70), which culminated in the destruction of the Jerusalem Temple, as we rehearsed in the last chapter. Roman society increasingly adopts a hostile position toward Jews as a defeated foe with a degraded faith. Jews are forced to pay a special tax to Rome in place of the biblical offering for the temple in Jerusalem. Christians are also perceived as having originated in Judea. They are viewed as a barbaric and superstitious group that calls into question the ultimate claims of Roman power. Especially in the East, the imperial cult of deified emperors is celebrated as a test of loyalty to the state. Domitian requires that his statue be worshiped as a god. He insists on being addressed as "Lord and god" (*dominus et deus*). He is remembered in ancient sources as a solitary man, suspicious and cruel. He reportedly enjoyed catching flies and stabbing them. He sponsored gladiatorial contests between women and dwarfs. He executed his political rivals and members of his own family whom he accused of atheism and Jewish manners, which was a charge usually given to those who had become followers of Christ. According to the early church historian, Eusebius, Domitian becomes the second Roman emperor after Nero to persecute the church. The persecution begins in Rome and varies in intensity throughout the provinces. Christians are forced to participate in the imperial cult. Those who refuse are punished with public beatings, confiscation of property, exile, and even death. Domitian's demonic claim of divinity locates this period in our study as a time of severe testing for Christians. They serve a King who is truly divine. They cannot offer their lives or their worship to any mortal man.

John in exile shares "tribulation, kingdom, and endurance in Jesus"

The apostle John suffers from imperial persecution while shepherding the Christian communities of Asia Minor from Ephesus. He is exiled to the small, arid island of Patmos "on account of the word of God and the testimony of Jesus" (Rev. 1:9). The Romans used Patmos as a place of banishment, much like the English later used Australia. The rocky island of Patmos formed a natural prison, thirty-six miles out into the sea. John is banished there, knowing that the people whom he loves so dearly face ongoing trials on shore. John identifies himself as "your brother and partner in the tribulation and the kingdom and the patient endurance that are in Jesus" (Rev. 1:9). Pastoral leadership does not insulate us from suffering, but demands our participation. John shares in the present tribulation, the reality of Christ's kingdom, and the patient endurance required for all who believe. Like Paul before him, John continues his ministry while in prison. He lifts up the communities in earnest prayer. He worships with them "on the Lord's day" (Rev. 1:10). He writes to them all that Christ would reveal to him.

The exalted Son of Man is Lord of the church (Rev. 1-3)

While John is in the Spirit on the Lord's Day, he hears a loud voice behind him like a trumpet saying: "Write what you see in a book and send it to the seven churches, to Ephesus and to Smyrna and to Pergamum and to Thyatira and to Sardis and to Philadelphia and to Laodicea" (Rev. 1:10-11). When he turns around to see the one who is speaking, he sees Jesus, the exalted Son of Man, as Lord of the church (Rev. 1:12-16). Jesus stands in the midst of golden lampstands that illuminate the heavenly sanctuary. He appears like the glorious Son of Man whom Daniel had seen centuries before (Dan. 7:13-14). He is clothed with a long robe and golden sash. His hair is white like wool. His eyes are like a flame of fire and his feet like burnished bronze. His voice resounds with divine authority like the roar of many waters. In his hand he holds seven stars, and from his mouth comes a two-edged sword. His face shines like the sun in full strength. Like everyone in Scripture who sees the Lord, John is overwhelmed by the glory of the Lord (Rev. 1:17; cf. Gen. 15; Exod. 3; Isa. 6; Ezek. 1; Matt. 17; Acts 9). He falls at his feet as though dead. Yet the exalted Jesus summons him to life. Jesus places his right hand upon John and calmly assures him: "Fear not, I am the first and the last, and the living one. I died, and behold I am alive forevermore, and I have the keys of Death and Hades" (Rev. 1:17-18). We see here again the centrality of Christ's death and resurrection for understanding the entire Bible. Jesus conquers death by his death upon the cross. Jesus now lives and reigns forever by his resurrection.

Jesus instructs John to write "the things that you have seen, those that are and those that are to take place after this" (Rev. 1:19). Jesus also explains to John that the Christian communities on earth are connected with those who worship in heaven throughout the extended vision of Revelation. The lampstands in the sanctuary represent the gathered Christian churches in Asia Minor. The stars signify messengers (lit. "angels") of the heavenly court sent by Christ to encourage faithfulness on the earth (Rev. 1:20). The divine Word of Christ reaches the churches through the human agency of his servant John.

Jesus addresses seven churches as exalted Lord and coming King (Rev. 2-3)

In Rev. 2-3, Jesus addresses seven churches in a circle of cities in Asia Minor. He speaks with heavenly authority as exalted Lord and coming King. It is important to remember that these cities are real places. These congregations are real people. The believers there face the same temptations that we have encountered in our study of the New Testament letters, such as persecution, false teaching, and compromise with the world. Christ speaks to his bride through the human agency of John in a similar manner as the rest of the New Testament letters. The letters of Revelation are specific with respect to local circumstances, geography, and people. However, they remain applicable for all believers in all places, just as Paul's letters provide ongoing teaching for the church today. There is no suggestion in the text for interpreting the churches as referring to successive periods of church history.

It is also important for us to recognize that we never leave this scene of heavenly worship throughout the book of Revelation. Jesus addresses the seven churches from the sanctuary as exalted Son of Man. Each of the letters begins with a preamble of self-identification that is taken directly from the vision of Revelation 1:10-16. Jesus then addresses the spiritual condition of each church and reveals his will for them. Each letter ends with a warning for those who disobey him and a promise of future blessing for those who overcome by faith. Jesus speaks in the letters within the controlling sanctuary vision of Rev. 1 and promises blessings that will be fulfilled in Rev. 21-22. In this way, the book of Revelation should really be understood as a single, extended vision of the exalted Jesus addressing his bride. The plot of Revelation should be seen as a single story that leads to a glorious ending. The imagery of Revelation should be interpreted consistently within the overarching vision. Revelation is best read or heard in a single sitting which takes about one hour. The result should purify our imagination, lift our hope, inspire our faithfulness, and banish our fear.

Jesus addresses his first letter to Ephesus, modern Selçuk. You will remember that Ephesus was the fourth largest city in the Roman world with a population of around 250,000. Paul ministered there extensively on his third missionary journey (Acts 19:1, 10). Timothy served the growing church in the city (1 Tim. 1:3). According to early Christian tradition, John moved to Ephesus to strengthen the church after leaving Jerusalem just before the Roman siege in AD 70.

To the church at Ephesus, Jesus identifies himself as the one "who holds the seven stars in his right hand, who walks among the seven golden lampstands" (Rev. 2:1). He knows the church and commends them for their good works, hard labor, and patient endurance (Rev. 2:1-2; cf. Eph. 2:10). They have tested and discerned false teachers without growing weary (Rev. 2:2-3; cf. Acts 20:28-31). However, in their battle for truth, the Ephesians have lost their first love for Christ (Rev. 2:4; cf. Eph. 3:14-19). Jesus admonishes them to remember the heights of love from which they have fallen, and to repent and do the works they had done at first. In the end, he warns them that a dead orthodoxy will only cause him to come and remove their lampstand. If they conquer by obeying his word, then he promises: "I will grant to eat of the tree of life, which is in the paradise of God" (Rev. 2:7; cf. Gen. 3:22-24; Rev. 22:14).

Jesus addresses his second letter to Smyrna, modern Izmir (forty miles northwest of Ephesus). The city was an important port with a well-protected harbor that opened to an inland trade route up the Hermes Valley. The city maintained an economic alliance with Rome and was home to a substantial Jewish community. It also boasted of having a temple dedicated to the imperial cult.

To the church in Smyrna, Jesus identifies himself as "the first and the last, who died and came to life" (Rev. 2:8). He knows their tribulation, poverty, and slander from those of the local synagogue (Rev. 2:9). The reference to the "synagogue of Satan" should not be understood as an attack on Judaism in general, but as a reference to Jews who denounced Christians as not being "true Jews." Since Jews were granted exemption from participation in the Roman imperial cult due to their antiquity, this accusation left Christians exposed to persecution. Jesus knows that the church of Smyrna is about to suffer greatly. Some will be thrown into prison. Others will bear testimony, even unto a martyr's death. Yet under Jesus' sovereign hand, the time of testing will have a temporal limit and achieve the weight of glory. He admonishes them: "Be faithful unto death, and I will give you the crown of life" (Rev. 2:10). This precious verse has inspired faithfulness — from the martyrdom of Polycarp, bishop of Smyrna in the second century, to the Korean martyrs in the twenty-first century. In the end, Jesus promises: "the one who conquers will not be hurt by the second death" (Rev. 2:11; cf. Rev. 20:6).

Jesus addresses his third letter to Pergamum, modern Bergama (fifteen miles inland and seventy miles north of Smyrna). The populous city of 150,000 was located on a towering, cone-shaped hill rising one thousand feet above the surrounding valley. The name Pergamum means "tower" or "citadel." The spectacular acropolis held temples to the patron deities of the city. Pergamum was also the site of the first temple erected for the imperial cult in Asia Minor.

To the church in Pergamum, Jesus identifies himself as the one "who has the sharp two-edged sword" (Rev. 2:12). He wields the authoritative word of God. He knows that the church dwells at the location of Satan's throne (Rev. 2:13). This is probably a reference to the cluster of idolatrous temples that dominate the city. Jesus commends them for holding fast to his name and not denying their faith, even as some members of the community like Antipas have suffered a martyr's death. He warns them against the teaching of Balaam, who lured God's people away from the Lord through sexual immorality and idolatry (Rev. 2:14; cf. Num. 25:1-3; 2 Pet. 2:15; Jude 1:11). He also rebukes them for the teaching of the Nicolaitans, who accommodate themselves to pagan society to avoid persecution (Rev. 2:15). Jesus urges them to repent of such a dangerous posture toward the world or "I will come to you soon and war against them with the sword of my mouth" (Rev. 2:16). He promises that those who conquer by obeying his word will be given "some of the hidden manna, and I will give him a white stone, with a new name written on the stone that no one knows except the one who receives it" (Rev. 2:17; cf. Rev. 22:3-4). The new name probably refers to the name of the Lord and the stone grants entrance into the City of God, the New Jerusalem.

Jesus addresses his fourth letter to Thyatira, modern Akhisar (twenty-five miles southeast of Pergamum). Thyatira was a significant commercial city on the broad plain between Pergamum and Sardis. Lydia, whom Paul met in Philippi, was from Thyatira and sold the expensive purple cloth dyed from the madder root (Acts 16:14). Numerous trade guilds held great influence in the city life. Membership in trade guilds often required participation in idolatry and thus placed Christians in a position of compromise.

To the church in Thyatira, Jesus identifies himself as "the Son of God, who has eyes like a flame of fire, and whose feet are like burnished bronze" (Rev. 2:18). He knows their works. He knows their faithful service and patient endurance (Rev. 2:19). Yet he rebukes them for tolerating the teaching of Jezebel, who is "seducing my servants to practice sexual immorality and to eat food sacrificed to idols" (Rev. 2:20). Jezebel was the queen of Israel who was condemned by Elijah for her idolatry and immorality (1 Kgs. 16:31). Jesus warns the church in Thyatira against spiritual compromise for worldly acceptance. He invokes the devastating end that came upon unrepentant Jezebel to stir repentance in the church (Rev. 2:21-23; cf. 2 Kgs. 9:29-37). Rather than spiritual compromise, Jesus exhorts the church to hold fast to his teaching until he comes (Rev. 2:25). He promises that those who conquer by faithful obedience will share in Christ's own authority over the nations (Rev. 2:26-27; cf. Ps. 2:9). They will receive "the morning star," signaling their participation in Christ's everlasting rule (Rev. 2:28; cf. Num. 24:17; 2 Pet. 1:19; Rev. 22:16).

Jesus addresses his fifth letter to Sardis, modern Sart (thirty-five miles southeast of Thyatira). Sardis had been the capital of the Lydian empire and the famed wealth of King Croesus. The city had been captured twice by surprise attack. Sardis had a reputation for complacency and lack of vigilance.

To the church in Sardis, Jesus identifies himself as the one "who has the seven spirits of God and the seven stars" (Rev. 3:1). He is present and active in the world. He knows their deeds and their reputation of being alive, but in fact they are dead. He admonishes them to "wake up, and strengthen what remains and is about to die, for I have not found your works complete in the sight of my God" (Rev. 3:2). He warns that "if you will not wake up, I will come like a thief, and you will not know at what hour I will come against you" (Rev. 3:3; cf. Matt. 24:43-44; 1 Thess. 5:2-8; 2 Pet. 3:10). The church at Sardis displays the spiritual danger of neglect and apathy. He promises that those who walk with him in active faithfulness "will be clothed thus in white garments, and I will never blot his name out of the book of life" (Rev. 3:5; cf. Dan. 12:1; Rev. 6:11; 7:9; 13:8; 20:12). The book of life represents the civic register of the City of God (Rev. 21:27; cf. Luke 10:20; Phil. 4:3; Heb. 12:23). Those who conquer by faithfulness to Christ will never lose their citizenship in the heavenly city. Jesus will openly acknowledge them before his Father and the heavenly host (Rev. 3:5; cf. Matt. 10:32; Luke 12:8).

Jesus addresses his sixth letter to the church in Philadelphia, modern Alascehir (thirty miles southeast of Sardis). The city was founded by the Lydian king Attalus II. The king's steadfast loyalty to his brother Eumenes earned him the nickname "Philadelphus" ("brotherly love"). Philadelphia was a commercial center located at the junction of several major roads. The city served as the gateway to the high central plateau of Asia Minor. After a devastating earthquake in AD 17, terrified residents were forced to leave the city and live in the surrounding countryside for months.

To the church in Philadelphia, Jesus identifies himself with all authority as "the true one, who has the key of David, who opens and no one will shut, who shuts and no one opens" (Rev. 3:7). The key of David signifies governing authority (Isa. 22:20-21; Matt. 16:19). Jesus knows their works, and with full authority he has set before them an open door of ministry, which no one is able to shut (Rev. 3:8; cf. Acts 14:27; 1 Cor. 16:9). Jesus commends them for keeping his word and for not denying his name. He warns those of the local synagogue who are slandering the Christian community. Like Joseph's reluctant brothers, they will one day "come and bow down before your feet and they will learn that I have loved you" (Rev. 3:9; cf. Gen. 37:10; Isa. 49:23; 60:14). Throughout the letters we see a correspondence between what is taking place on earth, and what will take place in heaven. This is expressed beautifully to the church of Philadelphia. Jesus assures them that "because you have kept my word about patient endurance, I will keep you from the hour of trial that is coming on the whole world" (Rev. 3:10). Trials refine genuine Christians. Temptations purify their faith. Jesus promises to keep us from stumbling and to present us faultless before his throne (Jude 1:24). God is our ever-present help in time of trouble (Ps. 46:1). He assures the church: "I am coming soon. Hold fast what you have, so that no one may seize your crown" (Rev. 3:11). He promises those who conquer by faithfulness: "I will make him a pillar in the temple of my God. Never shall he go out of it, and I will write on him the name of my God, and the name of the city of my God, the new Jerusalem, which comes down from my God out of heaven, and my own new name" (Rev. 3:12; cf. Rev. 14:1; 21:10; 22:4). They will be firmly established in the heavenly city. No earthquake will ever cause them to flee. They will abide with him in safety forever.

Jesus addresses his seventh letter to Laodicea, near modern Denizli (forty miles southeast of Philadelphia). Paul's letter to the Colossians was also read in Laodicea just a few miles away (Col. 4:16). Laodicea was founded by the Seleucid ruler Antiochus II and named after his wife Laodice. Laodicea stood at the intersection of two major roads at the head of the Lycus and Meander Valleys. The city thrived as a commercial banking center. After an earthquake in AD 60, Laodicea proudly refused financial assistance from the Roman Senate, boasting that their own funds were sufficient to rebuild the city. Laodicea was just six miles south of the famous hot springs at Hierapolis (modern Pammukale). Colossae was only eleven miles to the east and equally famous for cold springs. Laodicea received its water through the calcified pipes of a Roman aqueduct, which arrived in the city lukewarm.

To the church in Laodicea, Jesus identifies himself as "the Amen, the faithful and true witness, the beginning of God's creation" (Rev. 3:14). He rebukes the Laodiceans in that "you are neither cold nor hot. Would that you were either cold or hot!" (Rev. 3:15). They have neither the healing properties of hot springs, nor the refreshing properties of cold springs. They are lukewarm, neither hot nor cold. Jesus threatens that "I will spit you out of my mouth" (Rev. 3:16). Jesus exposes their pride and self-sufficiency with devastating clarity of expression: "You say, I am rich, I have prospered, and I need nothing, not realizing that you are wretched, pitiable, poor, blind, and naked" (Rev. 3:17). He admonishes them to acquire their wealth from Christ. He provides gold refined by fire, white garments to cover their shame, and salve to anoint their eyes that they might see. His strong words to Laodicea are motivated by love. Those whom the Lord loves, he disciplines (Rev. 3:19;

cf. Deut. 8:5; Prov. 3:12; Heb. 12:6). He urges them to be zealous and repent. He stands ready to receive them with a striking image: "Behold, I stand at the door and knock. If anyone hears my voice and opens the door, I will come in to him and eat with him, and he with me" (Rev. 3:20). He promises to those who conquer by faithfulness: "I will grant him to sit with me on my throne, as I also conquered and sat down with my Father on his throne" (Rev. 3:21; cf. Rev. 7:10; 20:11-12; 22:1-3). Those who humbly receive Christ's correction will be enthroned with him forever.

The seven letters to the churches are an important part of "the revelation of Jesus Christ" (Rev. 1:1). Jesus appears before us as exalted Son of Man and Lord of the church. He is not a distant, silent husband. We are reminded for our context that Jesus speaks to his bride with intimate awareness of our particular circumstances. He knows when to encourage and when to rebuke. He is familiar with the temptations and trials of this world. He empowers suffering witness, even unto to death. He arouses those who are complacent. He will honor faithfulness with generous reward. Above all, Jesus repeatedly invites the churches to listen to his voice. Each letter ends with the same summons: "He who has an ear, let him hear what the Spirit says to the churches" (Rev. 3:22; cf. Deut. 6:4; John 10:16).

The exalted Son of Man is worshiped in heaven (Rev. 4-5)

In Rev. 4-5, the revelation of Jesus Christ continues as John is invited further inside the heavenly sanctuary. He sees a door standing open and hears the same voice that he had heard in Rev. 1. Like Israel's prophets, John stands in God's heavenly council that he might be shown God's will (Rev. 4:1; cf. Amos 3:7). John enters into the heavenly throne-room where he sees the Lord God Almighty enthroned in splendor (Rev. 4:2-3). The scene is awesome and dynamic to behold. The glory of God radiates like precious stones. His voice is like the sound of rushing waters. Like Isaiah, Ezekiel, and Daniel before him, John sees the Lord surrounded by the heavenly host in royal majesty (Isa. 6; Ezek. 1; Dan. 7). Living creatures near his throne cry out: "Holy, holy, holy, is the Lord God Almighty, who was and is and is to come!" (Rev. 4:8; cf. Isa. 6:3). Twenty-four elders stand before him in the sanctuary (Rev. 4:4; cf. 1 Chron. 24:3-19; 25:1-31). They cast their crowns before him declaring: "Worthy are you, our Lord and God, to receive glory and honor and power, for you created all things, and by your will they existed and were created" (Rev. 4:11). God is known and worshiped as Creator of all things. We glimpse the identity and power of our heavenly Father. We are assured that God is in control. We are safe and secure from all alarm. His purposes and plans will surely be accomplished.

Jesus is worthy to open the seven-sealed scroll of God's will

As John gazes in awe, he sees a scroll in God's right hand. The scroll signifies God's will. The scroll is written inside and out, yet it is sealed with seven seals. An angel proclaims in a loud voice: "Who is worthy to open the scroll and break its seals?" (Rev. 5:2). The angel asks whether anyone has been found worthy to execute God's will. No one in heaven or on earth or under the earth is able to open the scroll or look into it. John begins to weep loudly, longing that the will of God might be understood and carried out. Precisely at this moment, one of the elders approaches him and declares: "Weep no more; behold, the Lion of the tribe of Judah, the Root of David, has conquered, so that he can open the scroll and its seven seals" (Rev. 5:5). The Messiah from the line of Judah to whom the obedience of all nations belongs has come (see Gen. 49:10). The son of David who will stand as a signal for all nations has conquered (see 2 Sam. 7:14; Isa. 11:1-10). This is Jesus Christ, whom heaven declares worthy to reveal and execute God's will for the salvation of the nations.

The Lamb of God, who purchased people from all nations, is slain

John looks toward the throne of God and sees a Lamb standing, having been slain (Rev. 5:6). Jesus is the royal Messiah who has given his life to carry the sin of the world (Isa. 53:4-5; John 1:29). He stands enthroned in heavenly glory after his resurrection. Jesus is the Son of David and the Suffering Servant. He conquers the nations by dying for them. His death and resurrection are the center of the biblical narrative (1 Cor. 15:3-4). The reigning Lamb is depicted with seven horns and eyes to signify the universal scope of his dominion over all the earth (Rev. 5:6; cf. Ps. 72:8). He takes the scroll from the Father and prepares to carry out his sovereign will and purpose. The court of heaven responds in praise. Those near the throne of God sing a new song: "Worthy are you to take the scroll and to open its seals, for you were slain, and by your blood you ransomed people for God from every tribe and language and people and nation, and you have made them a kingdom and priests to our God, and they shall reign on the earth" (Rev. 5:9-10). By the blood of our Passover Lamb, we become God's redeemed from every tribe, tongue, and nation (Gen. 12:3; Exod. 12:21-23; 1 Cor. 5:7).

Jesus makes us into a kingdom of priests and holy nation who will reign with him forever. This calling echoes the original commission to humanity in the Garden of Eden (Gen. 1:28), and to Israel at the base of Mount Sinai (Exod. 19:6). The realization of God's purpose fulfills the prophetic hope that the whole world would be filled with the knowledge of the glory of the Lord like the waters cover the sea (Isa. 11:9; Hab. 2:14). God's praise radiates out from the throne as myriads and myriads of angels join with a loud voice: "Worthy is the Lamb who was slain, to receive power and wealth and wisdom and might and honor and glory and blessing!" (Rev. 5:12). Then every creature in heaven and on earth and under the earth and in the sea joins in worship unto God and the Lamb who was slain. All together proclaim: "To him who sits on the throne and to the Lamb be blessing and honor and glory and might forever and ever!" (Rev. 5:13).

Allow this eternal scene of worship to fill your own heart. Take time right now to set your affection on the Lamb who was slain for you. Worship is our highest joy. Worship is the true meaning of our humanity. Worship is the ultimate purpose of global missions. The nations have been freed from idolatry so that they might worship and serve the living God. The next portion of Revelation shows how Jesus Christ, the exalted Son of Man, executes God's will and gathers in the harvest of the nations.

The exalted Son of Man releases wrath and gathers a people (Rev. 6-11)

John keeps his eyes fixed upon Jesus Christ, the Lion of Judah, the Lamb who was slain. We need to do the same. Throughout the "revelation of Jesus Christ," we remain before God's throne in the single, extended vision of the sanctuary. In Rev. 6-11, Jesus Christ opens the seven seals and begins to carry out the will of God. There is an escalating progression in these chapters. As each seal is broken, God's sovereign purpose in judgment and salvation is made known. There is also a recapitulating pattern in these chapters, so that the same point is made by the repetition of key ideas. This is a common feature in apocalyptic writing. Throughout this section, we see that the exalted Son of Man releases measured wrath in the world, even as he gathers a people for himself. God's kindness in delaying the full outpouring of his wrath is designed to lead the nations to repentance (see Rom. 2:4; 9:22-23; 2 Pet. 3:9, 15). God's salvation is made known to the nations through the faithful witness of the church in the world. This basic pattern is repeated three times as a series of measured judgments are released through a series of seven seals, seven trumpets, seven thunders, and finally seven bowls. At the end of each series there is a vivid portrait of the innumerable multitude that has been redeemed. This imagery reminds us of how God's series of judgments upon Egypt ends with the multitude of the redeemed at the Exodus. The symbolism of this section is deeply rooted in Scripture and should not be recast in terms of modern concepts that would have been meaningless to the original audience.

Seven seals of judgment on one-fourth of the earth as a multitude is redeemed (Rev. 6-7)

In Rev. 6-7, the first series of judgments is poured out upon one-fourth of the earth as a multitude is redeemed. God's judgment is revealed as the seals upon the scroll of his will are opened (Rev. 6:1-17). Christ opens the first seal and summons a white horse and an armed rider who goes out into the world to wage war. Christ opens the second seal and summons a red horse and a rider with a great sword who removes peace. Christ opens the third seal and summons a black horse and a rider equipped with a pair of scales. There is famine in the land to such an extent that a quart of wheat sells for a daily wage. This is about fifteen times the normal price of wheat during the late first century AD. At the same time, the wrath of the Lamb is measured, since the harvest of oil and wine are left unharmed. Christ opens the fourth seal and summons a pale horse and a rider named Death, followed closely by Hades. Judgment is carried out upon a fourth of the earth with sword, famine, pestilence, and wild beasts (Rev. 6:8). Christ opens the fifth seal and persecution breaks out against the church. John sees "the souls of those who had been slain for the word of God and for the witness they had borne" (Rev. 6:9). They are gathered under the altar and cry out with a loud voice: "O

Sovereign Lord, holy and true, how long before you will judge and avenge our blood on those who dwell on the earth?" (Rev. 6:10). Christ clothes them in white robes and answers that they must wait until the full number of their fellow servants who would be killed for the sake of Christ would be complete. Christ opens the sixth seal and summons a great convulsion of the created order. There is a great earthquake. The sun is darkened (probably with volcanic ash). The moon is eclipsed and appears blood-red in the sky. The stars appear to fall and the heavens vanish from sight. This is apocalyptic language used to describe the awesome reality of God's judgment upon the earth, echoing Old Testament descriptions (cf. Hag. 2:6-7). These symbols should not be pressed too literally. They signify the terrifying reality of God's wrath. This is evident in the reaction of the kings of the earth, rich and powerful, slave and free who call out to the mountains: "Fall on us and hide us from the face of him who is seated on the throne, and from the wrath of the Lamb, for the great day of their wrath has come, and who can stand?" (Rev. 6:16-17).

God's measured wrath upon one-fourth of the earth resolves with our eyes upon the great company of the redeemed. John sees four angels standing at the four corners of the earth holding back the wind. Again, the entire earth is in view. Yet, instead of a seal releasing judgment, an angel rises from the east with the seal of the living God (Rev. 7:2). The angel moves forward to place the seal of God upon the forehead of the redeemed. The seal signifies ownership. Just as the high priest bears the name of Yahweh upon his forehead (Exod. 28:36-38), the redeemed will bear the name of God and of the Lamb upon their foreheads (Rev. 14:1). Ezekiel 9 stands behind this image when God instructed angels to mark the foreheads of all who belonged to him. John first sees members of his own ethnic group. He recognizes twelve thousand people from every tribe of the sons of Israel before God's throne. Each of the traditional twelve tribes is multiplied by one thousand. This indicates the vast number of those who trust in Christ and are saved from God's wrath. Then John looks and sees a great multitude that no one could number, from every nation, from all tribes and peoples and languages (Rev. 7:9). Notice that our ethnic identity is not eliminated in heaven, but rather redeemed. People from every nation are standing before the throne and before the Lamb, clothed in white robes, with palm branches in their hands. They cry out with a loud voice: "Salvation belongs to our God who sits on the throne, and to the Lamb!" (Rev. 7:10). The vast multitude of the redeemed from Israel and from among all nations is interpreted as those who have come through the tribulation, distress, and the measured judgment upon the earth (Rev. 7:14). Like the highway through the sea at the Exodus from Egypt, the redeemed are delivered by the Lamb and led to the God's dwelling place. They have washed their robes and made them white in the blood of the Lamb. They are before the throne of God and serve him day and night in his temple. They abide in the shelter of God's presence. They neither hunger nor thirst "for the Lamb in the midst of the throne will be their shepherd, and he will guide them to springs of living water, and God will wipe away every tear from their eyes" (Rev. 7:17; cf. Isa. 25:8; Rev. 21:4).

Seven trumpets of judgment on one-third of the earth as his people are sealed (Rev. 8-11)

In Rev. 8-11, the pattern we have just observed now recapitulates with a series of seven trumpets sounded by seven angels before God's throne. Notice that we still remain inside the single, controlling sanctuary vision called "the revelation of Jesus Christ" (Rev. 1:1). The veil of the temple has been removed and we see Christ enthroned with glory and power. He executes the Father's will in heaven and on earth. The host of heaven and the innumerable multitude of the redeemed worship him. He hears and responds to the prayers of his people, even as he adds to their number daily (Rev. 8:3-5). He releases a measured wrath, now upon one-third of the earth. As the first four angels sound their trumpets, there is hail and fire that burn one-third of the earth (Rev. 8:7). Christ pours out a measured wrath upon one-third of the sea, and on one-third of the living creatures; even one-third of the ships are destroyed (Rev. 8:8-9). One-third of the rivers become bitter causing death (Rev. 8:11), and one-third of the moon, stars, and light of the sun grows dark (Rev. 8:12). These judgments again recall the imagery and intention of the Exodus plagues. An eagle flies overhead with a three-fold warning "woe, woe, woe to those who dwell on the earth" (Rev. 8:13). A fifth angel summons a terrifying plague of locusts released upon the earth, yet those who receive the seal of God are spared (Rev. 9:1-12). A sixth angel sounds forth a vast horde of mounted troops to devastate one-third of humanity (Rev. 9:13-19). However, those who remain and are not killed by these plagues refuse to repent of their idolatry and immorality (Rev. 9:20-21; cf. Exod. 8:15).

As God's measured wrath escalates on the earth, his great redemptive purpose again comes into focus. Just like the view of the innumerable multitude of the redeemed after the sixth seal (Rev. 7:1-17), we see the suffering, yet triumphant witness of the church after the sixth trumpet (Rev. 10:1-11:13). A mighty angel comes down from heaven, clothed with splendor and shining like the sun. John looks from his island exile toward the communities he knows and loves who are engaged in spiritual battle on shore. God's towering angel faces him, planting his right foot on the sea and his left foot on the land. The angel holds the scroll of God's will, which has been opened by the Lamb who has conquered (Rev. 10:2; cf. Rev. 5:5-10). He speaks with a loud voice and seven thunders sound. The seven thunders are not written down, but apparently describe Christ's measured wrath upon one-half of the earth (Rev. 10:3-4), as also inferred from the seven bowls that complete God's wrath upon all of the earth (Rev. 16). The mighty angel raises his hand and swears that there should be no more delay, but that the mystery of God would be fulfilled (Rev. 10:6-7). The mystery of God's will is the full realization of his redemptive plan. He plans to unite all things in heaven and on earth in Christ (Eph. 1:10).

This plan will be accomplished in and through the redeemed from every nation, created for his glory that they might declare his praise (Isa. 43:7, 21; Eph. 3:10). The church is entrusted with the revealed will of God and must remain on earth as living testimony to God's truth in Christ. John receives this sacred commission directly from Jesus Christ. The Lord speaks again, instructing him to take the scroll and to eat it (Rev. 10:8-9). The scroll of God's will is as sweet as honey, yet it is bitter with the message of God's wrath (Rev. 10:10). Like the prophet Ezekiel, John eats the scroll and is commissioned to prophesy "about many peoples and nations and languages and kings" (Rev. 10:11; cf. Ezek. 3:1-3, 10).

The prophetic witness of the church is vividly portrayed in Rev. 11. We remain inside the controlling sanctuary vision as John is given a rod to measure the sanctuary and the altar, alongside those who worship there (Rev. 11:1). The focus of the vision is on the faithful witness of the church.

It is important to see that throughout Revelation the church exists in the world as the very means by which the nations are converted. The innumerable multitude *from* all nations (Rev. 5:9) bears prophetic witness *to* all nations (Rev. 11:3-13). The prophetic role of the redeemed community is symbolically depicted as the story of two witnesses. Their story combines a set of recognizable apocalyptic images. These images, like the other symbols in Revelation, have established meaning in Scripture and should not be pressed out of context into a purely contemporary setting. The two witnesses are explicitly identified as lampstands (Rev. 11:4). Within the symbolic imagery of Revelation, lampstands represent the church in the world (Rev. 1:12, 20). The narrative of the two witnesses probably does not describe two literal individuals or a sequence of events. Instead, it depicts the nature and result of the church's prophetic witness in the world leading up to the return of Christ (Rev. 11:15-18).

The two witnesses bear faithful testimony in the sanctuary. They face opposition and persecution from the nations in the outer court (Rev. 11:1-3). They fulfill the biblical requirement that truth is established on the testimony of at least two witnesses (Deut. 19:15). The witnesses are clothed with sackcloth signifying repentance. They are given prophetic authority to address the nations. They issue a call to repentance toward a world addicted to idolatry and immorality. Their ministry recalls the prophetic role of Moses at the Exodus and Elijah during the dark days of Ahab and Jezebel (Rev. 11:5-6). The two witnesses suffer martyrdom when they are opposed by the satanic power animating from the beast, first introduced here (Rev. 11:7). Their death recalls the crucifixion of Jesus (Rev. 11:8). Peoples, tribes, languages, and nations gaze at their dead bodies. Those who dwell on the earth rejoice at their demise, even exchanging gifts with one another (Rev. 11:10). Yet after three and a half days, they are raised from the dead and stand upon their feet (Rev. 11:11). A loud voice from heaven calls them into heavenly glory. The two witnesses thus replay in the sight of all nations the death and resurrection of the Messiah. Even here in the concentrated apocalyptic imagery of Rev. 11 we see the absolute centrality of Christ's death and resurrection for the entire narrative of Scripture. CASKET EMPTY holds this before us so that we might recognize the fulfillment of God's redemptive purpose in

Christ. This purpose is received by faith and lived out in faithful witness to the world.

The church's prophetic witness achieves a glorious result. Although many are taken away by God's righteous wrath, those who remain repent and believe. They fear God and give him glory (Rev. 11:13). This language is used in Revelation to describe conversion and a genuine response to the eternal gospel (Rev. 14:6-7). In contrast to those who did not repent at the series of judgments (Rev. 9:20), the nations are gathered in through the faithful witness of the church. As we have seen throughout our study, God has poured out his Spirit and commissioned his people to teach the gospel to the nations (Acts 1:8). The church extends the gospel and issues a prophetic call for all nations to repent and believe (Luke 24:47; Acts 17:30). Faithful witness will encounter opposition and hostility. Persecution will at times even require a martyr's death. Nevertheless, throughout church history, faithful testimony, even unto death, often opens new frontiers of gospel witness and response.

"The kingdom of the world has become the kingdom of our Lord and of His Christ, and He shall reign forever and ever" (Rev. 11:15)

The faithful witness of the church in the world continues until the seventh angel sounds his trumpet in triumph at Christ's return. Loud voices in heaven proclaim the full realization of God's redemptive purpose: "The kingdom of the world has become the kingdom of our Lord and of his Christ, and he shall reign forever and ever" (Rev. 11:15). Here we reach the initial climax of Revelation. The heavenly court erupts in praise and thanksgiving to the Lord God Almighty (Rev. 11:16). He has taken up his great power and begun to reign. He has redeemed some from every nation for himself. The kingdoms of this world now rightly belong to Jesus Christ. All who believe are transferred into his glorious kingdom. Although the nations have raged against God and his church, the time has come for final judgment and reward. Those who destroy the earth will be destroyed. God's faithful servants will be richly rewarded (Rev. 11:18; cf. Isa. 62:11; Matt. 25:31).

The glorious sanctuary vision of Revelation resolves with God's temple open to all. The ark of his covenant, the throne of mercy, is visible to all. There are flashes of lightning and rolls of thunder at the mention of his name

(Rev. 11:19; cf. Exod. 19:16-20). God is enthroned in the midst of his people. He is God, and there is no other. He is God, and there is none like him. He has declared the end from the beginning and from ancient times things not yet done, for God will surely accomplish what he has planned (Isa. 46:10). Revelation 11 allows us to see the ending in advance. God's sovereign plan of redemption will be fully realized in all the earth. This certainty encourages our faithfulness today as the church is engaged in a spiritual battle for the hearts of the nations. The next section of the "revelation of Jesus Christ" will depict the nature of this spiritual battle and the ultimate triumph of the Lamb.

Chapter 10
YET-TO-COME Part 2

The spiritual battle between God and the Serpent (Rev. 12-15)

As WE CONTINUE with YET-TO-COME Part 2, the Lord shows John the spiritual battle in which the church is engaged. In Rev. 12-15, this spiritual battle is depicted as between God and the Serpent "who is called the devil and Satan, the deceiver of the whole world" (Rev. 12:9). These chapters introduce a new set of images into the controlling scene of Revelation that will be resolved by the end of the book. A pregnant woman is about to give birth, yet a great red dragon desires to devour the child (Rev. 12). A beast with a mortal wound rises from the sea and another from the earth in violent opposition to those who follow the Lamb who was slain (Rev. 13). Those who have been sealed with the name of God appear, in contrast with those who have received a mark of the beast (Rev. 14). We then see seven angels with bowls filled with the final outpouring of God's wrath upon the earth (Rev. 15-16). Despite the intensity of the conflict, God's kingdom will prevail. His wrath will be poured out upon the earth and evil will be condemned. His saving purpose will be made known to all nations and his righteousness rule will be established forever.

As God's wrath and saving purpose are fully displayed, the bride of Christ is contrasted with the whore of Babylon (Rev. 17-18). The New Jerusalem and Babylon the Great come into view as rival cities (Rev. 21). The tree of life is set against the lake of fire (Rev. 22). As with all of the symbols in Revelation, these images have established meanings in Scripture and should be interpreted in context. The images are presented as contrasting pairs, for in each case God's truth is counterfeited by satanic parody. God's truth is depicted with the beauty of holiness and sacrificial love. Satanic counterfeits are exposed with the garishness of sin and violent exploitation. The devil has no creative power in Revelation. He only deceives, distorts, and degrades what God has made. God alone creates and renews humanity made in his image and likeness by the power of the gospel. We will explore these contrasting pairs as we lead up to the dramatic ending of what still remains in the period of YET-TO-COME.

God is opposed by the Serpent

In Rev. 12:1, John sees "a great sign" in heaven. The explicit use of the word "sign" reminds us again that the imagery of Revelation is symbolic and should not be pressed too literally. The opening statement of the book tells us that the revelation of Jesus Christ is "signified" to the reader using symbols (Rev. 1:1). We should always interpret the visions God gives John with our eyes on the main point being represented. In Rev. 12, John sees an extraordinary woman. She is clothed with the sun, with the moon under her feet, and a crown of twelve stars upon her head. She is pregnant and about to give birth (Rev. 12:2-3). At the moment of her giving birth, he sees another "sign," as a great red dragon with seven heads and horns symbolizing vast domain and global power appears. The dragon sweeps down a third of the stars, depicting a great persecution against God's people in the world (cf. Dan. 8:10-12; 12:3). The dragon stands before the woman "so that when she bore her child he might devour it" (Rev. 12:4). Despite the dragon's looming threat, the woman gives birth to a male child. The child is extraordinary. He will shepherd all the nations with a rod of iron (Rev. 12:5). This imagery describes the promised Messiah, the Son of God who will defeat the serpent (Gen. 3:17; Ps. 2:7-9; Dan. 7:13-14). No wonder the dragon seeks to devour the child at birth! The child is then raised up before God and shares his heavenly throne (Rev. 12:5). As the Son is exalted, the woman flees into the wilderness where she is preserved and protected by God (Rev. 12:6). There is a war in heaven. The great dragon "that ancient serpent, who is called the devil and Satan, the deceiver of the whole world" is thrown down to the earth

(Rev. 12:7-9; cf. Luke 10:18). A loud voice in heaven proclaims: "Now the salvation and the power and the kingdom of our God and the authority of his Christ have come, for the accuser of our brothers has been thrown down, who accuses them day and night before our God" (Rev. 12:10). This dramatic vision shows us that the Messiah's birth signals the defeat of the dragon. His exaltation strips the power of the devil's accusation forever. God's people live in this reality without fear today, even though the dragon rages against all who place their trust in Christ.

When the dragon sees that he has been thrown down to the earth, he pursues the women with great violence, knowing that his time is short (Rev. 12:12-13). He attempts to drown her with a counterfeit flood of satanic judgment (Rev. 12:15). Unlike God's righteous judgment at the flood, the earth opens and swallows the waters. The serpent becomes furious and makes war on the rest of her offspring "who keep the commandments of God and hold to the testimony of Jesus" (Rev. 12:17). Yet they conquer him "by the blood of the Lamb and by the word of their testimony," even as they love not their lives even unto death (Rev. 12:11). The enraged serpent stands on the sand of the sea, searching for a way to defeat those who hold the testimony of Jesus (Rev. 12:18).

The vision of Rev. 12 shows us how God is opposed by the serpent. This is not a contest of equals. Although the Scripture does not tell us all that we might want to know about the origin of evil, Satan is present in the Garden of Eden, seeking to deceive, degrade, and dishonor humanity made in the image of God (Gen. 3:1). His initial success foretells an eternal defeat as God promises: "I will put enmity between you and the woman, and between your offspring and her offspring; he shall bruise your head, and you shall bruise his heel" (Gen. 3:15). Satan will be defeated by a descendant of the woman. The power of his accusation will be canceled forever at the cross. The apocalyptic imagery of Rev. 12 reveals Satan's rage against the Messiah and all who remain faithful to Jesus. The woman's heavenly appearance recalls Joseph's dream and probably should be understood as representing Israel (Gen. 37:9; Isa. 66:7-9). From this line of promise, the Messiah has been born (Matt. 1:1; Rom. 9:5). The vision calls forth faithfulness from those who keep the commandments of God and hold to the testimony of Jesus, knowing that Christ's victory is sure. The kingdoms of this world rightly belong to him (Rev. 11:15).

Son of Man counterfeited by the beast

In Rev. 13, John sees the enraged serpent upon the shore summon a beast out of the sea. This should remind us of Dan. 7, where a series of four hybrid beasts represented earthy kings. Their violent and temporary rule is contrasted with the eternal dominion of the Son of Man (Dan. 7:13-14). Remember from our study that these four beasts in Daniel signified a historical progression of four kingdoms: Babylon, Persia, Greece, and Rome. In Daniel's vision, these four kingdoms were destroyed by the everlasting kingdom of God. The beast in Rev. 13 is an ominous composite of all four beasts from Dan. 7. It has ten horns with the appearance of a leopard, feet like a bear's, and a lion's mouth (Rev. 13:1-2). Most disturbing of all, the beast receives its power and authority from the dragon. Satan stands behind any human expression of power that degrades humanity and diverts our worship away from the Lord. The whole earth marvels at the beast as he spews forth proud and blasphemous words. People are forced to worship the beast saying: "Who is like the beast, and who can fight against it?" (Rev. 13:4). This represents a satanic parody of Israel's Song at the Sea: "Who is like you, O LORD, among the gods? Who is like you, majestic in holiness, awesome in glorious deeds, doing wonders?" (Exod. 15:11).

The beast counterfeits the Son of Man in several ways. He has a mortal wound that has been healed in parody of the Lamb who was slain (Rev. 13:3, 12, 14; cf. Rev. 5:6). The beast compels worship through fear in contrast to the sacrificial love of Christ. The beast seeks authority over every tribe, people, language, and nation in imitation of the universal dominion of the Son of Man (Rev. 13:7; cf. Dan. 7:14). Although the beast seeks an everlasting reign, his dominion is limited to forty-two months (Rev. 13:5). Forty-two months is equivalent to 1,260 days or three and a half years in the lunar calendar. In Revelation, three and a half years is also expressed as a time, times, and half a time (Rev. 11:2-3; 12:14). All of these numbers are the same. This expression of time is used in apocalyptic literature to signify the limited duration and scope of evil. The beast's time is always half of seven, God's everlasting Sabbath. Though limited in time by God's decree and sovereign design, the beast makes war against the saints and seeks to conquer them (Rev. 13:7). Many suffer greatly, some are taken into captivity, and some into exile, like John himself. Still others are slain with the sword. This is a call for the patient endurance of God's people when evil seems for the moment to have the upper-hand (Rev. 13:10).

John then sees another beast rising out of the earth with two horns like a lamb, yet "it spoke like a dragon" (Rev. 13:11). The beast from the earth will be identified later as a false prophet performing spurious signs to deceive people into worshiping the beast (Rev. 13:12-14; 16:13; 19:20). The false prophet parodies God's truth by making an image for the beast (Rev. 13:14). In a demonic inversion of Gen. 2, the idol receives breath. The image of the beast appears to speak and demands worship. All those who do not worship the image of the beast are slain (Rev. 13:15).

The description of the beast in Rev. 13 reflects the demands of the Roman imperial cult in the late first century. Earlier emperors, like Julius Caesar and Augustus had been deified after their death. However, in the late first century, emperors such as Nero and Domitian demanded worship while still alive. The imperial cult had both a religious and political function. It became perceived as a test of loyalty to the state. Refusal to participate could result in economic punishment, exile, and even death. Yet believers in Christ are required to worship him alone. As believers today, we need the "revelation of Jesus Christ" to embolden our conviction that he is the ruler of the kings of the earth. He is worthy to receive the worship of all nations. His rule is everlasting. His dominion has no limits. Demonic counterfeits will always posture as though possessing great power. They will compel a worship that is utterly undeserved. Knowing that their time is short, they will force an immediate decision and threaten an early death. The real King conquers his enemies by dying for them on the cross. He lives forever by his resurrection and intercedes for them. He draws us freely to himself and promises eternal life for all who believe. The kingdom of God destroys the rival vision of earthly power represented by the beast and the false prophet. This was true in the first century and remains true of any contemporary expression of rule based on violence and the deification of power.

Mark of the Son counterfeited by the mark of the beast

Another important set of contrasting images is the mark of the Son counterfeited by the mark of the beast. We have seen in Rev. 7 that the servants of God are marked with a seal upon their forehead (Rev. 7:2; cf. Exod. 28:36-38;

Ezek. 9:4). The mark of the Son is the divine name of God and of the Lamb (Rev. 14:1). The seal signifies belonging to God. Believers are under his sovereign protection and covenant care. They are his and no one has the power to take them out of his hand (John 10:28). Jesus prayed to the Father: "I kept them in your name, which you have given me. I have guarded them, and not one of them has been lost" (John 17:12). The mark (or seal) of the Son of Man is by far the most important one in Revelation. All who bear the name of Jesus Christ will never be afraid. They belong to the most powerful, loving sovereign of all. They may lose their grip on him for a moment, but he will never lose his grip on them forever.

The false prophet counterfeits this mark of ownership. He requires all people regardless of their social or economic class "to be marked on the right hand or the forehead" (Rev. 13:16). The mark of the beast is a name, just as the mark of the Son of Man is a name (Rev. 13:17). The beast, however, is not worthy of our praise. He can only constrain it. Those who refuse to participate are threatened with economic damages (Rev. 13:17). They are denied commercial participation in society for refusing to comply. Those who do not bear the mark of the beast are branded as dangerous for the common good, enemies of the state, and traitors to a prosperous age. The concrete reality of this pressure calls for wisdom. John urges his readers: "let the one who has understanding calculate the number of the beast, for it is the number of a man, and his number is 666" (Rev. 13:18).

John employs here an interpretive technique in apocalyptic literature called *gematria*. In Greek, the first letter of the alphabet, *alpha*, equals one; the second letter, *beta*, equals two; and the third letter, *gamma*, equals three. This is the meaning of the term *gematria* (*gamma=tria* or "three). In this Greek system of counting, any noun can be encoded as a number. A number can represent the name of a person whose sum is the numerical value of its letters.

The exact identification of the number of the beast has generated speculation throughout church history. We need to remember that Revelation was written to make things clear. John assumes his original readers would understand the meaning. As we have just seen, the description of the beast in Rev. 13 corresponds to the demonic demands of the Roman imperial cult. The emperor Nero became a potent symbol in the first century of violence against early believers in Christ who worshiped God alone. When considering the significance of this number, it is important to remember that names could be given a numerical value in antiquity. With this background in view, the Greek form of the name "Nero Caesar" transliterated into Hebrew is equivalent to 666. The "mark of the beast" may signify this specific name as a symbol of imperial power, which counterfeits the name and power of God (Rev. 14:1). Within the symbolic imagery of Revelation, the number 666 also conveys the repeated failure to reach seven, the number of God's perfection. The mark of the beast is yet another demonic parody of God's truth in Christ.

True power and glory are set before our eyes in Jesus Christ. John sees the Lamb who was slain. The Lamb now stands on Mount Zion after his resurrection. John sees those who had "his name and his Father's name written on their foreheads" (Rev. 14:1). Heavenly worship resounds in praise. The great multitude of the redeemed sings a new song before the throne. They are undefiled with idolatry. They have an exclusive marriage with their covenant King. They follow the Lamb wherever he goes (Rev. 14:4). With authority like heavenly messengers, they are entrusted with "an eternal gospel to proclaim to those who dwell on the earth to every nation and tribe and language and people" (Rev. 14:6). They bear prophetic witness in the world: "Fear God and give him glory, because the hour of his judgment has come, and worship him who made heaven and earth, the sea and the springs of water" (Rev. 14:7; cf. Gen. 1:1). They remind the world that earthly power is short lived. The city of man will one day fall. They warn the nations that anyone who worships the beast and receives his mark will drink the wine of God's wrath (Rev. 14:10). There can be no neutrality or compromise with demonic power. Only Jesus Christ is Lord.

The exalted Jesus uses the faithful testimony of the church in the world to gather in the harvest of the nations. The harvest is depicted in two images: the harvest of grain (Rev. 14:14-16) and the harvest of wine (Rev. 14:17-20). Both of these images are used in Scripture to describe the full realization of God's redemptive purpose. The gathering of the grain harvest is a positive image of salvation. The exalted Son of Man gathers in the grain, which represents the redeemed from all nations. The people of God are "firstfruits for God and the Lamb" (Rev. 14:4; cf. Lev. 23:9-14; 1 Cor. 15:20). Jesus gathers his wheat into the barn as the earth is reaped (Rev. 14:16; cf. Matt. 3:12; 13:30). In contrast to the positive depiction of God's people, the gathering of the grape harvest is a negative image of judgment. The grapes are placed into the winepress of the wrath of God (Rev. 14:19). On a devastating scale, God's righteous judgment flows out upon all who refuse the gospel (Rev. 14:20). Jesus has drunk the cup of God's wrath for all who believe (Luke 22:42-44). For all who belong to him and bear his name, there is no fear of condemnation, future judgment, or coming wrath.

The spiritual battle depicted in Rev. 12-15 ultimately resolves in praise and worship. Seven angels appear with golden bowls which complete God's righteous wrath (Rev. 15:1). God's measured wrath has revealed the multitude of the redeemed. They conquer the beast, his image, and the number of his name through their faithfulness to Christ. In the controlling scene of the heavenly sanctuary, they sing together the song of Moses and the song of the Lamb: "Great and amazing are your deeds, O Lord God the Almighty! Just and true are your ways, O King of the nations! Who will not fear, O Lord, and glorify your name? For you alone are holy. All nations will come and worship you, for your righteous acts have been revealed" (Rev. 15:3; cf. Exod. 15:1).

The Bride of Christ is imitated by the whore of Babylon

As God's redemptive purpose unfolds in the remaining chapters of Revelation, there are three additional sets of contrasting images that we will encounter: the bride of Christ and the whore of Babylon; the New Jerusalem and Babylon the great; and the tree of life and the lake of fire. John first sees the bride of Christ being imitated by the whore of Babylon. These personified female figures signify rival communities, namely, the people of God and the people of the serpent. The bride of Christ wears pure white garments (Rev. 3:5; 6:11). The prostitute wears purple and scarlet, gold, jewels, and pearls (Rev. 3:4-5; 7:13-14; 17:4). The bride of Christ is betrothed to a single husband (Rev. 21:9). The whore commits adultery with the nations (Rev. 14:4; 17:2). The bride of Christ is undefiled. The prostitute is drunk with the blood of the saints (Rev. 14:4; 17:6). The bride of Christ prepares for her wedding. The prostitute rides upon a scarlet beast in drunken revelry (Rev. 17:3; 19:7-9). The bride bears the name of her faithful husband. The prostitute carries the name of "Babylon the great, mother of prostitutes and of earth's abominations (Rev. 17:5). The sharp contrast of these two images asserts a powerful point—we become like the one we worship (Ps. 115:3-8). Humanity has been made in the image and likeness of the living God. He is holy and righteous, faithful and pure. Those who belong to him reflect his character and likeness. The serpent has been a liar from the beginning. Those who follow him will inevitably bear his likeness.

The New Jerusalem and Babylon the Great

The second set of contrasting images is the New Jerusalem, the city of God, which is counterfeited by Babylon the Great, the city of man. Within the apocalyptic imagery of Revelation, these two cities represent rival structures of identity and power. They represent alternative kingdoms and contrasting ways of life. At the historical moment of Revelation, the harlot city seems to have the upper-hand, as God's people suffer under the Roman Empire. As such, there is need for the unveiling of the city of God; it must be seen and then proclaimed. "Babylon" is used as apocalyptic code for the city of seven hills, namely, the city of Rome (Rev. 17:9; cf. 1 Pet. 5:13). Babylon and Rome were closely associated in the first century for idolatry and immorality, and for having destroyed the temple in Jerusalem, recalling the Babylonian destruction in 586 BC under Nebuchadnezzar and the Roman destruction in AD 70 under Titus.

The New Jerusalem is the glorious city built by God himself (Rev. 21:2-3; cf. Heb. 11:10). The Bible begins in a garden, the paradise of Eden. As God's redemptive purpose moves forward, we eventually see the royal city that accompanies the garden. The New Jerusalem is the place where God dwells in the midst of his people. The city is beautiful, safe, and hosts a flourishing human community. Babylon perverts this ideal, as a home of idolatry and tyrannical rule. The city is dark, violent, and oppressive for all who reside there. Babylon must fall in Revelation (Rev. 14:8; 18:2). Her demonic parody must be exposed so that the nations might be drawn to God's true city.

The nature of these two cities is revealed through a series of vivid contrasts. The New Jerusalem is like a bride prepared for her husband (Rev. 21:2); Babylon is like a prostitute with whom the kings of the earth commit adultery (Rev. 17:2). The New Jerusalem is adorned with the glory of God (Rev.

21:11-21); Babylon is debased by abomination and immorality (Rev. 17:4-5). The New Jerusalem illuminates the nations to walk by her light (Rev. 21:24); Babylon deceives the nations to share in her ruin (Rev. 18:23). The New Jerusalem receives the willing offerings of the nations (Rev. 21:24); Babylon plunders the nations with commercial exploitation (Rev. 18:11-18). The New Jerusalem provides life and healing (Rev. 22:1-2); Babylon is a culture of death, filled with the blood of prophets, saints, and all who are slain upon the earth (Rev. 18:24). The nations are called into the New Jerusalem (Rev. 22:14); God's people are called out of Babylon (Rev. 18:4). The contrast of these cities strongly challenges the hearts of all who read Revelation then and now. The deceitful charms of Babylon must be exposed in order that we might see the genuine attraction of the New Jerusalem.

The tree of life versus the lake of fire

The third contrasting image is the tree of life and the lake of fire. The tree of life that grows within the New Jerusalem produces twelve kinds of fruit, yielding its fruit each month. The leaves of the tree supply the healing of the nations (Rev. 22:2). There is no longer anything accursed. God dwells with his people. They will see his face and worship him forever (Rev. 22:3-4). All of this imagery recalls the very beginning of Bible (Gen. 1-3). Humanity is made in the image and likeness of God. We are created for communion with God. We are designed to know him and respond to him in praise. Through our disobedience, sin, death, and the curse entered into God's world. The curse of sin is now removed by the atoning death of the Lamb. Blessing flows out from the place of God's presence and the whole earth is renewed by the knowledge of God (Rev. 22:1-3; cf. Isa. 11:9; Ezek. 47:1, 12; Hab. 2:14).

The tree of life is contrasted with the lake of fire. The lake is sterile and burns with sulfur. The lake of fire is a terrifying image of judgment. The lake is associated with the covenant curse. The birds of the air gorge themselves on those slain there (Rev. 19:21; cf. Deut. 28:26). The lake of fire is likened to a second death (Rev. 20:14-15). It is the final destination of the serpent, beast, and false prophet. All whose names are not written in the Lamb's book of life share their conscious torment day and night forever (Rev. 20:10, 15). The fearful reality of God's final judgment awakens our appetite for the tree of life. The certainty of judgment upon all who are without Christ motivates our mission. The eternal gospel alone offers forgiveness, redemption, healing, and everlasting life.

As we conclude this set of contrasting images, remember that one of greatest benefits of reading Revelation is to purify our imagination. We live in an image-saturated age that distorts our vision of reality. We see violence in the world and feel afraid. We see boastful, threatening earthly power and remain silent. We see worldliness as attractive and blindly follow along under bright, artificial lights. We see cultural compromise as necessary and are apathetic in our commission. We see evil and think only to defend ourselves. We tolerate the beast and false prophet to guard our own economic security. We see the city of man and lose sight of the City of God. We need "the revelation of Jesus Christ" to pull back the veil so that we can see God's reality. Renewed with the vision of God and the role of the church in the world, we see with renewed clarity. Temptations lose their power as evil is exposed. Hope rises when we see the accomplishment of the cross. Hearts are stirred to faithful witness and the gospel is openly proclaimed.

The exalted Son of Man returns in glory and final victory

The final chapters of Revelation depict the return of Christ in glory and final victory. As we return to the narrative of Revelation, it is important to remember the overarching unity of the book as a single, controlling sanctuary vision. In Rev. 1, Jesus is first revealed as he walks and speaks in the midst of the lampstands in the holy place (Rev. 1). He then addresses seven churches from the sanctuary as exalted Lord and coming King (Rev. 2-3). He calls them to faithfulness, perseverance, and uncompromising witness in the world. He promises great reward for those who conquer by faithful obedience and holding forth the testimony of Christ in the world.

We are then brought further inside the sanctuary to see the Lord enthroned (Rev. 4-5). The Lamb who was slain is seen as worthy to execute God's will. Remaining before the throne, we see the exalted Son of Man release a measured wrath as he gathers the nations to himself (Rev. 6-11). His church has a vital role in the conversion of the nations as they faithfully proclaim the gospel. The spiritual battle between God and the Serpent is depicted with a set of contrasting images, as God's truth is counterfeited by satanic parody (Rev. 12-15). These apocalyptic pairings compel the reader to decide who is worthy of our worship (Rev. 13:4; 15:4). There is no middle ground. The sanctuary is now open before us and filled with the glory of God (Rev. 15:8; cf. Exod. 40:34-35; 1 Kgs. 8:10-11). Seven angels with golden bowls stand ready to finish the outpouring of God's wrath and complete the harvest of the nations (Rev. 15:1).

The Lord now speaks again from the temple in Rev. 16:1. The time has now come for God's wrath to be poured out upon the whole earth. The seven angels pour out an escalating wrath in a series of plagues. The Exodus from Egypt again provides the visual and theological background. The plagues release God's righteous judgment that culminates in a vast multitude of the redeemed (Rev. 15:3-4; Exod. 15:11-13). The first bowl brings painful sores on those who worship the beast and bear his mark (Rev. 16:2). The second bowl turns the sea into blood as death abounds (Rev. 16:3). The third bowl turns the rivers and springs to blood, as an angelic voice announces God's judgment in vindication of his people (Rev. 16:4-6). Just as Pharaoh lost his own son because he had killed God's first-born son (Exod. 4:22-23), God turns the world to blood because "they have shed the blood of saints" (Rev. 16:6). The fourth bowl causes the sun to burn with intense heat, yet the people curse God and do not repent (Rev. 16:8-9). The fifth bowl turns the kingdom of the beast into darkness, yet the people curse God and do not repent (Rev. 16:10-11). The sixth bowl dries up the great river Euphrates, preparing the way for a great battle (Rev. 16:12). We see the dragon, the beast, and the false prophet spew demonic spirits who assemble the kings of the earth against the Lord God Almighty. They prepare to assemble at Megiddo, which in Hebrew is called *Har-Megiddo* ("the mount of Meggido"). Thus, the final battle will be known as Armageddon (Rev. 16:16).

At the seventh bowl, the Lord speaks from the temple: "It is done!" (Rev. 16:17). The Lord God Almighty appears in visible glory. There are flashes of lightning and the thunder of his voice (Rev. 16:18), echoing the divine presence at Sinai (Exod. 19:9). The earth shakes and cities fall. The mountains fall down and the islands flee. Hailstones fall from heaven and prompt those upon the earth to curse God. Babylon drains the cup of God's wrath. Such "cosmic upheaval" language is a feature of apocalyptic literature to convey the almost indescribable power of God at his appearing. Such language should not be read literally. Israel's prophets used similar "cosmic upheaval" language to describe the awesome reality of God's wrath and his judgment of evil at the day of the Lord (Ezek. 38:19-20; Joel 2:1-3; Hag. 2:6-7). At the same time, the day of the Lord is also a day of salvation for the redeemed. They are vindicated as evil is condemned. God's final victory displays his glory and leads to a renewed heavens and earth in which righteousness dwells (Rev. 21:1; cf. Isa. 65:17; 2 Pet. 3:13). The certainty of Christ's return inspires our faithful resolve and motivates our sacrificial service. The promise of his final victory banishes all of our fears.

Christ's judgment on the whore of Babylon (Rev. 17-18)

Revelation 17-18 describes Christ's judgment on the whore of Babylon. The city of man must fall in order that the City of God might fill the earth. One of the seven angels invites John to see "the judgment of the great prostitute who is seated on many waters with whom the kings of the earth have committed sexual immorality, and with the wine of whose sexual immorality the dwellers on earth have become drunk" (Rev. 17:1-2). He is carried away in the Spirit and sees the disturbing image of a drunken woman, riding the beast full of blasphemous names with seven heads and ten horns (Rev. 17:3; cf. Rev. 12:3; 13:1). The woman wears expensive clothing and imported jewelry. She holds a golden cup filled with abominations, sexual immorality, and the blood of those who bear testimony to Jesus (Rev. 17:4-6). She is identified by the name on her forehead: "Babylon the great, mother of prostitutes and of earth's abominations" (Rev. 17:5). The name Babylon is a "mystery" so that readers will not take it literally, but interpret it as a figurative expression for the imperial power of Rome. This becomes clear in the description of the woman as seated on seven hills, a common expression for the city of Rome (Rev. 17:9). The angel explicitly explains: "the woman that you saw is the great city that has dominion over the kings of the earth" (Rev. 17:18).

John marvels at the grotesque sight of the woman riding the beast. The angel explains the sign as a demonic parody of God's truth. The beast who "was, and is not, and is about to rise" only counterfeits the Lord God Almighty "who was, is, and is to come" (Rev. 17:8; cf. Rev. 1:4, 8). When the beast rises from the pit, he will be destroyed. When the Lord God comes down from heaven, he will reign forever. Those who first marveled at the beast later find that their names are not written in the book of life. Various interpretations of the seven kings have been given throughout church history. Within the imagery of Revelation, the main point is that the limited dominion of the beast is drawing to a close. Although earthly kings will make war, the Lamb will conquer them for he is "Lord of lords and King of kings" (Rev. 17:14). He is chosen and faithful. Those who stand with him will bear his likeness. The beast tries in vain to secure the glad obedience of the peoples, multitudes, nations, and languages through the seductive attractions of the woman and the city she represents (Rev. 17:15). They will turn against her in the end and she will be left desolate (Rev. 17:16). An innumerable multitude will leave her city. They will follow the Lamb wherever he goes. They will enter the city of God and rejoice with him forever.

John sees another angel coming down from heaven with great authority and radiant glory (Rev. 18:1). The angel announces the fall of "Babylon the great" (Rev. 18:2). Rome is exposed as a dwelling place for demons and unclean spirits. The nations of the world have drunk the wine of her immorality, kings have committed adultery with her, and the merchants of the earth have grown rich from her luxurious living (Rev. 18:3). God's people are called out of the city: "Come out of her, my people, lest you take part in her sins, lest you share in her plagues" (Rev. 18:4; cf. Isa. 48:20; Jer. 51:6, 45). Her sins have reached their full measure and the time of God's righteous judgment has come (Rev. 18:5; cf. Gen. 15:16). God's judgment will come quickly in a single day, even a single hour (Rev. 18:8, 10, 19; cf. Dan. 5:22-31). The kings of the earth will stand far off only lamenting their own economic loss (Rev. 18:11).

The list of twenty-eight imported luxury goods reflects a strong prophetic critique of wealth gained through exploitation and the intoxicating effect of conspicuous consumption (Rev. 18:12-13). Rome increased her wealth by plundering the nations. Gold was imported from Spain where mines had been confiscated as state property. Wealthy Roman families in the first century made gold a feature of extravagant luxury. Precious stones were imported from India. Pearls were imported from the Persian Gulf and India. Romans valued the pearl after the diamond, but for the largest and best they would pay more than for any other piece of jewelry. Nero at times scattered pearls among the people of Rome. He used to swallow them, dissolved in vinegar, at banquets for the thrill of consuming such vast expense at a single gulp. Purple was an extremely expensive dye extracted from murex snails and used to mark status and wealth. Silk was imported from China. Citron wood came from the citrus trees that grew along the North African coast and were valued for their unique graining patterns. Tables made from citron wood became one of the most expensive fashions of early imperial Rome, indispensable at banquets. Rome imported marble from Africa, Egypt, and Greece. Augustus famously stated: "I found Rome a city of bricks and left it a city of marble." Wine was in such surplus that Domitian passed laws to reduce viticulture by almost one half. Wheat was imported from Africa and Egypt in vast quantities. Thousands of ships were involved in the grain trade between Rome and Alexandria. Animals and chariots were used to gratify the Roman lust for entertainment. Lions perished in the Middle East and Mesopotamia at this time due to over-hunting. Nine thousand animals were killed on the opening day of the Colosseum. The most devastating cargo was "human souls" (Rev. 18:13). Slaves were frequently taken through conquest. The Jewish War alone yielded 97,000 slaves, glutting the market and driving prices down. Other sources of slaves were foundlings, children sold by their parents, adults selling themselves due to debt, and even kidnapping. Slaves formed thirty to forty percent of the entire population of the empire. The Roman Senate rejected a proposed law that slaves should wear a distinctive dress, lest they realize their strength of numbers.

The Lord pronounces a righteous judgment against the corruption, vice, and exploitation of the city: "The fruit for which your soul longed has gone from you, and all your delicacies and your splendors are lost to you, never to be found again!" (Rev. 18:14). The God of the Bible frees slaves (Exod. 6:5-7; Deut. 7:8). He defends the cause of the poor, gives deliverance to the children of the needy, and crushes the oppressor (Ps. 72:4). With righteousness, he shall judge with equity "for the meek of the earth; and he shall strike the earth with the rod of his mouth, and with the breath of his lips he shall kill the wicked" (Isa 11:4). Jesus pronounced to his disciples: "Blessed are the poor in spirit, for theirs is the kingdom of heaven. Blessed are those who mourn, for they shall be comforted. Blessed are the meek, for they shall inherit the earth" (Matt. 5:3-5).

Believers are therefore *called out* of the city of man and *invited into* the city of God. The city of man will exploit and degrade. The city of God will rescue and restore. The city of man will concentrate power and hoard personal wealth. The city of God will elevate human dignity and generously transform society. The kingdom of God can never be reduced to a means of increasing personal wealth. The so-called prosperity gospel brokers a counterfeit reading of the Bible. It makes no discipleship demands on those who teach or follow. It shares the essential theology of idolatry, as fallen humanity seeks to manipulate the gods for personal benefit. God's Word warns us that the love of money is dangerous and the pursuit of wealth can never be our highest virtue. The gospel of Jesus Christ calls us into servant leadership, ethical business practices, and a radical generosity in support of God's mission in the world.

The Messiah's final victory over the beast, serpent, and death (Rev. 19-20)

Within the controlling apocalyptic vision of Revelation, the sudden fall of Babylon prompts great rejoicing among the redeemed. John hears the voice of the great multitude declaring God's praise for his righteous judgment: "Hallelujah! Salvation and glory and power belong to our God, for his judgments are true and just; for he has judged the great prostitute who corrupted the earth with her immorality, and has avenged on her the blood of his servants" (Rev. 19:1-2). The heavenly sanctuary erupts in worship. All of God's servants praise him. The sound is likened to the roar of many waters and peals of thunder crying out in jubilation: "Hallelujah! For the Lord our God the Almighty reigns" (Rev. 19:6). God's righteous judgment will bring no regrets. We will praise him for his justice and celebrate our redemption. His final victory over evil will cause our hearts to rejoice. The character of God and the beauty of his city are compared to a wedding feast, the messianic banquet. God invites us to sit at his table for the marriage banquet of his beloved Son (Rev. 19:7-9; cf. Matt. 8:11). He will clothe us with fine linen, bright and pure. He will summon us to feast with him. We will see his face and be with him forever.

In final preparation for the wedding feast, Jesus Christ rides forth in final victory over the beast, the serpent, and death itself. John sees the sanctuary open and a white horse with a rider called "Faithful and True" (Rev. 19:11). We see the exalted Son of Man from Rev. 1, with his eyes like a flame of fire. He is crowned with many crowns of legitimate authority. He bears the divine name. His robe is dipped in redeeming blood. He is the Word of God. The armies of heaven follow him in triumph. He strikes down the nations with a sharp sword and rules them with a rod of iron (Rev. 19:12-15; cf. Ps. 2:8-9; Rev. 1:16). He treads the winepress of the fury of the wrath of God. He is "King of kings and Lord of lords" (Rev. 19:16). He is the divine warrior, mighty to save, righteous in all his ways (Exod. 15:3; Isa. 63:1-5; Luke 11:21-22).

John sees the beast and false prophet, along with their armies gathering to make war against Jesus Christ (Rev. 19:19). The outcome of the final battle is never in doubt. There is no suspense at all. The entire conflict is described in just three verses. God's people do not strike a single blow. They stand and see the salvation of the Lord (Rev. 19:20-21; cf. Exod. 14:13-14). The beast and the false prophet are captured. They are thrown alive into the lake of fire (Rev. 19:20). The rest of those who oppose the Son are slain by the sword that came from the mouth of him who rides in victory (Rev. 19:21). The birds of the air gorge themselves on the dead in a graphic depiction of the curse (Rev. 19:21; cf. Deut. 28:26; Matt. 24:28).

The Messiah's final victory also defeats the dragon, the ancient serpent. The serpent stands behind the power of the beast in any age (Rev. 13:1-2). Jesus Christ is the promised seed of the woman who will crush the serpent (Gen. 3:15). The dominion of the beast will be taken away and transferred to the Son of Man and his people. He will inherit the nations as the kingdom of God includes members of every tribe (Rev. 7:9; cf. Ps. 2:8). John sees the defeat of the beast and the serpent in close relationship with the vindication of God's people. He sees an angel coming down "with a key to the bottomless pit and a great chain" (Rev. 20:1). The serpent, identified as the Devil and Satan, is bound for one thousand years and is no longer able to deceive the nations (Rev. 20:2-3; cf. 2 Cor. 4:4).

John sees the heavenly court sit in judgment. The imagery is drawn from Dan. 7:9-14. In Daniel's vision, the beast that persecutes God's people is condemned and removed from power. The Son of Man is vindicated and exalted to power. Dominion, glory, and an everlasting kingdom are taken from the beast and given to God's people. This is the pattern that controls and informs what is described in Rev. 19-20. In Rev. 19:11-21, the beast, together with the kings of the earth and all who share in exploitation and violence, is defeated. In Rev. 20:4-6, the Son of Man is vindicated, together with the martyrs and all who hold the testimony of Jesus (Rev. 20:4-6). All those who had been persecuted for the testimony of Jesus and for the word of God now live in safety. All those who did not worship the beast or receive his mark come to life and reign with Christ for one thousand years (Rev. 20:4, 6).

While Christians have understood the millennium (Latin for "one thousand") differently, we should give our main attention to the meaning of the millennium within the controlling vision of Revelation. The image of Christ reigning with his people in the midst of a renewed earth replaces the demonic parody of the beast that had been inspired by the serpent. Within the symbolic vision of Revelation, the millennial reign of Christ with his people represents the positive counterpart to God's judgment upon the beast and the serpent. The serpent is bound in prison. God's people are set free from bondage. The beast and the serpent are thrown into the lake of fire, which is called the second death (Rev. 19:20; 20:10, 14). God's people are raised to everlasting life and the second death has no power over them. The beast's temporal kingdom is taken away. God's people inherit an eternal kingdom that will never be destroyed. Those who destroy the earth are destroyed (Rev. 11:18). The kingdoms of the earth now belong to Christ and his people (Rev. 11:15). They will live and rule with him as a kingdom of priests forever (Rev. 20:6; cf. Dan. 7:18, 27; Rev. 5:10). God's original calling for his people is now fulfilled in Christ (Gen. 1:28; Exod. 19:6). The decisive defeat of the serpent becomes evident when he is released from prison just before the final judgment. He gathers his forces in a desperate attempt to deceive the nations once more (Rev. 20:7-8). He is utterly unsuccessful. He is condemned forever and cast into the lake of fire (Rev. 20:10).

The final victory of the Messiah is over death itself. Paul had written to the Corinthian believers: "the last enemy to be destroyed is death" (1 Cor. 15:26). God is the author of life (Acts 3:15). He is not the God of the dead, but the God of the living (Matt. 22:32). Everything around him is alive, even his throne (Ezek. 1:5). John sees the Lord enthroned in the midst of the sanctuary (Rev. 20:11). He sees the dead gathered before the presence of the King of glory (Rev. 20:12). Death and Hades surrender the dead who were in them (Rev. 20:13). Every human being who has ever lived now appears before

Jesus, the righteous Savior and heavenly Judge (Matt. 25:31-32; Acts 17:31). This scene is awesome to consider. Books are opened and each one must give an account (Rev. 20:12). The Lord renders to each one according to what he or she has done (Rev. 20:13; cf. Matt. 16:27; 2 Cor. 5:10). God's judgment is impartial. All his ways are just and true (Rev. 15:3-4). Death and those who share the culture of death are cast into the lake of fire, making way for the ultimate triumph of life (Rev. 20:14-15).

John also sees the book of life, which records the names of all who belong to the Lamb (Rev. 20:12, 15; cf. Phil. 4:3). Those who trust in him will never be put to shame. Their names will never be blotted out (Rev. 3:5). Their names are written before the foundation of the world (Rev. 13:8; 17:8). They have received forgiveness and redemption through Christ's own shed blood (Rev. 5:9). They will live and reign with him forever (Rev. 5:10). He promises all who hear his voice: "I give them eternal life, and they will never perish, and no one will snatch them out of my hand" (John 10:28).

We should not pass too quickly from the description of God's final judgment. The certainty that we will all appear before Jesus Christ, the exalted Son of Man, makes us consider the state of our own soul. Israel's prophets described God's judgment as fiery anger and an overwhelming flood against sin and evil. He will appear like a refiner's fire and fuller's soap to purify the world. The prophets rightly ask: "Who can stand when he appears?" (Mal. 3:2; cf. Nah. 1:6). The kings of the earth ask at the great day of God's wrath: "Who can stand?" (Rev. 6:17). The answer to this most important question is found by the great multitude of the redeemed. They *are* standing before the throne and before the Lamb (Rev. 7:9). They stand because they are clothed in his righteousness by faith in his work upon the cross. They cry out in faithful confession: "Salvation belongs to our God who sits on the throne, and to the Lamb!" (Rev 7:10). He is the subject of their everlasting song. O Lamb of God who takes away the sins of the world! O Lamb of God who was slain for me! O Lamb of God cause my heart to rejoice in Thee!

The new creation of heaven and earth (Rev. 21)

The final scene of the Bible takes us back to the very beginning. After God's victory over evil, sin, and death, God creates "a new heaven and a new earth" (Rev. 21:1). The language recalls the first sentence of Scripture where we are introduced to the God who "created the heavens and the earth" (Gen. 1:1). God delights in his creation and calls the physical world "very good" (Gen. 1:31). Human beings created in his image are called to know God and respond to him in praise. They are to imitate his creativity in their work and the development of culture. They are to fill the earth with image-bearers who reflect God's righteousness and truth. As we know from our CASKET EMPTY study, God's good creation became corrupted by evil and sin (Gen. 3). Creation languished under God's curse (Gen. 3:14-19). Death and violence proliferated in the land (Gen. 6:5).

Israel's prophets longed for the day when God would recreate the heavens and the earth in which righteousness dwells (Isa. 65:17-25). Evil and sin would be banished. Death and violence would be no more. The new heavens and earth would endure as the sanctuary of worship for all of the redeemed (Isa. 66:22-23). It is important to emphasize that the biblical hope does not look toward a disembodied spiritual state for individuals. Bodily resurrection takes place within the context of a new heavens and a new earth. God may intend to create a completely new universe, but more likely, God intends to renew his creation, now purged of evil, sin, and death. God's people will be raised to everlasting life with physical bodies that will never grow old, sick, or die. There will be no more idolatry, for on that day the Lord will be one and his name the only one (Zech. 14:9). There will be no more dishonoring of his name. There will be no desecration of holy days, no disrespect of those deserving honor. There will be no murder, no adultery, and no theft. There will be no more lies, no curse, no coveting. The knowledge of God will fill the earth (Isa. 11:9). All nations will walk together in the light of the Lord (Isa. 2:5; 1 John 1:7). As God's people, we will live meaningful, everlasting lives in conscious praise of the Lord God Almighty, who is our Creator, Redeemer, and Savior. This life will be shared as fellow citizens of God's eternal city, the New Jerusalem, the centerpiece of the new heavens and new earth.

New Jerusalem descends like a bride for her husband (Rev. 21)

John sees God's holy city, the New Jerusalem, coming down out of heaven adorned as a bride adorned for her husband (Rev. 21:1-2). The city is the dwelling place of God with his people. They are together in an eternal covenant bond that echoes the formula: "I will be their God and they shall be my people" (Jer. 31:33; cf. Ezek. 37:28; Rev. 21:3). The Lord will wipe away every tear from their eyes and death shall be no more. There will no longer be mourning, nor crying, nor pain, for the former things have passed away. The Lord promises: "Behold, I am making all things new." (Rev. 21:5).

The city of God is holy, resplendent with the glory of God (Rev. 21:11). The city is secure with a great, high wall (Rev. 21:12). All cities in antiquity had walls. Gates built into the walls gave access to the city and usually held massive doors that could be closed at night to keep the residents safe. The New Jerusalem has a beautiful wall with strong foundations and twelve gates. However, there are no doors on the gates. The gates are never closed (Rev. 21:25). There is no danger, no evil, and no threat against the inhabitants of the city. They are free to work, play, and explore the surrounding lands. They can return to the city and enter the gates at any time. There are three gates on each side of the city, suggesting that a renewed earth lies open before us in every direction. The city has a noble heritage that unites the twelve Old Testament tribes and the twelve names of the New Testament apostles (Rev. 21:12-14). The city is massive in size, measuring twelve thousand stadia, approximately fifteen hundred miles on each side (Rev. 21:16). There is ample room for the innumerable multitude of the redeemed from every tribe and nation who walk by its light (Rev. 21:24). The kings of the earth bring their glory to adorn the city. The honor of the nations gladly enters within her gates (Rev. 21:26; cf. Gen. 49:10; Isa. 60:1-7).

The city of God is shaped like a cube. The Holy of Holies in the Jerusalem Temple is the only other cube in Scripture (1 Kgs. 6:20; Ezek. 41:4). The dimensions of the city communicate that the New Jerusalem is God's dwelling place that now fills the renewed heavens and earth. There is no separate temple in the city, for the entire city is the temple of the Lord God Almighty and the Lamb (Rev. 21:22). The glory of God illuminates the city with the radiance of God's own presence.

The city is built with precious stones and jewels that are first mentioned in connection with the Garden of Eden (Rev. 21:18-21; cf. Gen. 2:10-15). God's redemptive purpose through history began in a royal garden, the paradise of God (Gen. 2:8). Now we see clearly the royal city that accompanies the garden, the New Jerusalem. The city of God is the place of renewed relationship. God and humanity are reconciled. There is no anguish in the city. There is no pain or tragic death. Humanity made in his image enjoys the work of their hands. The curse of death is overturned. The harmony even among animals is a poetic depiction that all of life has been renewed. Creation is set free from futility and now enjoys the glorious freedom of the children of God (Rom. 8:21). "Your will be done, on earth as it is in heaven" is answered in full (Matt. 6:10). Redeemed humanity will live and reign with God forever (Rev. 22:5).

Redeemed humanity has access to the tree of life (Rev. 22)

When we look inside the New Jerusalem, we see "the river of the water of life, bright as crystal, flowing from the throne of God and of the Lamb" (Rev. 22:1). The river flows out from the place of God's dwelling through the middle of the street of the city and renews the earth (Rev. 22:2; cf. Gen. 2:10; Ezek. 47:1). Beside the clear, life-giving waters of the river, the tree of life grows alongside the banks (Rev. 22:2). The tree bears twelve kinds of fruit, one for each month. The leaves of the tree bring healing to the nations. You will remember from our study that humanity lost access to the tree of life in the Garden of Eden (Gen. 3:22-24). The intimate fellowship between God and humanity was shattered through the deception of sin. Redeemed humanity now has access to the tree of life. No longer will there be any curse (Rev. 22:3). God's people will live under his blessing. They will worship their Creator and Redeemer. They will see his face. The radiance of his glory will shine upon them. His name will be upon them (Rev. 22:4-5; cf. Num. 6:24-27). They will walk in newness of life. They will reflect his image in loving and wise care of the earth. They will fulfill their original mandate in the beauty of holiness and glorify him forever (Gen. 1:28; Ps. 86:2; Rev. 5:9-10).

"I am coming quickly. Amen. Come Lord Jesus!" (Rev. 22:20)

The revelation of Jesus Christ ends with the eager anticipation of all that is YET-TO-COME, according to what has been depicted in Revelation. God's words are trustworthy and true (Rev. 22:6). The exalted Son of Man promises his bride: "Behold, I am coming soon" (Rev. 22:7, 12). God's people are to live in expectation of the return of Christ. The words of Revelation are clear and understandable to all "for the time is near" (Rev. 22:10). Jesus urges his people to faithful witness until the day of his appearing. He will bring recompense upon evil and generous reward for all who love him. He is "the Alpha and the Omega, the first and the last, the beginning and the end" (Rev. 22:13; cf. Isa. 44:6; Rev. 1:8). His sovereign, redemptive purpose will be accomplished (Isa. 46:10). He blesses all who wash their robes in his blood so that they may have access to the tree of life and enter the New Jerusalem by the open city gates. Those who love and practice what is false will remain outside forever (Rev. 22:14-15). Jesus Christ is the root and offspring of David, the bright and morning star (Rev. 22:16; cf. Num. 24:17; Isa. 11:1; 2 Pet. 1:19). He stands today as the signal banner for all nations. His resting place will be glorious (Isa. 11:10).

In faithful response, the people of God, the bride of Christ, say: "Come!" Whoever hears the revelation of Jesus Christ says: "Come!" All who are thirsty are invited to come and drink from the water of life (Rev. 22:17). Revelation announces the end of the biblical canon with a warning. If anyone adds to Scripture, God will add to him the plagues described in this book. If anyone takes away from Scripture, God will take away his share in the tree of life and in the holy city, which are described in this book (Rev. 22:18-19). The canon of Scripture is complete. There is no new revelation. There are no additional books. There are no future prophets who could ever draw our attention away from Jesus Christ, the Lamb of God, who was slain for us. He alone is risen from the dead. He lives and reigns now and forevermore. He declares with everlasting authority: "Surely I am coming soon" (Rev. 22:20). His faithful, expectant bride answers in reply: "Amen. Come, Lord Jesus!"

Invitation of response

The CASKET EMPTY Bible study material has been written to help God's people understand his plan of redemption through history with Jesus at its center. We have journeyed together through the Word of the living God to discover who he is, what he has done for us, and who he calls us to be. As we conclude our study, it is eternally important to remember that God's redemptive plan addresses each one of us today. God invites us to become part of his story through faith in Jesus Christ. If you have never put your faith in Christ for salvation, I would like to personally invite you to do this now. You can use the following prayer as a guide:

> Almighty God, I have come to see the greatness of your person and your plan. I confess my own sinfulness before you and humbly repent of all of the ways in which I have dishonored or disobeyed you. I put my faith right now in Jesus Christ. I believe that you have placed my sin upon him. The righteous wrath that I deserve, you have poured out upon him at the cross. His righteousness is now my own. Christ's empty tomb is death's defeat. His resurrection is now my hope. Fill me now with presence of the Holy Spirit. Teach me to walk in newness of life. Use my life in any way you choose to extend your mission in the world. Keep my eyes fixed on you, Jesus, my promised Messiah and coming King. I will worship you with all of my heart both now and forever. In Jesus' Name, Amen.

If you have prayed this prayer, we would love to hear from you. You can send an email through the CasketEmpty website (www.casketempty.com). If you already know Jesus Christ and this material has strengthened your discipleship, or if you are using this material in a mission context, we would love to hear from you as well.

May the Lord bless each of you as you live and announce the good news of Jesus Christ in the power of the Holy Spirit. May he capture your heart and mind as you continue to study and delight in his inspired Word. May he use the Church as his instrument to reflect the radiant glory of God's renewed humanity in Christ. May he call each of us to join God's mission in the world today as the gospel of the kingdom continues to extend to all nations. Amen.

Made in the USA
San Bernardino, CA
15 January 2018